To Ban & Lyly,
Happy Holidays !

Warmly,
Ralph

CREATING A
QUANTUM
ORGANIZATION

Ralph H. Kilmann's Previous Books

The Management of Organization Design

Social Systems Design

Methodological Approaches to Social Science

Producing Useful Knowledge for Organizations

Corporate Tragedies

Beyond the Quick Fix

Gaining Control of the Corporate Culture

Corporate Transformation

Escaping the Quick Fix Trap

Managing Beyond the Quick Fix

Making Organizations Competitive

Workbooks for Implementing the Tracks

Logistics Manual for Implementing the Tracks

Holographic Quality Management

Managing Ego Energy

Quantum Organizations

The Courageous Mosaic

The Psychodynamics of Enlightened Leadership

CREATING A QUANTUM ORGANIZATION

The Whys & Hows of Implementing Eight Tracks for Long-Term Success

RALPH H. KILMANN

Published and Distributed by Kilmann Diagnostics LLC
1 Suprema Drive, Newport Coast, CA 92657
 www.kilmanndiagnostics.com
info@kilmanndiagnostics.com
949–497–8766

Book cover, interior design, and illustrations by Ralph H. Kilmann.

05 04 03 02 01   10 9 8 7 6 5 4 3 2 1
Printed in the United States of America

Library of Congress Control Number: 2021915815
Kilmann, Ralph H.
        Creating a quantum organization:
    the whys & hows of implementing
    eight tracks for long–term success / Ralph H. Kilmann
            p. cm.
    Includes bibliographical references and index.
    ISBN Hardback 978-0-9895713-3-3
    1. Change management. 2. Conflict management.
    3. Expanding Consciousness. 4. Organizational
    transformation. I. Title.
    658.4'06–dc21

TABLE OF CONTENTS

LIST
OF
ILLUSTRATIONS

FIGURES IN CHAPTER 7 – TEAM MANAGEMENT

FIGURES IN CHAPTER 8 – ALIGNING STRATEGY-STRUCTURE

FIGURES IN CHAPTER 11 – EXPANDING CONSCIOUSNESS

To Ian I. Mitroff

My "brother" in pursuing truth,
wisdom, and transformation

PREFACE
TO THE
BOOK

My most far-reaching and most comprehensive book in the past was published in 2001: *Quantum Organizations: A New Paradigm for Achieving Organizational Success and Personal Meaning*. That book integrated all my prior 20 books and 100-plus articles on change management and corporate transformation. In fact, my journey into this professional field began more than 50 years ago, way back in 1968, when I was first exposed to organizational theory and organizational development while I was a graduate student at Carnegie Mellon University in Pittsburgh, Pennsylvania.

I now see that my 2001 book, *Quantum Organizations*, ended up being much more intellectually challenging to read (and to thus comprehend) than I had planned, since that book integrated the streams of knowledge for organizational development from such diverse fields as quantum physics, relativity theory, philosophy, evolutionary theory, cosmology, psychology, neuroscience, and consciousness research.

During the next twenty years since *Quantum Organizations* was published, I've had the opportunity (1) to present my integrative theories and change methodologies to many senior management groups, (2) to coach scores of consultants on how to implement the sequence of eight tracks in their client organizations, and (3) to create a series of recorded online courses that were purposely designed to present my material on quantum organizations to a much larger audience in the most convenient format possible. As such, during the past decades since I wrote *Quantum Organizations*, I have acquired a much better understanding of my own work and thus I am now better able to explain it to others in a more "down to earth" and pragmatic manner.

To make a long story much shorter, my 2021 book, ***Creating a Quantum Organization,*** is my official answer to the literally hundreds of requests I've received that asked me to simplify – as well as update – all my knowledge and experience in bringing a quantum organization to life. If you know me and/or my work, you also know that in no way would I ever provide a simplistic discussion about a very complex problem, as in "the guaranteed formula for success or satisfaction," which could result in a major disservice to the challenging nature of quantum transformation. But there's a large gray area that exists between the one extreme of oversimplifying ("dumbing down") a highly complex subject into some doomed quick fix – and the other extreme of offering abstract theories and concepts that are much too vague to grasp and thus much too obtuse for immediate action.

As a result, for this new book, I have deliberately chosen the "middle path" that attempts to appropriately respect the complex nature of transformational change, but does so in a manner that allows many more people to deeply appreciate – and effectively use – my theories and methods without having to know all the scientific research and knowledge across many disciplines. Yes, in this book, I still refer to a few concepts from quantum physics and other scientific fields, but I only provide the bare essentials to make an important point. That's it.

But if it turns out that I have not entirely succeeded in my attempt to make my work more accessible and useful this time around (to make this 2021 book much more "user friendly" than the original 2001 *Quantum Organizations* book), I'll surely try again in another 20 years to be even more lucid and concrete – once I've had additional experience in the process of transformational change in many different kinds of organizations.

By the way, in 2013, I published a book that explored the key, underlying feature of a quantum organization, namely, how to awaken and expand the mind/body/spirit consciousness of its members, *The Courageous Mosaic: Awakening Society, Systems, and Souls.*

That book is autobiographical in its delivery, since I purposely made use of my own personal journey with various mind/body/spirit modalities in order to show how people can explore their self–aware consciousness. As such, *Creating a Quantum Organization* updates everything that I have learned and published since 2001, including what I presented in my 2013 book on the advent of the Consciousness Revolution that's sweeping the globe.

In sum, my new 2021 book presents ALL that I have created – and integrated – on the four timeless subjects that will always shape humanity's struggle with its destiny: conflict management, change management, consciousness, and transformation.

OVERVIEW OF CONTENTS

This book is organized into 12 chapters that include many illustrations to take full advantage of the old adage: "a picture is worth a thousand words." Although my previous book, *Quantum Organizations*, presented its 104 illustrations in full color, this 2021 book includes many more elegant figures (167 in total), but they are shown in shades of gray. I chose this Black & White scheme in order to keep the price of this book as low as possible – again, with the deliberate intention of reaching many more people.

Chapter 1 presents several "Big Pictures," also known as the Complex Hologram and the Quantum Wheel, which reveals all the interrelationships among systems, processes, and people – both inside and outside an organization. In that same chapter, I also present the seven features of a quantum organization, so you'll know how this totally new kind of approach for organized action is radically different from its still popular predecessor: the Newtonian organization. These Big Picture discussions will then lead us to the mega challenge for today's increasingly turbulent times, which can be stated this way: ***How can we transform our antiquated, sluggish, ineffective, and unfulfilling Newtonian organizations into vibrant, effective, and meaningful quantum organizations? In just two words, I call this mega challenge: QUANTUM TRANSFORMATION.***

Once you have become familiar with the Complex Hologram, the Quantum Wheel, and the eight tracks for creating a quantum organization, Chapters 2 and 3 investigate the essence of conflict management as well as change management – since conflict and change comprise two sides of the same coin. You can't have one without the other: *Change creates conflict and resolving conflict creates change.* The material on the Thomas–Kilmann Conflict Model (aka the TKI Conflict Model) along with the Kilmann Organizational Conflict Instrument (KOCI) allows us to assess the self–defeating conflicts that members have with their surrounding systems and processes. Examining such "systems conflicts" will enable us to pinpoint the barriers to long–term success *before* attempting to implement a completely integrated program that's intended to transform those Newtonian "barriers to success" into quantum "channels for success."

Chapter 4 provides an overview of quantum transformation, which is arranged into a completely integrated program of eight tracks: culture, skills, teams, strategy–structure, reward systems, and three process tracks (gradual, radical and learning process improvement). Included in the discussion are the five stages of planned change: initiating the program, diagnosing the barriers to success, scheduling the tracks, implementing the tracks, and then evaluating the results – and the cycle of transformational change continues.

Starting in Chapter 5, and proceeding chapter after chapter, I then present the most relevant and practical material for each of the eight tracks, which emphasizes why this particular sequence of change initiatives is crucial for achieving long–term success. Indeed, any program of change or set of change initiatives that implements the eight tracks out of sequence, or fails to address all eight tracks in their entirety, will inadvertently prevent people and their organizations from realizing their dreams.

In Chapter 11, I will then address the future of organizational development and quantum transformation by exploring how to expand the mind/body/spirit consciousness of all organizational members – and then bring that expanded consciousness directly into the workplace. ***We must continually encourage members to resolve their four INNER conflicts, which will then allow them to significantly improve how they will resolve all their OUTER conflicts — including their interpersonal and systems conflicts.***

Chapter 12 then summarizes twenty critical success factors that must be honored at all times in order to create a quantum organization and thus achieve long–term success. I also stress the importance of *reevaluating* the functioning of the organization's systems and processes to ensure that all organizational behavior always remains organically aligned – and completely on track – for effectively resolving all future problems and conflicts.

Lastly, visit the **Bibliography** for a listing of the publications that have had the greatest influence on my work, including the specific references that I cite for my chapters. Be sure to use the **Index** that has been especially prepared to help you find things, quickly and easily. If you want to learn about my background, see: **About the Author**.

Incidentally, you might have already observed that **I'm using bold-italic text to highlight key words, phrases, and sentences.** Why? Decades ago, various students would borrow one or more of my books. Upon returning them to me, they'd often comment that it was exceedingly valuable in their learning process to see the particular sentences that I had previously highlighted with a permanent yellow marker. Given those prior conversations with my MBA and Ph.D. students, for this "legacy book," I decided to provide you with that same learning experience by revealing to you – this time, using bold–italic text – precisely what I regard as the most vital points, principles, and practices during the process of creating a quantum organization.

ACKNOWLEDGMENTS

Many people have played a significant role in influencing the development of my theories and methods and then inspiring me to always do my very best in presenting my creations to others. My parents, Lilli and Martin, played that first big role and then continued their unwavering belief in me throughout their long lifetimes. My grandmother, Helena Loeb, provided me with the unconditional love that only a grandparent can give. My Uncle Morris provided the initial inspiration for me to study leadership and organizations when I worked as a management assistant for his company, Liberty Hardware, during my summers in college. My brother, Peter, a clinical psychologist, continues to be a great springboard for whatever personal and professional challenges appear in my life. My twin sister, Rosie, provides unconditional love and emotional support for everything I do.

Throughout my 30-year career as a research professor at the University of Pittsburgh, Dean Jerry Zoffer guided my personal and professional development. Many colleagues and friends also fostered my journey in science, humanity, and personal growth: Ken Mackenzie, Ken Thomas, Gail Thomas, Ian Mitroff, Jeanette and Dean Engel, Brandi and Tyler Kennedy, Teresa Joyce Covin, Richard MacDonald, Stan Grof, Judy Strauss, Joe Giwoff, Nancy Nicholas, Sunshine Smith, Michael McCormack, Theresa G. Lim, Malkara Smith, Donny Epstein, Vince Barabba, Adriana Fellipelli, Marjorie Panzer, Stephanie Shirley, and Marlee Winderman. Last, but not least, I appreciate the sustained support and inspiration from my Men's Group (12 years and still exploring): Jon Burras, Michael Cansler, Eric Nada, and Paul Villa.

I am dedicating this book to Ian Mitroff. For five decades, we have helped each other work through our challenging childhood traumas, while also coauthoring several professional books and many scientific articles on defining and solving a society's most wicked, chaotic, messy problems. We are Brothers – personally and professionally – always and forever.

CREATING A QUANTUM ORGANIZATION

The Whys & Hows of Implementing
Eight Tracks for Long-Term Success

*"I must create a system ...
or be enslaved by another man's"*

William Blake, poet, circa 1850

SEEING THE BIG PICTURE

SYSTEMS, PROCESSES, PEOPLE

Organizations are one of the greatest inventions of all time. They enable people to transcend their limitations of both body and mind to manage the problems of nature and civilization. Without organized activity, all the other great inventions either would not have been created or would never have been brought to market. It's hardly an overstatement to suggest that economic prosperity and the quality of life for the people of the world are largely determined by the functioning of our organizations.

There are two fundamental questions that must be addressed in humanity's continuing struggle to improve its organizations and institutions: (1) what is the essence of organized activity, that is, what makes an organization or institution successful? (2) How can this essence be explicitly managed – how can organizational success be created and maintained?

Creating and then maintaining organizational success is a very different kind of problem from that of only a few decades ago. The world has become increasingly *dynamic*, resulting from information technology and worldwide connectivity. At the same time, the world has become increasingly *complex*, resulting from the political deregulation and economic interdependence in our global village. This *dynamic complexity* means that organizations cannot remain stable for very long. Rather, *constant change on the outside requires constant change on the inside.* Long-term success is largely determined by how well the organization adjusts/adapts all its tangible and intangible properties in order to keep itself aligned with its incessantly changing environment.

3

The older and larger the firm, the more difficulty it has in changing. Eventually, a well-established organization can easily become rigidified. Just as hardening of the arteries sets in with age for individuals, hardening of the documents (and cultures and assumptions and psyches) seems to come with age and size for organizations. Making matters worse, if the organization has been successful in the past, its leaders may fall into the trap of "erroneous extrapolation." This occurs when executives make the false assumption that what worked in the last decades will also work in the next decade. Here, they draw a straight line from the past into the future. With dynamic complexity being the new rule, however, the line is dotted at best, and it twists and turns as well. In some cases, *the very thing that brought the organization success can bring about its sudden downfall.*

The temptation for executives and consultants is to gravitate toward every new approach that offers the promise of long-term organizational success. But this is like the search for the Holy Grail: *Each new approach looks for the one single answer.* In the 1950s, management by objectives was presented as the new solution to performance deficiencies. In the 1960s, organizational structure was presumed to be the missing solution. In the 1970s, corporate strategy was considered the new panacea. In the 1980s, the rage was corporate culture. In the 1990s, the magical cure was billed as total quality management (or TQM for short), business process reengineering (BPR), and organizational learning. Predictably, the quest for the single solution never ends: In today's world, the new touted remedies include digital technologies and artificial-intelligent systems, which are expected to introduce the missing ingredient for long-term success – and the beat goes on.

It's a real shame, however, that leaders and consultants will have to learn the hard way – once again – that new corporate cultures, quality circles, digital devices, or 5G networks cannot solve their long-term performance problems either. Eventually, executives will drop the current fad and move on to the next promised remedy. All too often, single approaches are discarded because they have not been given a fair test. It's not the single approach of improving the corporate culture, aligning strategy and structure, designing a new reward system, or speeding up process improvement that is inherently ineffective. Rather, each is ineffective only if it is applied by itself – as a quick fix – *while ignoring the other systems, processes, and people that also affect long-term organizational success.*

It is time to stop perpetuating the myth of simplicity. The system of organization established by humankind generates complex problems that cannot be solved by simplistic, quick fix solutions. The promising alternative is to develop a completely integrated program that explicitly examines ALL the tangible and intangible properties of an organization.

In this chapter, I will first present three very different ways of viewing the world: as a simple machine, as an open system, and as a Complex Hologram. These contrasting worldviews highlight why a completely integrated approach is so vital for long–term success and why any quick fix inevitably will result in failure. Second, I will present the Complex Hologram as the illuminating diagram that systematically displays the "barriers to success" that must be changed into "channels for success" in our holographic world – which reveals all the important interconnections among an organization's systems, processes, and people. Third, I will present the Quantum Wheel as a symbolic integration of conflict management and change management, since how well conflict and change are managed determines whether an organization will experience stagnation – or transformation. And fourth, **I will highlight the distinctions between a Newtonian organization and a quantum organization, which will surely inspire us to transform antiquated Newtonian organizations into enduring quantum organizations.**

THREE WORLD VIEWS FOR
IMPROVING ORGANIZATIONS

Viewing the world as analogous to ***a simple machine*** argues for single efforts at change and improvement, like replacing one defective part in some mechanical apparatus. The one defective part can be replaced without affecting any other part. This single approach only works for fixing a physical, nonliving system. The quick fix cannot hope to heal a human being, much less a living, breathing organization. The simple machine view demonstrates one–dimensional thinking at its best.

Viewing the world as analogous to ***an open system*** looks for a more integrated approach, in which numerous parts must be balanced simultaneously in order to improve organizations. In this case, a dynamic equilibrium exists between an organization and its environment. The organization consists of systems, such as strategies, structures, and rewards. The environment contains its own systems, as well, such as the competitors, suppliers, and customers. This worldview, however, remains at the surface level, where things can be readily observed and easily measured. The open system represents two–dimensional thinking at its best.

Viewing the world as a Complex Hologram argues for adding depth to the open system (and the simple machine) – analogous to forming a three–dimensional image by combining streams of light at different angles. ***The Complex Hologram explores below the surface to examine cultures (shared but unwritten rules for each member's behavior), assumptions (unstated beliefs behind all decisions and actions), and psyches (the deepest reaches of the human mind, heart, and soul, also known as mind/body/spirit consciousness).*** To neglect such deeper aspects of human and organizational life is to assume that what cannot be seen or touched directly is unimportant – and thus can be ignored.

The simple machine view of the world is already outdated. It had its heyday in the industrial revolution, a long time ago in the eighteenth and nineteenth centuries. Yet, looking at the way contemporary organizations are designed and managed would lead one to conclude that the simple machine conception is alive and well: *Quick fixes are all around us!* The open systems approach (emphasizing the interrelationships among all the elements that comprise any network) has been available since the 1950s, yet seldom is it put into practice. The Complex Hologram includes a variety of below–the–surface, subtle, hidden, unconscious, social, and psychodynamic forces to the interconnectedness of all living systems. Consequently, the worldview of a Complex Hologram captures the essential nature of the world today, although three-dimensional approaches are rarely utilized in change initiatives to improve organizations.

The Complex Hologram: Seeing the Big Picture

Figure 1.1 shows an image to represent space–time, the fabric of our universe, which consists of quantum waves and particles. These super tiny waves and particles then create all the invisible forces and visible forms that we experience, either consciously or unconsciously. Based on superstring theory in quantum physics, perhaps the smallest – and most fundamental – wave/particle in the universe consists of vibrating strings, as represented by the wiggly lines and patterns in this illustration.

This big picture image also hints at the donut (torus) shape of the universe, including its evolution over time, starting from the initial Big Bang. That energetic explosion, about 14 billion years ago, might have originated from within a gigantic black hole – eventually creating the first beam of *light* in the universe. This evolutionary process continued by then creating all the chemical elements on the periodic chart, including the essential life-giving subtle energies, which led to the creation and evolution of life on Planet Earth. ***This quantum/biological/energetic image of our universe also represents the evolution of consciousness, which is, simply put, the awareness by sentient beings that such a universe of waves and particles (including themselves) actually exist, which is the foundation for self-reflection, contemplation, scientific study, designing organizations, conflict management, and quantum transformation.***

FIGURE 1.1
SPACE-TIME — INVISIBLE FORCES AND VISIBLE FORMS

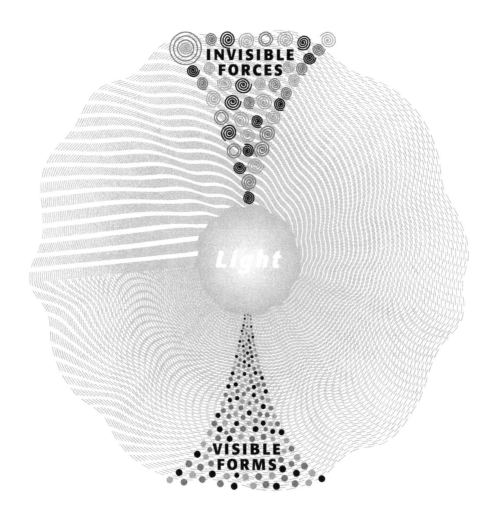

Now, let's further investigate the emergence of the deepest – holographic – aspects of human beings, which determines how organizations are created, managed, maintained, and improved.

Figure 1.2 shows the evolution from space–time to matter and then to the emergence and development of consciousness. In the initial stages of this process, individuals begin their journey as passive (unconscious) observers; then they become more active (conscious) participants in their own evolutionary process; and, eventually, **human beings can become enlightened participants**

who are fully aware of the consciousness that underlies every experience, decision, and action. Notice that the hourglass shape of the forces and forms in Figure 1.1 is the same as the hourglass shape of the evolution of human beings from passive observers into enlightened participants that's shown in Figure 1.2.

FIGURE 1.2
THE EVOLUTION OF HUMAN BEINGS

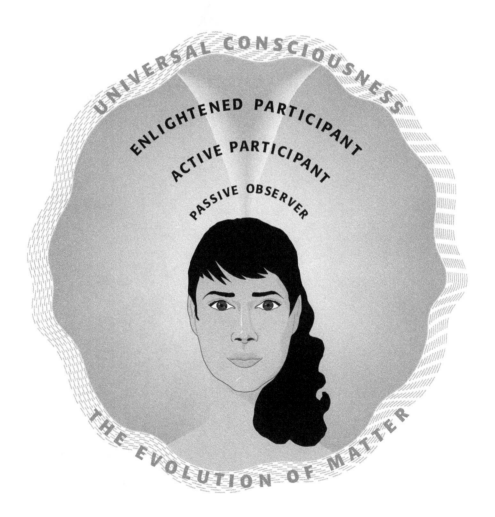

Figure 1.3 shows another big picture. In this instance, we see all the various forces and forms that make up our organizations

and institutions. I published a simpler version of this illustration in my 1984 book, *Beyond the Quick Fix*, to demonstrate the complex interplay of systems, processes, and people.

FIGURE 1.3
THE COMPLEX HOLOGRAM — SEEING THE BIG PICTURE

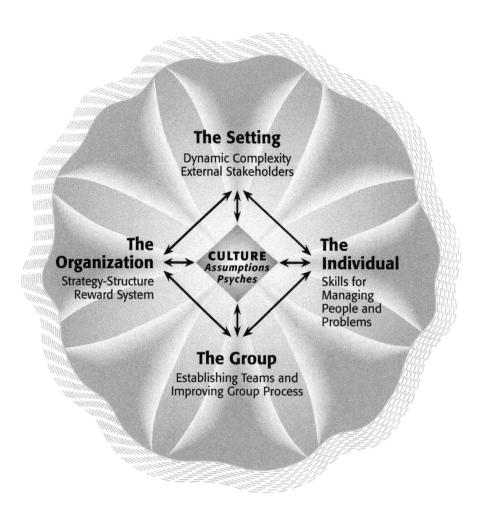

Starting on the right side of the Complex Hologram, I include all the individuals who are the members of the organization – particularly taking note of their styles and skills for addressing problems and conflicts. These individuals are *always* surrounded by the organization's culture, strategy, structure, reward systems, and the immediate work group, which includes, in most cases, a boss or manager. Of course, other organizations and institutions, identified as "The Setting" on the top of the Complex Hologram, completely surround the organization, which defines its external environment. These "External Stakeholders" also affect the kinds of problems and conflicts that members face on a daily basis.

Further, the various NODES in Complex Hologram represent the organization's informal and formal systems (culture, strategy, structure, rewards, groups, and individual skills and styles for managing people, problems, and conflicts). Meanwhile, all the double arrows that are IN BETWEEN these various system nodes represent the business, management, and learning processes that flow throughout the organization – which include all the tasks, decisions, and other activities that take place over time.

I now present the first key principle that derives from the Complex Hologram. Because this key principle is so relevant to life in organizations, I highlight it in bold: ***About 80% (or more) of what goes on in organizations is determined by its systems and processes, while 20% (or less) is determined by individual desires or preferences.***

THE 80/20 RULE OF SYSTEMS OVER INDIVIDUALS

I recall an unpublished experiment that revealed the power of the organization – its systems – over its members:

College students were randomly assigned to be members in one of two vastly different kinds of organization: a pyramid and a circle (to represent a Newtonian organization and a quantum organization, respectively). In the pyramid organization, fifteen students had to work on a number of mundane tasks. Within a strict hierarchical structure, those students at the bottom of the pyramid could only ask questions and receive answers by going through their bosses, who then had to communicate requests to *their* bosses, and so forth. When the one student at the top of the pyramid eventually received a request through this tall chain of command, he would then make his decision and communicate it through the identical chain of bosses down the hierarchy to the workers below. For every question or request, the students had no choice but to accept the rules, procedures, jobs, and bosses in their pyramid organization.

But another fifteen students had been randomly assigned to a circle organization. Sitting in a large, open circle without any preestablished (bureaucratic) procedures, they could accomplish the same tasks by talking to whomever they pleased, at any time, without having to go through a slew of bosses: Everyone in the circle was actively involved in making democratic decisions on the most crucial topics that concerned them. But if these students wanted to design specialized jobs and/or procedures, they could do that, which is known as ***self-designing systems.*** And if these students also wanted to design coordinating mechanisms among their specialized jobs, they were free to do that, which is referred to as ***self-managing systems.***

After having completed a few rounds of work, one member in the circle organization was switched with a member in the pyramid organization. Fourteen of the fifteen members in each organization still knew their system very well, while that new member only knew how the *other* organization got things done. After a few more rounds of work, however, the two new students had learned the new system with the help of the fourteen other students in their assigned organization. In fact, this procedure for learning the culture, "how things are done around here," is pretty much the same process whenever individuals join an established organization, and then learn "the rules of the road" directly from the more experienced members.

A little while later, another two "originally assigned" students (who had participated in the same organization from the start) were asked to switch to the other organization. Again, it didn't take much time for the switched students to learn the particular systems and processes in their new system. The same cycle then continued: switching two of the original students, proceeding with additional cycles of work (so the switched students could learn what was required of them in their new organization), then switching two more of the original students, and so it continued.

Eventually, all fifteen students who were first assigned to the pyramid organization were working in the circle organization; and all fifteen students who were initially assigned to the circle organization were now working in the pyramid organization.

It was entirely the system that predicted how the students functioned in their organization — regardless of their prior experience, personality style, or work preference: One at a time, pairs of switched students easily learned the autocratic or the democratic process of their newly assigned system. Even if those students who'd been initially assigned to the circle preferred that free-flowing decision-making process, once they were switched to the pyramid, they subsequently learned and applied the more regimented way of working together. And if those students who were first assigned to the pyramid preferred such a top-down decision-making process, once they were switched to the other system, they quickly learned how to function within the loosely structured, circle organization. By the way, if there'd been only two or three members in each organization, it would have been natural for these few students to discuss whether they wanted to redesign their structure – on their own. But once there were at least eight to ten members involved in each organization, as a critical mass for ensuring cultural indoctrination, the switched students accepted their new system and followed its procedures. It's worth emphasizing: The pyramid (Newtonian organization) and circle (quantum organization) both remained fully intact – even though each was entirely replaced by new members who had previously experienced a very different system of work.

This unpublished experiment showed the immense power of the system over its members, which is represented in that 80/20 rule: As I mentioned before, **at least 80% of what goes on in an organization is determined by its systems and processes, while only 20% is determined by the personal preferences and the inclinations of its members.**

Based on my 2001 book, *Quantum Organizations*, directly below I provide an even more elaborate diagram in Figure 1.4, which captures how a completely integrated program of eight tracks can identify – and resolve – the various problems and conflicts that become accessible only when seeing the world through the three–dimensional lens of the Complex Hologram.

FIGURE 1.4
THE EIGHT TRACKS AND THE COMPLEX HOLOGRAM

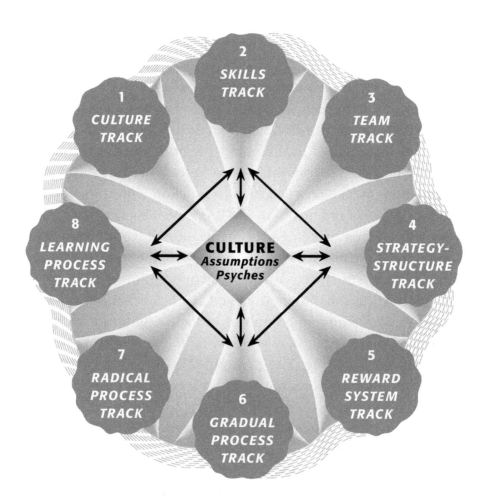

The first three tracks focus on the organization's **behavioral infrastructure** (also considered the *informal* organization), which addresses how well the culture, skills, and teams support long-term success. The next two tracks focus on the ***formal systems,*** which are generally documented on paper or in electronic files:

Figure 1.6 reveals the traditional organization chart that has become the trademark of bureaucratic, mechanistic, Newtonian organizations. Each shaded box on the chart designates a formal division, department, or work group. These formal subunits have specific, well-documented charters outlining the scope of their responsibilities. The members associated with each shaded box are assigned detailed job descriptions and standard operating procedures. The solid lines between the boxes depict the chain of command or the lines of authority that indicate who reports to whom and who is in charge of which department or group. Most often, there are many levels in this vertical (pyramid) command-and-control, management hierarchy. ***The "empty space" between subunits is often called the white space (or open space) on an organization chart — which represents the tasks and decisions that have not been assigned to any subunit's charter or domain and, therefore, suggests what "falls between the cracks."***

THE QUANTUM ORGANIZATION

Figure 1.7 provides a symbolic representation of a quantum organization that incorporates the quantum waves and particles that comprise space-time – and life itself. In comparison to the previous organization chart, clear (self-aware) circles now replace those shaded boxes (blinders). Furthermore, those solid lines on the Newtonian chart, characterizing hierarchy, are now replaced with dotted lines, representing interconnections. And what was previously shown as white space, open space, or dead space on the Newtonian organization chart has been transformed into the living, evolving Planet Earth on the quantum organization chart. Right below this figure, I'll then discuss more about each of the distinguishing features that define the quantum organization. I'll then conclude this chapter by emphasizing the dire need for ALL our organizations and institutions – worldwide – to proceed with quantum transformation, so all human beings can activate their full potential and then bring their essence to work.

FIGURE 1.7
THE QUANTUM ORGANIZATION

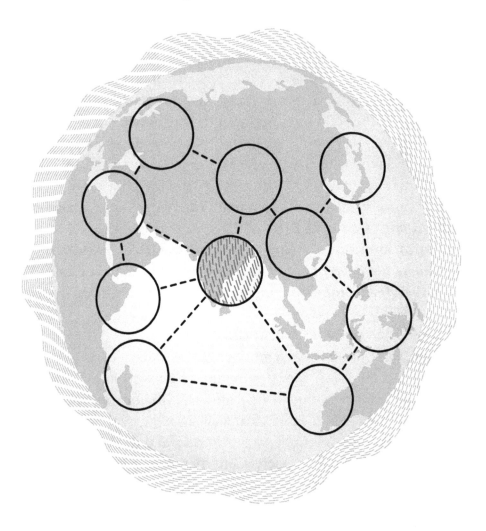

Seven Features for Defining a Quantum Organization

1. Members Actively Participate in Designing Their Surrounding Systems
2. Members Actively Participate in Designing Their Business Processes
3. Members Explicitly Manage What Flows Between the Cracks on the Organization Chart
4. Members Self-Manage Their Self-Designed Organization
5. Members Expand Their Mind/Body/Spirit Consciousness
6. Members Maintain Healthy Relationships with Key Stakeholders
7. Members Continually Transform Themselves and Their Organization

As a total set, these seven features represent a revolutionary, new kind of organization. Numerous names have been offered: an empowered organization, an organic–adaptive organization, a horizontal organization, a knowledge–creating organization, and a learning organization. Because of its newness, there's still little consensus concerning what this organization is like or what it's best to call it. It's not evident, for example, whether any existing organizations can serve as useful prototypes.

During this process of summarizing the seven distinguishing features of a quantum organization, it's worthwhile to point out THE SINGLE prime feature that defines this new revolutionary approach for self–designing systems, processes, and people: *A quantum organization continuously encourages its members to thoroughly examine — and expand — their mind/body/spirit consciousness and then utilize that expanded consciousness to resolve their many complex problems and conflicts in the most effective, efficient, and satisfying manner possible.*

1. Members Actively Participate in Designing Their
   Surrounding Systems

All members of a quantum organization would be actively involved in self–designing their formal systems (which include strategy, structure, and reward systems) – which might also rely on the active involvement of key external stakeholders (such as suppliers and customers). *This widespread participation means that members' hands-on knowledge regarding their work in the organization (including their wisdom, skills, interests, and experiences) will influence how strategy, structure, and reward systems are designed and aligned with one another.* And when these newly designed systems are put into practice, these same members will be in the best position to deeply understand the context of implementation, which allows them to appreciate how to apply their formal systems to achieve long–term success. This proactive, widespread, participative approach to the redesign of formal systems purposely relies on the self-aware consciousness of the membership and other key stakeholders – which, as noted previously, is THE SINGLE defining feature of a well–functioning quantum organization.

What often occurs in Newtonian organizations, however, is quite different: Here, formal systems are exclusively designed by senior executives (or by outside consultants who specialize in strategy, structure, and/or reward systems) with either meager or no participation by the "silenced membership" who'll determine the eventual success or failure of those formal systems. Perhaps even more incomprehensible, however, is when the uninvolved members are then required to follow all official procedures to the letter – even though they don't understand them.

2. Members Actively Participate in the Design of Their Business Processes

The actively involved members of a quantum organization would also use all their consciousness, knowledge, expertise, and experience for self-designing *value-added processes*, which would include business, management, and learning processes that can be explicitly described, controlled, and improved for long–term organizational success. **The active participation by all relevant internal and external stakeholders would help ensure that the organization's key processes will indeed address the needs of all its constituencies – which requires that same widespread participation that was used for designing the organization's formal systems.**

Through greater self–awareness and consciousness, members would also be more reflective about their processes. Aside from performing their portion of the relevant *business processes* in an effective and efficient manner, members would also be inspired to improve their *learning processes*. The subject of organizational learning will be examined in more detail in the last track of the completely integrated program (i.e., the learning process track), which is presented in Chapter 10. For the time being, however, it's enough to know that a key aspect of organizational learning is becoming more aware of how members acquire, store, and use knowledge. **This focus on learning in a quantum organization is in sharp contrast to what usually takes place in Newtonian organizations, in which all attention is focused on following well-established procedures exactly and faithfully, while never attempting to improve anything, let alone considering how to achieve better (and much faster) improvement during the next performance cycle.**

3. Members Explicitly Manage What Flows Between the Cracks on the Organization Chart

Another feature that helps to define a quantum organization is also based on the self-aware consciousness of members (and other key stakeholders). Continuous attention would be directed to what flows "between the cracks" on the organization chart – whether processes, information, responsibilities, or member's behavior and attitudes. A highly cooperative effort would have been undertaken to first self-design and then implement formal systems and processes so members can focus all their wisdom and energy on the most strategically significant activities. In our interconnected global marketplace, however, it isn't possible to organize work into perfectly contained, independent work units (whether jobs, departments, or entire organizations). **Some vital work, therefore, will always flow across subunit boundaries in any organization.**

A quantum organization, however, explicitly examines all its cross-boundary processes to manage these "cracks" in the most efficient and effective way possible. Declarations such as "it's not my problem," "that is not my job," and "it's not my department's responsibility" would rarely, if ever, be mentioned in a quantum organization. Instead, the usually ignored "white space" or "open space" on the chart would simply be regarded as presenting new opportunities for integrating systems and processes as well as suggesting entirely new ways to resolve old problems – which previously were addressed separately and, thus, incompletely.

Equally significant, members and other stakeholders would also be aware of early-warning signals that could identify when a redesign of their current systems and processes is warranted. Since members who work together within the same work group can best perform the most interdependent tasks and decisions, **it's necessary to know when it's the right time to rearrange the most troublesome cross-boundary processes into new subunits, so problematic task flow will be contained within (not across) subunit boundaries**.

4. Members Self-Manage Their Self-Designed Organization

All members of a quantum organization would be actively involved in self-managing their systems and processes – just as soon as they've been designed (and implemented). Of course, the active participation of other stakeholders would also be included in self-managing the quantum organization. Thus, as opposed to high–level managers being in complete charge of daily planning, coordinating, administrating, evaluating, and performing other such managerial activities, the members of subunits themselves would now be fully responsible for performing these traditional management functions. Recruiting, hiring, training, educating, developing, retaining, and promoting members would also be the responsibility of the subunit itself. As circumstances change, the members of these work units would also be involved in first formulating and then implementing improvements in all their systems and processes.

5. Members Expand Their Mind/Body/Spirit Consciousness

Members of a quantum organization would be passionately committed to enhancing their self–awareness and mind/body/spirit consciousness – as the primary driver of long–term success. Thus, avenues both inside and outside the organization would be made available so all members could continuously enhance all aspects of their self–aware consciousness. During educational programs, members would encourage one another to augment their self–knowledge in order to foster self–identity, self–esteem, and self–worth. By trying to identify – and then improve – these foundational aspects of self–aware consciousness, members will be capable of focusing all their time and energy on addressing important problems and conflicts in their organization – instead of being drained by psychological defense mechanisms or self–defeating interpersonal behavior. Therefore, *a deep commitment to self-discovery and self-understanding will inspire members to contribute to something larger than themselves, which will ultimately provide all members with more meaning, success, and satisfaction.*

Not surprisingly, Newtonian organizations have no place for self-awareness and consciousness. Such subjects are considered strictly private matters: to occur far away from the job and to be kept there. Only those "hired parts" of employees that specifically pertain to "doing the job" are accepted as under the jurisdiction of senior management. In a Newtonian organization, it would be viewed as inappropriate (and possibly unethical) for managers to encourage members to enhance their self-knowledge.

By the way, in Chapter 11, I will discuss HOW to expand the mind/body/spirit consciousness of all members and then bring that expanded consciousness into the workplace, where it can dramatically improve how members address all their complex problems and conflicts. In fact, there's no doubt in my mind that *expanding all members' self-awareness consciousness is the future mission in the fields of human resources management, organizational development, and organizational effectiveness.*

6. Members Maintain Healthy Relationships with Key Stakeholders

The members in a quantum organization would maintain their relationships with all the other individuals they have ever worked with before, including members in other subunits and external stakeholders – notwithstanding transfers, promotions, restructurings, reorganizations, and consolidations.

Forming, developing, and sustaining both within–group and across–group connections builds organization–wide commitment and thus fosters a greater potential for systemwide collaboration. Moreover, preserving those cross-boundary connections enables members to manage the typically ignored space between formal systems and processes. Consequently, rather than identifying this in–between space as white space, empty space, open space, and someone else's space, *it is vital that members remain actively*

2 BASIC, GROUP, AND ADVANCED TRAINING IN CONFLICT MANAGEMENT

THOMAS–KILMANN INSTRUMENT (TKI)

It's a great pleasure to share with you the evolution of my decades of research and consulting work in conflict management and change management, which, of course, includes all that I've learned from using the Thomas–Kilmann Instrument (TKI) with many organizations since the early 1970s. That evolution of my work with the TKI led me to create the Kilmann Organizational Conflict Instrument (KOCI) almost 50 years later. In essence, the KOCI measures how frequently an organization's systems and processes (i.e., culture, strategy, structure, rewards, and so forth) are interfering with members achieving organizational success, which thus makes it difficult for them to resolve their complex problems and conflicts.

Incidentally, I chose the title of this chapter to correspond to the same titles of my three TKI-based online courses on conflict management that are available on my website: (1) my two-hour BASIC Training course that enables participants to learn how to accurately interpret their own as well as other people's *Individual* TKI Profiles; (2) my three-hour GROUP Training course, which helps participants learn how to develop and interpret the more complex *Group* TKI Profiles; and (3) my eight-hour ADVANCED Training course that helps participants learn how to use the five conflict-handling modes to identify and resolve an *organization's* most complex problems and conflicts.

The Big Picture of the Complex Hologram, which I introduced in Figure 1.3 (Chapter 1), reveals the great variety of conflicts and problems that arise in our organizations and institutions – not only the interpersonal conflicts between two or more people, but also the variety of conflicts between the individual members in the organization and their surrounding systems and processes, as well as all the conflicts that are set in motion by the particular needs, requirements, and expectations from the organization's external stakeholders (such as customers, suppliers, government agencies, competitors, the community, and so forth). But before I say more about the KOCI instrument and how it can be used to diagnose an organization for the "barriers to success" that must be transformed into "channels for success", I will first explain the essence of conflict and present the TKI Conflict Model, both of which take center stage in the *Quantum Wheel*, which is illustrated in Figure 1.5 (Chapter 1).

THE ESSENCE OF CONFLICT

Just like death and taxes, conflict is inevitable. Consequently, there's no escape from conflict and there's no way of eliminating conflict. This "reality" about the persistence of conflict seems to be the case for both physical systems and human society.

If you've ever studied quantum physics, you'll know that the essence of physical reality is composed of sub-atomic particles, larger elements, and chemical chains that are ALWAYS in some opposition to other particles, forces, and energies. Essentially, it's through those tensions, polarities, dialectics (and experiencing all those resulting conflicts) *that the physical world and life itself continue to evolve into more elaborate physical arrangements and various stages of consciousness.* It is important to remember that the great German philosopher, Georg Wilhelm Friedrich Hegel, saw **the evolution of society as a perpetual struggle between a thesis and its anti-thesis. Through that struggle between such polar (dialectical) opposites, a synthesis eventually emerges that includes – and**

yet transcends — all the previous theses and anti-theses that came before.

In time, that new synthesis then finds itself in opposition to another, new, anti-thesis, and then the process of synthesis – and evolution and revolution – continues to untangle. *In both human and physical systems, we always have a thesis and an antithesis, which, in essence, produces what we experience as conflict.* But with that existence of conflict, we now have the potential of creating a higher–order synthesis, as we address – and resolve – the differences between the most recent thesis and its opposing anti–thesis. As a result of this recurring dance between thesis and anti–thesis, it might be said that the chief role or prime purpose of conflict is to inspire creativity, which thus sows the seeds for the further evolution of both the material world and human consciousness.

Another key principle to keep in mind is that conflict itself is neutral. Yet, I still meet people who think of conflict as bad, and who genuinely believe that it would be a much better world if we eliminated all conflict. But then I tell these people: "If we eliminated all conflict, we'd all be dead!" So the crucial questions to address are as follows: How do we *manage* conflict? How can we benefit from confronting conflict? And how can we minimize the ineffective approaches to conflict (since conflict is not going away any time soon)?

THE TKI CONFLICT MODEL

On Figure 2.1, you can see the two underlying dimensions on the TKI Conflict Model, which define the entire space for conflict management. The first dimension is **assertiveness,** which defines the extent to which you attempt to get *your* needs and concerns met in any situation. The second dimension is **cooperativeness,** which is the extent to which you try to satisfy the *other* person's needs and concerns in that same situation.

FIGURE 2.1

THE TKI CONFLICT MODEL — TWO UNDERLYING DIMENSIONS

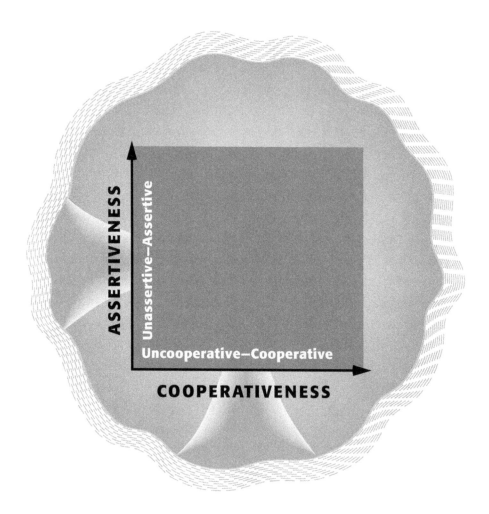

Figure 2.2 reveals the five conflict modes that cover the space of assertiveness and cooperativeness on the TKI Conflict Model. Of course, we could have defined a larger number of behaviors on that same conflict management space. But the convention of using these five conflict modes follows from the original model that Blake and Mouton first presented in their 1964 book, titled, *The Managerial Grid,* even though they used two different labels, "Concern for People" and "Concern for Production" for those two underlying dimensions and different names for the five modes.

FIGURE 2.2

THE TKI CONFLICT MODEL — FIVE CONFLICT MODES

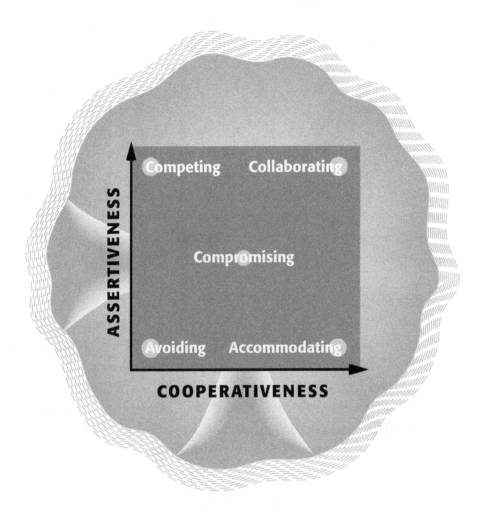

I'll now discuss what each of these five conflict modes is all about. Let's start with the competing mode, which is defined as high assertiveness and low cooperativeness. **When you use the competing mode,** you are only trying to satisfy your own needs and concerns; you're not at all concerned about satisfying the other person's needs in that same situation.

The opposite of competing is accommodating. **When you use the accommodating mode,** your prime concern is to satisfy the *other* person's needs. In fact, in the extreme, you don't get any of your needs met, and the other person gets all of his or her needs met. Thus, the accommodating mode is high on cooperativeness and low on assertiveness.

In the very center of the conflict management space, we place compromising. **When you use the compromising mode,** you are attempting to get *some* of your needs met and *some* of the other people's needs met. You might try to split the difference between the two of you, so both of you are at least partly satisfied with a middle-ground solution to your conflict – since compromising is moderate in both assertiveness and cooperativeness.

Now let's consider the avoiding mode, which is low on both assertiveness and cooperativeness. **When you use the avoiding mode,** you essentially leave the situation – physically, mentally, and emotionally – so no person gets her needs met, not even partially, which is why the avoiding mode was originally called: withdrawing.

It's now time to examine the remaining conflict mode, which I saved for last. Make no mistake about it: **Collaborating is the most complex and challenging conflict mode.** At first, it sounds ideal: "If we can collaborate, we'll get all our needs met. Let's use the collaborating mode for every conflict situation!"

And yet, we have to realize that the collaborating mode is only suited for a particular situation: For collaborating to do its magic, there must be a culture that engenders trust, openness, and candor among all the people involved in the conflict. The participants must also be able to communicate very clearly and respectfully with one another, because to get all your needs and other people's needs met, everyone has to openly express what they really want and need. Said differently, if there is mistrust, people won't share their true needs with others. In addition, for the collaborating mode to be effective, you also have to listen very intently to what the other person has to say and what he or she needs and wants. Therefore, speaking clearly and listening intently are both essential conditions for making effective use of the collaborating mode.

However, if the various conditions for using the collaborating mode are not yet in place, using this ideal-sounding mode will predictably waste everyone's time and, besides, cannot possibly achieve the desired outcome.

WHEN TO USE EACH CONFLICT-HANDLING MODE

Here is the first key principle I introduced to you in Chapter 1 when I presented the Complex Hologram: *About 80% of what takes place in an organization is determined by its systems and processes, while only 20% is determined by individual desires or preferences.*

Here's the second key principle to always remember (which follows directly from that first principle): *Choose the particular conflict-handling mode that best matches the key attributes of the situation.* Therefore, do NOT use any mode out of habit or based only on your typical preferences. Instead, choose – and use – one or more of the five conflict modes based exclusively on how you would answer these eight questions:

THE EIGHT KEY ATTRIBUTES OF A CONFLICT SITUATION
1. Is there overwhelming stress?
2. Is the conflict simple or complex?
3. How important is the topic to each person in the situation?
4. Is there time to discuss the issues?
5. Is there sufficient trust to openly share needs and concerns?
6. Do people have good listening and communication skills?
7. Does the culture and reward system actively encourage people to share their true needs and concerns?
8. How important are relationships to each person in the situation?

Depending on these eight attributes, members should choose the conflict mode that has the best chance of satisfying not only their most important needs but also the most important needs of their organization and its key internal and external stakeholders.

Below are five listings that summarize when it is best to use each of the five modes, depending on the particular quality and nature of those eight key attributes of a conflict situation. Note: Each numbered item on these lists (1, 2, 3, etc.) corresponds to the same numbered attribute that appears on the above list of eight key attributes.

WHEN TO USE COMPETING
1. Stress is high or moderate
2. Problem is simple: unidimensional
3. Problem is more important to you than to others
4. There is little time for discussion
5. Low or moderate levels of trust exist
6. People can communicate their views
7. The culture and reward system support members who argue their positions in a win/lose manner
8. People are not concerned with sustaining their relationships

WHEN TO USE COLLABORATING
1. Stress is stimulating
2. Problem is complex: multidimensional
3. Problem is equally important to all
4. There is much time for discussion
5. High levels of trust exist
6. Interactions are effective
7. The culture and the reward system actively encourage exploration, cooperation, and teamwork
8. People want their relationships to last

WHEN TO USE COMPROMISING
1. Stress is high or moderate
2. Problem is simple: unidimensional
3. Problem is moderately important to all
4. There is little time for discussion
5. Moderate or low levels of trust exist
6. Interactions are respectful
7. The culture and reward system encourage quick fixes
8. People are indifferent about their relationships

WHEN TO USE AVOIDING
1. Stress is overwhelming
2. Problem is simple: unidimensional
3. Problem is not important
4. There is little time for discussion
5. Low levels of trust exist
6. Interactions are ineffective
7. The culture and reward system discourage confrontation
8. People don't particularly care about their relationships

WHEN TO USE ACCOMMODATING
1. Stress is moderate or high
2. Problem is simple: unidimensional
3. Problem is more important to others
4. There is little time for discussion
5. Moderate or low levels of trust exist
6. Interactions are ineffective
7. The culture and reward system encourage compliance
8. People are eager to please others to maintain their relationships

With regard to the first key attribute of a conflict situation, **I always begin by determining the relative level of stress among the participants.** Is it high, medium, or low? If I sense that the stress is overwhelming, I already know that the several people in the conflict situation can't possibly use the collaborating mode. It might even be difficult for the parties to use the compromising mode, which requires some back–and–forth dialogue in order to propose a middle–group resolution.

Let's take a look at the other three conflict modes, competing, avoiding, and accommodating, which are feasible options when there is low or moderate stress. **But when there's overwhelming stress, competing, avoiding, and accommodating immediately morph into fight, flight, and freeze.** Specifically, when there is overwhelming stress, competing turns into fight, avoiding turns into flight, and accommodating turns into freeze.

Technically speaking, a fight, flight, or freeze reaction is the sympathetic nervous system's automatic way of protecting the person from possible harm or death. Thus, overwhelming stress makes it exceedingly difficult, if not impossible, to be conscious about anything, so it's usually best to postpone the conversation regarding the conflict until the people in the situation can regain their composure, are no longer stressed out, and therefore are no longer prone to react in a defensive, protective, or dysfunctional manner, whether at home or at work.

By the way, in my Expanding Consciousness Course, I present a modified TKI Conflict Model in order to emphasize the primal reactions that happen when members are feeling overwhelming stress, which I reproduce in Figure 2.3 below. As you can see, I eliminate the usual space that surrounds the collaborating mode and the compromising mode, since these two modes are simply unavailable when people are so stressed out that they can't even think clearly or have a thoughtful conversation. **On that reduced conflict management space, competing becomes fight, avoiding becomes flight, and accommodating becomes freeze.** In terms of the two underlying dimensions, assertiveness reverts to attacking behavior and cooperativeness reverts to retreating behavior.

FIGURE 2.3
THREE CONFLICT MODES UNDER HIGH STRESS

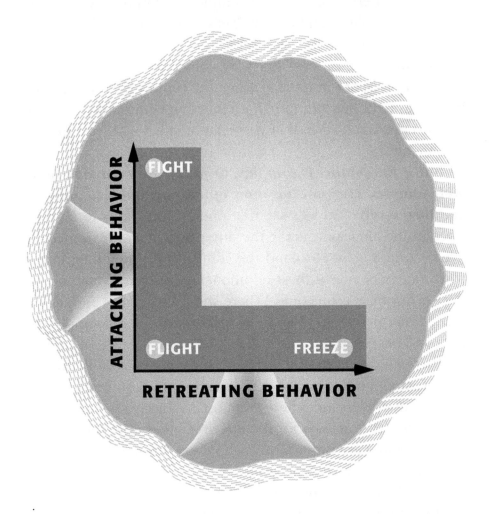

The second key attribute of a conflict situation concerns this question: **Is the conflict simple or complex?** By that distinction, I mean: Is the conflict on one dimension (as in unidimensional), or are there several aspects or numerous issues involved that also pertain to the conflict in question (as in multidimensional)?

Here's an example. If two people are trying to decide when to hold a meeting, one might say, "Let's meet at three o'clock in the afternoon." The other person might say: Let's meet at five o'clock." Yes, this discussion begins as a very simple conflict to resolve!

Both people may then realize that they're likely to choose a starting time for their meeting somewhere between three and five in the afternoon. A great example of compromise is when they quickly split the difference: "Let's meet at four o'clock."

Although that middle-ground solution does not satisfy either person super well, at least they have come up with an acceptable compromise. That can happen when the conflict is rather simple, in this case, the starting time for a meeting with no other issues or concerns involved in that particular conflict – at least for the time being.

But if the conflict is complex, or purposely expanded to be more complex, everyone has more options available to consider and then resolve. So let's say that one person wants to meet at three in the afternoon while the other person wants to meet at five o'clock. But they expand the conflict into something larger when one person asks these additional questions: "What will we discuss during our meeting? Where should we meet? Should we invite other people to attend our meeting? Who will supply the food and beverages?"

These kinds of questions expand the conflict from the initial focus that was only about agreeing on the starting time for their meeting to now include these additional subjects: the location of the meeting, the agenda for the meeting, other attendees for the meeting, and, very importantly, who should bring the food and beverages to the meeting.

The initial conflict was only about the meeting time (which is strictly unidimensional and therefore would be rather simple to address). But by asking several more questions, the initial conflict has been expanded into additional dimensions for the meeting – which then makes the expanded conflict multidimensional and more complex, rather than only have to agree on a starting time.

As a result of expanding the conflict from one dimension to several matters to consider, thus transforming a simple conflict into a more complex one, it's now possible to pick a synergistic resolution by making use of the collaborating mode, whereby the two participants now have the opportunity to come up with a multifaceted resolution that satisfies everyone in the situation, in one way or another. In the case of just two people, one person might say: "I wanted to begin the meeting at three in one of our offices, so we would be done by dinner time."

The other person then says, "If you come to my home at five o'clock, I'll have a delicious dinner already prepared for us, so we can thoroughly enjoy ourselves while we get our work done."

Next, they can now consider what particular issues should be discussed during their meeting. Indeed, perhaps one or both of them realize that by being removed from their everyday work environment, they can now discuss some challenging issues that have concerned them in the past, but they haven't yet been able to address them back in the workplace where there's usually too much stress, competing demands for their attention, and limited time. Ironically, when they finally come up with a multifaceted resolution, they may find that their initial conflict concerning when to start their meeting turns out to be quite elementary. In fact, the problem of agreeing on the meeting time has become a rather trivial conflict as compared to what topics would actually be discussed at the meeting and who else should attend.

The third key attribute of a conflict situation concerns the relative importance of the topic, relative to everything else that needs to be addressed by the persons in the situation – whether it is personal or work related.

This third attribute, just like the others, helps you to choose – and use – one or several of the five conflict modes in order to resolve the current situation.

For example, if the topic is crucial to both people, all things being equal, the collaborating mode has the best opportunity of satisfying both people's needs, so long as the other key attributes to effectively use the collaborating mode are also present in the situation: such as low to moderate levels of stress, sufficient trust for the parties to share their true needs, sufficient time to discuss the issues, and so forth.

However, if the topic is much more important to one person than it is to the other, that's when a combination of competing and accommodating can effectively be used, so the person who's most concerned about that topic gets his needs satisfied when he asserts himself – while other person, who's not as affected by the outcome, graciously accommodates.

But if the conflict is, at most, only of moderate importance to both persons, then choosing and using the compromising mode is recommended, so both people can at least get some of their needs met, even though the issue is not of prime importance to either of them.

When the subject isn't important to either person, however, then the use of the avoiding mode is clearly suggested, so both people can move on to address a much more important conflict or problem.

The fourth key attribute of a conflict situation concerns this question: Is there sufficient time to have a probing discussion on this issue? As I have suggested previously, the collaborating mode can take a lot of time for each person to share and discuss what they really need and want. And then, it usually takes even more time to generate and discuss different possible resolutions to the conflict, which would then allow the participants to create an integrated – synergistic – resolution that effectively addresses all the multifaceted aspects of their complex conflict. If sufficient time is not available for a thorough, probing discussion, then it's best to use one of the other conflict modes.

Nonetheless, even using the compromising mode can take a little time for people to discuss several middle–ground solutions and then to select or negotiate a workable resolution for both parties. If there's very limited time, however, then one of the two persons, the boss, for example, might use the competing mode and thereby assert, hence officially announce, his resolution of the conflict and then expect the other members to accommodate and fully accept that decision.

If an executive uses the competing mode to authoritatively determine the final resolution to the conflict, such an approach usually takes very little time, and may be completely acceptable in certain situations, so long as the most important needs and concerns of the group members are not being ignored during other conflicts. Naturally, if there is little or no time for even a brief interaction of the competing and accommodating modes, then the avoiding mode might be the best choice in the situation until the parties have the necessary time (or *make* the time) for a more engaging discussion.

The fifth key attribute of a conflict situation has to do with trust. If people don't trust one another and thus have trouble in trusting the other person's words or intentions, you can forget about using the collaborating mode. People will not share what they really need and want if they believe what they share might be used against them sometime in the future. And when there's low trust, people won't engage in a creative, open, and candid dialogue to develop a synergistic solution to a complex conflict. Instead, with fairly low levels of trust, all conversations will be guarded, as people deliberately withhold vital information and withhold their true feelings in order to protect themselves from actual or perceived harm.

But if there *IS* sufficient trust among the participants in the conflict, then the use of the collaborating mode is now possible, so long as the other key attributes of the situation also support the effective use of the collaborating mode.

The sixth key attribute of the conflict situation concerns the quality of the interactions among the key participants in the conflict. If their interactions produce defensiveness (because of blaming or judging behavior, let alone mean–spirited behavior), and if there's hardly any listening going on (since the parties are only interested in expressing their own needs without a genuine desire to learn what others need), then trying to use the conflict modes that require quality interaction will simply not work – namely collaborating and, to a lesser extent, compromising.

Basically, when the interactions among the participants in the conflict are ineffective or even demeaning (that is, when there is defensive–producing behavior combined with no listening, only the competing/accommodating combination of conflict modes is a viable choice in such a situation.

Nevertheless, if you choose to use the competing mode, you still have to clearly – and convincingly – express what you need and want, and why it is so important to you, so the other person has the best chance to understand and also accept your position. Naturally, choose the avoiding mode when people's interactions are dysfunctional or mean-spirited.

Let's discuss the seventh key attribute of a conflict situation, which concerns all those surrounding systems that affect how conflicts are addressed. In particular, we can ask this question: Do the cultural norms in the group, department, or organization encourage members to express their true needs and concerns? So often, the surrounding culture compels members to use the avoiding mode by expecting them to follow these silent cultural norms: "Keep your opinions to yourself since you have to play it safe around here." Similar cultural norms that support avoiding behavior might be expressed as follows: "Don't step on the toes of senior management; don't rock the boat; don't make waves; let the other fool take the chance of openly expressing new ideas and alternative solutions during group meetings."

Essentially, regardless of what your personal preferences are with respect to using one conflict mode or another, the usually implicit – but highly influential – cultural norms may have something else to say about what conflict mode is safe to use in your organization. And never ignore the potential impact of the reward system on how conflicts are being addressed in your group or department. You may, in fact, get seriously penalized when it's time for your annual performance appraisal if you've openly confronted other members, let alone your boss or other managers, about certain topics, which nobody really wanted to discuss. If you stir up trouble and bad feelings, as other members or managers experience your continued efforts to openly discuss certain sensitive conflicts, you might later be the recipient of a negative performance appraisal. In most organizations, it's quite evident which members receive bonuses, raises, and promotions, and whether those fortunate persons have actually played it safe or, instead, have openly expressed their opinions on one conflict or another. As members notice the relationship between playing it safe and later getting rewarded for such protective behavior, the reward system becomes one more attribute that may limit the use of the more assertive conflict modes, such as competing, collaborating, and compromising.

The eighth key attribute of a conflict situation considers how important the relationship is to both people and if they want their relationship to last. It has become quite apparent that unless each person in the situation gets some of his most important needs met over an extended period of time, he will either disengage from the situation and only do the minimum to get by — or he'll leave the situation altogether. As a result, if, over time, the avoiding mode is used again and again, or if some members are expected to regularly accommodate others, many members will gradually disengage from work and, at some later time, simply take another job somewhere else. Even if all or most conflicts are resolved by using the compromising mode, people in the situation will only be partially satisfied – which does NOT lead to an engaged, enthusiastic, and empowered workforce.

Always remember this principle: *If it's important to you to stay on good terms with the other people in the situation, then over a period of time, you have to make sure that those others will get their most important needs met.* This principle means that all members in the family, group, or organization must be able to use the more assertive conflict modes of competing and collaborating from time to time, which must, of course, also be supported by the other key attributes of a conflict situation.

THE BEST APPROACH TO CONFLICT MANAGEMENT

Many times, people have asked me: "What is the best conflict mode for managing differences between two or more people?" As you can imagine, I always respond to this kind of question by letting people know that there's not a single best conflict mode to use in all situations, since the effectiveness of each of the five conflict mode always depends on how well the requirements of that mode match the key attributes of the situation. Each conflict mode, therefore, has its time and place; there is not a single best conflict mode for all occasions.

But even after I explain that situational perspective, people often repeat that same basic question: "Yes, I hear you, but I still want to know: What's the best approach for managing conflict?" Because people are always so eager to know the "best approach" for addressing conflict, the list below allows me to answer that popular question:

THE BEST APPROACH TO CONFLICT MANAGEMENT
- Know that you have all five conflict modes available to you at all times, in all situations
- Develop the ability to read (assess) the eight key attributes of any conflict situation
- Choose the conflict mode that best fits the specific situation
- Enact the chosen mode with care, sensitivity, and respect
- Switch to a different conflict mode as you experience changes in the key attributes of the situation
- Continue to improve your listening and communication skills — and your ability to engender trust

At the start, it's vital to know that all five conflict modes are available to you at all times, which first becomes apparent when you examine your results from taking the TKI assessment tool. Even if you discover that you typically rely on one or two modes most the time, you still get to see the *other* modes that you have inadvertently neglected, since those underused modes have not previously been incorporated in your behavioral repertoire. **But from taking the TKI, you can now discover that you have more behavioral options than you previously realized you had. With** *self-awareness and then trying out how to use those underused modes, you WILL have more behavioral choices in the future — for everyone's benefit, including your own.*

The next step is to accurately assess — to read — the eight key attributes in a conflict situation, as we've just discussed. So after you're aware that you theoretically have access to all five conflict modes and after you've also had a chance to practice using all five modes in one situation or another, **you now have to learn how to read the situation — so you can pick the best mode to use and, therefore, you are most likely to satisfy your needs as well as the other person's needs.**

As I noted before, the very first thing to assess is the level of stress in the situation, since that powerfully affects which of the five modes can be used under different levels of stress. Then we consider such additional key attributes as the complexity of the conflict, the relative importance of the conflict to each person, if there is enough time to discuss the issues, is there sufficient trust between the two people, and do we have good interaction skills, with regard to (1) conversing in non–defensive ways and then (2) listening attentively to what the other is saying? We also read the situation to access the following additional questions: What does the culture say about how to address and resolve conflicts in this family, group, or organization; what are the implications of the reward system on conflict–handling behavior; and do we intend to address this conflict in a manner that will help preserve our relationship well into the future? Once we assess those eight key attributes in the situation, we then can choose to use the one or more conflict modes that can be expected to be most effective in addressing and resolving the conflict in that particular situation.

After we have selected a conflict mode, however, we must still enact that chosen mode with great care, sensitivity and respect.

Perhaps an example would be helpful here: Let's consider the competing mode. I can assert myself by being forceful, dogmatic, authoritarian, and aggressive. Or I can try to win my position by wearing the other person down. Perhaps I'm even going to shout my point of view right in his face and hopefully intimidate him to accept my proposal. That's one way to compete.

But a different way to enact the compete mode is along these lines: "I'd like to explain why this subject is so important to me, and why I've worked so hard to devise my proposed resolution to our conflict.

"And since this conflict seems to be much more important to me than it is to you, perhaps you can let me have my way in this instance. And then, sometime in the future, when the situation is reversed, and we're then addressing an issue that's much more important to you than it is to me, I'll support your position on that issue. How's that?"

The latter approach is also using the competing mode, but it comes across very differently, precisely because it expresses care, sensitivity and respect to the other person in the situation.

I would like to emphasize that each of the five modes can be enacted in an emotionally intelligent manner, thus displaying a large dose of interpersonal sensitivity, dignity, and respect. Not only will most people respond in kind, but it's also a good way of sustaining a relationship among the participants. But if you enact a conflict mode without any regard to other people's feelings, needs, fears, and concerns, such a defensive-producing approach usually has some negative consequences – both short term and long term.

The next item on this list of "Best Approaches" is concerned with developing the skill of being able to quickly switch from using one conflict mode to using another conflict mode, as the key attributes of the situation change. If trust goes up or goes down, that change might encourage you to switch to a different conflict mode, say from compromising to collaborating or from collaborating to compromising. Or if you discover that the issue is not as important to you as you had thought at the outset, you might then switch to a different mode, perhaps from competing to accommodating. As a result of your interactions with others, whether deliberate or not, you might wind up changing one or more key attributes of the situation, which then suggests the use of a different mode. Conflict management is dynamic, regardless of which mode you first use to begin the discussion.

In sum, rather than initially reading the conflict situation and then using the same mode throughout the entire discussion, it's therefore critical to *keep reading the situation* – and every time you sense that something has shifted, anything that pertains to those eight attributes of a conflict situation, you can then choose a different conflict mode to use. That is the height of adaptability when it comes to effectively choosing – and using – a sequence of one conflict mode after another, as the situation changes.

The last bullet on this list of "Best Approaches" emphasizes the importance of always trying to improve your listening and communication skills, and your ability to engender trust. Even though the collaborating mode is not ideal in all situations, the more you can use this mode over a period of time, more people will get their most important needs met. Sustaining a high level of trust with other people in the situation, therefore, will allow you to use the collaborating mode more often than not, so long as the other key attributes also support that conflict mode. And then, if you can also keep the level of stress in the moderate to low range, and if you are able to expand the size of the pie by introducing additional aspects or concerns to the initial conflict situation, it's then more likely that you can use the collaborating mode effectively. ***But never forget that it won't be productive to collaborate under adverse conditions, such as when the issue is not that important or you have little time to have a through discussion on the relevant aspects of the conflict situation.***

THREE ADDITIONAL DIMENSIONS ON THE TKI CONFLICT MODEL

The TKI Conflict Model is deceptively simple, since it reveals so much about your five behavioral choices in any situation. But besides defining the two underlying dimensions of assertiveness and cooperativeness, I can define three diagonal dimensions that can be displayed on that same TKI Conflict Model, as shown in

Figure 2.4, **which provide even more insight and depth into the meaning of the five conflict modes and conflict management.**

FIGURE 2.4
THE TKI CONFLICT MODEL — THREE DIAGONAL DIMENSIONS

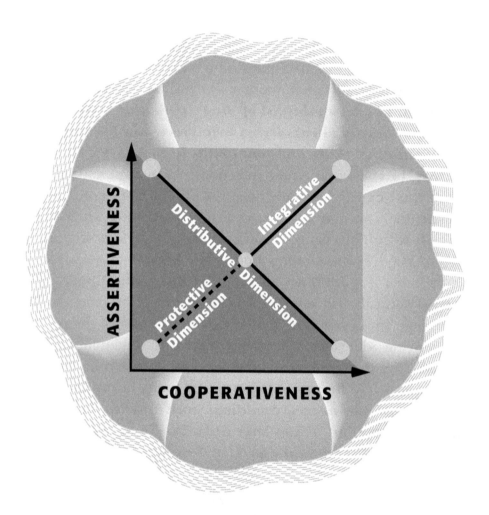

Let's proceed by first examining the **distributive dimension,** which moves back and forth from the competing mode through compromising to accommodating. In fact, as we move along this diagonal, we vary the relative percentage of what you get versus what I get in the final resolution of our conflict. For example, if we focus only on my needs, I'm 100% satisfied by the outcome, while you're 0% satisfied, since none of your needs or concerns has been addressed by our final resolution: I used the competing mode to get my needs met and you used the accommodating mode to concede to my preferences, which is represented by the upper–left circle on the distributive dimension.

At the other extreme, if I focus exclusively on satisfying *your* needs, then, in the end, I accommodate your preferences, while I get none of my needs and concerns addressed in the resolution, which is represented by the lower–right circle on the distributive dimension. Naturally, if we split our differences between us, we wind up with a compromise, whereby we both get our needs at least partially satisfied (e.g., a 50/50 split), which is shown at the midpoint on the distributive dimension.

Basically, when we stick to only those three conflict modes on the distributive dimension, the more I get, the less you get, and the more you get, the less I get. In a sense, the size of the pie (all that is available for us to distribute between us) remains fixed; we are only negotiating over the size of the piece of the pie that I will get versus the size of the piece of the pie that you'll get. *Our two pieces always combine to make up the entire pie.* Sometimes, the distributive dimension is referred to as a zero–sum game, or as the give–and–take dimension, or the win/lose dimension: Thus, the more you win, the more I lose – since the size of the pie is fixed. Many conflicts in life are approached and resolved on this diagonal dimension. As a result, when the conflict is regarded as simple, meaning that the issue concerns only one dimension of disagreement, the discussion usually moves along this diagonal. But at other times, people assume that they only have two stark behavioral choices: (1) We do it *my* way. (2) We do it *your* way. But there's much more to conflict management than having to make either/or choices that are situated on the distributive dimension.

Let's now consider the diagonal dimension that moves from compromising to collaborating, what I refer to as the **integrative dimension**. By moving up the integrative diagonal, *we can expand the size of the pie by adding more aspects and topics to the initial conflict.* By having several items to consider, we have the chance to first develop – and then agree upon – a multifaceted resolution that satisfies the most important needs of all the participants in the conflict situation.

Perhaps it would be worthwhile to provide an example that conveys the main differences between the distributive and the integrative dimension. Let's use a union–management dispute on the subject of wages for the union employees.

The union wants its members to receive $25 per hour for the next two years, while senior management wants its employees to continue receiving the current $20 per hour. On the distributive diagonal, it's easy to go back and forth on that seesaw between $25 and $20 an hour for union wages. This is a useful example of a give–and–take or win/lose discussion on a unidimensional topic, which identifies a rather simple conflict about the hourly pay for union members over the next two years.

But let's suppose we are able to expand the size of the pie, so we can travel up the integrative dimension. Let's add on a few more issues to the conflict, such as working conditions, flextime, greater union involvement in decisions that are important to its members, and so forth. Let's say we also include fringe benefits, or tuition benefits. As we add on more aspects and concerns to the original conflict, we expand the size of the pie to include not just wages, but also working conditions and the quality of work life. If the eight key attributes in the conflict situation support the use of the collaborating mode, it's now possible to create a multifaceted, multidimensional resolution, whereby both union members and the organization's senior management get their most important needs met.

It's worthwhile to emphasize this key point: To move up the integrative dimension, there must be considerable trust between union and management. There must also be excellent listening and communication skills. The cultural norms must encourage candor, openness, and deep respect. The union and management representatives must be willing to devote the time to have more probing discussions on all those relevant issues that make up the expanded pie. And both parties must also realize that it's very important to satisfy everyone's needs as best as possible, so a healthy working relationship between union and management continues well into the future. Clearly, a satisfied workforce that trusts senior management is much more likely to be engaged, empowered, and enthusiastic about its job and about its role in the organization, short term and long term.

Let's now examine the **protective dimension** – the diagonal that runs between avoiding and compromising. I purposely use the word "protective" to emphasize when people tend to avoid conflicts, even though not resolving those issues will negatively affect their personal satisfaction and organizational success.

There are a number of good reasons to avoid conflicts, such as when you need more time to examine an important decision, since you first have to learn more about the subject, speak to a few more people, and so forth. But if the topic is very important to both people, then we have to develop the conditions, the key attributes of the situation, so that people can satisfy their most important needs.

But if you're in a conflict situation that initially falls on the protective dimension, you and the other person are probably experiencing fear or spite. In the case of fear, people say: "I'm not going to share with others what I really need or want, since, at some later time, they'll use what I said against me. I've been hurt in the past from sharing my true feelings and I don't intend to set myself up for additional hurt in the future." By definition, if people are holding back from sharing what they really need and want, they're protecting themselves. If one or both parties don't talk about the topic or only do so in superficial ways, nobody is getting their needs met. No satisfactory resolution can possibly occur when people believe they have to protect themselves from either real or imagined harm.

In the case of spite, the person is saying something like this: "To make sure that you'll get less than what you want, I'm going to take less myself." Spite is evident when one person purposely withholds their own need satisfaction, just so the other persons won't get their needs met.

Let's be clear: **Whenever people act out fear or spite during any conflict situation, the size of the pie shrinks**. As fewer issues are considered, any resolution on the protective dimension will provide the two parties with much less than if they'd been able to arrive at a resolution that fell on the distributive dimension.

Specifically, on the distributive dimension, if one person gets 100% of their needs met, while the other person gets 0%, at least one person is totally satisfied. But when both persons avoid the topic, they both get 0% of their needs met. If there is a superficial resolution on the protective dimension, maybe one person gets 25% of his needs met, while the other person gets 15%. That 25% and 15% on the protective dimension adds to 40% in total, while arriving at a one-sided resolution on the distributive dimension still adds to 100% – the total size of the distributive pie.

In sharp contrast, a resolution that moves up the integrative dimension can satisfy 90% of one's person's needs and 90% of the other person's needs, which creates a much larger pie that now totals 180% in combined need satisfaction!

CONCLUDING THOUGHTS

The particular conditions that surround a conflict (as based on those eight key attributes of a conflict situation) significantly determine whether that conflict is addressed on the protective, the distributive, or the integrative dimension. In the short term, however, the surrounding systems might prevent certain modes from being used effectively – notably the more assertive modes, and particularly the collaborating mode. **But in the long term, the surrounding systems and processes can be transformed via the eight tracks of quantum transformation in order to support the effective use of all conflict-handling modes.**

But even if the systems and processes can be revitalized to support the use for all five conflict modes, the participants must still be able to read the situation, choose the right conflict mode, adjust the mode as the situation changes, and then enact each conflict mode with great care, sensitivity, and respect.

DIAGNOSING SYSTEMS CONFLICTS

KILMANN ORGANIZATIONAL CONFLICT INSTRUMENT (KOCI)

In the early 1970s, Kenneth Thomas and I developed the TKI assessment tool in order to measure how individuals attempt to resolve their interpersonal conflicts, **but without specifying any particular situation**. In fact, directly below are the standard TKI instructions that are printed on every TKI paper booklet and are also shown on your computer or mobile screen whenever you take the online version of the TKI assessment tool:

Consider situations in which you find your wishes differing from those of another person. How do you usually respond to such situations?

The respondent is shown 30 pairs of statements that describe different behavioral responses to any interpersonal conflict. For each pair of A/B choices, the respondent is asked to select either the A or B choice based on which statement best characterizes his or her behavior, which represents the five conflict–handling modes: collaborating, competing, compromising, avoiding, and accommodating. After a person completes her responses to all 30 items on the instrument, the results reveal which conflict modes that person might be using too much or too little, as compared to a large normative sample.

It's important to reemphasize this key point: **Respondents to the TKI are NOT presented with any interpersonal situation.** Instead, respondents are asked to provide their typical responses to conflict across ALL such situations. In fact, when a trainer or facilitator provides the TKI's standard instructions for a group of participants, there is always someone in the audience who asks this question: "Since I respond to conflict differently, depending if I'm at home or at work, which setting should I keep in mind while responding to the items on this instrument?"

In response to that popular question, the trainer or facilitator is expected to provide this standardized answer: "Don't think of any particular situation when you respond to the 30 A/B items on the TKI instrument. Just provide your *typical* response, your **average** response to conflict, across all the situations in your life."

By 1974, just before the TKI was officially published, Ken and I already knew that a few people had some difficulty with taking the TKI by mentally averaging, so to speak, their typical response to interpersonal conflicts across all possible situations – rather than focusing entirely on their conflict-handling behavior in the workplace or focusing only on their behavior in their home with family or friends, or in some other specified social setting. But despite this dilemma, we still decided to word the standard TKI instructions to illicit the typical or average behavioral response a person has to conflict in general, since our exclusive use of the TKI at that time (as young assistant professors) was in teaching graduate students who were either unemployed or held jobs in altogether different organizations.

MODIFYING THE STANDARD TKI INSTRUCTIONS

By the late 1970s, I became regularly involved in conducting management training workshops and implementing consulting programs INSIDE various organizations. Not surprisingly, I made considerable use of the TKI assessment, since almost everyone needed to be more comfortable with conflict and also learn how to manage workplace conflict much more effectively.

I don't recall exactly when I first tried modifying the TKI for a specific situation, but I began experimenting with modifying the TKI's standard instructions so that participant responses to the assessment would exclusively be focused on how conflicts were being addressed INSIDE the organization. So instead of using the standard TKI instructions, which ask people to consider ALL situations in their life, I began asking participants to respond to the TKI's 30 A/B items along these lines:

In this organization, or in this group, or in this department ... how do you usually respond when you find your wishes differing from those of other members?

When I modified the TKI's standard instructions in this way, respondents never again asked me whether they should respond to the TKI in terms of their conflict experiences at home or at work. I had now provided them with a particular situation that they could easily keep straight in their mind as they responded to all 30 A/B items on the TKI assessment tool.

USING TWO TKIS WITH MODIFIED INSTRUCTIONS

After having modified the standard TKI instructions for many organizations and work situations in the 1970s and 1980s, by the early 1990s, I thought it might be interesting to ask each person to take TWO TKIs, each with different modified instructions. This approach seemed pretty radical at the time, but revealed some valuable information that one TKI, by itself, could never provide.

To make a long story short, whenever I conduct management training programs or provide consulting services to any group or organization, *(1) I ask the members to take their first TKI from the specific perspective of INSIDE their group*, department, or organization (however they wish to focus on conflict at work), and then, directly afterwards, *(2) I ask those same members to take their second TKI from the general perspective of OUTSIDE their group* (meaning, how they typically respond to conflicts in *other* settings of their life, excluding their current group).

Basically, the second TKI asks respondents to provide their "average" or typical approach to conflict across all those other situations, which necessarily includes conflicts with their family members, friends, neighbors, other organizations, and so forth.

In contrast to the OUTSIDE perspective, when respondents focus on their conflict–handling behavior INSIDE their group, team, or organization, there are various systems and processes in an organization that tend to encourage or require members to use certain conflict modes more than others, in contrast to what modes these members typically use across all the *other* settings in their life.

So what did I learn from having members take two TKIs, each with modified instructions for (1) INSIDE their group or organization and (2) OUTSIDE their group or organization? Figure 3.1 provides one way of answering that question: Here we see an abridged organization chart with the senior executives at the very top of the hierarchy (i.e., the pyramid), the next level of managers immediately below them, followed by the next level of managers or non–supervisory personnel, and so forth. Naturally, very large organizations have many more levels, divisions, and groups, but this organization chart is sufficient for our purposes.

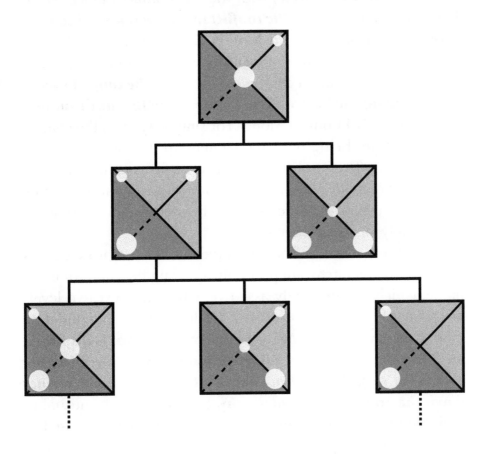

FIGURE 3.1
AN ORGANIZATION'S INSIDE TKI RESULTS

As you can see, I have found it particularly useful to replace each box on the organization chart, which represents a division, department or work group, with the TKI Conflict Model, which then graphically displays **the conflict modes that are being used most often, as shown by the large circles** where a conflict mode is positioned on the TKI Conflict Model. At the same time, each box on the organization chart also highlights t**he conflict modes that are being used least often, as shown by the much smaller circles** on the TKI Conflict Model. For simplicity sake, the conflict modes that are being used moderately are not shown by any symbol on the TKI Conflict Model. Instead, focusing primarily on those conflict modes that each group or department is possibly using too much or too little presents the most useful information in a visually clear–cut manner.

On this organization chart, observe that the senior executives on top of the hierarchy are primarily applying the compromising mode, which is moderately assertive, while the next two levels are primarily making use of the avoiding and accommodating modes, which are the LEAST assertive modes. **What is displayed on this chart is, in fact, a rather common result, revealing the overuse of avoiding and accommodating as we move farther down the organization's hierarchy.** In fact, it is not unusual to find that the senior executives at the top of the hierarchy use lots of competing, compromising, and collaborating to address their conflicts inside the organization, while members at the bottom of the hierarchy frequently use avoiding and accommodating in order to comply with the bosses and managers above them.

On Figure 3.2, the TKI results displayed on each box on the organization chart captures the OUTSIDE perspective, meaning that these results were based on members' responses to their SECOND TKI, with those modified instructions to measure their conflict–handling behavior OUTSIDE their group, department, or organization. As you can see from this figure, the more assertive modes are frequently being used outside the organization, and, most striking, **this same pattern of conflict-handling behavior emerges up and down the hierarchy and this pattern is also the**

same as we look across the various departments and groups at the same level in the organization. Said different, every box on the organization chart shows that members are rather assertive when they approach any conflict OUTSIDE the work setting, as indicated by the frequently used conflict modes of competing, collaborating, and compromising across the entire chart.

FIGURE 3.2
AN ORGANIZATION'S OUTSIDE TKI RESULTS

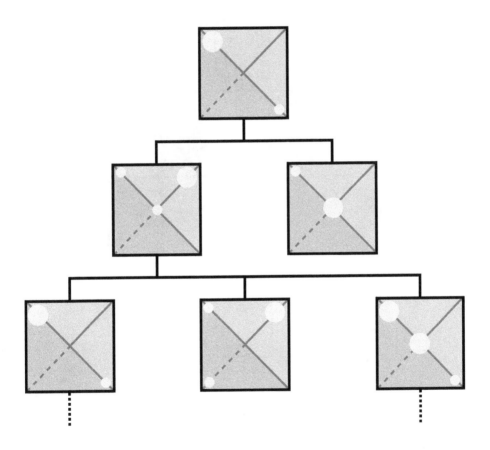

Now look back and forth between the INSIDE and OUTSIDE perspective, as vividly portrayed by the two organization charts reproduced in Figure 3.3. Sometimes, the INSIDE and OUTSIDE charts are very similar for an organization. But most of the time, the two charts are noticeably different, which usually shows that **the avoiding and accommodating modes are being used more frequently INSIDE the organization, particularly as you move from the senior management levels down the hierarchy to the frontline employees at the bottom of the chart:**

FIGURE 3.3
COMPARING THE INSIDE AND OUTSIDE TKI RESULTS

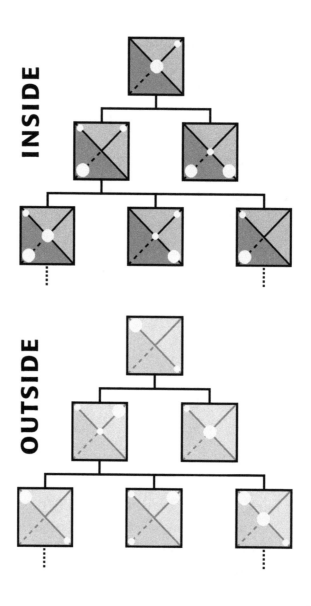

CHAPTER 3

But now I must confess: Even though it's easy to suggest the *probable* causes of any large discrepancies between the inside and outside perspective (e.g., the organization's culture, the group's culture, the reward system, and the leader's behavior, which are collectively known as the organization's systems and processes), technically speaking, my suggested list of probable causes for the differences in the INSIDE and OUTSIDE perspectives is only a guess – even if it's a good guess – based on all my knowledge of organizations and systems. Those two TKI assessments are only measuring the use of those five conflict–handling modes INSIDE and OUTSIDE the group or organization. Let me be crystal clear: **The TKI only assesses conflict-handling behavior. That's it. The TKI does NOT measure anything having to do with the systems and processes, let alone what impact each of those systems and processes is having on conflict-handling behavior.**

Even if the culture, reward system, and leadership behavior are the principle causes for any observable differences between the inside and outside organization charts, we still don't know the *relative* influence of an organization's different systems and processes. Are all of these aspects of the organization playing an equal role in shifting members' conflict–handling behavior? Or is the culture the primary culprit? Or is it the reward system that compels members to use some modes more than others? Or are members more likely to use avoiding and accommodating at the lower levels in the organization primarily due to very assertive, autocratic leaders?

When using two TKI assessments per person, it is still only a guess as to which particular systems and processes are primarily causing members to use certain conflict modes to address their workplace conflicts, which might not be effective or desirable. As such, to stop guessing as to why people are approaching conflict differently, whether they are inside or outside their organization, *we have to find a way to assess the impact of systems and processes directly and explicitly and, of course, accurately. Transforming organizations must be based on an accurate understanding of which SPECIFIC systems create the eight attributes of a situation that govern when to use each conflict mode.*

REVISITING THE COMPLEX HOLOGRAM AND THE QUANTUM WHEEL

Before I say more about the Kilmann Organizational Conflict Instrument and how it explicitly assesses the particular systems and processes in organizations that could be negatively affecting how conflicts are being addressed and resolved, I would like to remind you about our previous discussions about the Complex Hologram (Figure 1.3 in Chapter 1). That diagram captures what I mean by an organization's systems, and why those systems and processes have such a huge impact on how members approach their workplace conflicts, which, as I've illustrated, might be very different from how members approach conflicts in all the other settings in their life.

I would also like to remind you about the "Quantum Wheel," which integrates my work on conflict management and change management (Figure 1.5 in Chapter 1).

It's so important that you remember this key point: **It takes revitalized and aligned systems and processes for members to use all five modes effectively, depending on the key attributes of the situation. And members must then be able to use those five conflict-handling modes for managing all their organization's business, technical, and management problems.** Basically, for any organization to achieve long-term success, its systems must support effective conflict management and change management for its most complex problems and challenges.

WHEN IS IT BEST TO USE EACH ASSESSMENT TOOL?

Given the several choices that are now available for assessing conflict-handling behavior, it should not be surprising that I'm regularly asked to help people decide when it's best to use each available assessment tool. Specifically, I am often asked two basic questions. The first type of question is this: "When is it best to use 1 TKI per person with those STANDARD TKI instructions – or when is it best to use 1 TKI with MODIFIED instructions for INSIDE your group? The second type of question is along these lines: When is it best to use two TKIs per person, each with the modified instructions for INSIDE and OUTSIDE your group – or when is it more informative to use the Kilmann Organizational Conflict Instrument instead of either 1 or 2 TKIs per person?

Regarding the first type of question, having each participant take **1 TKI with those standard TKI instructions** is still the best choice when teaching students or conducting training programs **when the respondents are either not employed or come from different organizations.** Using that 1 traditional TKI per person helps people learn more about their conflict–handling behavior across all their interpersonal conflicts, since there's no immediate interest in learning about their behavior in any specific work or family setting.

However, **when the people all come from the same intact group or intact organization** and the focus of the training is on improving behavior in that particular group or organizational setting, that's the time to modify the standard TKI instructions to a focus on "inside your group" in order to make the assessment more accurate for that specific group or organization – and thus not to "dilute" the results by members possibly thinking about *other* situations as they respond to the TKI, which they might be prone to do if they are given the TKI's standard instructions.

Regarding the second type of question that I'm often asked, in those cases **when the consultant or facilitator wants to know the overall – general – effect of an organization's systems and processes on members' conflict-handling behavior,** it is then a good idea to ask each member to take two TKIs, so it becomes possible to discover if group members are using different conflict modes INSIDE versus OUTSIDE their group or organization.

But as I've stressed earlier, although the two TKIs provide a *general* impression, an educated guess, about whether or not the organization's systems are causing a negative effect on members' conflict–handling behavior, asking members to take two TKIs per person with modified instructions cannot possibly provide any information about WHICH systems are the culprit – and WHICH particular systems are inspiring members to do their very best.

THE KOCI FOR ASSESSING SYSTEMS CONFLICTS

Now that I've provided a detailed account of how to measure conflict-handling behavior in organizations (including my work on change management and quantum transformation), you can appreciate what the Kilmann Organizational Conflict Instrument can provide for organizations and its members.

First, I'll summarize the two parts of the instrument. Next, I'll describe the kind of diagnostic information that this instrument reveals, which can then inspire the top executives to implement the completely integrated program of eight tracks – so the entire organization can resolve any identified systems conflicts that are clearly getting in the way of long-term success.

PART 1 OF THE KOCI INSTRUMENT

For Part 1 of this instrument, you're asked to respond to 27 systems conflicts that derive from the Complex Hologram (Figure 1.3 in Chapter 1). Incidentally, I purposely constructed separate items for strategy and structure, since each of these two formal systems is so important in its own right as a guide to member behavior. Later, these two formal systems will be combined into one strategy-structure category, since structure is always needed to implement strategy – which conveniently corresponds to the strategy-structure track.

Specifically, for Part 1 of the Kilmann Organizational Conflict Instrument (KOCI), you're asked to indicate **how often you are negatively affected by each of the various "systems conflicts"** by selecting your response on the five-point scale: (1) when you are **never** affected negatively by that systems conflict; (2) when you are **rarely** affected negatively by that systems conflict; (3) when you are **occasionally** being affected negatively; (4) when you are **frequently** affected negatively; or (5) when you are **always** being negatively affected by that systems conflict.

So you can get a good sense of what is meant by a "systems conflict," here's one of the items that concerns the **structure** of the organization:

I have neither the necessary authority nor the sufficient resources to achieve my assigned goals and objectives, yet I'm held accountable for the results.

Here's an item about a systems conflict with **teams:**

During meetings, some members are more reserved than others, but no one makes a special effort to ask those quieter members to express their opinions or ideas.

Essentially, Part 1 of the Organizational Conflict Instrument explicitly – and directly – measures which particular systems conflicts might be limiting your choice of the conflict modes that you can safely use INSIDE your group or organization, which might be very different from the comfort that you experience in using those same modes OUTSIDE your group or organization. Thus Part 1 explicitly assesses what the results from two TKIs per person can only infer, which, at best, is just an educated guess. As I suggested previously, having members take two TKIs each still doesn't allow a facilitator to pinpoint which one (or several) systems conflicts are having a negative influence on members.

PART 2 OF THE KOCI INSTRUMENT

Here are the instructions for Part 2 of the online version of the instrument: *For each of the nine systems conflicts (treating strategy and structure separately for the time being), you are asked to indicate your relative use of the five conflict-handling modes* – by arranging five statements from 1 to 5, where the statement you would drag into the #1 position on your screen is the mode that you tend to use most often in approaching – or trying to resolve – that particular kind of systems conflict. Then, you would drag the statement that represents your next used approach to that systems conflict into the #2 position, and so on, until you drag your least used mode into the #5 position.

Although this instrument is measuring the same five classic conflict modes as the TKI assessment tool, the KOCI Instrument wants you to think of those particular systems conflicts and how you tend to approach them, which is very different from simply taking the TKI according to how you approach *interpersonal conflict* INSIDE your group or organization. Always remember that the TKI and the KOCI are assessing two different kinds of conflicts.

Because of this distinction, I word the conflict modes on Part 2 of the KOCI very differently from the way in which the TKI's 30 items are worded. For example, the **avoiding conflict mode** is always worded as follows for each of the nine systems conflicts:

> **Sometimes, it's simply not worth the extra time and effort it would take to discuss and examine this particular aspect of the organization, since we're unlikely to find a good solution.**

The **collaborating mode** is always worded as follows for each of the nine systems conflicts:

> **I always ask my boss or team members to take the necessary time to thoroughly discuss this particular aspect of the organization, so we can develop a creative solution.**

The three other conflict modes (competing, compromising, and accommodating) are also worded with respect to addressing systems conflicts in organizations – NOT interpersonal conflict.

Regarding how the systems conflicts are worded on Part 2 of the KOCI instrument, consider the systems conflict between the organization's **reward system** and its individual members:

How are you likely to respond when you experience the negative aspects of your organization's REWARDS – regarding the design and functioning of the performance appraisal system?

For this item, you would arrange those five statements into positions 1 through 5 to indicate your relative tendencies to use those conflict modes to approach your reward systems conflicts.

As another example of the items from Part 2, here is a conflict that can occur between **teams** and individuals:

How are you likely to respond when you experience the negative aspects of TEAMS – regarding how meetings are conducted and whether the boss makes sure that all the wisdom in the group is used for its major decisions?

For this item, you would arrange those same five statements into positions 1 through 5 to indicate your relative tendencies to use those conflict modes to approach your team conflicts. You would then do the same for the remaining items in Part 2 of the Kilmann Organizational Conflict Instrument.

INTERPRETING AN INDIVIDUAL'S KOCI RESULTS

Let's now interpret the results for an individual: As displayed on Figure 3.4, the raw scores for the systems conflicts are placed in the outer ring or SPOKES of the Quantum Wheel, including which ones are H, M, and L, as based on the established ranges for High, Medium, and Low, which are given in the instrument's interpretive materials.

FIGURE 3.4
KOCI RESULTS FOR AN INDIVIDUAL (FIRST TIME)

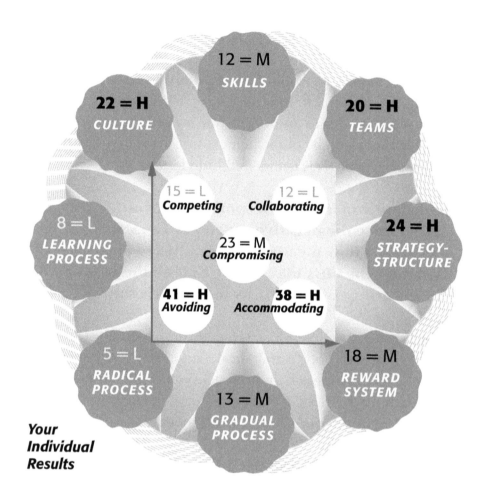

As you can see on this illustration, there are **three systems conflicts that scored in the HIGH range,** which suggests that this individual is *frequently* being hampered by negative experiences with the culture of her organization or group, the way in which her team's meetings are being conducted, and the lack of clarity in the organization's strategy–structure. The three high scores for these three systems conflicts suggest some very serious barriers to long–term organizational success.

Three other systems conflicts are MEDIUM in their impact, because they are *only occasionally* interfering with the individual's performance and satisfaction: skills, the reward system, and the processes that flow within her group. Yet two systems conflicts are LOW in their impact, shown by the grayed letter L: radical process improvement and learning process improvement. But not until those HIGH systems conflicts in the earlier tracks of the Quantum Wheel are resolved might the last two process tracks become more challenging.

In the HUB of that same Quantum Wheel, you can also see the person's results on the TKI Conflict Model, which shows that avoiding and accommodating are in the HIGH range. As a result, this person is almost always being negatively affected by cultural norms and team behavior that seem to pressure the members to remain quiet, not to express different points of view, and not to disagree with the boss (to avoid such conflicts); or, alternatively, to defer to the experience of other members or managers, which means to accommodate others when deciding how to improve the formal systems in the organization.

Indeed, **the assertive modes of competing and collaborating are in the LOW range,** which confirms that this member is not bringing all her talent, wisdom, ideas, and experience into the workplace. But once implementation of the change program is well underway, members will be given the chance to learn more about how to use the five conflict modes, and especially how to *change* the informal systems regarding their culture, skills, and teams so all five modes are always available to all members – and can be used effectively as needed.

As shown on Figure 3.5, let's interpret the results for the same individual after she responded to the Kilmann Organizational Conflict Instrument **nine months later.** As we'll see, **much can be learned from such quantitative, before-and-after comparisons.**

FIGURE 3.5
KOCI RESULTS FOR AN INDIVIDUAL (SECOND TIME)

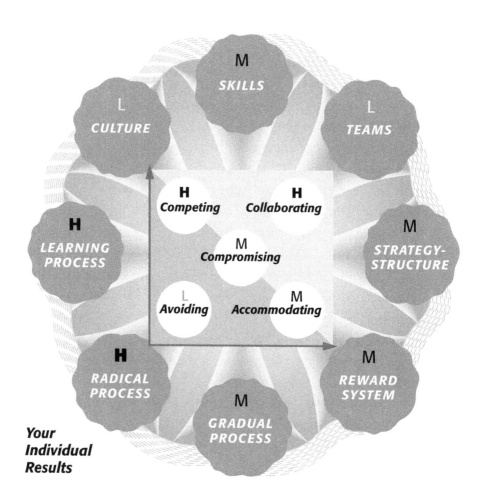

**Your
Individual
Results**

For these KOCI results, only the H, M, and L are displayed – which makes it visually easier to focus on the significant systems conflicts. These results show that the integrated program of eight tracks has been proceeding – since the culture, skills, and teams are no longer *frequently* distracting this member, although more skill training might still be needed. Progress is also occurring for strategy–structure and the reward system – which sets the stage for resolving the remaining systems conflicts.

In the HUB of this Quantum Wheel, you can also review the nine-month follow-up results for how she tends to approach her systems conflicts: ***The assertive conflict modes are now HIGH while avoiding is LOW***, so the "pendulum" has obviously swung from unassertive (based on the previous KOCI results) to highly assertive (using a lot of competing and collaborating behavior). Usually, before the results display a balanced TKI profile (which is revealed by the presence of mostly medium scores on the five conflict modes), members go from the extreme use of one or two modes to the extreme use of the other modes!

INTERPRETING A GROUP'S KOCI RESULTS

Figure 3.6 illustrates the KOCI results for a twelve-member group in a large organization. Such a graph can be developed by simply calculating the average scores of group members for each of their systems conflicts on the outer SPOKES of the Quantum Wheel, as well as calculating the average scores of members for their relative use of the conflict modes on the inner HUB of the Quantum Wheel, which are used for addressing and resolving their identified systems conflicts.

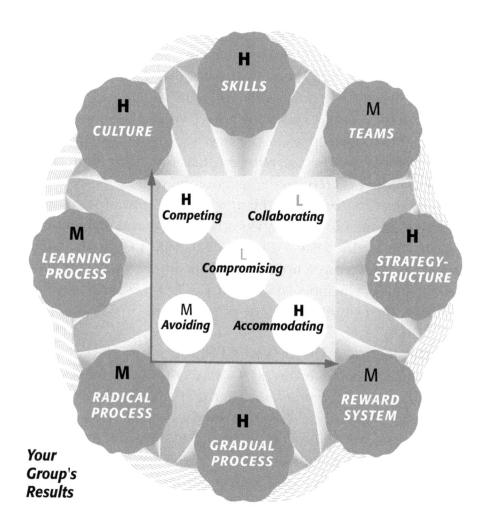

Figure 3.6
KOCI Results for a Group (N = 12)

On the SPOKES of this group's Quantum Wheel, the results show four systems conflicts, marked by a bold **H,** which reveals what has ***frequently*** been affecting group members in a negative way: both the culture and skills in the behavioral infrastructure, strategy–structure in the formal systems, and business processes that take place inside each group (gradual process improvement).

These HIGH systems conflicts that are revealed within all the major categories of informal systems, formal systems, and processes clearly suggest that this work group is facing quite an assortment of roadblocks to performance and satisfaction, which severely undermines what members can provide to their organization. The other systems conflicts (namely teams, reward systems, radical process, and learning process improvement) are **occasionally** interfering with the work group's performance and satisfaction, as designated by the M for medium in those outer circles. Yet, there are no systems conflicts that are **rarely** affecting these twelve group members: Every systems conflict is negatively affecting them, either **frequently** or **occasionally**.

In the HUB of this Quantum Wheel, the KOCI findings that are shown on the TKI Conflict Model indicate that these group members are heavily relying on competing and accommodating for resolving their systems conflicts (shown by the H for HIGH for these two conflict modes), which means that members either get their own needs met or they do their best to get the needs of other members met. Yet there is little compromising (shown by the L for that conflict mode), whereby each person gets at least some of his needs met. Indeed, the collaborating conflict mode is not being used much at all (shown by the grayed letter L for that mode), so members aren't taking the necessary time to generate creative solutions to their systems conflicts – which would help them get their most important needs met, while also helping the organization achieve long–term success.

For this group, the avoiding mode is being used more often than compromising and collaborating (shown by the letter M for the avoiding mode), but the latter mode is being used less often than the competing mode or the accommodating mode. During the culture, skills, and team tracks, members will find it useful to discuss how their informal systems might be discouraging them from discussing challenging subjects, even though members are being negatively affected by those particular systems conflicts – which puts a real damper on achieving long–term success.

Interpreting an Organization's KOCI Results

On Figure 3.7, I present the KOCI results for an organization, based on calculating an average of all the members' individual scores on system conflicts and conflict modes.

FIGURE 3.7
KOCI RESULTS FOR AN ORGANIZATION (N = 135)

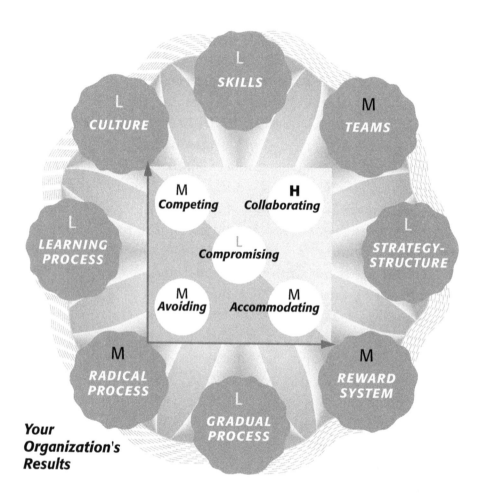

As you can see, not one of the eight systems conflicts have been **frequently** affecting the members of this organization in a negative manner. In particular, five systems conflicts are **rarely**

being experienced negatively, which suggests that members can spend most of their precious time contributing all their wisdom and passion to the strategic mission of their organization. Only three systems conflicts (i.e., teams, reward systems, and radical process improvement) are being **occasionally** experienced in a negative way, which identifies the few remaining organizational systems that still need to be investigated and improved – as the process of quantum transformation continues.

Based on the benefits of implementing the first three tracks, there are predictable changes that have been revealed on the TKI Conflict Model: ***The collaborating mode, displaying the bold letter H, is often used to resolve systems conflicts, which results in creative solutions that satisfy the needs of both internal and external stakeholders.*** Further, three of the other conflict modes (i.e., competing, accommodating, avoiding) are now being used moderately, as revealed by the letter M, while members are not making much use of the compromising mode. Perhaps, affected by the spirit of openly discussing their systems conflicts in depth (due to the program of eight tracks), members might be missing opportunities to arrive at a middle-ground resolution when the issue is not that crucial for success, and thus more time could be spent on resolving their other, more important, organizational conflicts and business conflicts. As mentioned before, members initially tend to use certain conflict modes to the extreme before they develop a more balanced use of all five modes.

THREE KEY PRINCIPLES FOR
RESOLVING SYSTEMS CONFLICTS

At this point, I'd like to remind you of the ***first key principle*** that derives from the Complex Hologram (Figure 1.3, Chapter 1): ***About 80% (or more) of what takes place in an organization is determined by its systems and processes, while 20% (or less) is determined by individual desires or preferences.***

Now, I'll also remind you of the **second key principle** to keep in your mind (Chapter 2), which follows from the first principle:

Choose the particular conflict mode that best matches the eight key attributes of the situation.

And here is the **third key principle** to remember at all times: *In the short term, the organization's systems and processes are fixed, so the use of one or more modes might be significantly constrained by the nature and quality of the key attributes of the situation, which are mostly shaped by the organization's systems and processes. But in the long term, those systems and processes can be transformed — which then modifies the eight key attributes of any conflict situation to support the use of all five conflict-handling modes, as needed.*

CONCLUDING THOUGHTS

Regularly visualize the images of the Complex Hologram and the Quantum Wheel, which will hopefully inspire you and your organization to use all the wisdom, knowledge, talent, passion, and experience of its members for satisfying the needs of all key stakeholders – and thereby achieve long-term success.

QUANTUM TRANSFORMATION FOR ORGANIZATIONS

IMPLEMENTING EIGHT TRACKS FOR LONG-TERM SUCCESS

As I have emphasized throughout my long academic career, any attempt to improve the functioning of an organization that ignores the context and all the interrelated dynamics that drive that entire complex problem will most likely fail. Yet, whenever senior executives are asked what can be done to transform their organization into a highly adaptive, market–driven, innovative, and competitive enterprise, their usual reply conveys that they are still waiting for a magical quick fix to come along. Most are not even aware of any alternatives to the quick fix. Nobody even knows what to call "it" other than a *non*-quick fix. Nonetheless, more than ever, we must now use a systematic, comprehensive, broad–based approach for achieving long–term organizational success in today's highly interconnected world: It is the only way to create – and maintain – high performance and satisfaction for all key internal and external stakeholders.

For the lack of a popular term, I refer to a non-quick fix for improving organizations as "a completely integrated program." It is made up of at least three major elements: (1) a holistic, three dimensional worldview, represented by the Complex Hologram, which can interrelate all the systems, processes, and people that together determine performance and satisfaction, short term and long term; (2) all the multifaceted methods that are included in the eight tracks – including instructional materials, assessment tools, experiential exercises, case studies, feedback sessions, and group discussions for transforming an organization's barriers to success into the fundamental channels for success; and (3) all the ongoing, behind-the-scene logistics – from beginning to end – that enable the members to effectively resolve all their complex problem and conflicts.

THE FIVE STEPS OF PROBLEM MANAGEMENT

As members implement the completely integrated program, they often use the five steps of problem management whenever they experience a barrier to long-term organizational success.

As displayed on Figure 4.1, Step 1 in problem management is **sensing the problem,** which is identifying a GAP between "what is" and "what could or should be" that clearly exceeds a certain threshold of acceptability, which then initiates the formal cycle of problem management for one or more organizational members. Not surprisingly, the cost-effective goal for this endeavor is to resolve the problem (hence, close the identified GAP) in a single cycle of problem management, which indeed can be achieved if the members do not commit any of the classic errors in any of the five steps of problem management.

In Step 2 of problem management, members must investigate the root cause of the problem – often referred to as **defining the problem**. Basically, members have to decide what exactly caused that GAP to appear in the first place. Naturally, it might take a number of diverse participants an extended period of time to uncover the cause (or causes) of the identified GAP, especially for a very complex problem that affects many internal and external stakeholders and thus involves different areas of expertise and varieties of experience.

Once the root causes of the GAP have been defined, Step 3 of problem management is **deriving a solution** that is expected to close that initial GAP. Some solutions, of course, are better than others in terms of how well they address the root causes of the problem in a cost-effective manner. But if the problem has been defined *incorrectly* during Step 2 of problem management, *then any* derived solution cannot possibly achieve its intended results, no matter how well that solution has been implemented.

FIGURE 4.1
THE FIVE STEPS OF PROBLEM MANAGEMENT

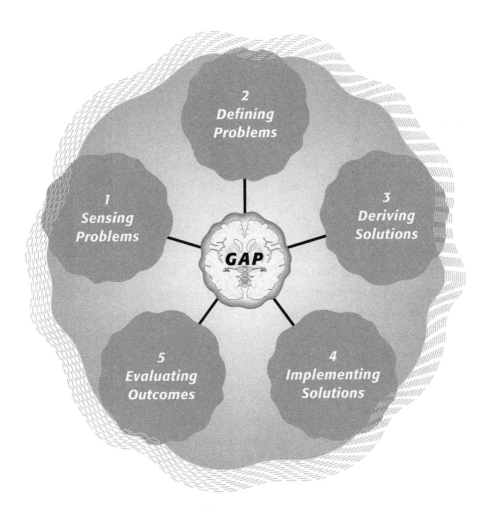

Step 4 is ***implementing the solution*** to the problem, which is hopefully based on up–to–date, valid assumptions about all key stakeholders, which includes valid assumptions about the best ways to create lasting improvement in any organization. But if implementing the solution is based on false assumptions about how members will (or won't) participate in the change process, implementation will fail – no matter how valid the definition of the problem and the quality of the derived solution.

Lastly, Step 5 of problem management involves **evaluating outcomes:** Did members close the GAP or did the GAP stay the same? Or did the GAP become even worse (larger)? Essentially, if the GAP that initiated the five steps of problem management did not close as a result of all the decisions and actions in the four prior steps, then an error was probably made somewhere along the way: (1) Perhaps the GAP didn't turn out to be as important as the members had anticipated, so they eventually lost interest in closing that GAP. (2) Perhaps the root causes of the problem were defined incorrectly, so no solution, no matter how carefully conceived or implemented, could possibly have closed the initial GAP. (3) Perhaps a solution was derived that didn't address the root causes of the problem. (4) Perhaps the derived solution was implemented in a manner that annoyed the membership, which then made the initial GAP even larger.

Nevertheless, if the members address each and every step in problem management without making any significant errors, they can then close the initial GAP in just one cycle of problem management. In the worst cases, by not understanding how to perform every step in problem management, the members will continue to go through the five steps, again and again, without success – which will only serve to increase their frustration and dash their hopes for ever closing the initial GAP.

Keep this in mind: *Two errors in problem management are most damaging: defining problems (Step 2) and implementing solutions (Step 4).* Essentially, if a problem is defined incorrectly at the beginning, everything else that follows is a big waste of time and resources. In addition, if a solution is not implemented effectively, that major error then negates everything that came before: Therefore, if an important problem is sensed, correctly defined, and then a viable solution is derived to close the GAP, all of that time and effort will be entirely wasted if the solution is not implemented effectively in the organization. Incidentally, the errors in sensing problems and evaluating outcomes tend to be either/or choices: either we address the problem or we don't; either we continue working on closing the gap or we move on to something else. Moreover, even choosing a mediocre solution (instead of the very best solution) is not that crucial, so long as the problem has already been correctly defined: Indeed, a weak solution to an accurately defined problem is always much better than implementing any solution to a poorly defined problem.

Each of the eight tracks addresses one or more GAPS that require the members to regularly use the five steps of problem management, effectively and efficiently. Indeed, virtually every organization (before implementing the eight tracks) experiences a lively stream of culture–gaps, skills–gaps, team–gaps, strategy–structure gaps, reward system gaps, and process gaps, whereby the problem (the GAP) must be sensed, then root causes must be accurately defined, then quality solutions must be derived, then solutions must be implemented effectively, and, finally, outcomes must be evaluated accurately – to improve the performance and satisfaction of all key stakeholders.

PROBLEM MANAGEMENT AND CONFLICT MANAGEMENT

Every GAP in the organization (the difference between "what is" and "what could or should be") is likely to be experienced very differently by different organizational members, especially among those members who have received their education and training in different specializations (e.g., engineering, finance, marketing, medicine, law, information technology, and so forth). In addition, those diverse experts have been working in different specialized work units (functional areas in the organization) for months or even for years – which highly reinforces their vastly different experiences with culture–gaps, skills–gaps, team–gaps, strategy–structure gaps, reward system gaps, and process gaps. Essentially, *every GAP in an organization generates conflict – a dialectic – in every step in problem management, since every expert from a different specialized subunit in the organization will, by design, experience organizational problems differently, as they make their way through the steps of sensing problems, defining problems, deriving solutions, implementing solutions, and evaluating outcomes.*

More specifically, when specialized experts begin to discuss whether a GAP needs to be investigated (Step 1), **they experience conflict** – precisely BECAUSE they have been purposely trained (conditioned) to focus on different aspects of their organization and its mission. When the members decide to move forward and thus devote time and effort for closing that identified GAP, **they experience conflict** – precisely BECAUSE they must now debate their very different proposed definitions of the root causes of the GAP, based on their different educational background, training, experience, and allegiance to a different specialized work unit in the organization.

Let's say these diverse experts have agreed on a definition of the problem (its root causes). But when they now consider what solution to implement in order to close the GAP to that defined problem, **they generate even more conflict** – precisely BECAUSE each expert has been purposely trained to propose very different solutions for resolving organizational problem – primarily based on their specialized training and work experience (e.g., deriving financial solutions, marketing solutions, engineering solutions, technology solutions, and so forth).

Once these specialized experts have resolved their conflicts on what solution to implement, when they then have to decide on the process for implementing their solution, **they experience additional conflict** – precisely BECAUSE of their different views about how to bring about change and transformation in people, organizations, and for society as a whole.

And then, in Step 5 of problem management (i.e., evaluating outcomes), when the different experts have to decide (a) whether the initial GAP disappeared, stayed the same, or became worse, so they can then decide (b) whether they should continue their efforts to close the initial GAP on that same problem or if they should switch to investigating another, more important GAP on another problem, **they once again experience conflict** – precisely BECAUSE of their vastly different, ingrained perspectives on the impact of various GAPS on long–term organizational success. As such, problem management embraces conflict management.

Figure 4.2 shows the different approaches for resolving the many conflicts – the *dialectics* – that must be addressed whenever specialized experts attempt to manage organizational problems through the perceptual lens of the Complex Hologram.

FIGURE 4.2
MANAGING CONFLICT FOR THE COMPLEX HOLOGRAM

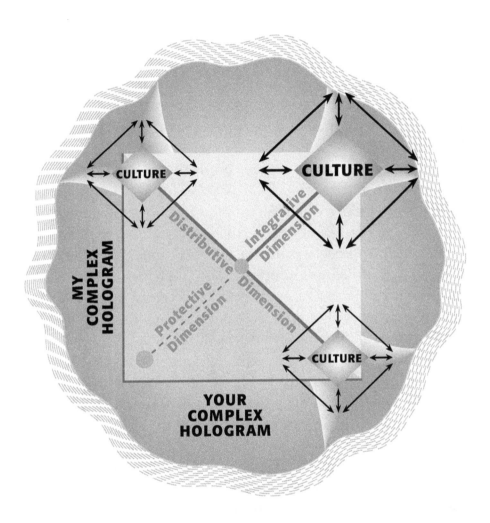

Indeed, making good use of the TKI Conflict Model, we can see that one expert's perspective – his *thesis* – on how to identify and close the GAPS that emerge on the Complex Hologram can be placed at the upper–left corner on the distributive dimension. Meanwhile, another expert's completely different perspective – her *anti-thesis* – on how to identify and close the numerous GAPS that emerge from the Complex Hologram can then be placed at the lower–right corner on the distributive dimension. By using a combination of competing, accommodating, and compromising, perhaps these two experts can eventually choose one approach over another (i.e., one person wins the argument, while the other person accommodates) or perhaps the two of them can find a practical way to "split their differences" and thereby arrive at a compromise solution.

However, in order to minimize those two most costly errors in problem management (defining problems and implementing solutions), I recommend using the collaborating mode on the integrative dimension for those two steps in the cycle – instead of using the three conflict modes on the distributive dimension. Conveniently, if the eight key attributes of the situation already support the effective application of the collaborating mode, then the diverse experts can integrate their *thesis* and *anti-thesis* to form a synergistic approach to the *dialectics* that emerge during those crucial steps of defining problems and implementing solutions. Incorporating the different expert perspectives into those two crucial steps would not only lead to a high–quality resolution for the benefit of all internal and external stakeholders (a resolution that includes and yet transcends the prior thesis and anti–thesis), but would also lead to satisfaction for all the experts themselves, since they would certainly enjoy seeing their unique perspective integrated into the definition of the problem and in their plans for implementing a viable solution.

But there is an added benefit that materializes when using an integrated approach for not only defining problems but also for implementing solutions: It's more likely that the identified

GAPS in various systems and processes can be closed in just one cycle of problem management, which is shown by the symbolic image of the Complex Hologram that is placed on the top–right corner of the TKI Conflict Model. But if those two crucial steps of problem management (i.e., defining problems and implementing solutions) are discussed on the distributive dimension (because the eight key attributes of the current situation only support the use of competing, compromising, and accommodating, it's more likely that those specialized experts will go through repeat cycles of problem management – without success.

THE FIVE STAGES OF QUANTUM TRANSFORMATION

As shown in Figure 4.3, I find it especially informative to sort all the tasks and decisions for a completely integrated program into *five stages of quantum transformation, which correspond to the five steps of problem management. To be successful, all change initiatives that strive to create and maintain long-term success must address each of the five stages in an effective and efficient manner*. Just as the five steps in problem management, movement from each stage in quantum transformation to the next stage should not occur until all the criteria for the earlier stages have been met. What is the danger in not following this principle? Any glossed–over stages will result in more difficulties later, such as one or more errors in problem management. Since most organizations have lagged behind the many revolutionary changes that have taken place in our fast–paced, interconnected global village, they usually conduct transformational change for the first cycle of the completely integrated program. During the next cycles of improvement, organizations conduct incremental change, since they will be able to keep up with all subsequent shifts in the expectations of all key stakeholders.

FIGURE 4.3
THE FIVE STAGES OF QUANTUM TRANSFORMATION

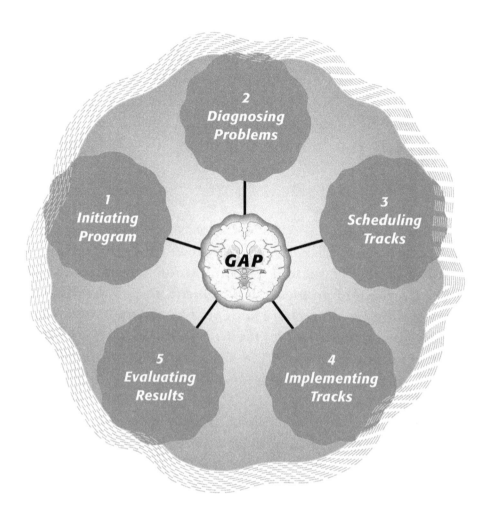

The remainder of this chapter will examine each of the five stages of quantum transformation in depth, which provides the basic framework for learning more about each track in its proper sequence, one chapter at a time. Once I've explored each of the eight tracks in Chapters 5 to 10 in this book, then in Chapter 11, I'll suggest how to expand the mind/body/spirit consciousness of members and then bring that expanded consciousness into the workplace – which is likely to be the futuristic direction for human resource management, organizational development, and quantum transformation. Lastly, in Chapter 12, I will discuss the twenty critical success factors for quantum transformation.

By the way, the current chapter was given the same title as my online course: "Quantum Transformation for Organizations." That five-hour recorded course also includes several assessment tools that will enable participants to examine their influence and courage to transform a Newtonian organization into a quantum organization: The *Kilmann-Covin Organizational Influence Survey* and the Kilmann, O'Hara, and Strauss *Organizational Courage Assessment*.

STAGE 1: INITIATING THE PROGRAM

The main concern during the "initiation" stage is whether the essential preconditions are present for a successful improvement effort. Four questions must be answered in the affirmative before the second stage (diagnosing problems) proceeds. The following questions pertain to the "critical mass" of senior executives of the organization who are deciding whether they should implement the completely integrated program:

1. Do senior executives understand (a) the various systems and processes that are depicted in the Complex Hologram, (b) the five stages of quantum transformation, (c) the sequence of eight tracks, and (d) what it takes — logistically — to coordinate such a large-scale effort, while, at the same time, still getting all the organization's other work done? It would be unrealistic to expect senior management to make a well-informed decision about whether to implement a completely integrated program of quantum transformation if they neither understand the concepts nor have the language to debate the major issues. If the program is to succeed, the executives must know beforehand exactly what it entails – alongside all their other corporate responsibilities.

2. Will senior executives fully commit to implementing the completely integrated program? Once the leaders know what to expect, the program's success requires their full commitment – in deed and not just in words. Despite their commitment to follow through on the entire program, senior executives often view the change initiatives as being relevant to the *rest of the organization*, rather than being relevant for themselves. True commitment is evidenced when the "powers-that-be" openly acknowledge that they themselves are part of "the problem" and therefore need to change as well. Such an admission sets the best example for all the other members and thus encourages everyone to participate in a learning mode, which is essential for trying out new ways of managing people and problems, as well as transforming systems and processes.

3. Will senior executives lead the implementation process for the completely integrated program and will they accept full responsibility for the outcome? Although most change initiatives are led by staff units in the organization (i.e., human resources or organizational development), the completely integrated program for transformational change must be led by line management, preferably by senior management – and they must use their full authority to implement the program. With senior management behind the mission, the resources needed to conduct the entire program are more likely to be forthcoming. Moreover, with top management leading the charge, top priority will be assigned to implementing the completely integrated program in spite of all the pressures to focus on the organization's nagging, day-to-day, business problems.

4. Will the senior executives arrange for expert consultants to diagnose the organization's "barriers to success" (its GAPS)? While managers might believe they can diagnose the problems themselves, this is the one area in which it is imperative to get an objective reading of the organization's well-being and health (its barriers and channels for long-term success), which can only be performed by well-trained and experienced consultants who come from outside the organization. All the remaining stages of quantum transformation rely on the diagnosis for confirming (a) WHY the organization is implementing a completely integrated program and (b) WHAT instructional materials, assessment tools, experiential exercises, feedback sessions, and group discussions should take place in each track. **If the diagnosis is simplistic, or,**

worse yet, inaccurate, all the remaining stages of quantum transformation — particularly scheduling and implementing the tracks — will be jeopardized.

Generally, one or two senior executives lead the search for suitable external consultants. These key managers are often the chief advocates of the improvement program and those who feel a special responsibility for its success. Indeed, implementation is helped immensely if these key managers also happen to be the senior executives. Having the formal authority of the hierarchy behind the completely integrated program — from beginning to end — helps ensure a successful outcome.

STAGE 2: DIAGNOSING THE PROBLEMS

When the senior executives and external consultants believe that all the conditions for success are present (which means that the program has been initiated properly), the diagnostic stage of quantum transformation can now proceed. Specifically, the goal is to develop a deep understanding of all the problems (barriers) in the organization and its opportunities (channels) for success.

I suggest that the organization use two methods to diagnose its barriers and channels for success: (1) a "preliminary diagnosis" based on members taking the Kilmann Organizational Conflict Instrument and (2) a "probing diagnosis" derived by conducting one–on–one, in–person (or virtual) diagnostic interviews with a representative sample of the membership from different levels, areas, and locations in the organization.

PRELIMINARY DIAGNOSTIC RESULTS WITH THE KOCI

As we discussed in the previous chapter, Part 1 of the KOCI instrument assesses which particular systems and processes are interfering with members' performance and satisfaction. As you know, the systems and processes on the KOCI instrument were purposely chosen to correspond to the eight tracks of quantum transformation. Part 2 of the KOCI instrument measures which conflict modes are members using too much or too little, while addressing their systems conflicts in the organization.

If it is economically feasible, I suggest that every member in the group, department, or organization carefully respond to the KOCI instrument. Such a comprehensive survey of all relevant members will generate the most confidence that the ineffective systems in the organization have been diagnosed accurately and thoroughly. If the cost of the KOCI instrument is an issue, then a representative sampling of members from different parts of the organization will have to be sufficient. But I always emphasize to senior managers: Having all members involved in defining the organization's problems will likely motivate everyone to actively participate in a genuine, positive, and engaging manner during the subsequent implementation of the program. In contrast, if members are excluded from the process of uncovering the root causes of what is undermining long–term success (by *not* taking the KOCI instrument or *not* being interviewed by a consultant), that exclusion at the outset could then affect their subsequent participation in the next stages of quantum transformation: "Yes, they're now expecting me to participate in monthly workshop sessions, but why didn't they ask me to share *my* experiences of our organization's problems at the very start of this program?"

As discussed in the last chapter, the members' individual KOCI scores on Part I of the instrument can be averaged for the entire organization in order to identify the generic root causes of its identified barriers to success (i.e., culture, skills, teams, strategy-structures, reward systems, and process management). Moreover, member responses can be averaged separately for the organization's divisions, departments, and work groups as well as sorting the KOCI results into the vertical distinctions of senior management, middle management, supervisory personnel, and frontline employees – or using some other statistical breakdown of the KOCI results in order to decipher the relevant *patterns* of problems, GAPS, and barriers to long–term success.

Let's now consider the organization's results from Part 2 of the KOCI instrument: It's especially informative to discover if the membership is using certain conflict modes "too much" or "too little" when addressing their systems conflicts. More specifically, as I discussed in Chapter 2, we can replace each box (subunit) on the organization chart with the TKI Conflict Model. And then, for each box on the chart, we can determine if there are significant differences in how frequently each of the five conflict modes is being used to address the most significant systems conflicts: (1) horizontally across different departments at the same level in the organization and (2) vertically (traveling down) the management hierarchy. For example, **it's often good to know if the frontline employees are mostly using the avoiding and accommodating modes in response to their most debilitating systems conflicts, while the managers above them, because of their positions of formal authority, are able to enact the more assertive conflict modes (i.e., competing, collaborating, and compromising) for examining what can be done to resolve their most troublesome systems conflicts.**

Although much can be discovered when carefully examining the KOCI results for any organization (especially if most or all members have responded to the instrument), much more can be uncovered by subsequently conducting one–on–one, in–person diagnostic interviews with a sample of members throughout the organization. Indeed, from examining the KOCI results from Part 1 and Part 2 of the instrument, both horizontally and vertically across the organization chart, **expert consultants can develop a list of probing, follow-up questions to ask members so a more interactive, collaborative, and in-depth understanding of the organization's systems, processes, and people can be achieved,** as well as learning more about WHY and HOW various systems conflicts are currently being addressed (or are being suppressed) throughout the organization.

Probing Diagnostic Results from In-Person Interviews

After having analyzed and discussed the KOCI results from different organizational perspectives, expert consultants, with the aid of a few key managers, develop a plan to gather face–to–face diagnostic information from the members (in real and/or virtual meetings). The objective is to interview members at each level in the hierarchy, and from each division and department, in order to obtain a representative sample of the organization. Everyone in the senior management group should be interviewed, simply because their views, and especially their commitment to change, are so important to the success of the program. If there are more than 5,000 employees in an organization, interviewing about 100 members should provide sufficient information to diagnose the organization's problems and opportunities (based on the "law of large numbers" through stratified random sampling). For smaller organizations, conducting between 25 to 50 interviews should be sufficient. Nevertheless, if the KOCI results are self-explanatory and fairly comprehensive already, then fewer members need to be interviewed. But if the KOCI results are inconsistent and/or incomplete in any way, then a larger number of interviews are needed to develop a more thorough and accurate understanding of the particular barriers to success that have been undermining performance and satisfaction in one subunit or another, let alone for the organization as a whole.

Each one-on-one, one-hour interview with a member begins with the external consultant briefly sharing the background and expectations of the meeting. He (or she) then lists the questions that will be asked and summarizes what will be done with the responses. The consultant takes the time to explain the purpose and principles of the five stages of quantum transformation and responds to any questions the interviewee may have about what to expect as the program unfolds. By openly expressing what the interviewee might be silently contemplating – and by sincerely responding to his concerns and questions – the consultant gives the interviewee the needed confidence and comfort to reveal the organization's problems.

SEEING ALL THERE IS TO SEE IN THE BIG PICTURE

It is essential to be absolutely clear about the worldview that is used as the lens for asking questions about the organization's systems and processes during those one-on-one interviews. For your convenience, Figure 4.4 shows organizational life through a multidimensional lens. This model, which was first displayed in Figure 1.3 in Chapter 1, is used for diagnosing the full range of "barriers to success" and "channels for success."

FIGURE 4.4
THE COMPLEX HOLOGRAM — SEEING THE BIG PICTURE

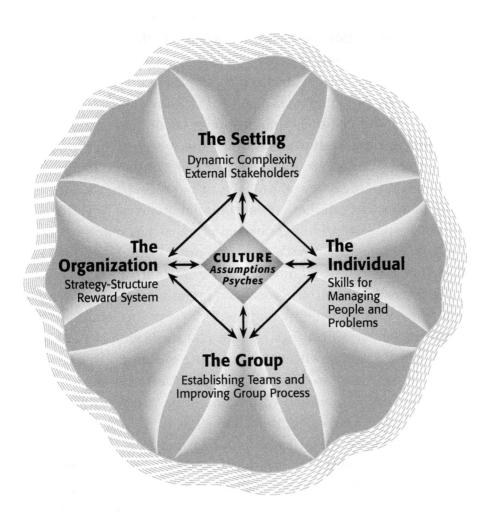

I'll now share the primary inspiration for my developing the Complex Hologram. The design of this model gradually emerged through the process of interviewing hundreds of members in a great variety of organizations over a ten–year period (from 1972

to 1982), which was then published in my 1984 book: *Beyond the Quick Fix*. In those diagnostic interviews, members spoke of what organizational qualities facilitated their work and what qualities interfered. The facilitating qualities became known as "channels for success," while the identified roadblocks became known as "barriers to success." ***Later in the 1980s, the double arrows in between all the system NODES in the Complex Hologram were recognized as processes (business, management, and learning processes) that flow within and across all the organization's formal and informal systems.***

Decades later, the interrelated dynamics that are displayed in the Complex Hologram still beautifully capture the great variety of barriers and channels that reappear (again and again) while diagnosing organizations. Naturally, there are differences from one organization to another and from one continent to another; there always are some unique circumstance that moderates the extent and variety of these organizational qualities. Nevertheless, I must emphasize the uncanny pattern that has emerged in all the consulting work I have done for organizations: Rarely do I find that having all members learn new skills about complex problems will – by itself – solve the organization's performance problems. I have never encountered a case in any nation in the world in which only the corporate culture lagged behind and there already was an effective formal organization in place with everyone applying up–to–date skills. The "culture–gap problem" has *always* been associated with many other problems (GAPS) in the organization, group, and individual as well.

Incidentally, the KOCI results for the organization also tend to show the striking interrelationship of all those systems and processes. Rarely, if ever, do the results from a KOCI analysis show that members are being negatively affected by only one or two systems, while all the other features in the organization are "not at all" or "rarely" interfering with their performance and/or satisfaction. In most cases, members negatively experience many (if not all) of the systems and processes that are sorted into the eight tracks, *BECAUSE* the members are completely surrounded –

and thus deeply affected – by all those highly intertwined forces and forms.

Once the diagnostic interviews have been conducted (which also includes what was previously discovered from the KOCI results), the external consultants organize all their findings into the same categories on the Complex Hologram. Then the consultants recommend how implementing the eight tracks can remove all the identified barriers to success and transform them into channels for success.

A diagnostic report is presented first to the top managers (or whoever represents the "critical mass" of leaders who have the authority and the resources to implement the entire program of transformation). When these top managers have discussed and accepted the diagnostic results, it's time to share these findings with the entire membership. Naturally, it takes conviction for the top managers to be willing to present the diagnostic report, in its entirety, to the membership. But this desire to openly discuss the diagnostics findings is critical, for it demonstrates commitment to removing the identified barriers to long-term success.

MOBILIZING THE SHADOW TRACK

Primary responsibility for managing the remaining stages of quantum transformation is neither delegated to the consultants nor assigned to any group in human resources or organizational development. Instead, a "shadow track" (running parallel to all eight tracks) is formed just after the decision is made to proceed with implementing the program: The dedicated members of the shadow track consist of senior executives and an equal number of members who represent all levels, areas, and locations in the organization – are selected by the senior management group. Knowing that the rest of the membership will judge the fairness of the selection process always seems to motivate the executives to develop a process that they can defend – easily, rationally, and publicly. The number of selected shadow trackers can vary from fifteen to twenty-five, depending on the size of the organization. Once formed, the members of the shadow track regularly meet to monitor the impact of the program on the functioning of the organization and to create additional approaches for improving the implementation process.

The shadow track is also expected to keep in regular contact with the subunits they are representing. They develop and use a special-purpose information system – so attitudes, feelings, and any difficulties with the change program can surface. In this way, the shadow trackers (relying on the professional judgment of the consultants) has a basis for modifying its efforts to address the evolving needs, concerns, and problems of the organization.

STAGE 3: SCHEDULING THE TRACKS

Let's further explore how the eight tracks can revitalize all the systems, processes, and people that affect long-term success, to clarify what each track does for the organization, and to explain why the tracks must be implemented in the prescribed sequence to bring about lasting change and continuous improvement.

Figure 4.5 displays the "Arc of Transformation" for sequencing all the change initiatives that conveniently sort into three major components of transformation: behavioral infrastructure, formal systems, and process management. As you can observe on the left-hand side of this illustration, the **behavioral infrastructure** of the organization must first be addressed in order to generate a healthy culture, critical thinking skills, and effective teamwork within and across all subunits in the organization. With such an adaptive behavioral infrastructure (also referred to as the *informal organization*), members would then be able to self-design their **formal systems** (strategy-structure and the reward system). As these formal systems are being revitalized – and fully aligned – for the future, members can also enhance their performance and satisfaction by gradually and radically improving the quality and speed of their business, management, and learning processes – known as **process management.** The three components that are shown on the Arc of Transformation, in sequence, can effectively close the various GAPS that were identified during the diagnostic stage of quantum transformation.

FIGURE 4.5
THE ARC OF TRANSFORMATION — THREE COMPONENTS

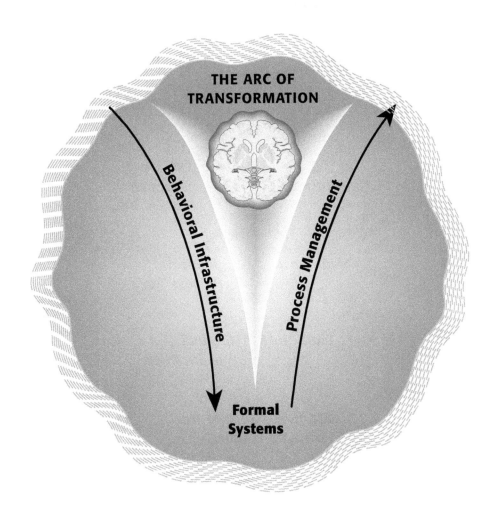

Figure 4.6 shows the sequence of eight tracks sorted into the three components of quantum transformation: The **culture track** establishes the trust, communication, information sharing, and willingness to change among members – the preconditions that must exist before any improvement effort can succeed. The **skills track** provides all members with improved ways of managing problems and conflicts. The **team track** infuses the new culture and enhanced skills into each work unit in the organization.

FIGURE 4.6
THE ARC OF TRANSFORMATION — EIGHT TRACKS

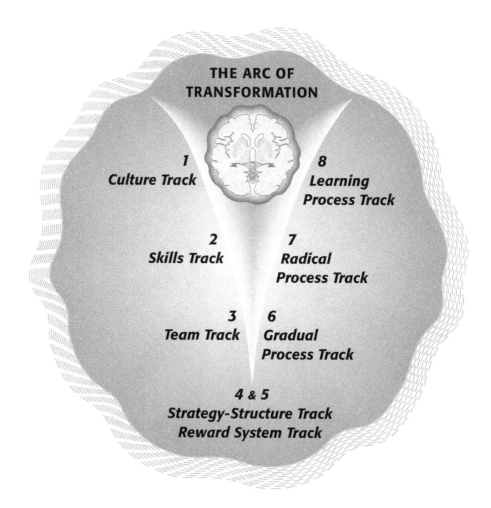

Building on an improved behavioral infrastructure from the first three tracks, the **strategy-structure track** develops either a completely new or a revised strategic plan – and then aligns all divisions, departments, work groups, jobs, and all resources with that new strategic direction. The **reward system track** develops a performance–based reward system that regularly appraises the new culture, the use of updated skills, and effective team efforts within and across all work units.

The **gradual process track**, building on a healthy behavioral infrastructure and aligned formal systems, enables members to speed up and improve the quality of the key processes that flow *within* their work group. The **radical process track**, also building on all the improvements from the prior tracks, enables members to design their work units around their most important business processes that currently flow *across* the preexisting work groups, so important decisions and actions will no longer fall between the cracks on the open space on the organizational chart. Lastly, the **learning process track** determines how the organization can dramatically improve the way that it acquires, stores, retrieves, shares, and uses knowledge, so it can do everything faster and better than it did before – which includes not only how it can speed up the next round of transformational change, but how the organization can also speed up and enhance the quality of its business and technical decisions.

This carefully developed sequence of eight tracks is the most important principle to understand and honor. As first presented in Chapter 1, while it might be tempting to try to improve things by first modifying the formal aspects of the organization (with the middle two tracks that are shown on the bottom of the Arc of Transformation), such an approach inevitably leads to failure: Changing the formal systems on paper (or on electronic files), for example, cannot result in behavioral change on the job – unless members are completely willing and able to change. But if there is mistrust, defensive communication, deficient problem–solving skills, and only superficial cooperation across departments, then formal systems and process management will remain off track.

Alternatively, by first proceeding to improve the behavioral infrastructure of the organization (via the first three tracks), the membership can develop the necessary culture, skills, and teamwork for effectively managing all its important business, technical, and organizational problems – including its formal systems. Even so, the first three tracks – by themselves – are not enough: If the formal systems (particularly the reward system) are not eventually redesigned to support the performance and behavior that are essential for long-term success, any short-term improvements in the informal organization will soon fade away.

CHOOSING THE CONTENT OF WORKSHOP MATERIALS

Scheduling the eight tracks involves two types of decisions: (1) determining the content of all the workshop materials that will be utilized in each track for organizational members and (2) arranging and managing the logistics by which the eight tracks will be conducted for all participants in the program – typically in one-day, monthly workshops (whether in person or in virtual meetings). The outcomes of these two scheduling decisions are guided by the diagnostic stage of quantum transformation and are made by the consultants and the shadow trackers (with the aid of organizational members who are skilled at planning large meetings and formal educational programs). Once the schedule has been outlined in as much detail as possible, the consultants and the shadow track will work together to apply it in the next stage – implementing the tracks. Many adjustments will be made as the improvement program unfolds – because of the changing circumstances, problems, and needs of the organization.

Regarding the content of what gets presented, examined, and discussed during each track in the program, the key issue here concerns how to make use of two different types of workshop materials for quantum transformation:

(1) How to select and use the already available presentation slides, assessment tools, experiential exercises, feedback sessions, and group discussions that can transform the **typical barriers to success** that almost all organizations experience into the typical channels for success that most organizations need to succeed in today's world. The materials for closing those typical GAPS in the functioning of all organizations are available for purchase in pdf files (for facilitators who have already received their certification in the completely integrated program): Kilmann, R. H., *Workbooks for Implementing the Tracks: Volumes I, II, and III.*

(2) How to develop and use the special instructional materials that are expected to remove the **unique barriers to success** that

were identified during the diagnostic interviews (and, therefore, cannot be resolved with the already available materials that only focus on the *typical* barriers to success that are common to most organizations today).

Incidentally, based on prior experience, roughly 80% of the barriers to success that are identified during the diagnostic stage tend to be common to most organizations (as in the case of the usual culture–gaps, skills–gaps, team–gaps, etc.). Meanwhile, the remaining 20% of the barriers to success are rather unique to the organization, which requires some specially designed materials in order to close those unique GAPS during the implementation stage of quantum transformation.

Essentially, all the instructional materials that are combined from (1) my previously published workbook materials (for those traditional GAPS in systems, processes, and people) and (2) any new, specially designed workshop materials (that are developed for the unique GAPS that were uncovered during the diagnostic interviews) are then sorted into the eight tracks and subdivided into one–day, monthly workshop sessions within each track. For some guidance on how much time to spend on the key topics in each workshop session, see: Kilmann, R. H., *Consultant Schedules for Implementing the Tracks: Volumes I, II, and III.*

Regarding the logistics involved in scheduling the program, a number of additional decisions must be made. Specifically: Who will be involved in each track? How many one–day workshops in each track should be scheduled? On what particular calendar day is each workshop scheduled to take place for each group of participants? See Kilmann, R. H., *Logistics Manual for Implementing the Tracks,* for all the logistical details involved in implementing the program of quantum transformation for tens, hundreds, or thousands of participants.

Now I'll provide some of the key principles for scheduling the tracks, although many modifications are usually necessary given what is learned about the organization and its members during the first two stages of quantum transformation: (1) initiating the program and (2) diagnosing the problems:

Scheduling the culture track and the skills track generally includes every work group in the entire organization. As might be expected, ensuring every member's involvement in workshop sessions is the only means to change something as ingrained as culture and the only way to learn new skills that the members are expected to use in the workplace. Since, in most cases, an open and trusting culture won't be evident in the organization for several months to come (at least not until the team track has begun), every work group is subdivided into *peer groups* for each workshop session during the first two tracks of the program. In virtually all cases, these peer groups are arranged by separating bosses from their subordinates, since this kind of arrangement provides the best opportunity for holding safe, open, candid, and forthright conversations – until the culture changes.

Scheduling the team track first involves reuniting the bosses with their direct reports in their intact work groups. This is the only way to make sure that all the new knowledge gained from the prior workshop sessions can be applied directly to the job – in the workplace – where it counts. If, however, the intact group (which includes the immediate boss) is brought together before the new cultural norms and skills have been internalized, almost everyone will fall back on their old practices (and will continue to play it safe). It does take a fair amount of time in a relatively safe environment for members to develop new skills for tackling very complex problems *before* they can be expected to approach emotionally charged work situations in new ways.

Scheduling the middle two tracks involves the formation of two separate task forces of about fifteen to twenty–five members each, referred to as a Problem Management Organization (PMO). ***One PMO is established to address the strategy-structure gaps that were identified during the diagnostic stage of quantum transformation, while another PMO is established to address the reward system gaps.*** The members selected for these special missions not only represent all levels, areas, and locations in the organization, but they also have demonstrated leadership during the prior tracks. (The shadow track develops and then manages the process for selecting the participants for these middle two tracks of the program.) Following their deliberations, those two PMOs present their recommendations to senior management for revitalizing – and aligning – the organization's strategy–structure and reward system. Later, those two PMOs play a leadership role in helping to implement the recommended changes.

Scheduling the gradual process track is done much like the team track: intact work groups, with both bosses and members together, learn how to describe, control, and improve processes within their subunit, since this is the best way to learn the tools of process management and then practice using those tools on short process chains – since these business processes flow *within* the subunit itself as compared to the longer and more complex process chains that flow *across* subunit boundaries.

Scheduling the radical process track proceeds much like the middle two tracks, whereby the shadow track carefully selects about fifteen to twenty–five participants who represent all areas, levels, and locations in the organization to form another PMO, since describing, controlling, and continually improving cross-boundary processes is an especially complex problem that needs the wisdom and knowledge of diverse experts – once an effective behavioral infrastructure along with revitalized formal systems have been established throughout the organization.

Last but not least, **scheduling the learning process track** also involves forming another PMO of fifteen to twenty–five diverse members, since describing, controlling, and improving how the organization collects, stores, retrieves, and uses knowledge is a most complex and far–reaching problem. **This additional PMO addresses how the organization can improve both the speed and quality of its learning processes, which directly builds on all the system-wide improvements that were achieved during the prior tracks in the program.**

Figure 4.7 displays a rough timeline – as one example only – for scheduling the complete program of eight tracks of quantum transformation. Employing the metaphor of railroad tracks, this figure illustrates a time schedule that is reasonably accurate for the first three tracks (for the behavioral infrastructure). The times for the subsequent tracks, however, are more difficult to predict since they are very complex problems (i.e., the transformation of formal systems and process management) that are significantly affected by the changing expectations of external stakeholders.

FIGURE 4.7

SCHEDULING THE EIGHT TRACKS ON A TIMELINE

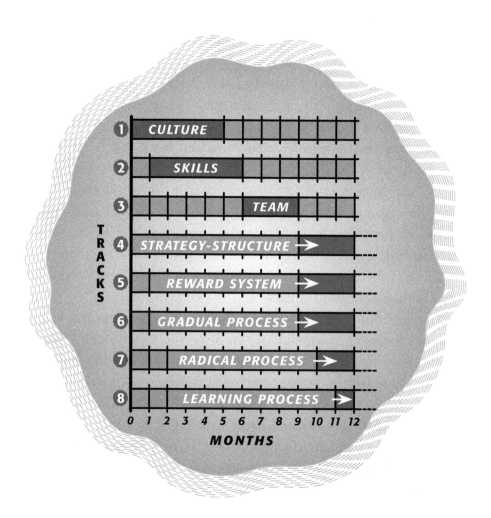

As displayed on this figure, the horizontal bar for each track represents a series of ongoing off-site meetings (held in one-day workshops) and on-site meetings (held at the workplace) that are arranged to pursue the topic in question. As can be seen, a track does not have to be completed before the next track can begin. In most cases, the first two tracks are conducted via alternating sessions, since a healthy culture is necessary to learn new skills – and vice versa. The team track should not begin, however, until the first two tracks have accomplished their purposes. For similar reasons, the middle two tracks (the formal systems) and the last three tracks (improving processes) should not be initiated until sufficient members throughout the organization enact the new cultural norms and apply their updated skills effectively – both within and across all work units.

STAGE 4: IMPLEMENTING THE TRACKS

It is rather easy to schedule the eight tracks in a neat, logical, and linear way. Such an elegant schedule, however, never takes place as planned: There are always surprises. Human nature and living systems do not follow a predictable path.

A core challenge throughout implementation, therefore, is flexibility. As the schedule of tracks is being implemented, the shadow trackers and consultants look for cues, take suggestions, and, in short, adapt. For example, special requests will be made for various feedback sessions, staff meetings, additional culture workshops, more skills development, and so on. In each case, the consultants and the shadow track must consider the request and respond according to their best sense of what will work in the given situation. Sometimes requests may be turned down, but the reasons should always be stated. At other times, the requests may be acted upon – but in a fashion that is very different from what was first suggested.

The railroad track metaphor that I applied for scheduling the tracks might appear much too precise or structured for quantum transformation. But, as illustrated in Figure 4.8, **the tracks should be considered as quantum channels through which all change initiatives and workshop sessions take place, with considerable flexibility and ongoing responsiveness to the members who are actively participating in the program.**

FIGURE 4.8
THE EIGHT TRACKS AS QUANTUM CHANNELS

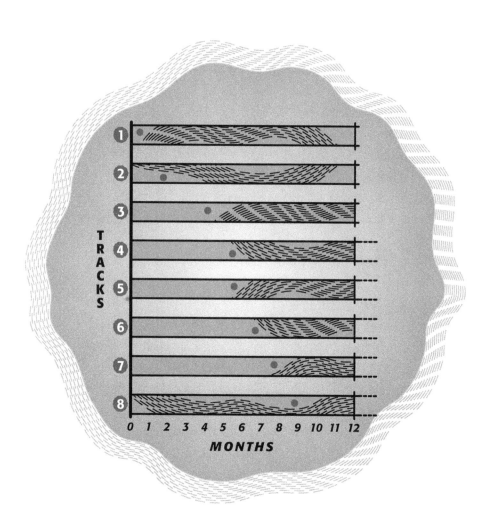

By far, the most enjoyable aspect of the implementation stage is seeing actual changes and improvements take hold. Initially, everyone is a little leery of what to expect and somewhat unsure as to whether the organization has the ability to change. But as early successes are achieved and observed, confidence develops, and this inspires an even greater effort at improvement. This is not to say that the path will be smooth and without challenges. Week by week, some things will get a lot worse before they get better. When an event seems to reinforce the traditional ways or attitudes of the past, it's easy to be discouraged and believe that nothing has changed.

These fluctuations in perceived accomplishments and moods highlight the importance of setting realistic expectations in the beginning – what should happen and when – and making sure that impatience doesn't raise expectations to unattainable levels. Disappointment and frustration result when expectations are out of line with reality, which can later affect member confidence to continue learning, changing, and improving. **Expectations must be managed proactively – and very mindfully – throughout the completely integrated program.**

A nagging issue that always surfaces during implementation is whether members will take personal responsibility for change. Even after having participated in several workshop sessions on culture and skills, members keep waiting for something different to occur: "My manager still doesn't keep me informed of what's going on in the company." "The other groups still don't cooperate with us." "My subordinates still don't finish their work on time." "When will this organization change?"

The key distinction between Internal Control and External Control is exceedingly useful in challenging all participants to look at themselves – rather than point their fingers at others (Rotter). *External Control* is apparent when a person believes that what happens to him is caused by external forces (luck, politics, fate, other people's behavior). *Internal Control* is apparent when a person believes that what happens to him is caused by what he does (*his* decisions, attitudes, and behavior). Naturally, Internal Control helps members take responsibility for change; External Control shifts the attention elsewhere.

Who *is* the source of quantum transformation? Discussions of this question translate into action when they are supplemented by this simple exercise, repeated as often as necessary: First, each member lists all the various things he's done differently since the improvement program began. Then each member shares his list with the others in his work group. Next each member asks his associates if they have witnessed what he claims. If they have *not* observed these reported changes, the member must be prepared to act on his stated intentions – to demonstrate Internal Control and personal responsibility for organizational change. Gradually, members begin to talk about their experiences in a different way from before: "I've convinced my boss that I can do a better job if I know more about *her* priorities." "I've spent more time getting to know the people in those *other* departments." "I now explain to my subordinates the specific reasons *why* I need something done on a given date." "This organization is really changing!"

After a number of months go by, it becomes more and more obvious that the members have learned – and internalized – the desired behavior. Now the new behavior is being applied much more naturally. At a particular point – sometime during the team track when the new culture and skills become internalized – the hump is crossed and the old transforms into the new. So long as these behavioral changes are subsequently guided and rewarded by the formal systems, continuous adaptability will have become ingrained in the organization.

How long will the process of implementation take? One can expect the first round of implementing the eight tracks to take anywhere from one to five years. A period of less than one year might work for a small division in which the identified barriers to success were fairly minor. A program taking more than three years might be necessary for a large, established organization that must break with its traditions in virtually every way. But if the completely integrated program were to take more than five years, I would assume that there was insufficient commitment to follow through with the implementation stage – and thus little or no momentum for change to prevail.

STAGE 5: EVALUATING THE RESULTS

Typically, this final stage of quantum transformation receives the least time and attention. Indeed, by the time the participants have redesigned their formal systems via the middle two tracks and are already describing, controlling, and improving their key business, management, and learning processes in the last three tracks, the members are primarily focused on "getting the work done" rather than attending additional workshop sessions.

A comparable shift in focus is experienced by the external consultants: Once they've initiated the process for the last three tracks, they generally spend most of their time sitting in the back of the room, simply observing how the members manage their learning processes. In fact, soon after the start of the learning process track, the consultants disappear altogether. At that point, members and their bosses are already convinced of the results of the program without needing a formal assessment. They can see and experience the system–wide improvements themselves.

What is the need, then, for a formal evaluation beyond such widespread impressions and experiences? **Formal evaluations tend to confirm these informal assessments and systematize these results for the organization.** Perhaps the more outspoken members aren't a fair representation of the membership. It might be that the quieter members are dissatisfied with the results of the program than are their more vocal counterparts. Or it could be that the more vocal individuals are more negative about the results while the "silent majority" is fairly satisfied. It's therefore important that a "streamlined diagnosis" be undertaken in order to develop a more balanced – and more accurate – evaluation of the results from implementing the program of eight tracks.

There are at least three approaches to evaluation that can be utilized to determine the impact of the program in a systematic manner: (1) diagnostic interviews, (2) diagnostic surveys, and (3) "bottom–line" measures.

Regarding the first approach, we can consider "evaluating the results" as similar to conducting another round of "diagnosing the problems." But it wouldn't be necessary to interview as large a number of members as was the case for the initial diagnosis. Having learned the language during the program, any subset of members should find it rather easy to zero in on the key issues and even use the Complex Hologram to share their perceptions during the diagnostic interview. Nor is it essential to use external consultants as interviewers: With increasingly open and candid conversations occurring in each work unit, internal consultants can obtain valid information – even in group settings. Thus, one can feel certain that the full range of real issues will be revealed during an internally conducted "mini–diagnosis" – so long as a representative sample of members is interviewed.

Besides using diagnostic interviews to assess perceptions and opinions in an anecdotal manner, the Kilmann Organizational Conflict Instrument (KOCI) can be administered, once again, to assess in a quantitative manner whether and to what extent one or more of the organization's systems are still interfering with member performance and satisfaction. In fact, it'll be very useful to compare the KOCI results that were first presented during the diagnostic stage of the program with what the KOCI results are six to twelve months later. Such a before–and–after comparison (comparing the results *before* the tracks were scheduled with the results *after* most or all of tracks have been set in motion) usually provides a meaningful evaluation to the membership. And just as was done for the first KOCI assessment, the individual scores from the latest KOCI assessment can be collected, averaged, and graphed according to levels, divisions, and subunits in order to determine which particular areas in the organization still need some additional work in improving their systems and processes.

In addition, The Kilmann, O'Hara, and Strauss *Organizational Courage Assessment* (OCA) is another useful survey instrument for evaluating the results after implementing most or all tracks in the program. ***The OCA focuses on a particular aspect of human behavior that turns out to be a very telling indicator of what life is like, which signals if the organization is still Newtonian, has become Quantum, or is somewhere in between.*** Specifically, the OCA measures: (1) if members **observe** bad behavior taking place in their subunit or organization (e.g., when members are being bullied by others) and (2) if members are **afraid** to engage in the "acts of courage" that could protect their colleagues from being harmed, abused, ridiculed, or demeaned.

I realize, of course, that the transformation from a Newtonian to a quantum organization involves several more features than just ensuring that people are kind, decent, and compassionate. ***But it's also rather obvious that no organization could possibly be considered to be a quantum organization if its members are still being harmful and hurtful to one another.*** If members are living in fear and don't strive to counteract bad behavior when they observe it, they must still be complying with the antiquated practices of their still flourishing Newtonian organization.

The OCA instrument officially presents "twenty possible acts of courage," which include: "I have observed members coming to another's aid when that person was being unfairly treated or ridiculed." "I have observed people speaking out against illegal or unethical actions." "I have observed minority members speaking out to defend their ideas in white, male–dominated groups."

Members are asked to respond to all twenty acts of courage in two different ways: In Part I of the OCA instrument, members are asked to indicate how often they *observe* these acts of courage (or if any of these acts are not necessary because the members have already been doing what is needed for long–term success). In Part II of the instrument, respondents are asked to indicate how *afraid* people would be of receiving negative consequences if they actually performed those same twenty acts of courage in their organization.

As shown in Figure 4.9, combining (1) high or low observed acts of courage with (2) high or low fear of receiving negative consequences for engaging in those particular acts then results in these four basic types of organizations: Fearful Organizations, Bureaucratic Organizations, Courageous Organizations, and also Quantum Organizations.

FIGURE 4.9
FOUR TYPES OF ORGANIZATIONS

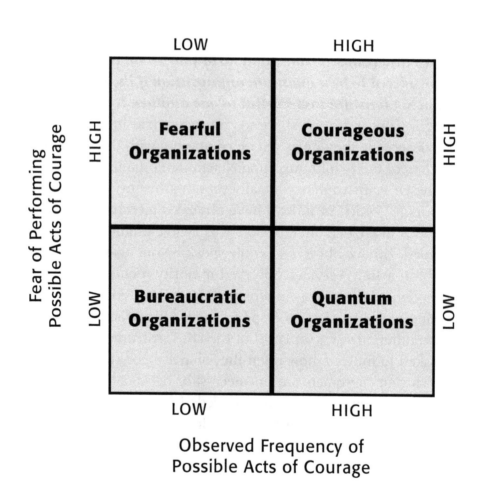

Observed Frequency of
Possible Acts of Courage

From my experience, the Fearful Organization, which reveals few observed acts of courage with lots of fear, is clearly a classic type of Newtonian organization. Even worse off, however, is the Bureaucratic Organization: Besides experiencing only a few acts of courage, members in this organization have already given up trying to make a difference, since they have totally succeeded in suppressing their fears; as such, these members don't even try to counteract the bad behavior they observe. Basically, members in a Bureaucratic Organization ignore (hence, avoid) what they see and then proceed with other activities. Perhaps the "healthiest" kind of Newtonian organization is when its members frequently engage in acts of courage to protect their colleagues from harm, as in Courageous Organizations, but those members are always living in fear of the negative consequences they'll experience for speaking up whenever they observe others are being harmed or bullied in any way.

But why do organizational members have to live in fear?

Being in a Quantum Organization, according to the OCA's survey results, is indicated when members acknowledge that they speak up whenever they observe bad behavior, but these members experience very little or zero fear that they'll receive any negative consequences for their confrontational behavior. In this case, you can bet that the desired cultural norms and an effective sanctioning system are being employed in each subunit in the organization, which helps to ensure that bad behavior is being confronted explicitly – and then resolved. In addition, if there were any troublemakers identified through the diagnostic interviews, they have since been constrained. Consequently, bad behavior is rarely observed in a quantum organization.

I'll now show you how the average scores from all members taking the Organizational Courage Assessment can be plotted on a diagram to reveal one of those four types of organizations. To begin, Figure 4.10 displays a typical result when members first respond to the OCA during the start of the completely integrated program, which reveals a Fearful Organization.

FIGURE 4.10
A FEARFUL ORGANIZATION

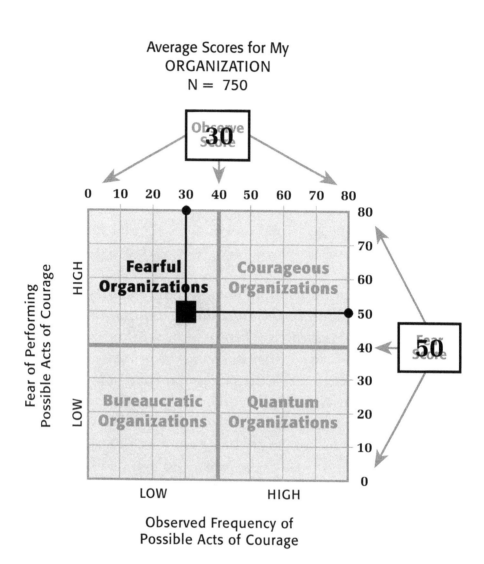

Average Scores for My
ORGANIZATION
N = 750

Now let's examine the survey results from the same members after their organization has successfully completed the first three tracks of quantum transformation. Perhaps, these same members have also been redesigning the organization's strategy–structure and establishing a performance-based reward system.

Figure 4.11 reveals a Quantum Organization, where members are now doing the right things to care for one another (in case any acts of courage are still needed from time to time) and they confront any kind of bad behavior without any fear of reprisals.

FIGURE 4.11
A QUANTUM ORGANIZATION

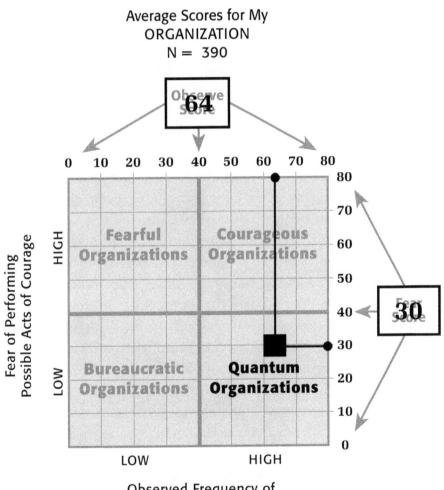

Average Scores for My
ORGANIZATION
N = 390

In most applications of the eight tracks, the first OCA results usually illuminate either a Fearful Organization or a Bureaucratic Organization. And then, with the second OCA survey, say six to nine months later, the results reveal a Courageous Organization, since members are now being more assertive (effectively using the competing, collaborating, and compromising conflict modes) and thus speaking up whenever they observe or experience bad behavior, as supported by their desired cultural norms and their sanctioning systems. But the members still experience some fear, since they probably remember how things used to be (less than one year ago).

But when the OCA is administered to those same members about a year or two after the completely integrated program was initiated, the results may reveal a Quantum Organization. Members continue to assert themselves, as encouraged by their desired cultural norms of behavior, which are reinforced by their sanctioning systems. But their previous fears have dissolved into the distant past. Again, although the OCA only assesses a limited aspect of what might have changed in the past months or years since the program began, this survey captures a distinguishing feature of Newtonian versus quantum organizations – whereby the latter drives out fear so members can behave in a dignified and ethical manner for the benefit of all key stakeholders.

Regarding the third approach, professional evaluators often emphasize "bottom–line" measures: return on investment (ROI), earnings per share, profit, sales, number of clients served, market share, budget increases, number of patents or new products, new contracts and orders, and several other performance measures. From the point of view of any stakeholder – such as customers, suppliers, stockholders, government agencies, and so forth – one usually can suggest some "hard" outcome measures. Making a before–and–after comparison on any of these measures should provide a solid basis for evaluating the impact of the program. If the program is successful, then the differences in these measures should be evident – or so the argument goes.

While these quantitative, bottom–line measures certainly can be convincing, one has to recognize their numerous limitations. Improvements in the quality of decision making and actions, for example, do not translate into one-for-one increments in profit or performance. Normally, a sequence of decisions and actions is combined in complicated ways before their effects are evident. Moreover, one shouldn't forget the time lag between decisions and actions on the one hand and performance improvements on the other hand. Some bottom–line measures will not be affected for months or even years after a key decision has been made: Improved decision making that results in much faster and better product development, for example, won't be experienced in the marketplace for years. If the before–and–after comparisons on bottom–line results are made right after the workshop sessions have concluded, one cannot expect external stakeholders to take note of any observable differences in outcomes. Ironically, if such before–and–after comparisons showed major improvements (or declines), they probably would be spurious. In fact, only if these bottom–line measurements were made over a reasonable period of time can we take the results of such an evaluation seriously.

When all is said and done, the most comprehensive — and convincing — evaluation of the completely integrated program requires all three approaches: Conducting a second round of diagnostic interviews and examining additional results from the KOCI instrument can be used to assess short-term results, while bottom–line measures can be used to assess long-term outcomes. Keep in mind, however, that short–term success might not result in long–term success: If another round of diagnostic interviews and additional KOCI surveys show good short–term results, then positive bottom–line measures *may* be expected in the future, if all the other dynamics favor the organization. This is the nature of dynamic complexity. Although using those three methods for evaluating the results of the improvement program isn't a perfect solution, it is the very best that can be done when treating the organization as a living system.

CONCLUDING THOUGHTS

While the five stages of quantum transformation might seem fairly complex, so are the organizational problems that members now face in today's fast-pace, interconnected global village. A completely integrated program must be able to influence all the interrelated systems and processes in an organization, not just one or two. At the same time, if the improvement program isn't initiated properly with top management's full support and if the organization's barriers to success are not accurately identified, the program cannot possibly produce its potential benefits. The program's implementation must be especially flexible and given sufficient time to unfold. Attempting to shortcut a program for transformation would do any organization a great disservice.

CULTURE
MANAGEMENT
FOR ORGANIZATIONS
THE CULTURE TRACK

The culture track is the first of eight tracks for implementing the completely integrated program of quantum transformation. ***The prime reason for starting with the culture track is because culture-gaps produce the most insidious barriers to long-term success*** — the difference between "what is" and "what could or should be" with respect to the cultural pressures that members put on one another to think, feel, see, and behave a particular (acceptable) way in their organization. Said differently, unless the work group or organization's culture actively supports an open, candid, probing, and engaging dialogue among diverse experts, it will be most difficult, if not impossible, for members to use the five steps of problem management for first identifying and then closing their *other* significant GAPS in the remaining seven tracks, especially for complex problems that flow across the traditional functional areas (specialized departments) in their organization.

To ensure an effective learning environment for all members to openly explore what might never have been discussed before, bosses are purposely separated from their direct reports in the off-site workshop sessions throughout the first two tracks of the program. Why? A candid dialogue for closing culture–gaps and learning critical thinking skills can best be accomplished in **peer groups** – without the immediate boss present. Then, at the start of the team track, all those peer groups that have met separately during the first two tracks of the program are reunited with their boss or manager for all the subsequent workshop sessions in the completely integrated program.

This chapter presents a very practical method for uncovering the "unwritten rules of the road," or **actual norms** as I call them, which shape people's behavior in any social group – whether a family, a group of friends, a work unit, or an entire organization. Once these previously unwritten, unspoken "cultural rules" are open for inspection, the members of a work group are then able to discuss which cultural norms are getting in the way of their performance and satisfaction (i.e., barriers to success) and which cultural norms facilitate high performance and satisfaction (i.e., channels for success). Group members can next develop a *new* set of more effective cultural rules, or **desired norms** as I call them, which will subsequently support long-term success.

A culture-gap is defined as the difference between the actual norms and the desired norms of behavior. To identify and then close their most challenging culture-gaps, members can use the same five steps of problem management that I presented in the previous chapter: (1) sensing problems (i.e., identifying GAPS); (2) defining problems (determining the root causes of those GAPS); (3) deriving solutions (selecting specific action steps in order to close those same GAPS); (4) implementing solutions (taking steps to close GAPS); and (5) evaluating outcomes (reassessing GAPS).

As a key component of any solution for closing culture-gaps, I'll describe an effective "social tool," what I call the **sanctioning system.** Essentially, this social tool is an informal reward system to help group members stop acting out their dysfunctional *actual norms* and begin enacting their newly established *desired norms*. Because it's so difficult to break old habits, especially habits that were never previously discussed out in the open, it's essential for members to always use a sanctioning system for creating – and maintaining – cultural change in the workplace.

Incidentally, the title of this chapter is identical to my 6-hour recorded online course on the same subject, which includes the two assessment tools that I discuss a little later in this chapter: *The Kilmann-Saxton Culture-Gap® Survey* and *Kilmanns Organizational Belief Survey.* My online course also provides you with two sets of work sheets that organize the problem management process for groups: *Work Sheets on Identifying Culture-Gaps* and *Work Sheets on Closing Culture-Gaps.*

THE ESSENCE OF CULTURE

The likelihood that an organization will achieve success in a dynamic and complex setting is not determined just by the skills of its leaders; nor will its adaptiveness be primarily determined by the strategy, structure, and reward systems that comprise its visible features. Rather, every organization and its work units has an invisible quality – a certain style, a character, and a way of doing things – that ultimately determines whether success will be achieved. Ironically, what cannot be seen or touched may be more influential than the behavior of any one individual or the dictates of any formally documented system. **To understand the essence or soul of the organization requires that we penetrate deep below the charts, policy statements, procedure manuals, machines, buildings, and individual members themselves, so we can explore the third dimension of the Complex Hologram.**

Culture is the invisible force behind all the surface tangibles and observables in any organization, a social energy that moves people into action. As an analogy, culture is to the organization what personality is to a person: a subtle, nonphysical, unifying theme that gives meaning, direction, and mobilization. A person has to experience the social energy that flows from such shared commitments among group members to know it: the energy that springs from mutual influence, "one for all and all for one," and "esprit de corps."

An **adaptive culture** is demonstrated when members actively support one another's efforts to identify troublesome problems and to then implement workable solutions. There is a feeling of confidence: The members believe, without a doubt, that they can successfully approach the new problems and opportunities that will come their way. There is a widespread enthusiasm, a spirit of doing whatever is needed to achieve organizational success: The members are receptive to quantum transformation.

A ***dysfunctional culture*** is evident when the social energy of the organization steers members in the wrong direction: Work groups pressure their members to persist in behaviors that may have worked well in the past, but that clearly are inappropriate today. Gradually, the organization falls into a classic **culture rut:** members do their work blindly and unconsciously out of habit. There is no adaptation or change; routine motions are enacted again and again, even though success is not forthcoming. Here the social energy not only works against the organization, but is also contrary to the wishes of the members. Nobody wants to be ineffective and dissatisfied, but everyone pressures one another to abide by the unstated, below-the-surface, behind-the-scenes, invisible culture. Such a mindless rut can go on for years, even though performance and satisfaction suffer. Bad habits die hard.

Eventually, a dysfunctional culture may fall into a collective depression as the organization's social energy is deactivated: It's not mobilized toward anything. Most members seem apathetic or listless about their jobs. They no longer pressure one another to do well. Formal pronouncements by top managers that they will improve the situation fall on deaf ears. The members have heard these promises before. Nothing seems to matter. The soul of the organization is slowly dying.

Culture shock occurs when the sleeping organization awakes and finds that it has lost touch with its mission, its setting, and its assumptions. The new world has left the insulated company behind. Rather than experience this shock, the organization may decide not to wake up. Its managers simply continue to endorse erroneous extrapolation: What made the organization successful in the past will make it successful in the future.

To understand and then succeed at cultural change, we must first address two questions: (1) How do cultures form? (2) How do cultures persist? Understanding the answers to these questions is essential for identifying and closing culture-gaps.

How Do Cultures Form?

A culture comes into being rather quickly in direct response to the organization's mission, its setting, and what's required for success: quality, efficiency, product reliability, customer service, innovation, hard work, and/or loyalty. When the organization is born, a tremendous energy is activated as members struggle to succeed. The culture captures everyone's drive and imagination. As the reward systems and rules governing work are formally documented, they also have a profound impact on shaping the initial cultural norms, suggesting what behaviors and attitudes are important for success.

Such forces in shaping culture are further heightened by the impact of key individuals. For example, the founder's objectives, principles, values, and behavior provide important clues as to what is expected from all members both now and in the future. Other top executives follow the founder's lead and pass on the culture of the company to their subordinates. Edson W. Spencer, the former CEO and chairman of Honeywell, Inc., realizes what impact he has had on his company's culture ("Conversation...."):

"Most of us, very humbly, don't wish to acknowledge that
fact, but nonetheless the chief executive's tone, his
integrity, his standards, his way of dealing with people,
his focusing on things that are important or not
important can have a profound impact on the rest of the
organization. What I am saying is that the way the chief
executive and senior managers of the company conduct
themselves as individuals has a more profound impact
on how other people in the company conduct *themselves*
than anything else that happens." (page 43)

Employees also take note of all critical incidents that stem from any management action – such as the time that so-and-so was reprimanded for doing a good job just because he wasn't asked to do it beforehand. Incidents such as these become the folklore that people remember, indicating what the organization really wants, what really counts in getting ahead, or, how to stay out of trouble. Work groups adopt these lessons as *norms* on how to survive and how to protect oneself from the organization. Roy Lewicki suggests how the double standard – managers asking for one behavior while rewarding another – motivates employees to develop the necessary unwritten rules to survive and prosper:

> "What an organization says it expects should be consistent with what it rewards – but that's not always so. If an organization says it wants to aggressively develop new businesses, then presumably it should reward those who are the most aggressive in new business development. However, if it consistently promotes those who have done the best job in nurturing current accounts and ignores the entrepreneurs, employees will soon get the message that an organizational double standard exists. Employee discontent about this duplicity will soon find its way into lunch table or cocktail circuit conversation, where the "dos and don'ts" of organizational life are shared, evaluated, and communicated to new members. 'Don't listen to what management says,' old–timers will warn; 'do what others have been rewarded for.'" (pages 8–9)

As a culture develops around particular needs, settings, and specific task requirements, it may be very functional at first. **But, over time, the culture appears to become an entity unto itself, independent of the reasons and critical incidents that formed it.** As long as it is supportive of – and aligned with – the mission of the organization, the culture remains in the background. But if management attempts to make significant changes that impact on everyone's behavior, the culture quickly rises to the occasion and asserts its powerful influence on the membership.

Indeed, the informal power of the culture is apparent when management attempts to make a major strategic shift or tries to adopt entirely new work methods. Management cannot pinpoint the source of apathy, resistance, or rebellion and is puzzled as to why the new work methods are not automatically embraced by the members. To management, it is obvious that these proposed changes are necessary and desirable. Why can't everyone else see this? *The reason is that the proposed changes run counter to the culture that underlies the organization.*

Managers are also held in the firm grip of the organization's hidden culture. Employees from below wonder why managers "play it so safe" and why their bosses keep applying the same authoritarian styles even though such mandates from above do not work. Employees wonder why their managers are so blind to the world around them. They wonder if management is "mean" or just "stupid."

How Do Cultures Persist?

Cultural norms become embedded in the organization when a strong consensus develops among group members concerning what constitutes appropriate behavior. If a norm is violated – if a member behaves in opposition to a behavioral norm – there are immediate and persistent pressures to get the offending party to change his behavior. For example, one norm in an organization might be: Don't disagree with your boss in public. Consider an individual who insists on presenting his reservations about the company's new product at a group meeting just after his boss has argued for making a very large investment in an advertising campaign for the product. The individual is stared at, frowned at, looked at with rolling eyes, and given other nonverbal messages to shut up and sit down.

Solomon Asch designed a simple experiment to demonstrate just how powerfully "a group" can influence the behavior of its members. The experiment was presented to subjects as a study in perception. As you can see on the left side of Figure 5.1, three lines – A, B, and C – all of different lengths, were presented on a card. Subjects were asked to indicate which of these three lines was identical in length to line, D, displayed on another card.

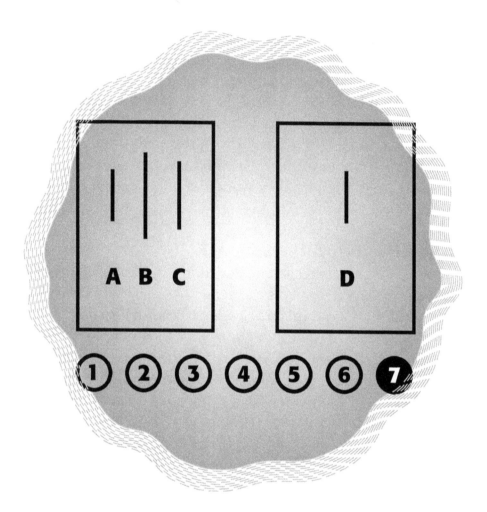

FIGURE 5.1
ASCH'S EXPERIMENTS ON SOCIAL REALITY

As shown on the bottom of Figure 5.1, seven persons sat in a row. One by one, they indicated their choice. While line D was in fact identical to line A, each of the first six persons, confederates of the experimenter, reported that line D was identical to C. The seventh person in the row was the only unknowing subject. As the six confederates each announced the agreed–upon incorrect response, the unknowing subjects became increasingly uneasy, anxious, and doubtful of their own perceptions – and sense of reality. **When it was their turn to respond to the length of those lines, the unknowing subjects seated in Position 7 agreed with the fraudulent responses from those six confederates about 40 percent of the time. When no other persons were present, the subjects chose the wrong line less than 1 percent of the time – a research finding that has been replicated many times.**

FIGURE 5.2
GROUP PRESSURES ON THE DEVIANT MEMBER TO CONFORM

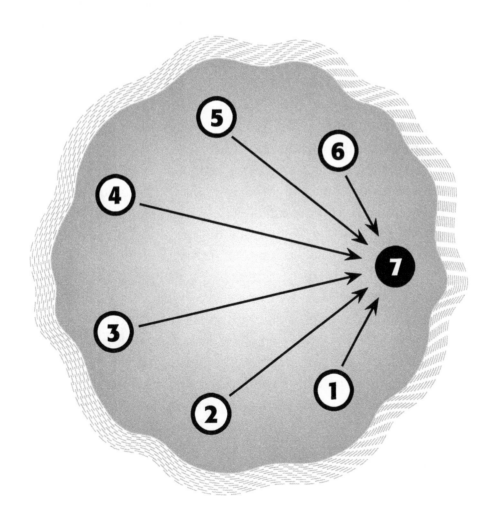

In this social experiment, there wasn't an opportunity for the seven individuals to discuss the problem among themselves. As vividly portrayed in Figure 5.2, however, if there *had* been such an open discussion among the individuals, the effect would have been much stronger, because the six confederates would attempt to *influence* the seventh person.

It's not easy being the sole deviant in a group (i.e., sitting in Position 7) when everyone else appears to be against you. Every human being has a need to be accepted by the group – family, friends, coworkers, or neighbors – which gives a group leverage to demand compliance with its behavioral norms. If people did not care about acceptance at all, a group would have little hold, other than formal sanctions, over its individual members. Most people, in fact, will deny their own perceptions when confronted with the group's norms of "objective" or physical reality. **Physical reality thus becomes a social reality.**

In all likelihood, that 40% compliance for persons in Position 7 without any group discussion would probably increase to 75% (or more) compliance, if the six other members would have the opportunity to put considerable social pressure on Person 7 to conform to the group's majority view the reality of the situation.

Now consider when the topic for a group discussion involves a highly subjective matter, such as defining a complex problems or planning how to implement a solution – and not just being asked to assess the relative lengths of three different black lines on a large card. When discussion topics are highly subjective, the compliance for individuals sitting in Position 7 would probably rise to well over 90%, especially if the six other group members put a lot of social pressure on the deviant to conform with the group's majority position on that highly subjective matter.

Now, imagine just how easily such distorted perceptions of reality can persist when backed by formal sanctions such as pay, promotions, and other rewards. The subunit or the entire organization can reward its members so they literally ignore the fundamental changes taking place in their external environment.

The members collectively believe that everything is totally fine, and they continue to reinforce this myth while they reward one another for maintaining it. In essence, everyone agrees that the dysfunctional ways of the past can continue without question. Any deviant who thinks otherwise is punished and eventually "banished from the tribe."

IDENTIFYING AND CLOSING CULTURE-GAPS

Why does one organization have an adaptive culture while another has a culture that lives in the past? Is one a case of good fortune and the other is simply a consequence of bad luck? On the contrary, it seems that *any organization can easily find itself with an outdated culture if its culture is not being managed explicitly.*

If left alone, and thus never discussed, a culture eventually becomes dysfunctional. Human fear, insecurity, oversensitivity, dependency, and paranoia seem to take over unless a concerted effort to create an adaptive culture is undertaken. People have been badly hurt at one time or another in their lives, particularly in their childhoods. It is, therefore, very easy to scare people into worrying about what pain or hurt will be inflicted in the future, even in a relatively nonthreatening situation. As a result, people cope by protecting themselves, by being cautious, by minimizing their risks, by going along with a culture that builds protective barriers around its units and around the whole organization.

If we understand how cultures form and then persist, we can prevent them from becoming dysfunctional. With a completely integrated program, it's possible to transform a long–standing dysfunctional culture into an adaptive one. Although corporate culture manifests itself in several ways (e.g., through stories, rites, rituals, symbols, slogans, and songs), the most effective approach to redirect dysfunctional organizational behavior is by managing norms. Even cultural norms that dictate how one should behave, the opinions one should state, and even one's facial expressions can be surfaced, discussed, and altered.

Step 1: Sensing Problems

In a workshop setting of peer groups, without any superiors present in any intact group (so everyone feels safe and secure), the first step in the culture track is for all group members to list the *actual norms* that are currently guiding their behaviors and attitudes. In order to get the process started, it only takes a little prodding and a few illustrations to move the discussion along. But once the process begins, members are quick to suggest many norms. In fact, they seem to delight in being able to articulate what previously was never stated in any document and rarely, if ever, mentioned in any conversation.

For an organization whose culture is dysfunctional, some of the **actual norms** that members might list are: Look busy even when you're not; don't be the first to disagree; don't step on the toes of senior management; laugh at those who suggest new ways of doing things; complain a lot; don't be the bearer of bad news; shoot the messenger who brings us bad news; don't trust anyone who seems sincere; ridicule the work of other groups. Ironically, the one norm that must be violated so this list can be developed is simply this: Don't make norms explicit!

Next, group members are asked to develop a list of the *desired norms* that would result in long-term organizational success. At this point in the process, members usually recognize the impact that their unwritten cultural norms have had on their behavior. They typically experience a sense of relief as a new way of life is considered. They recognize that they no longer have to pressure one another to behave in dysfunctional ways. The members can create a new social reality within their own groups and within their own organization. Part of this sense of relief comes from recognizing that their dissatisfaction and ineffectiveness are not the result of their being incompetent or bad individuals. It is much easier for members to blame the invisible force known as *culture* – so long as they take responsibility for changing it.

Some of the **desired norms** often listed as necessary for an organization to adapt to its dynamic complexity are as follows: Be willing to take on responsibility; initiate changes to improve performance; treat every person with respect and as a potential source of valuable insight and expertise; congratulate those who suggest new ideas and new ways of doing things; enjoy your work and show your enthusiasm for a job well done; speak with pride about your work group; be helpful and supportive of the other groups in the organization; don't criticize the organization in front of customers.

The difference between the actual and the desired norms, as I noted before, is officially termed: a culture-gap. Conveniently, the *Kilmann-Saxton Culture-Gap Survey* is a measurement tool that can be used to detect the gap between what the current culture is and what it should be, in a *quantitative* manner, which allows for some meaningful cultural comparisons across the subunits in the organization, up and down the management hierarchy and, months later, as a before–and–after comparison of culture–gaps: comparing the particular GAPS that were first sensed in Step 1 of problem management (sensing problems) with the size of those same GAPS in Step 5 (evaluating outcomes).

The Culture–Gap Survey was initially developed by collecting more than four hundred behavioral norms from employees in more than twenty different types of organizations. These norms were organized as paired opposites in order to draw attention to contrasting normative pressures in any work environment. An example of a norm pair is: (A) share information only when it benefits your own work group versus (B) share information to help other groups. Each respondent is asked to select the item in (A) or (B) in two ways. In Part 1, the respondent is asked to reveal the *actual norms that are currently operating in her work unit.* Then in Part 2, the respondent is asked to pick the *desired norms that should be operating to promote high performance and satisfaction.* The final set of twenty–eight norm pairs that appear on both Part 1 and Part 2 of the Culture–Gap Survey were considered to be the most relevant norm pairs across a variety of organizations and industries.

The organizations that participated in early research studies to develop the Culture–Gap Survey were located in the United States. Subsequent uses of the instrument, however, took place in various European countries, with the survey translated into the appropriate languages, such as Dutch, French, Finnish, German, and Spanish. While the survey was initially used cross–culturally with great caution (since national cultures can surely influence organizational cultures), all experience to date has demonstrated the worldwide relevance of four very basic types of culture–gaps, each assessed through seven norm pairs:

1. **Task Support** — behavioral norms having to do with information sharing, helping other groups, and concern with efficiency, such as: "Support the work of other groups" versus "Put down the work of other groups."
2. **Task Innovation** — behavioral norms for being creative, being rewarded for creativity, and doing new things, such as: "Always try to improve" versus "Don't rock the boat."
3. **Social Relationships** — behavioral norms for socializing with one's work group and mixing friendships with business, such as: "Get to know the people in your work group" versus "Don't bother."
4. **Personal Freedom** — behavioral norms for self-expression, exercising discretion, and pleasing oneself, such as: "Live for yourself and your family" versus "Live for your job and career."

As shown in Figure 5.3, these four culture–gaps are defined by two underlying distinctions in the workplace: technical versus human and short term versus long term. The technical/human distinction contrasts norms that speak to the technical aspects of work in organizations with cultural norms that guide the social and personal aspects of life in an organization. The short–term/long–term distinction contrasts norms that focus on day–to–day concerns versus norms that significantly affect the future of the organization. The latter includes cultural norms that emphasize work improvements (rather than just getting today's work done) and norms that define the relationship between the individual and the organization (rather than focusing only on daily social interactions). Since these two underlying distinctions cover such a broad spectrum of work experiences, the resulting four types of culture–gaps capture the great variety of cultural norms that impact on organizational success.

FIGURE 5.3
DEFINING FOUR TYPES OF CULTURE-GAPS

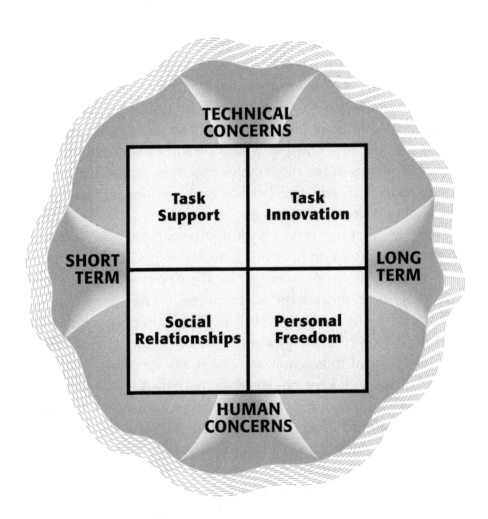

A group, department, division, or an entire organization can be surveyed with regard to its four culture-gaps. By calculating the differences between the actual versus the desired norms, the four culture-gap scores are derived. Naturally, the larger the gap, the greater is the likelihood that the current norms are hindering performance and satisfaction. As such, large culture-gaps signal significant barriers to success that should be further investigated. Indeed, if significant culture-gaps are allowed to continue, work groups are likely to ignore any attempts at work improvements and provide lip service when changes in strategic directions are announced. Even organization-wide efforts to improve member satisfaction will be met with either apathy or active resistance.

Figure 5.4 shows how the culture-gaps are displayed for easy interpretation. Each work group calculates its four average scores and then transfers them onto the four respective bar graphs. A positive culture-gap score is plotted as a filled bar (+1 to +7), a negative culture-gap score is plotted as an unfilled bar (–1 to –7), and a zero score is simply ignored. A positive culture-gap score means that the organization would be improved by modifying the actual norms in the direction of *more* Task Support, *more* Task Innovation, etc. A negative culture-gap score means that *less* of that quality is desired for success.

This sample Culture-Gap® Profile reveals that the technical norms of the group do not encourage the necessary information sharing and task support for getting the day-to-day work done. Even more pronounced, the actual norms do not encourage the necessary creative and innovative behavior that is necessary for the future. However, the group believes that the current norms that foster social interaction are essentially identical to what is desired. Regarding Personal Freedom, perhaps there is too much discretion in following policies and regulations, and members realize that a much closer adherence to organizational guidelines is needed to achieve success. Since three of the four culture-gaps are considered significant (i.e., three or more difference points), a broad-based problem is evident: The culture of the work group is holding back performance and satisfaction in several ways.

FIGURE 5.4
CULTURE-GAP® PROFILE

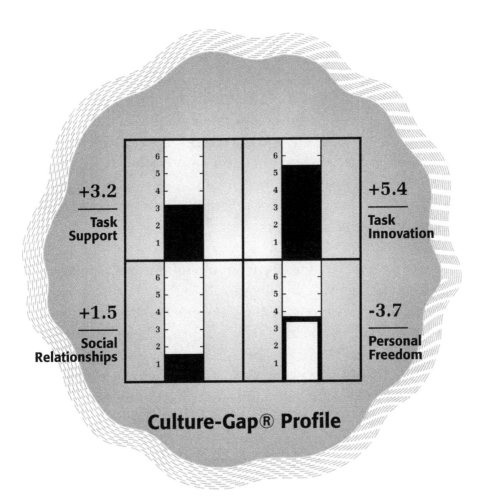

Do all members throughout an organization experience the same culture–gaps? Apparently, that's not the case. The smallest culture–gaps are usually found at the top of the organization's hierarchy. Executives believe their own publicity: For example, they *say* that they reward innovation, as they point to the widely distributed brochures that describe the organization's revamped innovation program – but they do not seem to realize that their actions speak louder than their words. **Culture-gaps tend to be**

largest at the lowest levels on the organization chart, where members continue to experience the inconsistencies that have trickled down the management hierarchy. Using the example of the innovation program, frontline employees probably view it as a joke: "Innovation? You've got to be kidding! Nobody here even remembers the last time when someone was rewarded for a new approach to a problem. If someone *did* propose something new, they wouldn't be here long enough to talk about it!"

Just as the *size* of culture-gaps often parallel the shape of the organization pyramid, the *type* of culture-gaps can differ division by division in the identical organization. Divisions have different histories, critical incidents, strategies, markets, and managers. E. J. Wallach vividly describes how different cultural norms can exist within the same organization:

> "Organizational cultures are not monolithic. Although strong cultures will be pervasive throughout an organization, coloring each employee's reality of the company's "personality," many cultures exist within the corporate reality. We all work for the same company, but the norms will vary somewhat from division to division, location to location, and functional area to functional area.... What might be totally appropriate behavior in one divisional or geographical piece of your company might be totally inappropriate in another." (page 33)

Figure 5.5 presents the Culture-Gap® Profile for each box on an organization chart. As you can tell, one should NOT assume that an organization currently has – or should have – only one culture; it totally depends on the nature of the work and what behavior is required for success in each subunit.

Figure 5.5
Plotting Culture-Gaps on an Organization Chart

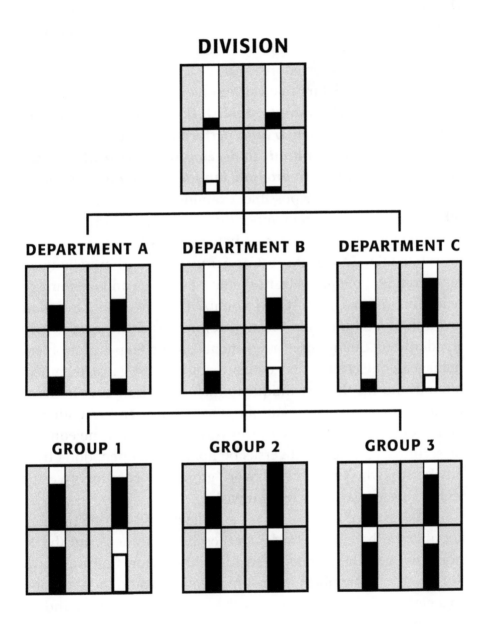

Consider what happens, however, when each subunit in an organization has different cultural norms: Communications and conflicts across divisions become much more difficult to manage. The various subunits have different jargons, values, work habits, and attitudes. If divisions need to share information, technology, personnel, and other resources, the different cultures can get in the way of cooperative efforts.

A general procedure that can resolve this cultural dilemma is as follows: ***Let each subunit establish the particular subculture that's conducive to its own high performance and satisfaction, but encourage each subunit to develop the organization-wide norms that are likely to promote long-term success:*** Help other departments whenever possible; examine the problem from the other's point of view; remember that we are all working for the same organization and we must behave accordingly.

While taking the Culture–Gap Survey is useful in helping all organizational members learn the new language and meaning of behavioral norms, it must be recognized that every organization has unique cultural qualities that cannot be anticipated in any standardized, quantitative assessment. During Step 1 of problem management (sensing, hence identifying culture–gaps), members often list norms that are unique to their organization in terms of language or focus. Those unique norms can then be written as paired opposites: Show favoritism versus treat everyone equally; be secretive and deceitful versus be honest and open; don't trust any person who's not in your work group or department versus feel free to trust whomever you wish.

Any listing of unique norm pairs developed by one or more subunits in the culture track can then be combined with the 28 norm pairs of the standardized Kilmann–Saxton Culture–Gap® Survey. All the members in the organization would then respond to a *modified* Culture–Gap Survey that includes both the standard norm pairs as well as the unique norm pairs.

STEP 2: DEFINING PROBLEMS

Once group members have identified their most troublesome culture-gaps (combining the usual and their unique set of actual and desired norms), attention shifts to discussing what is causing the existence and persistence of those culture-gaps. Discussing "the causes" will help members realize what they must now do to close their culture-gaps, so they are no longer pressuring one another to follow outdated "rules of the road" that are negatively affecting their performance and satisfaction – and undermining the long-term success of their organization.

From my prior discussion in this chapter ("How Do Cultures Form?" and "How Do Cultures Persist?"), you should already have a good idea of how culture-gaps first develop and why they are then so difficult to close – especially since those invisible cultural norms (which are powerfully sustained by peer-group pressure) are rarely, if ever, discussed openly in any group meeting.

In this section, I will concentrate on what members need to know about the root causes of their significant culture-gaps, so they can be inspired to derive solutions (selecting action steps) and then implement their solutions (applying those action steps) to close their most troublesome GAPS.

When members and their culture are at least open to change, it's miraculous to see what impact any list of desired norms has on the members of a work unit – let alone reviewing the results from the Culture-Gap Survey. As mentioned previously, there's often a sense of great relief as members become aware that they can choose to live according to different cultural norms and that they have the power to transform not only their cultural norms, but also "who pressures whom" to abide by the group's cultural norms. ***Spontaneously, members start trying out their desired norms immediately after they list them.***

When the members and their immediate culture are cynical and depressed – as when the social energy in the organization has been deactivated – their response to those results from the Culture–Gap Survey or those lists of actual and desired norms is quite different. Even when large culture-gaps are shown to exist, the members are often apathetic and listless. Members respond by saying that their work units can't change for the better *until* the next level of management above them and the rest of the organization first changes. Members believe that their immediate working environment is keeping them down.

When a Culture–Gap Survey is conducted at the next–highest level, the very same arguments are heard once again: "We have no power to change; we have to wait for the next level to let us change; *they* have the power." It's astonishing, after conducting a Culture–Gap Survey for the entire organization, to then present the results to the top management group only to find the same feelings of helplessness. Here top management is waiting for the *economy* to change! In reality, it's the culture that's saying: Don't assume responsibility; protect yourself at all costs; don't attempt to change until everyone else has changed; don't lead the way, follow; if you avoid the problem, maybe it'll go away.

This is a perfect example of a **culture rut,** where the shock of acknowledging the large discrepancy between actual and desired norms is just too great to face. Instead, the organization "buries its head in the sand" and hopes everything will sort itself out. Even in the face of strong evidence of a serious culture problem, this sort of **collective denial** persists and, not surprisingly, it is a much more insidious and perhaps more destructive force than any isolated case of *individual denial.* ***The group's power to define reality clouds each person's judgment.***

A major lesson to learn from work group cultures that have successfully changed, especially from cultures that were initially dysfunctional, is that people do NOT have to feel powerless and inept. If members decide that change should occur, then change can and will occur. It seems that ***power and control are more a social reality than any kind of physical reality.*** Members have often moved forward and achieved great success when everyone else "knew" that such an outcome was impossible.

Bottom line: Through such open group discussions at all levels and areas in the organization, members begin to realize that one of the common ROOT CAUSES of culture-gaps has to do with feeling helpless, hopeless, powerless, and not in control of directing the course of one's thoughts, feelings, and behavior. Said differently, in most cases, the source of large culture–gaps is a conditioned belief in External Control (i.e., "what happens to me is determined by outside events and what other people do") instead of a mindful, fully conscious belief in Internal Control (i.e., "what happens to me is mostly based on what I do").

Unless the membership realizes that it is the primary cause of its own culture-gaps, everyone will be waiting around for someone else "to fix the culture," which will subsequently derail all the remaining steps of problem management. Therefore, no matter what solutions are derived to close the culture–gaps, and no matter how extensively those solutions are discussed in work units throughout the organization, if members continually and blindly believe that cultural change is well beyond their reach, you can be sure that the existing culture–gaps will remain intact or will even get worse (larger).

To expand every member's understanding of the root causes of large, persistent culture–gaps, I find it helpful to ask members to take the *Kilmanns Organizational Belief Survey*. This survey invites participants to respond to 30 items: 15 items present instances of Internal Control, while 15 items focus on External Control.

Here are two survey items that represent **Internal Control:** "Management will seriously review my ideas for organizational change and improvement;" "If I need more education or training, I can get it." Here are two items that express **External Control:** "I cannot get the resources I need to do my job effectively;" "I have a hard time inspiring my coworkers to do their very best."

Members are then asked to respond to each of the 30 items on a five–point scale, ranging from "I strongly disagree (1 on the scale) to "I strongly agree: (5 on the scale). Based on normative data, a score between +11 to +60 represents a belief in Internal Control, while a score between −60 and −11 suggests a belief in

External Control; and a score in the middle, between −10 to +10, suggests Mixed Control (i.e., beliefs that often fluctuate between Internal Control and External Control).

In some situations, people's beliefs are exactly aligned with reality: They believe they cannot influence much of what goes on and, indeed, they can't: Insurmountable barriers continuously undermine their attempts at change and improvement. In other situations, however, people's beliefs are out of touch with reality. For example, it may be possible for organizational members to influence what goes on – but because they do not *believe* they can succeed, they do not even test whether their beliefs are true or false. **Worse still is the case in which an organization gives its members the opportunity to improve their performance and satisfaction; yet members do not want to believe they can make a real difference – so they refuse to try.**

At first, it's difficult to know which of these three scenarios is true: (1) whether beliefs in External Control are rooted in reality, because members cannot improve their performance no matter how hard they try, (2) whether such beliefs in External Control are *unknowingly* out of touch with reality – because those beliefs have never been tested, or (3) whether those beliefs are *knowingly* out of touch with reality – simply because people prefer, quite intentionally, not to be responsible or accountable for their own behavior. If an organization showed little interest in attempting to improve itself, perhaps the first scenario would be plausible. But when any organization is in the process of implementing a completely integrated program of quantum transformation, it's hard to argue that real improvement can't and won't take place.

Figure 5.6 illustrates an Organizational Belief Profile in which a particular individual and, to a lesser extent, his work group are pessimistic about being able to improve performance while the department and the organization as a whole are more optimistic. These relative profiles might suggest that the individual and his work group don't believe that change is possible and, as a result, cannot take advantage of what most others are able to influence in the same organization.

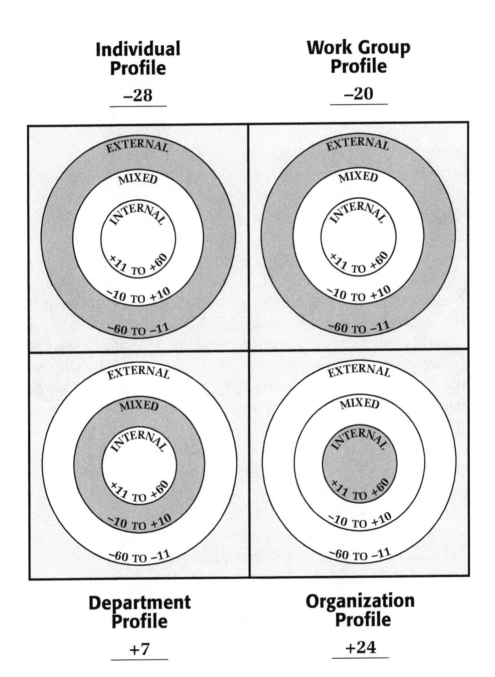

FIGURE 5.6
AN EXAMPLE OF ORGANIZATIONAL BELIEFS (1)

Individual Profile
−28

Work Group Profile
−20

Department Profile
+7

Organization Profile
+24

By examining these results from the Organizational Belief Survey and then discussing their many implications, however, the particular individuals and their work groups will be able to consciously reexamine whether their perceptions of various constraints, limitations, and restrictions in the situation are actually real — or primarily imagined. Having an open, candid, and thoughtful discussion along these lines might enable these members to align their beliefs with reality – which is more likely to foster constructive action than continued resignation.

Now consider the Organizational Belief Profiles displayed on Figure 5.7. In this second example, this individual and her work group believe they can actually influence what determines their performance, but the larger department and the organization do not! Somehow, these particular group members have not been negatively affected by the various obstacles that others *in the same organization* seem to experience (or imagine). In this case, it's not unusual for other members of the same organization to declare: "Hasn't anyone told them they can't do that? They're acting as if they can really make a difference here!"

By sharing the Belief Profiles in Figure 5.7 with the rest of the organization, however, members in the other subunits can now be encouraged to mindfully rethink whether they are as helpless and out of control as they envision themselves to be. In particular, to discover that some members *in the same organization* have not succumbed to beliefs in External Control may very well stimulate a fresh look at the reality that stands before them.

To enhance Internal Control, therefore, here are the profound guidelines for every member: **See** the connection between what you do and what then occurs all around you. **Think** as though you can effectively influence what goes on in your organization. **Act** as though you can make a big difference on everything that affects you. **Encourage** others to believe in their ability and will to determine the quality of their work life – short term and long term. One thing is certain: **Without developing a collective belief in Internal Control, the members cannot and will not improve their performance — even with the best of intentions.**

FIGURE 5.7
AN EXAMPLE OF ORGANIZATIONAL BELIEFS (2)

**Individual
Profile**

+22

**Work Group
Profile**

+14

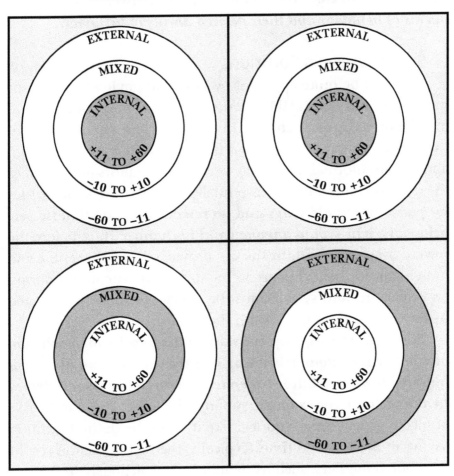

**Department
Profile**

−5

**Organization
Profile**

−18

Once all the peer groups in the culture track have had the chance to identify their most troublesome culture-gaps (Step 1), and have also had the opportunity to discover and discuss their collective beliefs about WHO controls what happens to them in their organization and WHY an effective sanctioning system is definitely needed to break bad habits and reward more adaptive behavior (Step 2), members are now ready (Step 3) to **self-design an effective sanctioning system as the prime solution that will enable them to close the identified GAPS between their actual norms of behavior and their desired norms of behavior.**

STEP 3: DERIVING SOLUTIONS

It should be quite apparent by now that having peer groups merely list and discuss their desired norms is never sufficient to instill more adaptive behavior in the workplace and throughout their organization: As noted, each work group must self-design and use an informal *sanctioning system* that monitors and enforces the desired cultural norms. Essentially, **if there were no penalties for persisting in old ways and no reward for engaging in new behaviors, why would anyone want to change?** Thus, before the reward system – the fifth track – provides formal incentives to individuals for behaving according to those new cultural norms, an *informal* reward system must be developed and then utilized by every subunit in the organization.

Basically, every group is asked to develop its own solution of what will be done when any member acts out an old norm (referred to as a violation) or enacts a desired behavior (referred to as a victory). For example, suppose the actual norm is: "Arrive at meetings whenever you feel like it;" and the desired norm is: "Arrive at meetings on time." Typically, the first infraction results in subtle reminders, such as members conspicuously looking at their watches whenever one of them arrives late to the meeting. Subsequent infractions incur stronger sanctions, such as placing someone's problem with lateness on the formal meeting agenda or reporting a short description of the incident in the company's e-newsletter. And then, those members who set the best example of showing up to group meetings on time are treated to a lavish dinner by those who have violated the agreed-upon norm!

As long as the sanctioning system developed by each work group is ethical and legal, every group can be encouraged to be as creative as possible in determining how to reward desired behavior and how to penalize bad habits. If each sanctioning system also involves some gentle humor, the cultural change will not be as difficult as might have first been thought. However, if members insist that they are too adult-like and mature for such a "social game," undoubtedly they have failed to grasp the extent to which their work groups have been using powerful sanctions to maintain the dissatisfying status quo. Undiscussable sanctions, such as "one mistake and you're out," are more debilitating than any work group's sanctioning system that's created during the culture track: Indeed, bringing the previously silent sanctioning system to the attention of group members will motivate them to create an open system that is more equitable – and effective.

For example, in one organization that was implementing the culture track, a senior management group agreed that each new cultural norm should be written on an index card and given a number. Each member in the group was given responsibility for monitoring several norms and calling attention to behavior that did not conform. Eventually, group members no longer needed to cite the actual norms – only their numbers. Members would state: "You just committed a number twelve error," or "You pulled a number seven on me." These people were able to enforce their new culture in this lighthearted and humorous manner, yet the point of adopting the norms was made unequivocally.

In another organization, the senior executives designed their sanctioning system by humorously making use of the corporate pin of the American eagle that they proudly wore on their shirts and blouses. The first time that a member violated a norm, one wing of the eagle would be broken off *and* the executive still had to wear the partially broken eagle pin. When a second violation occurred, the other wing of the eagle would be broken off. Thus, after just two violations, the slow-to-change executive would be wearing the pin of the eagle, showing the body of the bird, but the wings were gone. And if that weren't enough to convince the executive to change his behavior, the third time this same person violated the new cultural norms, he'd have to sit in the corner of the room, facing the wall, throughout the next group meeting! Although this third sanction probably was never utilized, every executive got the point that *behavior had to change.*

STEP 4: IMPLEMENTING SOLUTIONS

The first three steps of problem management can usually be conducted in just one or two workshop sessions. But for there to be real cultural change throughout the organization, additional discussions, further reinforcement, and more group sanctions are surely needed in order to sustain what has begun in those early workshop sessions.

Kurt Lewin defined three overlapping phases of behavioral change that explains what generally takes place throughout the culture track: unfreezing, change, and refreezing.

The **unfreezing phase** begins when group members accept that their behavior must change, as dramatically discovered by their self–assessed culture–gaps and their organizational beliefs about External Control versus Internal Control. These members also accept that their newly devised sanctioning system must be used in actuality if there is to be any real incentive for change. But knowing something intellectually is never the same thing as behaving differently.

The **change phase** is evident when members begin to behave according to their new cultural norms: Unlike before, members now share information with other subunits, arrive at all group meetings on time, and offer opposing viewpoints during group discussions. At first, behaving in these new ways is awkward and somewhat forced. Anybody who attempts to break an old habit and replace it with a different behavior will initially experience uncomfortable feelings. Naturally, the easiest thing for anyone to do is to revert back to the old habit even if it violates new norms and results in various sanctions. It is also much easier to wait for other members to change first, rather than to take (on one's own) those embarrassing first steps.

The **refreezing phase** begins when the new ways of behaving in the workplace become more natural and automatic. Members no longer need to remind one another of the desired norms: The new behaviors have developed into new habits.

Moving from the unfreezing phase through the change phase and then to the refreezing phase, however, can take a lot of time and effort. From the start of the culture track, perhaps four to six months will usually pass before organizational members have significantly modified their behavior. Members quickly discover that it's very difficult switching from talk to action – from the discussions in a safe workshop setting to behavioral changes on the job. Most often, there's a great deal of frustration since some members expect the cultural change to take place immediately. Even when these members admit that they themselves have not done much of anything differently, they still wait for something to happen. Discussing these experiences in terms of "unfreezing, change, and refreezing" helps to alleviate the usual pressure for immediate success. Knowing those three phases also encourages everyone to be more patient with themselves and others while implementing their solutions for closing their culture–gaps.

To reinforce the change process, follow–up workshop sessions are conducted at least once every month. In addition, the work groups are asked to have several meetings at the workplace, in between these formal workshop sessions, so they can continue their cultural discussions (and how to improve the use of their sanctioning system). In these subsequent workshop sessions and on–the–job discussions, work groups are asked to address several questions relative to when the culture track first began: What has improved? What has stayed the same? What has become worse? Then, attention focuses on identifying the obstacles that are preventing cultural change from occurring or, more exactly, understanding the *root causes* of what's making it so difficult for members to move from awareness to behavior. Next, numerous solutions are derived that can remove the obstacles to cultural change. Following the selection of the best solutions, action steps are developed to implement the chosen solutions.

During the next group meeting, the members again inquire as to the results of their efforts (by sharing what has improved, stayed the same, or become worse), and this cycle of reflection, discussion, and more effective action continues. As the process of behavioral change transitions into the refreezing phase, the most troublesome culture-gaps become smaller and smaller.

STEP 5: EVALUATING OUTCOMES

Approximately six to nine months after the culture track was initiated, the Kilmann–Saxton Culture-Gap Survey (expanded by the addition of several unique norm pairs) can be administered once again to reassess which areas, levels, and locations in the organization have improved, stayed the same, or become worse with respect to their GAPS. Each work group then analyzes its own culture-gap results to consider what additional work needs to be done in order to bring their remaining culture-gaps within acceptable limits.

Figure 5.8 shows before-and-after Culture-Gap comparisons for the 217 members of a division in an industrial corporation, about six months after the culture track was initiated. As these profiles illustrate, the culture-gap for Task Support was reduced from +3.2 to +1.3, the latter GAP now being insignificant. The culture-gap for Task Innovation, which initially was the largest at +5.4, was reduced to 2.1. The culture-gap for Social Relationships increased a little from +1.5 to +2.8, perhaps due to the greater interaction now taking place in the workshops and also in the workplace. The culture-gap for Personal Freedom was reduced from a minus 3.7 (suggesting the members desired *less* freedom on the job) to an insignificant +0.3. This pattern of culture-gap comparisons was similar in most work units in this division. In fact, only a few work groups still had some lingering difficulties in Task Support and Task Innovation, which then required some additional discussion, solutions, and action.

FIGURE 5.8

BEFORE-AND-AFTER COMPARISON OF CULTURE-GAPS

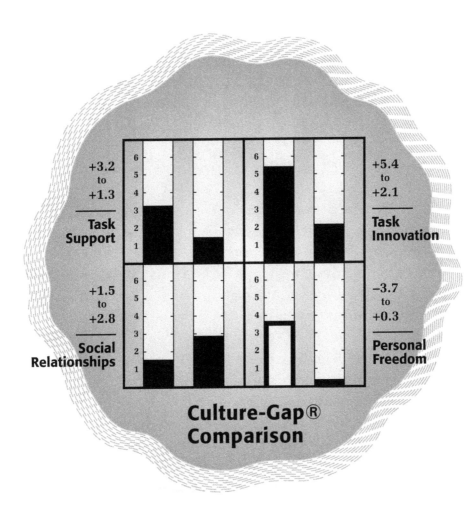

It's generally worthwhile to also reassess member results on the Organizational Belief Survey. A before–and–after comparison usually confirms that there's been a significant transformation from External Control to Internal Control. After participating for several months in the culture track, members now believe that they *can* influence what happens in their work group: They have experienced for themselves the different manner in which they interact with one another (both within their subunit and with members of other subunits), which typically demonstrates more open, candid, and forthright discussions on all their problems and conflicts. On the other hand, if their identified culture–gaps have stayed the same (or have become worse), you can bet that members have not transformed their earlier beliefs in External Control into new beliefs in Internal Control – so instead of their taking deliberate steps to close their GAPS, they've been waiting around for someone else to fix their culture for them.

CONCLUDING THOUGHTS

A healthy, supportive, candid, open, and adaptive culture sets the proper stage for the successful completion of the remaining seven tracks of the completely integrated program. In contrast, a dysfunctional culture, breeding a lack of trust, little confidence, and not much sharing of information across work units, would make it most difficult to improve anything of importance.

Only with an adaptive culture will all members be willing to accept their skill deficiencies and to then learn new approaches for addressing complex problems; they need an adaptive culture to recognize the many changes going on in the external setting, so they can surface and revise any false assumptions. With an adaptive culture, the membership can partake in team building to improve the quality of decision making and action taking on complex problems, where sustaining a cooperative spirit is vital, especially when working across subunit boundaries. Only with an adaptive culture will the membership be able to examine and then revitalize their formal systems – strategies, structures, and reward systems – representing very sensitive and close–to–home problems. Lastly, with an open, candid, and adaptive culture, it'll now be much easier – and effective – for members to describe, control, and improve the business, management, and learning processes that flow within (and especially across) all the formal and informal systems in the organization.

CRITICAL
THINKING SKILLS
FOR ORGANIZATIONS

THE SKILLS TRACK

The skills track is the second of eight tracks for implementing the completely integrated program of quantum transformation. At least one workshop in the culture track should be conducted BEFORE the first session of the skills track begins. Why? It'll be so much easier for participants to enhance their critical thinking skills if the desired cultural norms throughout the organization are already encouraging a safe and engaging learning process.

As also noted at the start of the last chapter, to ensure a safe learning environment, bosses are purposely separated from their direct reports in the off-site workshop sessions throughout the first two tracks of the program. Why? An effective dialogue for closing culture-gaps and learning critical thinking skills can best be achieved in **peer groups** without the immediate boss present. Then, at the start of the team track, all the peer groups that have met separately during the first two tracks are reunited with their boss or manager for all subsequent workshop sessions in the completely integrated program.

Typically, the diagnostic results from the one-hour interviews with a representative sample of members across the organization reveal what further skill development is necessary for long-term success. The skill deficiencies that are often identified during the diagnostic interviews vary from one organization to another, but usually fall into these major categories: technical skills, conflict management skills, problem management skills, listening skills, communication skills, leadership skills, team management skills, time management skills, and critical thinking skills.

Since there already are many available training programs for enhancing what is often called, *people management skills*, and since the essential technical, professional, and administrative skills are usually unique to the organization in question, **this chapter will concentrate on learning the critical thinking skills that remain seriously undeveloped throughout our entire society**, primarily due to our increasingly fast-paced, highly interconnected, global village. Not surprisingly, most university degree programs and typical corporate training programs teach participants to define and solve only SIMPLE problems, even though the world is now facing COMPLEX problems. Please note: **Even when members have already developed social and technical skills, if members have not yet developed the key skills for managing dynamic complexity, then all their other organizational, technical, and business skills cannot be put to effective use.**

Bottom line: Learning how to resolve complex problems and conflicts is THE nagging challenge for all our organizations and institutions: As highlighted in Chapter 1 (Seeing the Big Picture), we must now approach the world as a complex hologram – not as a simple machine.

In this chapter, I will begin by discussing the **key differences between a simple problem and a complex problem** – and how those crucial differences are highly relevant to the five steps of problem management (which I presented in Chapter 4, Quantum Transformation for Organizations). Following, I'll summarize **two different inquiry systems**, the Lockean Inquiring System and the Hegelian Inquiring System, to help us inquire into the nature of TRUTH for the most important steps in problem management: In particular: **How do we know that we have correctly defined the root causes of a complex problem (Step 2)? And how do we know that the GAP will close after we have implemented our chosen solution (Step 4)?** Using the metaphor of decision trees (including branches, trunks, and roots) will allow us to deeply appreciate WHY different people with very different knowledge, expertise, and experience must be included in those two steps of problem management – which epitomize dynamic complexity.

After this background discussion on simple versus complex problems, the distinction between the Lockean Inquiring System and the Hegelian Inquiry System, and why it's so important to take note of the particular distribution of decision trees in the quantum forest, **I'll formally present one of the most powerful analytical methods that utilizes all the foregoing material on managing dynamic complexity: Assumptional Analysis**. Much like the process in the culture track for surfacing actual cultural norms (so those troublesome culture-gaps can first be identified and then closed), I will discuss a profound process for surfacing all the hidden assumptions that implicitly support any proposed conclusion, decision, or plan. Next, any false assumptions can be revised, which will then allow active participants **to convincingly deduce a NEW conclusion for correctly defining the root causes of a complex problem and then successfully implementing the best solution.**

Next I'll present a psychological framework, based on the work of Carl G. Jung, for highlighting – and then magnifying – the fundamental differences that are always the heart and soul of a complex problem. The *Kilmanns Personality Style Instrument* can then be used to identify **four personality styles for managing complex problems**, which will allow organizational members to form four personality-style groups (each group based on very a different personality style) for the purpose of investigating the tangled roots that are underneath all the decision trees that are scattered across the quantum forest. But once those personality differences for defining problems and implementing solutions have been purposely magnified (to clearly see the differences in a bright light), we must then use each of the **five conflict modes for resolving those exaggerated personality-style differences** – depending on the eight key attributes of the situation.

In the concluding section of this chapter, I formally present the establishment and functioning of the Problem Management Organization (PMO), which is staffed with fifteen to twenty-five participants who represent all areas, levels, and locations in an organization. In essence, the PMO is designed to make the best use of radically different perspectives for defining and solving the most complex problems facing the organization. As you will see, the PMO effectively integrates all the foregoing discussions on the method of assumptional analysis, the inquiring systems, the four personality styles, and the five conflict-handling modes.

By the way, just as I've done for the previous chapters in this book, I have titled this chapter the same as my six-hour, online course: Critical Thinking Skills for Organizations. After learning the three stages of assumptional analysis (surfacing, classifying, and synthesizing assumptions), my online course provides you with some valuable practice in applying this unique method to a business case: Atwater County Hospital East (ACHE). Specially designed work sheets are also included in this recorded course for going through all the stages of assumptional analysis in the most efficient and effective manner possible.

Simple versus Complex Problems

A **simple problem** is apparent whenever one individual CAN HAVE all the necessary knowledge, expertise, and experience to solve the problem. In contrast, a **complex problem** is apparent when one individual CANNOT POSSIBLY HAVE all the relevant knowledge, expertise, and experience to solve the problem.

This sharp contrast between a simple and complex problem is squarely rooted in the biological, physical, social, emotional, and cognitive limitations of human beings. Indeed, if a human being *were* capable of knowing everything about each subject, it would be entirely unnecessary to distinguish a simple problem from a complex problem. But given the inherent limitations of every human being, it takes several people (or multiple groups) to have ALL the necessary knowledge, expertise, and experience to understand ALL the interrelated aspects of complex problems, so organizational members can accurately sense problems in the beginning, define the root causes of those problems, next derive solutions, implement solutions and, finally, evaluate their results (as per the five steps of problem management). Said differently, since human beings are highly specialized (especially when they have received all their education in their chosen profession and have worked in only a few functional areas in an organization), there are many problems that, by definition, are well beyond the knowledge, expertise, and experience of any one person.

To truly appreciate the essential differences between simple and complex problems, I will modify the old Sufi tale about the six blind men and the elephant, so I can demonstrate how each person, no matter how accomplished in his own profession and occupation, cannot effectively address a complex problem from that one limited perspective.

Let's imagine that six blind persons are each placed next to a different part of a live elephant – as a metaphor for a very messy and complex beast before them (problem). When the blind men are asked what they experience right in front of them, they each assume that their own perceptions capture the whole problem. One person, feeling the elephant's tail, says: "This beast must be a snake." The blind person touching one of the elephant's legs says: "This beast must be a tall tree with a large trunk." The blind person rubbing the tusk of the elephant says: "This beast must be a special kind of sword," and so forth. In essence, each blind person can only experience "the problem" by making use of his limited perspective, since his *blindness* (his specialized profession or vocational focus) prevents him from seeing the whole beast.

This Sufi tale beautifully illustrates the limited range of our mental, emotional, and professional abilities – since we're blind to all the other relevant perspectives about which we know little or nothing, or we've never had the chance to live and experience firsthand in our lifetime. However, if a person has 20/20 vision and can also be in a position to see all aspects and nuances of the complex problem, he would be more likely to announce, "It's obvious: This is an elephant!"

During the skills track, members learn that they'll fail to correctly define the root causes of a complex problem and also fail to implement their chosen solution unless they are able to integrate the different perspectives of different experts.

TREES, BRANCHES, TRUNKS, ROOTS, AND FORESTS

Figure 6.1 shows *a single decision tree that reveals a simple problem*. The trunk or base of the tree represents the definition of the problem that has already been determined and specified (either unconsciously or deliberately) through a single discipline. The branches on this tree represent alternative solutions. Smaller branches represent additional mini–steps for deriving a detailed solution to the simple problem. A solving error would be picking the wrong branch on the tree.

FIGURE 6.1
SIMPLE PROBLEMS HAVE ONE DECISION TREE

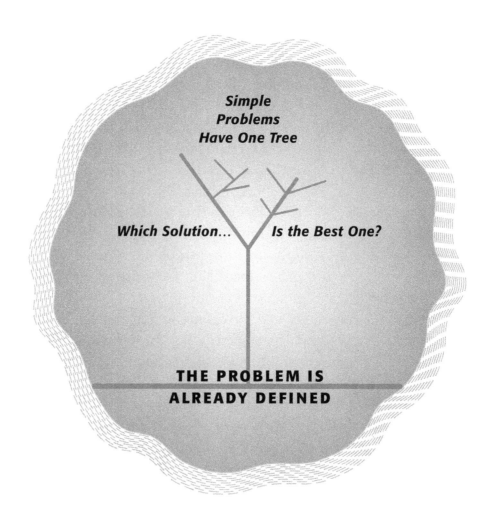

Figure 6.2 displays the **two (or more) decision trees that exist for every complex problem**. The trunk or base of each decision tree represents a different definition of the problem. Incidentally, although decision trees are generally drawn from left to right as if they were lying on their sides (and therefore dead and rotting away), I find it more inspiring to draw trees from the ground up (as being alive and growing). Each flourishing tree is thus rooted in its below–the–surface assumptions that can now be untangled and revised for managing the organization's complex problems.

FIGURE 6.2
COMPLEX PROBLEMS HAVE MANY DECISION TREES

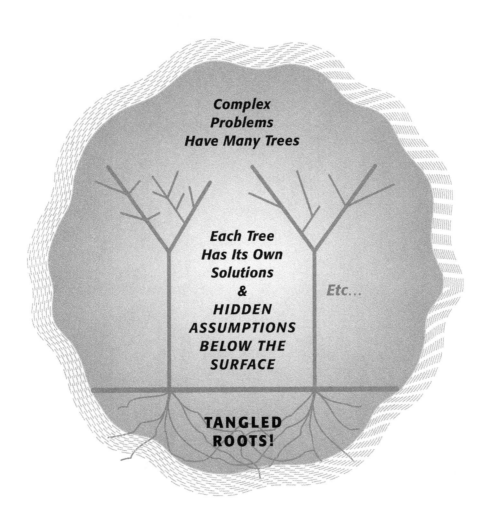

As shown in Figure 6.3, **once those underlying assumptions have been surfaced, revised, and synthesized — by untangling and rearranging the roots underneath several decision trees — it is possible to create an altogether new decision tree in the forest.** Most importantly, this new decision tree offers completely new alternative solutions – branches – that none of the previous trees could have provided. As we will see, synthesizing previous decision trees into a new tree in the forest is a beautiful example of using the integrative dimension on the TKI Conflict Model.

FIGURE 6.3
CREATING A NEW TREE IN THE FOREST

Figure 6.4 represents the ***quantum forest***. Essentially, for any complex problem that arises in today's world, a diverse group of experts (based on their divergent educational backgrounds and work experiences) can easily generate a large forest of decision trees, which will allow those diverse experts to debate different definitions of the problem (i.e., the trunk of each tree) and then to derive one or more solutions to the problem (i.e., the branches on each tree). Establishing and analyzing this quantum forest is the best way to resolve an organization's complex problems.

FIGURE 6.4
THE QUANTUM FOREST OF DECISION TREES

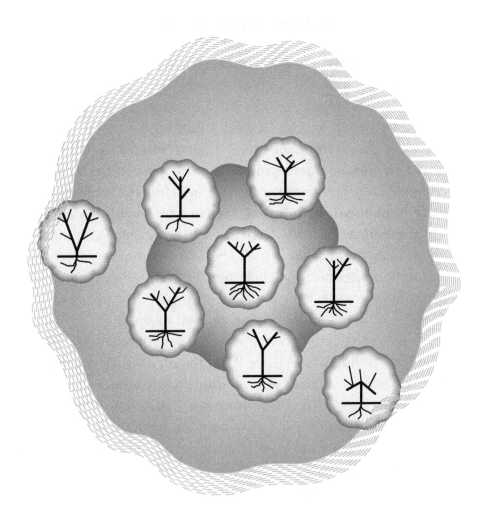

Check out the particular distribution of decision trees in this quantum forest: The tree in the dead center of the illustration is the most obvious problem definition for members – based on the history (and culture) of the organization. The middle area in the forest depicts the accepted, mainstream **grove of trees,** which the majority of experts can easily acknowledge and appreciate. But the outer edge of the forest, closest to those quantum waves, captures the most radical perspectives: These revolutionary trees can only be acknowledged and appreciated if the organization's behavioral infrastructure encourages their formation – based on functional cultural norms, critical thinking skills, and teamwork within and across all subunit and organizational boundaries.

TWO INQUIRING SYSTEMS

As shown on Figure 6.5, there are two Inquiring Systems that reveal two very different ways of determining the TRUTH about anything (Churchman). First, looking at the top portion of the diagram, let's consider the Lockean Inquiring System (based on the work of the philosopher, John Locke): **Truth for the Lockeans is based on seeking agreement: If you can get a majority of the members in a group to agree on how to define the problem and how to implement the solution, they must be right – while the deviant members in that group must then be wrong.** Truth lies in the middle of the normal (bell-shaped) distribution of trees in the quantum forest; for the Lockeans, the endpoints on a normal distribution are viewed as aberrations ("misguided" opinions).

Second, looking at the bottom portion of the diagram, let us now consider the Hegelian Inquiring System (based on the work of the great philosopher, Georg Wilhelm Friedrich Hegel). **Truth for the Hegelians is based on investigating disagreement: How can different people view the same exact situation differently? Isn't that interesting!** By focusing only on the deviants and then struggling to understand WHY they perceive that same situation differently, all potential aspects of the problem become apparent and eventually accessible.

FIGURE 6.5
TWO INQUIRING SYSTEMS

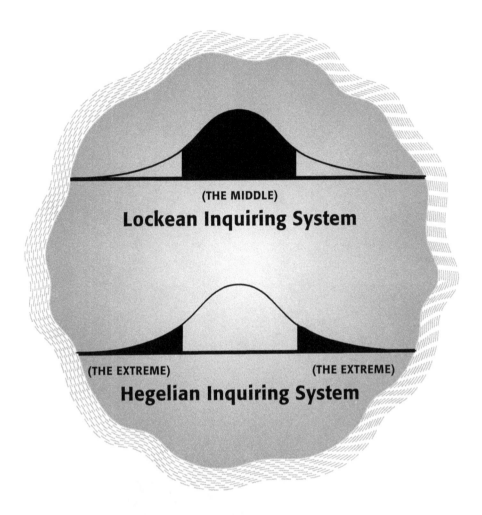

Furthermore, regarding the Lockean System shown in Figure 6.6, by ignoring or denying the extremes of the distribution, it's rather easy to determine a conclusion in a short amount of time: The majority of members only have to agree on that perspective. Virtually all groups in organizations use the Lockean approach: If people can agree, they must be right. If you are not sure of the agreement, then vote: That will convince the minority that the majority has discovered the truth. However, quickly selecting the

majority's perspective can only work well for a simple problem –
when there's a lot of redundant expertise and experience among
group members.

FIGURE 6.6
THE LOCKEAN INQUIRING SYSTEM

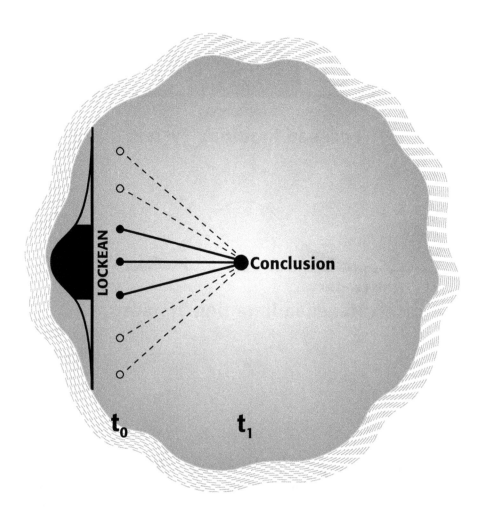

As Figure 6.7 shows, the Hegelian process takes the necessary
time to first recognize and then debate the most extreme points
on a normal distribution. By intensely discussing what is behind
the extreme views on the radical decision trees in the quantum

CHAPTER 6

forest (particularly those underground, underlying assumptions), complex problems become more deeply understood – and come to life for all to see.

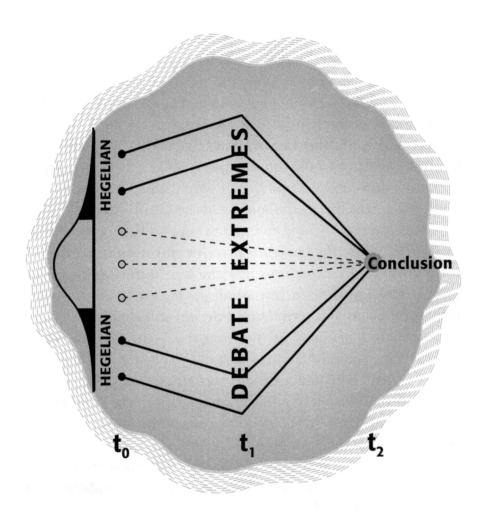

FIGURE 6.7
THE HEGELIAN INQUIRING SYSTEM

After the members of a group have debated all the different perspectives (especially the extreme ones), they become more at ease with complexity, since they now can see the *elephant* – the whole beast that stands before them. However, once the experts have surfaced and debated the underlying assumptions behind the different problem definitions or implementation plans, they then come to agreement on a single – integrated – approach. *But how do they achieve such agreement?* Ironically or not, they use the Lockean approach! But they do so only AFTER their differences have been thoroughly discussed and debated. Whereas the pure Lockean approach is based on immediately dismissing any and all extreme perspectives and then arriving at a quick agreement about the obvious, middle–of–the–road perspective, the Hegelian approach first conducts a fairly intensive, time–consuming, and probing debate among the extreme perspectives on a complex problem BEFORE seeking a Lockean agreement on defining the problem and/or implementing a solution.

As Figure 6.8 further demonstrates, the Lockeans quickly zero in on the most obvious, commonplace, and well–defined grove of centrist decision trees and then, to top it all off, they select the most prominent tree in the middle of the grove – because most members can quickly be convinced to support that most familiar perspective. Thus, **the Lockeans perceive only a small portion of the quantum forest (perhaps just one tree in the middle of the grove), which provides a very small pie for satisfying the most important needs of internal and external stakeholders.**

As captured in Figure 6.9, however, the beauty of discovering and debating the extreme trees in the forest is that ALL the trees and ALL their potential solutions (branches) will automatically be included in the analysis of the complex problem. Any centrist decision trees (those in the middle grove of the forest) are easily accessible to all the members and, as a result, will naturally be incorporated into the group's analysis of the problem situation. To reiterate: **It's the extreme views on a complex problem that typically get ignored and, therefore, must always be pursued proactively in the spirit of the Hegelian Inquiring System.**

FIGURE 6.8
THE LOCKEAN FOREST OF DECISION TREES

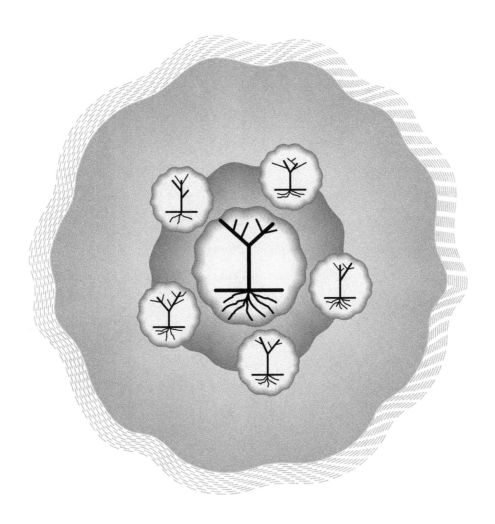

FIGURE 6.9
THE HEGELIAN FOREST OF DECISION TREES

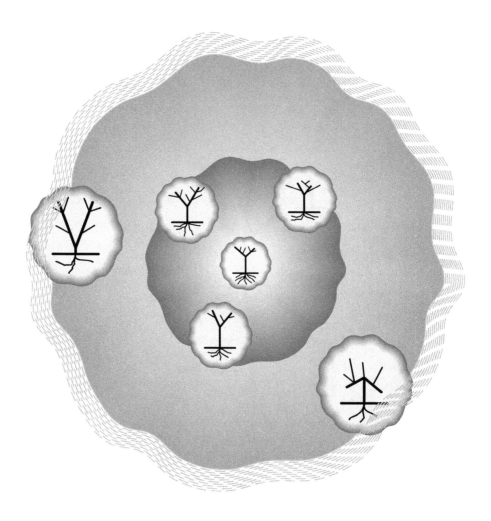

Notice: The two big trees on the outer edge of the forest look radically different from the other "typical" decision trees that are shown within the Lockean grove. Basically, radical perspectives ARE very different from what is typical, which is why it's so easy to ignore them (let alone suppress them).

On Figure 6.10, I present the connection between the classic tug-of-war along the TKI Model's distributive dimension and the intense kind of dialectical debate that takes place when applying the Hegelian Inquiry System on a complex problem or conflict. Both the distributive dimension and the Hegelian debates focus on the extreme positions of choosing "my perspective" OR "your perspective" or choosing my ***thesis*** versus your ***antithesis,*** with no interest, at least for the time being, in creating a ***synthesis.***

FIGURE 6.10
THE HEGELIAN DEBATE ON THE DISTRIBUTIVE DIMENSION

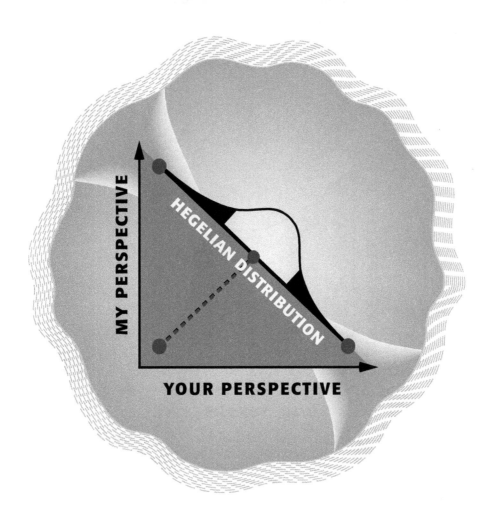

As depicted on Figure 6.11, **the original Hegelian debate on the distributive dimension eventually creates the conditions for a Lockean agreement on the integrative dimension of the TKI Conflict Model.** However, please remember: It's not a matter of choosing which one of the several different trees is "right" while regarding all the other trees as "wrong." **We can only synthesize a new tree by creatively INTEGRATING all the relevant wisdom and specialized knowledge that's contained within and across ALL the decision trees in the quantum forest.**

FIGURE 6.11
THE LOCKEAN AGREEMENT ON THE INTEGRATIVE DIMENSION

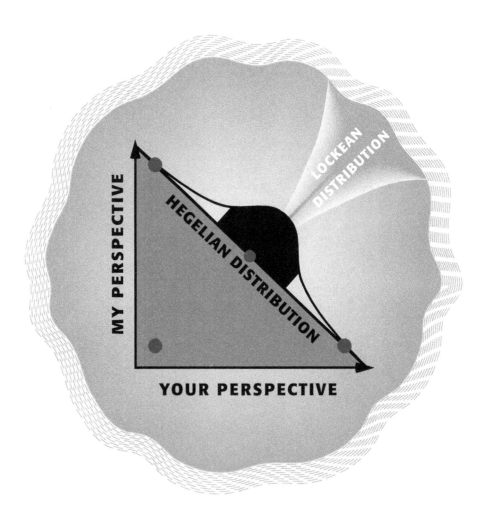

THE THREE STAGES OF
ASSUMPTIONAL ANALYSIS

Assumptional analysis is a systematic method for addressing the two most complex steps in problem management: defining problems and implementing solutions. This unique method not only reveals all the different decision trees in the quantum forest that pertain to defining problems and implementing solutions, but it also probes below the surface of every tree to thoroughly analyze its roots – the hidden assumptions that keep each tree alive and well.

Assumptional analysis makes effective use of both inquiring systems. As seen in Figure 6.12, the **Hegelian Inquiring System** is first used for going below the surface – to expose the hidden assumptions that support the initial conclusion. This reflective process on the left side of the figure, called **retroduction,** allows the participants to return to the source of the problem that lives below the surface (below the ground) of their direct experience. The **Lockean Inquiring System** is then used to move above the surface (above the ground) – to derive a new conclusion based on a majority agreement about the group's revised assumptions. This synergistic process, called **deduction**, allows participants to create a new conclusion for the problem at hand. **Cycling back and forth between the two inquiring systems brings the entire quantum forest to life – and ensures that the group's problem definitions and implementing plans will be based on TRUTH, as best as can be known at the time, given the uncertainties in today's increasingly turbulent world.**

Assumptions (A) are all the various things that one has to take for granted as TRUE (e.g., Human Nature, Mother Nature, Father Time, and Lady Luck) to argue, most convincingly, that the Initial Conclusion (C) as stated, is correct, true, and/or the best thing to do. However, assumptions usually remain unstated, untested, and thus hidden from view, which makes it impossible to uncover the roots of each tree. Nevertheless, those previously hidden assumptions can be thoroughly analyzed, debated, and then revised by systematically following a series of three stages: **(1) Surfacing Assumptions** from below each decision tree in the forest; **(2) Classifying Assumptions** into a matrix to determine the relative importance and certainty of each assumption; and **(3) Synthesizing Assumptions** by revising what is known – now that assumptions have been examined, revised, and rewritten via both the Hegelian and the Lockean Inquiring Systems.

FIGURE 6.12

ASSUMPTIONAL ANALYSIS AND THE TWO INQUIRING SYSTEMS

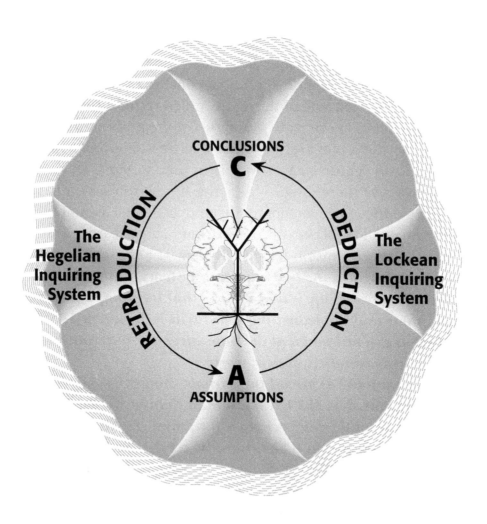

STAGE 1: SURFACING ASSUMPTIONS

Whenever a participant concludes that her definition of the problem (or plan for implementation) is correct, her arguments are sound only if her underlying assumptions are true.

Most experts are blind to their own assumptions, since they can't go about their specialty *without* taking certain things as a given. **But what one expert takes as a given, another expert, in another field, takes as an unwarranted assumption.** As it turns out, each professional and vocational specialization has a set of hidden assumptions, which are automatically and unconsciously treated as facts – since any single, specialized perspective could not exist without an underlying set of assumptions that govern "how things work from this profession's base of knowledge and specialized expertise."

Let's now explore the first stage of assumptional analysis by defining an **initial conclusion** as anything argued for or against, such as a decision, action, problem definition, or implementation plan. It's called an "initial" conclusion, because it might undergo significant change after its underground assumptions have been thoroughly analyzed, revised, and rewritten – which then results in a "new" conclusion.

As demonstrated in Figure 6.13, the assumptions underlying a conclusion can be surfaced by initially listing all the relevant **stakeholders** – those inside and outside the organization – who are associated or connected with the initial conclusion in some manner and, therefore, have a vested stake in what takes place. Whether clearly articulated or not, members make all kinds of assumptions about what internal and/or external stakeholders believe, expect, value – and what they need or want.

For example, **consider an initial conclusion that pertains to Strategic Change.** Some of the typical stakeholders that directly influence whether the organization will improve its performance and satisfaction as a result of its strategy change include: current customers, prospective customers, suppliers, employees, public agencies, shareholders, senior executives, unions, competitors, and more (depending on the organization and its industry).

FIGURE 6.13
STAKEHOLDERS FOR AN INITIAL CONCLUSION

As Figure 6.14 suggests, members next list their assumptions for each stakeholder: **What would have to be true about any and all aspects of a given stakeholder in order to argue, most convincingly, that the initial conclusion, as stated, is true?** In fact, every assumption should purposely be written to provide maximum support for the initial conclusion, regardless of how credible, obvious, or, instead, how ridiculous that assumption may appear. The "truth" of each assumption will be investigated later. Just as with surfacing cultural norms during the culture track, members usually experience delight during the skills track when they first access and then examine additional holographic features of their organization (i.e., hidden assumptions) that have previously been out of sight and thus out of reach.

FIGURE 6.14
WRITING ASSUMPTIONS FOR EACH STAKEHOLDER

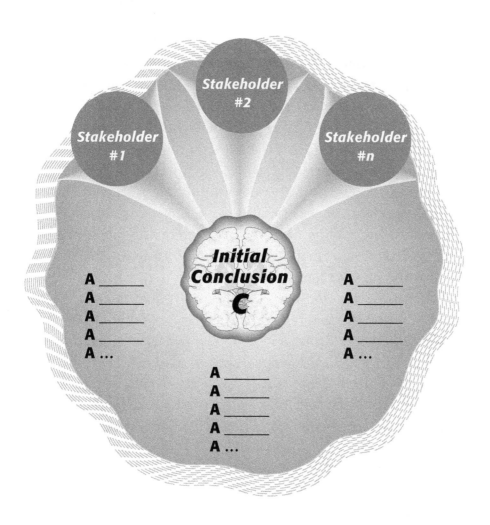

Essentially, there's a two-way relationship between those key stakeholders and any initial conclusion: *The actual properties of stakeholders determine the TRUTH of any initial conclusion* (as presented in the various assumptions that are made about those particular stakeholders). Meanwhile, *any new conclusion and its subsequently implemented solutions will affect whether those stakeholders really do get their most important needs met and whether the organization achieves long-term success.*

STAGE 2: CLASSIFYING ASSUMPTIONS

Are all assumptions of equal importance? As shown in Figure 6.15, there are usually tangential (least important) assumptions that, even if they are false, still don't prevent you from arguing for the initial conclusion. *But there may be assumptions that, if they turn out to be false, would significantly undermine your argument. In this latter case, you can no longer argue for the conclusion when the fallacy of such a major assumption has been revealed.* For example, the assumption, "We can perform all three stages of assumptional analysis in an efficient and effective manner," is most important to any initial conclusion that relies on assumptional analysis for achieving long-term success.

Do all assumptions have the same credibility? It seems that some assumptions are more certain – or uncertain – than others. On the one hand, a fact is an assumption that is believed to be true (or false) with complete certainty: 100%. On the other hand, an assumption has great uncertainty when no one can predict or control its eventual outcome. Actually, *the most uncertainty is represented by a 50/50 proposition: The stated assumption is just as likely to be true as it is likely to be false.* For example, the assumption that "our boss will encourage us to apply in the workplace what we have learned in the workshop sessions" may be 100% certain to be false, since every member already knows he's against doing things in new ways. Or that same assumption could be highly uncertain (50%) in a situation when the boss is new to the job and the members, therefore, have no idea how he might respond in them.

FIGURE 6.15

DISTINGUISHING ASSUMPTIONS BY THEIR IMPORTANCE

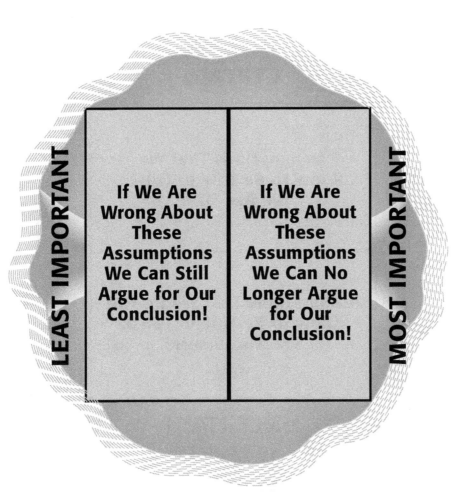

Figure 6.16 highlights the certainty distinction: The top line defines a 100% level of certainty that the assumption, as stated, is true (or false); the bottom line on the diagram represents a 50% level of certainty (which is the most *uncertainty* that is possible in any situation); meanwhile, any assumption that's placed near the middle line on this diagram defines a 75% level of certainty (and thus a 25% level of uncertainty) that the assumption, as stated, is either true or false.

FIGURE 6.16
DISTINGUISHING ASSUMPTIONS BY THEIR CERTAINTY

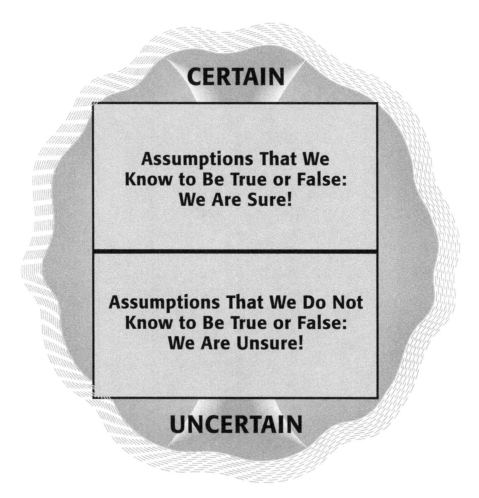

CERTAIN

Assumptions That We Know to Be True or False: We Are Sure!

Assumptions That We Do Not Know to Be True or False: We Are Unsure!

UNCERTAIN

Figure 6.17 illustrates the **assumption matrix** for classifying assumptions according to their relative importance AND relative certainty. Is the assumption, practically speaking, most important to arguing for the initial conclusion – or is it least important? Is the assumption, as stated, fairly certain to be true (or certain to be false), or is its truth (or falsity) uncertain? Combining the two distinctions creates the four distinct categories of assumptions: (1) certain and least important; (2) certain and most important; (3) uncertain, least important; and (4) uncertain, most important. ***This assumption matrix thus enables members to untangle the roots underneath the decision trees in their quantum forest by explicitly classifying assumptions so they can be systematically analyzed, revised, and synthesized to deduce a new conclusion.***

FIGURE 6.17
THE ASSUMPTION MATRIX FOR CLASSIFYING ASSUMPTIONS

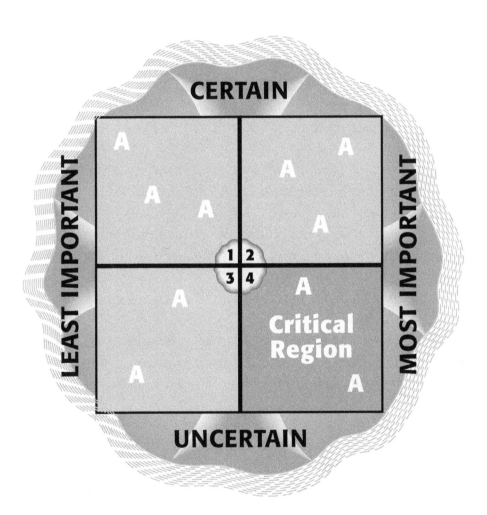

The first category on this matrix (i.e., certain/least important assumptions) represents trivia: highly certain facts that have little bearing on the subject at hand. The second category (i.e., certain/ most important) represents important facts: if we know them to be true, these assumptions do not provide anything new. In this second category, however, it might be surprising to discover that some important assumptions that support our initial conclusion (now that these assumptions have been surfaced for study) – are clearly false, when all along we have been assuming exactly the opposite. The third category (uncertain/least important) reveals what is not fully known to be true or false but, either way, these assumptions are not primary to the arguments being presented.

The fourth category (uncertain/most important) epitomizes the principal reason for surfacing and classifying assumptions: This highly informative category classifies assumptions that are most important to the initial conclusion (if you're wrong about any of these assumptions, your arguments fall apart), yet there's considerable uncertainty about whether these assumptions are actually true OR false. Recall: Maximum uncertainty presents a 50/50 proposition. These most important assumptions, as stated, are just as likely to be false as they are likely to be true.

The fourth category is named the **critical region**. This area is where the ultimate challenge to any argument will be addressed. Too frequently, this critical region is not only ignored, but is also deliberately repressed. Individuals and groups arguing strongly for their conclusions do not want to expose their "Achilles' heel," the fatal flaw in their argument. But let it be known: **Building a problem definition or implementation plan on assumptions in the critical region is like building a house on quicksand.**

STAGE 3: SYNTHESIZING ASSUMPTIONS

The final stage in the method is to examine the assumptions that were classified into those two most important quadrants on the right–hand portion of the matrix – so these most-important assumptions can be revised (if necessary) and subsequently used to deduce the new conclusion on a new decision tree. Regarding the critical region, it's now essential to collect information from people, books, magazines, journals, the Internet (and elsewhere) to discover the actual "truth" of these assumptions.

Figure 6.18 shows how rewriting assumptions that are now known – with high certainty – to be false into new assumptions that are now believed to be true creates revisions in the matrix. ***Symbolically, I surround each such revised assumption with a BOX to show that this assumption could be rewritten to reflect the truth – without having to gather any more information.***

FIGURE 6.18
REVISING THE ASSUMPTION MATRIX

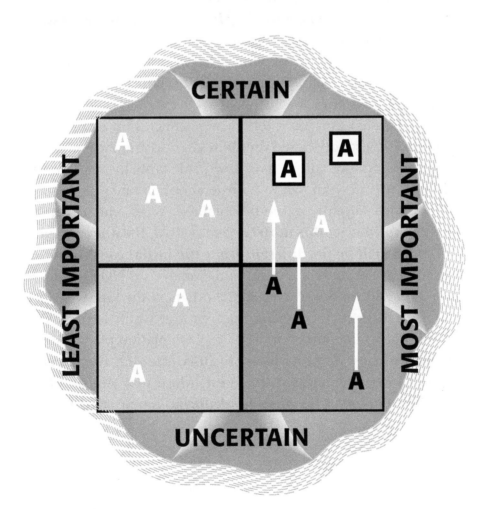

Further, it's also helpful to know that new information may move previously uncertain assumptions into the certain region, although those assumptions might also have to be rewritten to assimilate what was learned about them. I show those changes in the critical region by placing an arrow above the assumption to show its movement to greater certainty. But the big advantage of removing uncertain assumptions from this critical region is that you can then argue for your initial conclusion with much more confidence. However, given the nature of the world today, you can never assimilate sufficient information to eliminate ALL uncertainties about the truth of those assumptions. Instead, **we can only hope to minimize the uncertainties in the situation by collecting additional information on the most important and uncertain assumptions, once they have been classified as such.** Although the least important assumptions aren't investigated for the moment, they should be monitored from this point forward: What was once *least important* may easily become *most important* at any time in the future.

As illustrated on Figure 6.19, a new conclusion can now be deduced that's solidly based on the revised assumption matrix – whose assumptions might have been substantially rewritten to reflect what is now known to be true about all key stakeholders with as much certainty as can be obtained at this time. **The more the assumptions on this matrix were revised, the more the new conclusion will be far different from the initial conclusion.** As a reminder: The goal for assumptional analysis is NOT to simply choose one decision tree over all the others in the forest – which would result in only choosing that one tree's initial conclusion as THE problem definition or THE implementation plan. Instead, **we must always do our utmost to integrate ALL the relevant decision trees in the quantum forest into a new decision tree, which then becomes the basis for deducing a new conclusion.**

FIGURE 6.19
DEDUCING THE NEW CONCLUSION

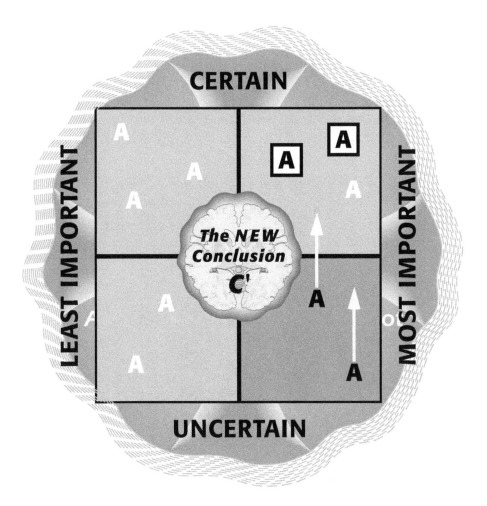

Figure 6.20 provides a summary of assumptional analysis: To minimize the errors of problem management, it's essential to first surface assumptions (i.e., write them out explicitly); next, classify assumptions according to their relative importance and certainty

of being true/false; and then we synthesize assumptions, that is, we collect additional information about the validity of the most important/uncertain assumptions and then, depending on how extensively those assumptions were rewritten, we create a new decision tree for deducing a new conclusion. Note: The **C** at the top of the illustration refers to the *initial conclusion* that started the process, while the **C´** at the very bottom of the diagram refers to the *new conclusion*. By the way, if you understand ALL the symbols and flows on this diagram, you have already learned a lot!

FIGURE 6.20
A SUMMARY OF ASSUMPTIONAL ANALYSIS

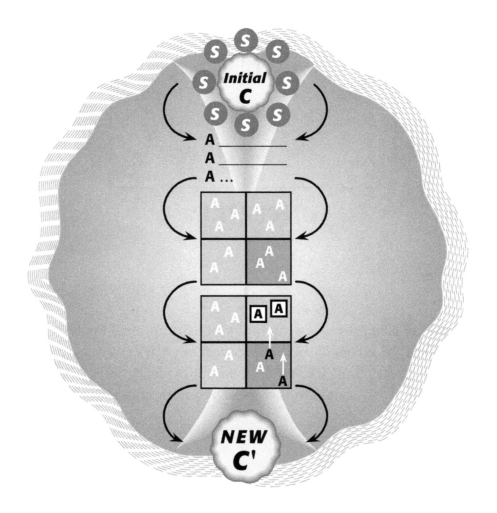

CHAPTER 6

Once members have practiced using assumptional analysis during several workshops in the skills track, they often make a startling discovery: ***Assumptions do not have to be regarded as fixed properties of stakeholders.*** Such a grand insight is rather ironic, since assumptions have been defined as the givens in the situation – as the uncontrollable, fixed properties of internal and external stakeholders that must be accurately described in order to deduce a new, viable, accurate, and truthful conclusion about any complex problem. But now, enlightened participants in the organization develop a different assumption about the nature of assumptions themselves: ***Assumptions change as stakeholders are changed.*** A conclusion that is desired, with concerted action, can become true! It's the resourceful members who now take the necessary steps to influence the qualities of the key stakeholders: ***By determining which assumptions about which stakeholders must provide maximum support for their desired conclusions (now classified on the assumption matrix as strategic targets), members attempt to INFLUENCE the behavior, attitudes, and beliefs of key stakeholders so they will now support the desired conclusions for long-term organizational success.***

FOUR PERSONALITY STYLES FOR PROBLEM MANAGEMENT

While addressing complex problems, members spend most of their time collecting information and making decisions. But there are FOUR different ways of doing these things, depending on the member's personality style and the nature of the problem itself.

The personality typology of C. G. Jung has been shown to be very useful in explaining the influence of individual differences on organizational behavior. More specifically, Jung's framework is based on his astute observation that people have a variety of ways of taking in information and then making decisions. Jung refers to these personality preferences as "psychological types" or simply "types," while I refer to these preferences as "personality styles" or simply "styles." Regardless of the different terminology, the point is to acknowledge the personality characteristics that members bring with them into their organization, which serve to focus their attention on different ways of collecting information and making decisions while addressing complex problems.

As shown in Figure 6.21, there are two basic ways in which people take in information: ***sensation and intuition***.

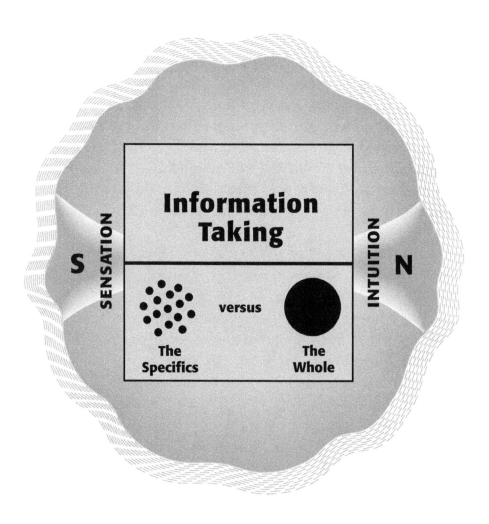

FIGURE 6.21
TWO WAYS OF COLLECTING INFORMATION: SENSATION AND INTUITION

Let's explore this personality style in more detail: Sensation refers to the preference for taking in information directly by the five senses. It focuses on the details, the facts, and **the specifics** of a situation, the here and now, the hard data, the itemized parts – what can be seen, heard, touched, smelled, and such. In contrast, intuition is a preference for **the whole** rather than the parts, for the possibilities, hunches, or future implications of a situation, the extrapolations, interpolations, and unique interrelationships among pieces of information – what cannot be seen or touched directly. With intuition, information is beyond the parts; with sensation, information is the specific parts themselves. According to Jung, people develop a preference for one of the two ways of taking in information. Although people can make use of either sensation or intuition when required, they may be unable to do each equally well. In fact, the information–taking mode that's not preferred is regarded as a person's shadow side or blind side.

As shown in Figure 6.22, there are two basic ways in which people make decisions: **thinking and feeling**. Thinking refers to an impersonal, logical, analytical approach for making decisions: using **the head.** If such and such is true, then this and that must follow, based on perfect logic. Feeling, in contrast, is a personal, subjective, value–based method for making decisions: using **the heart.** Does the person like the alternative? Does it fit with her values and the image she has of herself? While the development of such a conclusion is not logical per se, it is not illogical either. Feeling is simply based on a different style of reaching decisions. Just as they do regarding sensation and intuition, people develop a preference for using either thinking or feeling. Although they can apply either preference when required, they may be unsure of themselves when they rely on their blind side, especially for important decisions and complex problems.

FIGURE 6.22
TWO WAYS OF MAKING DECISIONS: THINKING AND FEELING

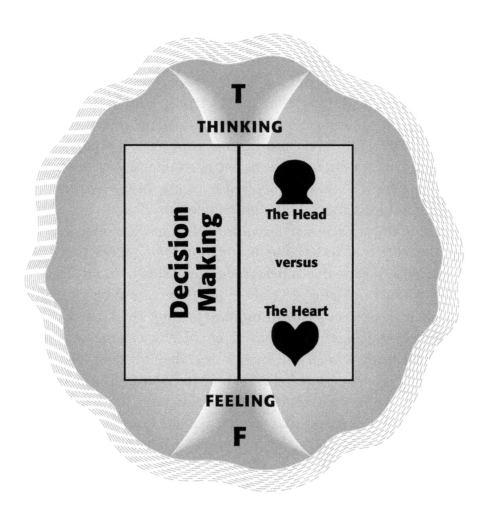

As shown in Figure 6.23, the two personality characteristics that are associated with information taking and decision making result in four personality styles that are organically contained in every person's mind: **intuition-feeling (NF), intuition-thinking (NT), sensation-thinking (ST), and sensation-feeling (SF).** Let me now provide a little more detail about each of these personality styles for problem management.

FIGURE 6.23
THE FOUR PERSONALITY STYLES

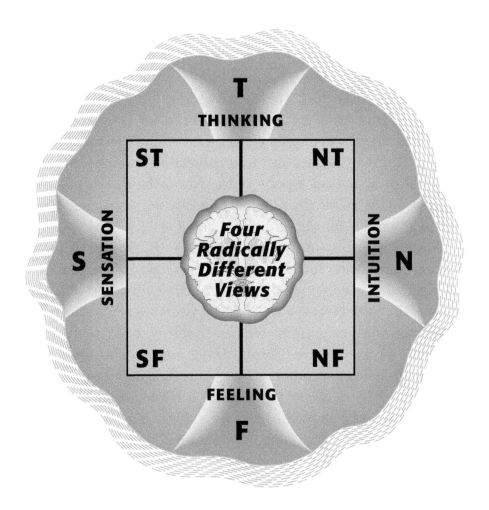

STs enjoy the well-structured steps of problem solving. Such people choose a solution to a problem on the basis of a logical, impersonal analysis. ST people generate single answers to most questions and prefer those answers to be clearly right or wrong according to some quantitative assessment. It is not surprising, then, that ST persons are most confident and competent while working with details, facts, and well-established rules.

NTs enjoy investigating a complex problem from different – global – perspectives. Such individuals are particularly attracted to abstract discussions; they get bored with well-structured and routine problems, and they hate details. NTs are especially good at developing theories, diagrams, and classification schemes to intellectually structure their universe – which largely consists of ideas, possibilities, and conceptual frameworks.

SFs enjoy socializing. This activity satisfies their focus on the immediate experience as well as their need for interacting with friends. SF people are highly concerned with the personal needs of their fellow associates in the organization – rather than the technical or analytical aspects of the work. Their personal style and sensitivity enable them to feel how any decision might affect the quality of life for organizational members.

NFs enjoy uncertainty and ambiguity. Such individuals prefer looking far into the future and using their personal criteria for deciding what is vital to address. Such people thrive on dynamic complexity; they function at their best when there's a minimum of structure and when problems have not even been defined yet. NFs are especially focused on meaning, impact, and the future welfare of their organization, society, and the entire universe.

By taking the *Kilmanns Personality Style Instrument* or the *Myers-Briggs Type Indicator*, all members in the skills track can assess their own preferences for collecting information and making decisions from an ST, NT, SF, and NF perspective. By receiving their scores from such an assessment tool, each participant becomes more aware of not only his personality style but also his blind spots. This knowledge helps everyone compensate for his or her own strengths and limitations. Members will now deeply appreciate that interpersonal conflicts can sometimes be explained by the collision of opposite personality styles, types, or traits. Indeed, a member's reaction to problems can sometimes be explained by the fit – or lack of fit – between his personality preferences and what steps of problem management he needs to perform well – particularly during the more crucial steps of defining problems and implementing solutions.

On Figure 6.24, I present the striking connection between the diagonal dimensions on the TKI Conflict Model (particularly the distributive and integrative dimensions) as they relate to each of the five steps of problem management.

FIGURE 6.24
CONFLICT MODES AND PROBLEM MANAGEMENT

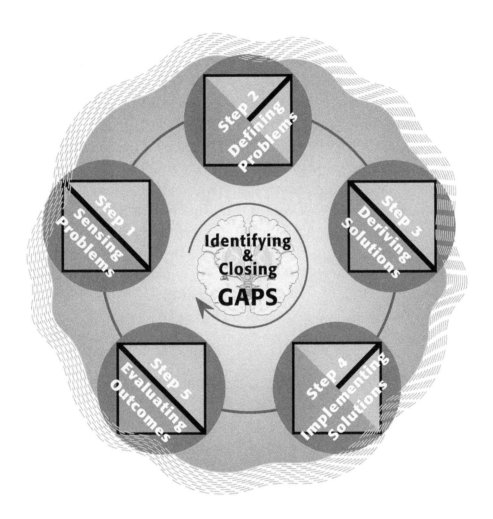

As you can see from the TKI symbol on each step, using the three conflict modes on the distributive dimension (competing, compromising, and accommodating) perfectly suits several steps:

go/no-go decisions that pertain to sensing problems and the same kind of go/no-go decisions that are needed for evaluating outcomes. Essentially, do we proceed with the process, or do we redo one or more of the prior steps, or do we cease our efforts altogether? The step of deriving solutions is also well structured, once the problem has already been defined: Do we pick Solution A or Solution B from the branches on our decision tree? **Notice the highlighted distributive dimension for those three simpler (much less complex) steps of problem management: (1) sensing problems, (3) deriving solutions, and (5) evaluating outcomes.**

Regarding the two most challenging and error-prone steps of problem management (i.e., Step 2 for defining problems and Step 4 for implementing solutions), it is vital to move up the integrative dimension, *instead of* seeking an either/or resolution on the distributive dimension. In fact, the surest way to close any identified GAP on those two steps requires that members *integrate* their very different definitions of the problem and their plans for implementing a viable solution. Said differently: Expanding the size of the pie during those two steps is the best way to resolve a complex problem in one single cycle of problem management. **Please notice the highlighted integrative dimension for Step 2 and Step 4.** But always keep in mind that the eight attributes in the situation must support the use of the collaborating mode on the integrative dimension.

The Problem Management Organization

This next section officially presents the Problem Management Organization (PMO) as a DUAL structure for addressing the most complex problems that affect the entire organization. As we shall see, PMOs make extensive use of critical thinking skills in order to minimize the most disastrous errors of problem management: defining problems and implementing solutions. In fact, if you truly understand the formation and functioning of a PMO, you must already understand quite a lot about conflict and change, consciousness (personality styles), and quantum transformation.

The initial use of a PMO, as discussed in the previous chapter on Quantum Transformation, is for mobilizing a special steering committee (referred to as the **shadow track**) that is responsible for guiding and advising the implementation of the completely integrated program. Once the diagnostic report has pinpointed the transformation GAPS (and hence, has accurately sensed the organization's barriers and channels to success), about fifteen to twenty-five representatives from all levels, areas, and locations in the organization are selected to be members of this steering group for the duration of the program.

The second application of a PMO is to revitalize and realign the strategy and structure of the organization via the **strategy-structure track**. This second PMO is staffed with a different set of fifteen to twenty-five members who also represent all the levels, areas, and locations in the organization. The third use of a PMO is to design and then implement an effective performance-based reward system through the **reward system track**. This third PMO is composed of another set of fifteen to twenty-five members who represent all levels, areas, and locations in the organization. Thereafter, additional PMOs are utilized for the **radical process track** and the **learning process track** – and for all subsequent complex problems that affect the entire organization.

Active participation among the members within each of these PMOs helps ensure the successful creation of a self-designing – and self-managing – quantum organization. But it's important to keep this key principle in mind: ***Only if an organization has already developed a healthy culture, only if its members have already learned the skills for managing complex problems and hidden assumptions, and only if a cooperative team spirit has already been activated within and across all subunits – will all members have established a healthy behavioral infrastructure for achieving long-term success.*** Please note: At this point in the completely integrated program, the culture and skills tracks are already underway and the team track (which is discussed in the next chapter) will soon proceed to further establish the necessary behavioral infrastructure for all PMOs.

Figure 6.25 presents the Problem Management Organization. The top portion of the diagram depicts the **operational structure** of an organization. The bottom portion of the diagram illustrates the **collateral structure** of C-groups (abbreviated for Conclusion groups) and one S-group (i.e., the Synthesis group) that expands any typical organization into a full-blown Problem Management Organization. Indeed, discussions flow back and forth between the day-to-day operational structure and the collateral structure, which addresses the organization's most complex problems.

FIGURE 6.25
THE PROBLEM MANAGEMENT ORGANIZATION (PMO)

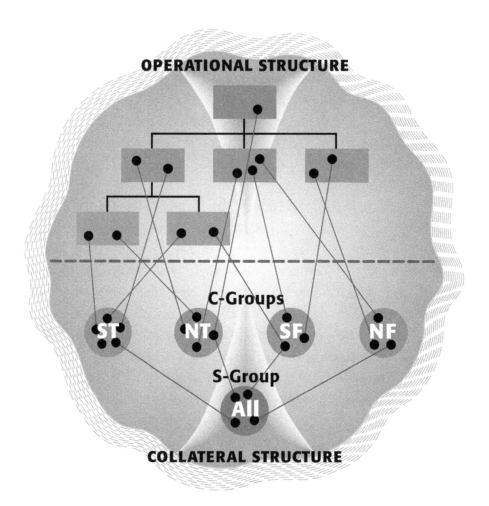

The reason for using these two parallel, DUAL organizational structures – with overlapping memberships – is to increase the probability that creative/effective solutions to complex problems will be derived and implemented: *A collateral structure allows diverse members to be directly involved in defining and solving complex problems; and these same members are then directly responsible for effectively implementing their solutions back in the operational structure, thus establishing a well-functioning, self-designing, and self-managing quantum organization.*

You can see that each of the four C–groups in the collateral structure is made up of active participants who share a particular personality style: ST, NT, SF, or NF. When a group is made up of one dominant style, all the members in that personality–based C–group will automatically reinforce that particular approach to collecting information and making decisions. Even more to the point, those personality–based C–groups will *extremely exaggerate* (magnify) their member's individual ST, NT, SF, or NF preferences, regardless of the problem being investigated (strategy, structure, rewards, learning processes, etc.). In a sense, when all individual members in a group share the same ST personality style, their interactions – and their conclusions – become ST^2; similarly, the NT group acts as if it were NT^2; and so forth.

As suggested in Figure 6.26, knowing that each C–group will examine (and argue for) its unique, personality–style perspective on a complex problem ensures that all the decision trees in the quantum forest (even the extreme decision trees at the very edge of the forest) will readily be available for discussions within each C–group as well as for all the debates across the four C–groups.

After the C–groups have concluded their discussions/debates on a complex problem, one or two members from each C–group will be asked to form a single S–group. In this way, **the S-group will contain members who reflect ALL four personality styles (ST, NT, SF, and NF), so that all decision trees will be available for additional S-group discussions/debates, which will enable them to grow – synthesize – a new tree in the quantum forest. That goal is the whole point of establishing an effective PMO.**

FIGURE 6.26
FOUR PERSONALITY STYLES AND THE QUANTUM FOREST

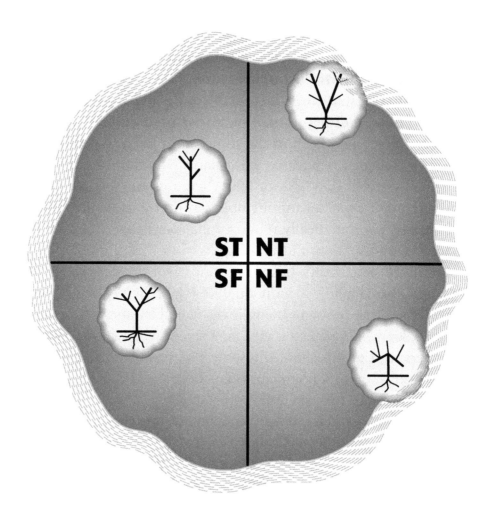

Figure 6.27 illustrates the sequence of C-group and S-group activities in a PMO on the right portion of the diagram. On the left portion of the diagram, I show the corresponding (parallel) stages of assumptional analysis. Using a PMO with assumptional analysis is the most practical – and effective – way to minimize both the defining and implementing errors for the most complex problems facing an organization (e.g., strategy–structure, reward

systems, and organizational learning). However, as you should know by now, the first three tracks MUST precede the formation of the collateral structure, C–groups, and S–group in the PMO. ***Without healthy cultural norms, enlightened critical thinking skills, and effective teamwork within – and across – all the boundaries in the operational structure, we could hardly expect much sharing of knowledge, expertise, and experience in the collateral structure.***

FIGURE 6.27
ASSUMPTIONAL ANALYSIS AND THE PMO PROCESS

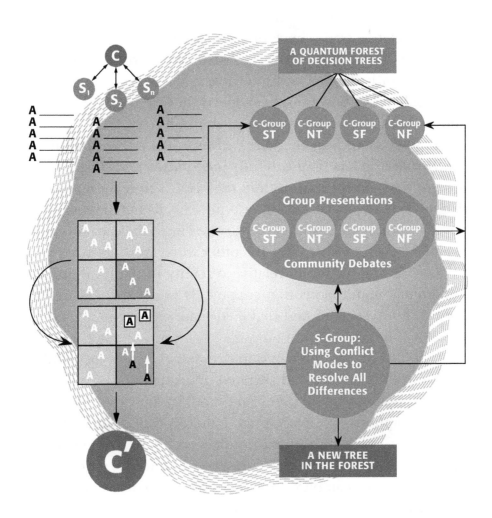

Once the fifteen to twenty-five members have been arranged into one of the four personality-based C-groups, each group is instructed to meet, introduce its members, establish the desired cultural norms and sanctioning systems for all group meetings (based on what was learned in the culture track), and confirm its knowledge of problem management and assumptional analysis.

Then each of the four C-groups plans the process by which it will develop its initial conclusion: its position statement on the root causes of the complex problem or its plan for effectively implementing the chosen solutions. Each C-group then uses the method of assumptional analysis to first surface its underlying assumptions, which are then sorted into a matrix according to the certainty/uncertainty of the assumption being true or false and the relative importance of each assumption for supporting the group's initial conclusion. As you already know by now, how the problem is defined will limit the available options for how the problem can best be solved (given the selection of branches and subbranches on that particular decision tree).

As soon as each of the four C-groups has refined its initial conclusion and has then carefully formulated and classified its assumptions on the assumption matrix, it's time for a probing debate: One by one, each C-group presents its initial conclusion and its underlying assumptions to the entire PMO community. Following each presentation, the other three groups are allowed to question the truth and relative certainty of the focal group's underlying assumptions that support its initial conclusion, but always in a respectful and dignified manner – as mandated by the PMO's desired cultural norms.

Typically, during the C-group debates, especially benefitting from a healthy culture and a shared understanding of problems and assumptions, many significant modifications to conclusions and assumptions take place quite naturally. But no matter how open and candid the community debates, there will always be some core issues that remain unresolved, since they get at the heart of why the complex problem *is* viewed so differently across a diverse community of participants. As a result, **we now need** *another arrangement to help resolve the unresolved conflicts that still remain among the four C-groups, so the entire PMO community can use ALL its knowledge, experience, and talent to develop the most comprehensive, inclusive, and promising approach to its complex problem.*

Now another group is formed from the community of PMO members, which is named a "Synthesis Group" or S–group for short. **The S-group is composed of one or two members from each of the four C-groups.** Ideally, each S–group member should have a balanced repertoire of the five conflict–handling modes, as measured by the *Thomas-Kilmann Conflict Mode Instrument*.

In essence, those unresolved issues that emanated from the community debates represent all the underlying conflicts – the "dialectics" – that arise from the various perspectives of the PMO members, which could not be resolved during the discussions and debates among those four personality–based C–groups. But now the PMO's mission is to approach and resolve those most fundamental differences with the use of one (or more) conflict modes. Ideally, the collaborating mode for approaching conflict will be applied in order to synthesize the remaining unresolved conflicts on the **integrative dimension** of the TKI Conflict Model, which provides the best opportunity for creating a new tree in the quantum forest.

When it's not possible to develop a synergistic resolution for a complex problem, the compromising mode might enable the S–group to include some aspects of each C-group's conclusions (and assumptions) on the **distributive dimension**. Perhaps one expert is clearly more knowledgeable than the other members in the S–group, so he should assert his knowledge (hence, use the competing mode) for resolving that particular conflict. Naturally, other members in the S–group will accommodate other experts (when those others know more about a particular topic or area of expertise); and a few members will choose to avoid debating topics that turn out to be much less important to them than was first thought. This is why it helps for each S–group member to be able to use each of the five conflict–handling modes – easily and effectively – for both a Hegelian and a Lockean approach on the distributive and integrative dimensions, respectively.

Occasionally, it's useful to form a few S-groups (from two to four), each being composed of two representatives from each of the four personality-style C-groups. Such an arrangement allows for greater participation for all the PMO members, rather than relying on only a handful of members to form a single S-group that deduces the PMO's synthesized – new – conclusion.

When multiple S-groups can be used for a complex problem, it's fascinating to discover that each S-group's resulting synthesis is not noticeably different from one another. In fact, the S-groups usually make similar presentations, regarding: (1) how to define and resolve those remaining conflicts that divided the C-groups and (2) how to deduce an altogether new conclusion that takes into account all the different experiences and areas of expertise in the PMO community. Not surprisingly, such striking similarity across the multiple S-groups serves to confirm the validity of the PMO process for everyone who has the chance to witness the process in person. So unless there are logistical constraints that must be considered, I encourage the use of multiple S-groups to address the unresolved conflicts of the four previous C-groups.

As all the members in the skills track are learning the critical thinking skills for assumptional analysis, they become eager to apply these new skills to real problems and not just to workshop exercises. The members now recognize the various errors they've made in the past: sensing errors, defining errors, solving errors, implementing errors, and evaluating errors. They make a public statement that they, henceforth, will always search for members with different personality styles and different areas of expertise when defining problems and implementing solutions for their most complex problems. The members also realize that only by surfacing, classifying, and revising assumptions will they be able to successfully cope with dynamic complexity. Thoughtfully, but deliberately, the members enter their new holographic world.

CONCLUDING THOUGHTS

In the spirit of assumptional analysis, it seems appropriate to examine the assumptions behind the method, so its benefits and its shortcomings can be better understood – and appreciated.

Assumptional analysis assumes that the participants want their hidden assumptions exposed. This is a most-important yet uncertain assumption, since its TRUTH heavily depends on the particular people in the situation. Exposing assumptions is not only confronting an individual's precious truths, but can also be a painful experience: It may become public that the assumptions a person has been living with for years are clearly false, once exposed and subjected to the collective wisdom of the diverse members in a Problem Management Organization. Individuals often make every possible effort to protect their "tried-and-true" assumptions rather than take the chance of discovering that they have been "mistaken" all these years. It is also much easier for a person to argue for his point of view if other members are not able to expose his false assumptions.

Assumptional analysis also assumes that people are mostly rational; meaning, that they will make decisions for the greater good of their organization, for effectiveness and efficiency, and for all the other "good" characteristics that we like to ascribe to human nature. Consider an opposite set of assumptions – that members are largely a-rational if not irrational; that they make choices to protect themselves and their place in society (as they perceive it), and that they often act on fears, anxieties, fantasies, etc., for all sorts of defensive reasons or as a result of intrapsychic conflicts. These latter assumptions about human nature might be closer to why it's worthwhile to establish multiple S-groups, so members' vested interests will give way to the rational synthesis of assumptions. Assumptional analysis is a very rational, logical procedure, but it may not be used as intended if its underlying assumptions about "rational human beings" are just not true.

A final set of assumptions to consider concerns the implicit influence dynamics that take place among members using this methodology. ***Assumptional analysis strives to be nonpolitical, at least at the outset, by setting up equal C-groups, without weighting one group above the others in synthesizing the new conclusion.*** The assumption being that relying on a democratic process with equal influence (e.g., only one vote per member or group) will lead to a "better" synthesis than a politicized process where individuals and groups are free to gain and use unequal power and influence (e.g., a person's position of formal authority in operational structure determines that member's influence in surfacing, classifying, and synthesizing assumptions within the PMO's collateral structure). If organizations are mostly networks of coalitions, whereby each person and subunit is attempting to gain power over the others, then assumptional analysis might be trying to establish a social arrangement that is both foreign and unacceptable to the PMO participants and the other members in the organization. One reason that assumptional analysis won't work in some settings is because it prevents the members and their subunits from engaging in their usual political processes. Even if the synthesized conclusion from using the three stages of assumptional analysis were high in quality, it might still not be accepted because the process itself is unacceptable, regardless of the outcome.

Surfacing, classifying, and synthesizing assumptions about human nature is expected to be essential for further developing quantum transformation. But what would be particularly ironic is whether the underlying assumptions behind methods such as assumptional analysis turn out to be false and, as a result, will serve to prevent these problem management approaches from contributing to long-term success. Whether this is as it should be depends on the assumptions one is willing to make.

TEAM
MANAGEMENT
SKILLS TRAINING

THE TEAM TRACK

Much of the work that goes on in today's organizations takes place in small groups – which includes cross-functional teams, task forces, project teams, and all kinds of different committees. The reason for all this group–based and team–based functioning, of course, is that organizations are increasingly facing complex problems that need radically different perspectives from diverse experts – within and across subunits – concerning how to satisfy the most important needs of internal and external stakeholders. This rationale should be reason enough for organizations to use groups extensively – but never indiscriminately.

The culture track emphasizes how each group must pressure its members toward more effective behavior and attitudes on the job. The skills track emphasizes that the newly developed skills for using problem management and assumptional analysis must be transferred from the safe workshop to the actual workplace. Now we will see how the team track continues what these earlier tracks started: Team building fully activates both the new culture and the new skills throughout the organization. Alternatively, if certain "transfer of learning" issues are NOT explicitly addressed in the team track, members will experience what I have labeled, *The Three-Day Washout Effect: In just three days after having learned a new behavior or skill in a relatively safe workshop, it's as if that training never took place. Instead, upon returning to the workplace, it's back to business as usual — as members hear the battle cry: "Get back to work!"*

Indeed, I estimate that billions of dollars are spent every year for all kinds of training programs and, yet, the very sad reality is that all (or most) of what is learned in such off-site classrooms or workshop settings never changes behavior and attitudes on the job – where it counts. To overcome the threat of the "three-day washout effect," one key objective for the team track is to directly address this classic **transfer-of-learning problem**. Otherwise, the huge investment of every member's time and effort during the first two tracks will be completely wasted, except for the possible benefits that some members might experience when they apply their new skills in *other* settings in their life (but NOT in their work group in their organization).

In fact, applying in the workplace what is learned in a safe workshop setting is not an easy task for members, particularly for those employees at the lower levels in the organization who are most vulnerable to unscrupulous, autocratic managers. Even though all members have learned the importance of behaving according to the new cultural norms that foster trust, openness, and candor in all interpersonal and group discussions, asserting one's opposing views to other group members, which might also include disagreeing with your boss in public, can be an awkward (to say the least), if not a frightening experience.

During the first two tracks, bosses and their direct reports are deliberately separated from each other during off-site workshop activities: All discussions, assessments, and experiential exercises during the first two tracks are conducted in peer groups – which gives everyone the best (and safest) opportunity to learn about identifying and then closing culture-gaps – as well as learning to surface, classify, and synthesize previously hidden assumptions. As we'll soon see, **the first workshop in the team track officially reunites the bosses and their direct reports in intact work units, so every work group – with the immediate boss present – will enact its desired cultural norms and apply its critical thinking skills to the group's most challenging problems and conflicts.**

This chapter presents three related approaches for fostering successful teamwork both within and across all work units: (1) managing troublemakers, (2) team building *within* work groups, and, lastly, (3) interteam building *across* work groups. The first approach considers how to manage the painful problems created by troublemakers – those persons whose behavior and attitudes severely disrupts the development of trust, openness, and candor throughout the organization. Once the troublemakers have been put in check, attention then switches to developing every work group into an effective team. Lastly, once every work group is a well-functioning team, the third approach, interteam building, addresses the special problems created by interconnected groups that compete with each other for resources, power, and glory. As a result, uncooperative cliques soon become cooperative teams.

Just as I have done for some of my previous chapters, I have also titled this chapter to match my four–hour recorded course: Team Management Skills Training. In that online course, people take the two assessment tools that I'll discuss a little later in this chapter, *Kilmanns Time-Gap Survey* and *Kilmanns Team-Gap Survey*, both of which will help members identify the significant GAPS between their team's dysfunctional behavior in the present and what behavior is required for higher performance and greater satisfaction in the future. Further, my Team Management Course provides each participant with these consulting materials: (1) the Process Observer Form, (2) Work Sheets on Closing Time–Gaps, (2) Work Sheets on Reuniting the Work Group, (3) Work Sheets on Identifying Team–Gaps, and, lastly, (4) Work Sheets on Closing Team–Gaps. ***These work sheets enable members to go through the five steps of problem management so they can identify and then close their most challenging time-gaps and team-gaps. As a result, each work group will then be able to develop into a well-functioning team — by effectively applying directly in the workplace all that was learned during the first two tracks of quantum transformation.***

Managing Troublemakers

In every organization that I've ever encountered, there have always been at least one or more troublemakers: people who are preoccupied with expanding their own power and control, often at the expense of all others. ***To acknowledge the dysfunctional behavior of troublemakers (and the extensive damage they do to members and organizations) means that we must seriously question our longstanding assumptions about human nature.*** Currently, managers and members in most organizations prefer to rely on an especially rational model of human behavior. Such an overly optimistic model assumes that all people work for the greater good of their organization and society; include all the relevant criteria and information when making their decisions; and implement all solutions exactly as planned.

More valid assumptions about human nature reflect other qualities, such as: (1) Human beings are not entirely rational and have inherent limitations in their mental capacity, memory, and objectivity. (2) Human beings often experience their life through negative feelings of self-worth, which can result in all kinds of defensive reactions and dysfunctional behavior styles. (3) Human beings may have strong desires to gain power and control (and maintain what they have already acquired), which may override any stated intentions to bring about long-term organizational success. (4) Human beings resist change when they perceive that their security and position may be threatened. (5) Human beings do not automatically have the ability to learn, grow, and adapt; sometimes, all they can do is attempt to survive by staying safe and secure – no matter what is needed for success.

These five most-important assumptions about human nature allow for the persistence of troublemaking behavior. Only when we naively assume that human beings are primarily rational, all knowing, honest, good, and pure, are we surprised and shocked at just how badly people behave. Even if many people do fit the rational/functional model of human behavior, others clearly do not. Rather than assume that those others can simply be ignored because they are a minority, *I assume that troublemakers must be curtailed because they can be so incredibly disruptive to the rest of the organization.*

In an attempt to be more realistic about the distribution of healthy behavior in our society, I will discuss the psychological dynamics of troublemakers, explore why any effort to transform organizations seem to bring the troublemakers out into the open (out of the woodwork), and then I will summarize a process for managing the troublemakers – so they either can get on board with the vital mission of the completely integrated program, or else they can choose (or be forced) to leave the organization for another job. PLEASE NOTE: The third dimension of the Complex Hologram (Chapter 1; Figure 1.3) reveals the below–the–surface, subtle, informal systems of Culture, Assumptions, and Psyches. *Managing troublemakers is an excellent example of explicitly acknowledging and addressing Psyches*, and thus not foolishly trying to improve an organization by only addressing its surface aspects, which occurs when you view the organization as either a one–dimensional simple machine or a two–dimensional open system. The latter two worldviews ignore Troublemakers!

However, we must always distinguish between troublemakers (destructive individuals) and what has been called objectors or dissenters (i.e., well–intentioned deviants). This distinction should never be confused. Objectors, according to Ewing, are mentally healthy people who just happen to disagree with some decision or action by those holding – or controlling – the majority view. The skills track emphasizes the importance of listening to the deviants (based on the Hegelian Inquiring System), since they are the ones who have the specialized knowledge for their piece of the puzzle. Overruling them may minimize conflicts for the moment, but will quickly result in numerous errors in problem management, since surfacing and debating extreme differences are the key ingredients for resolving the organization's complex problems and conflicts.

In contrast, troublemakers are not well–intentioned deviants who simply express disagreement with some decision or action.

Quite the contrary: ***Troublemakers enact rather unhealthy and even destructive behavior: lying, cheating, stealing, harassing, intimidating, and deliberately hurting other members. When troublemakers are implicitly "given the green light" to act out their destructive tendencies on others, it is nearly impossible to have a useful discussion on complex problems. Troublemakers prevent the majority as well as the minority views from being expressed openly and publicly.***

Unfortunately, top management often seems to inadvertently support troublemakers by quietly enabling that bad behavior to continue without being confronted. In part, that's because many troublemakers are often highly intelligent, hardworking people, who contribute to the organization and its mission, despite their disruptive behavior. Making such matters worse, most "normal" people are uncomfortable dealing with "abnormal" behavior and so avoid any confrontations with troublemakers. By looking the other way, everyone (including top management) can somehow pretend that the problem doesn't exist – and, at the same time, ignore their own fears of acting out the intrapsychic conflicts and controlled aggression that exist in most human beings.

Let's take a deeper journey into just how badly people can actually behave: What happens when a person's deepest animal instincts and their most aggressive fantasies go unchecked? What behavior is actually possible when the culture and the system of organization do not curtail people's dark side?

Troublemakers (also called "bullies") come in many varieties. Bramson, in his book *Coping with Difficult People*, profiles some of these troublesome people as Sherman tanks, snipers, exploders, and bulldozers. It doesn't take much imagination to picture these types in action or to identify people we have met who perfectly exemplify these bullying types of behavior.

Lombardo and McCall, in an article titled, "The Intolerable Boss," show how some bosses – described as snakes-in-the-grass, heel grinders, egotists, dodgers, and detail drones – torment their subordinates: "He was a living snake and a pathological liar. His decisions were based on whoever talked to him last. He was a little dictator.... If anyone else tried to make a decision, he took it as a personal insult. Does this sound like anyone you know – your current boss, perhaps, or one you've endured in the past? Most people have met up with at least one impossible boss – someone who fully deserved unflattering characterizations like the ones above." (page 45)

In a *Fortune* article titled "The Ten Toughest Bosses in America," Flax summarizes comments made by subordinates about their tough bosses: "Working for him is like a war. A lot of people get shot up; the survivors go on to the next battle.... Unwilling to entertain ideas that don't fit with his.... Employees are scared to death of him.... firing threats commonplace." (pages 18–23).

It would take much too much space to provide a full account of each type of troublemaker and the inner psychodynamics that make these problematic individuals the way they are. Suffice it to say that deep within each type is an insecure and unhappy person, one who copes with his inner conflicts and his negative self-image by projecting them onto other group members – and then attacking those others for displaying those highly negative characteristics. Indeed, troublemakers spend most of their energy surviving, protecting, projecting, attacking, and thus living out their problems on others. There is a stark and extreme intensity in their life-and-death struggle with the rest of the world. And make no mistake about it, troublemakers are at war – they have little or no inner peace.

For some types of troublemakers (i.e., bullies), they must win every argument (at any cost} and must receive all the credit for every success. For other types of troublemakers who have grown up in an atmosphere of suspicion, insufficient love, and constant disappointment, there's a deep mistrust of others in everything they do. Such troublemakers demand blind loyalty and steadfast obedience – anything less is taken as a personal affront. For still other troublemakers, there's a strong need to control everything and everyone. No matter how much power and authority such a person has, it still isn't enough: Their incessant need to control others is insatiable.

Figure 7.1 summarizes the coping styles that troublemakers use to satisfy three primary ego needs: the need for achievement, the need for affiliation, and the need for power (John Atkinson). "Normal" people vary in the relative strength of their ego needs for competing with some standard of excellence, being accepted by coworkers, and controlling the means of influencing others – as shown by the MIDDLE areas under each of the three normal (bell-shaped) distributions.

But any member who attempts to satisfy his ego needs in a more extreme form, either by attacking others or by retreating from the situation, will probably be viewed as a troublemaker. Thus, as shown by the two shaded areas at the two ends of the three normal distributions, troublemakers act out the needs for achievement, affiliation, and power in an extreme manner. While the "attacking" portion of the three distributions might appear to characterize the most disruptive coping styles that interfere with long-term success, a manager who acts out the "retreating" side of those three ego needs can also be exceedingly frustrating and debilitating for members who are genuinely willing to take risks, work together in harmony, and influence one another.

Recall how the five conflict-handling modes reduce to three defensive reactions, fight, flight, and freeze, when the situation is characterized by overwhelming stress. In Chapter 2 (Figure 2.3), I showed you a revised version of the TKI Conflict Model for high stress: I changed assertiveness to reflect **attacking behavior** and cooperativeness to **retreating behavior,** which underscores those three high-stress reactions. **Troublemaker behavior is shaped by intense INTERNAL stress that has never been resolved.**

The connection between how one was treated in years gone by and how one copes with the world today is apparent with all the troublemakers. Thus, if a person was shattered or abused in his childhood (physically, sexually, mentally, or emotionally), has never felt good about himself (because he was somehow taught to see himself as bad and guilty; how else can a child explain the abuse?), and has never acquired a sense of responsibility for his actions, then becoming a troublemaker is likely to occur.

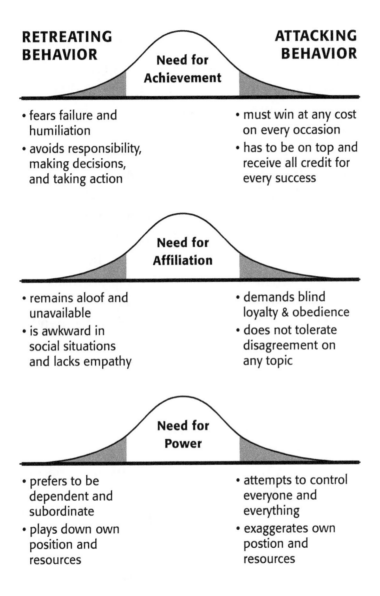

FIGURE 7.1
THREE EGO EXTREMES AND TROUBLEMAKING BEHAVIOR

RETREATING BEHAVIOR

Need for Achievement

ATTACKING BEHAVIOR

- fears failure and humiliation
- avoids responsibility, making decisions, and taking action

- must win at any cost on every occasion
- has to be on top and receive all credit for every success

Need for Affiliation

- remains aloof and unavailable
- is awkward in social situations and lacks empathy

- demands blind loyalty & obedience
- does not tolerate disagreement on any topic

Need for Power

- prefers to be dependent and subordinate
- plays down own position and resources

- attempts to control everyone and everything
- exaggerates own postion and resources

If we understand these powerful psychodynamics, it should not be surprising that troublemakers are not likely to learn from reading self-awareness books, from observing how others seem to examine themselves and then change their behavior for the better, from participating in discussions on closing culture-gaps, from attending the skills track, and thus from learning all about managing conflict and surfacing assumptions. Troublemakers do not see that they themselves need to question their behavior in general, consider how they negatively affect the culture in their group and organization, and then learn new skills for resolving complex problems and conflicts. Troublemakers are too troubled to look inside, see what is there, and change it.

I used to believe (perhaps "hope" is the better word) that the eight tracks could reach troublemakers and they would – *on their own* – choose to curtail their destructive behavior as a result of the relevant material that's covered during the first two tracks of the completely integrated program. But that turnaround never happens on its own. More often than not, troubled individuals attest to the value of the material for all the *other* members in the organization who "desperately need to change."

Any dedicated effort to improve long-term success requires all members to explore their behavior, culture, and assumptions. A troublemaker may interpret any change initiative as an act of war, as an invasion into his territory, and as a threat to his very existence. Immediately resistant to any program for improving the organization, a troublemaker might try to undermine, if not sabotage, every potential change initiative that comes along. If a troublemaker is one of the top executives in the organization, a completely integrated improvement program is not likely to be entertained, let alone implemented. In those rare cases when the "top troublemaker" *does* choose to proceed with transformation, the executive's public statements are probably driven by ulterior motives, such as a new political strategy to gain more power and control in the midst of the upheaval and uncertainties of "change and improvement."

Understandably, some people feel that troublemakers should be confronted at the start of the completely integrated program. **But I have discovered that not until an improvement program has been underway for six months is the organization actually prepared to confront these troubled people.** Generally speaking, members must already have acquired effective skills for people management and problem management before they are able – and willing – to confront disruptive behavior. At the same time, all members must be encouraged to openly question behavior that does not support the new cultural norms. Only when the organization is ready to address on-the-job problems with the new culture and new skills (with both bosses and subordinates present in each work group) is the organization really ready to manage troublemakers.

If the troublemakers are NOT confronted at this time (at the beginning of the team track), victimized members (and anyone else who knows of a troublemaker's abuse) quickly lose faith in the completely integrated program: "How can we possibly take such an improvement program seriously if it doesn't address all the fear and torment that this organization continues to inflict on innocent members? How can top management excuse such emotional, physical, and sexual harassment while they claim to be improving things?"

In Chapters 2 and 3, which addressed interpersonal conflict and organizational conflict, respectively, I mentioned that there's often a marked difference between the conflict-handling modes that members apply INSIDE their organization versus how they prefer to manage conflict OUTSIDE their organization (in all the other settings in their life). *Typically, members tend to overuse the avoiding and accommodating conflict modes INSIDE their organization (particularly at the lower levels in the hierarchy), even when they are inclined to use the assertive conflict modes (competing, collaborating, and compromising) OUTSIDE their organization.* We then spent some time on discussing WHY the INSIDE and OUTSIDE use of conflict modes can be so different.

Although the actual cultural norms and reward systems can cause such a huge difference in the conflict-handling behavior that is experienced INSIDE versus OUTSIDE an organization, **it should not be surprising that the overuse of the avoiding and accommodating modes in the workplace can occasionally be explained by the presence of one or more troublemakers who bully and intimidate members into silence and compliance.** But once troublemaking behavior has been contained, members will then find it much easier to use the more assertive conflict modes to address both their interpersonal and systems conflicts in the organization. Of course, closing culture-gaps (which encourages greater openness, honesty, and assertiveness) will also inspire the desired switch to more effective conflict management on the job, whereby all five conflict modes are readily available for use, as the situation requires.

Indeed, **as soon as culture-gaps are being closed and the troublemakers are being controlled, the eight key attributes of situation undergo significant change** (e.g., much less stress in the organization, greater trust among members, better listening and communication in all interactions, etc.). In addition, getting troublemakers to curb their bad behavior also makes it easier for members to reinforce their collective beliefs in *Internal Control* ("I can determine what happens to me") – whereas troublemaking behavior always reinforces the more confining belief in *External Control* ("I cannot make much of a difference in what takes place here"). Managing troublemakers thus creates a much healthier social environment for addressing all varieties of organizational problems and conflicts – while ignoring troublemakers seriously sours the organization's behavioral infrastructure.

Managing troublemakers initially involves identifying who they are, and then counseling them to curtail their disruptive behavior. Although troublemakers have a tough time receiving any kind of feedback, a counseling session (via an in-person or virtual meeting) is the most direct way to convey the corporate message: **Troublemaking behavior will no longer be tolerated in this organization.** Because of the deep psychological conflicts that drive troublemakers to act in such dysfunctional ways, an experienced consultant is needed to confront these emotionally wounded people. Most members have not received the training to deal with behavioral pathology and mental illness.

IDENTIFYING TROUBLEMAKERS

Often the organization's troublemakers come to the attention of the external consultants in the diagnostic stage of quantum transformation (Chapter 4). *While the diagnostic interviews are being held, certain names are inevitably mentioned again and again. Stories are told of mean and hostile acts that have hurt other people or the organization as a whole.* While such stories might be exaggerated, distorted by years of repetition, one must be careful not to discount them, especially when told by several interviewees. Sometimes, the stories are so alarming that even if they were only 10 percent true, they should be taken seriously.

The consultants also become introduced to troublemakers during the workshop sessions in the culture and skills tracks. Since troublemakers are usually unaware of how their own disruptive behavior affects others, they create trouble right in front of everyone: making hostile remarks that are not germane to the discussion, showing anger in verbal and nonverbal ways, and discouraging others from taking the discussion seriously. As the earlier tracks proceed, numerous members may speak to the consultants about the difficulty of applying their new skills back on the job: Their own managers ridicule them and even threaten them with bad performance reviews if they continue to attend the workshop sessions in the completely integrated program.

Identifying troublemakers is a more sensitive process than it might first appear. *When there's been widespread intimidation on the part of a manager, his victims may be afraid to come forth and reveal injustices.* Sometimes they're convinced that if the troublemaker even suspects that others have signaled him out, he'll take revenge. It's not uncommon for members to fear that this troublemaker will fire them for revealing anything to the consultants. Whether this is all due to fear or has some basis in reality is not clear. But it does cause members to hold back information on who is causing trouble for others. Ideally, as the team track proceeds, these members will begin to draw attention to troublemaking behavior when they see others taking risks for organizational success.

The number of identified troublemakers may range from a few people to as many as a dozen; every organization seems to have at least one such troubled individual. The great majority of troublemakers are typically in management positions that are scattered throughout the hierarchy – where they exploit formal authority to their full advantage. Often times, non-management personnel use their unique technical expertise or their informal "ringleader" status in order to get away with disruptive behavior.

COUNSELING TROUBLEMAKERS

Each identified troublemaker is then scheduled for a separate counseling session with a trained consultant. During this session, the consultant explains why the person was asked to attend. The consultant mentions several reported incidents and impressions (while protecting the confidentiality of the sources), emphasizing that these stories might be totally distorted. Any single incident can be explained away quite easily. But as a whole, as a pattern, is there any plausibility to these accounts of bad behavior? How can this person explain the similar perceptions that *several* others have of him or her?

Although the person is always alarmed at being considered a troublemaker, in rare cases he does seem to appreciate being given this feedback. After he recovers from the shock, he begins to explore how the incidents developed and how the perceptions must have formed. The individual then outlines how he plans to correct the perceptions, as well as his behavior. Here the person *accepts* the problem, takes *responsibility* for his own behavior (and how it impacts on other members), and thus wants to *improve* the situation. Such an adaptive response could indicate that he was mislabeled as a troublemaker, due to his unintentional abrasive behavior or a few inadvertent, embarrassing incidents. In these rare cases, perhaps no one has previously tried to tell him about the negative effects of his behavior on others and, consequently, he has never had the chance to benefit from such specific (and well-intentioned) feedback from other individuals. But now this situation can be corrected.

In most cases, as can be expected, the troublemaker becomes defensive, argumentative, and nasty as the consultant tries to offer compassionate feedback. Should the consultant point out that the person's response confirms exactly what others in the organization have previously experienced? If the troublemaker is so defensive, there is little likelihood that he'll even hear the message. Instead, he'll work very hard at protecting himself, as always. But the organization message has been given, and the individual has been "put on alert." The consultant concludes the meeting by encouraging the troublemaker to think about their discussion, since there will be several follow-up meetings to see "how things are going."

Some troublemakers will act as if their behavior has changed, hoping that the external consultants will leave shortly and that everything will go back to "normal." But a few weeks after the first meeting with each troublemaker, the consultant schedules the next round of counseling sessions in order to review what has transpired. Often, the exact same discussions are held again. *The troublemaker insists that her behavior is fine — why can no one else see this? She claims she is a victim of circumstance or of misunderstanding. She just does not see how her motives and behavior can be so misconstrued. Perhaps other members are jealous of her energy, intelligence, and accomplishments.*

During these sessions, the consultants see creativity at work. The troublemaker can turn, rationalize, distort, and justify almost anything. These emotionally wounded people, because of their wartime tactics, have learned to twist and turn reality so that it matches the image they have of themselves. If the facts do not fit their needs, they proceed to change the facts: They come up with a new reality to explain the worth of their net contributions. *The most striking example of these distortions is illustrated by the*

***troublemaker's insistence that she likes certain individuals —
who just happen to be the very ones who have been hurt by her,
time and time again.*** Often, these are the very same people who
reported that troublemaker to the consultants in the first place.
Such is the power of psychological compensation!

There may be as many as four to six one-on-one counseling
sessions over a period of a few months in order to convince each
troublemaker to squelch/contain his or her disruptive behavior.
***It should be clear, therefore, why senior management support
must be behind such a confrontation.*** Without this support, the
troublemakers will not show up for their scheduled counseling
sessions and, even if they attend, will surely ignore all the related
feedback and suggestions for changing their behavior. Without
this senior management support, members won't confront the
troublemakers for fear of reprisal. ***Yet when everyone is told the
SPECIFIC kinds of behavior that will no longer be tolerated in
the organization, the message will be received.*** Gradually, the
members become more assertive in confronting troublemakers
in a timely manner – as they're leaning to use their sanctioning
systems to reward behavior that conforms to the desired cultural
norms, while penalizing disruptive (troublemaking) behavior.

Accepting all sides of human nature allows us to recognize –
and directly confront – troublemakers who are inclined to take
advantage of the fears, doubts, insecurities, and other anxieties of
group members. When we assume that everyone is rational and
genuine, we allow those who are not to use the organization as
their own social battlefield. Achieving long-term success requires
seeing human nature as it is (with updated assumptions), not as
we wish it to be (based on false assumptions from the past).

TEAM BUILDING WITHIN WORK GROUPS

The purpose of team building is to help each work group use
its knowledge, expertise, and experience in managing complex
problems and conflicts. ***Every work group must know how to
establish an effective group process for all their deliberations,***

based on all the material learned in the prior tracks. In this section, I will make use of the following tools for resolving the transfer-of-learning problem and thus making sure that what is learned in a safe workshop setting is put to full use in the actual workplace: (1) the Process Observer along with using the Process Observer Form; (2) Work Sheets on Reuniting the Work Group; (3) Kilmanns Time-Gap Survey; and, importantly, (4) Kilmanns Team-Gap Survey. These special materials are used during the five steps of problem management, which is when the members in each work unit strive to identify and close the GAPS between their actual and desired behavior on matters that determine the group's performance and satisfaction.

Here are the five basic steps for team building: (1) reuniting the work group (and using a Process Observer during all group meetings); (2) sensing and defining GAPS; (3) developing action plans to close GAPS; (4) implementing solutions to close GAPS; and (5) monitoring and evaluating outcomes. As you can see, the five steps of team building are quite similar to the five steps of problem management: **Team building IS problem management applied to every work group in the organization. The challenge remains the same: first discovering what is wrong (identifying GAPS), doing something about it, and then finding out if the solution worked — and, if it did not, trying again.**

STEP 1: REUNITING THE WORK GROUP

At the beginning of the team track, the managers and their subordinates are brought together in their natural work groups for the first time in the program for quantum transformation. Since most groups range in size from three to fifteen members, the consultant or facilitator can handle numerous groups in one workshop session, so long as the total number of members is manageable (less than 100). Furthermore, just as with the earlier tracks, these sessions in the team track will be conducted at least once every month — and these off-site workshops are reinforced through several interim group meetings in the workplace, which include homework assignments and additional exercises.

Since virtually every manager is a member of two groups – the group in which he's the boss and the other one in which he reports to someone else – many managers may have to do team building in two groups. If most of a manager's time is devoted to just one of these groups, however, he only needs to participate in that primary work group throughout the team track.

The first topic for team building focuses on the work done in the culture track. Because the bosses and their direct reports were previously separated into their peer groups, each of these two "communities" may have developed some different desired norms as well as different sanctioning systems to enforce those new norms of behavior. Now that the work group is intact, it is essential to develop a consistent approach to the culture track. Usually, it doesn't take much effort to resolve cultural differences and to integrate the two sanctioning systems into one. After all, the bosses and subordinates generally have experienced similar problems in the same work group. Thereafter, any further work in the culture track takes place for the entire intact group with every member and boss present. The group also shares its results on the Kilmanns Organizational Belief Survey – so the boss and her direct reports can be sure to reinforce their *beliefs in Internal Control*, whenever they're facing complex problems and conflicts.

The second topic for team building concerns the work done during the skills track. The reunited members first discuss when to use each of the five conflict modes (competing, collaborating, compromising, avoiding, and accommodating) to make sure they have a shared understanding of how the eight attributes of the situation determine which conflict–handling mode is best to use for resolving every significant conflict that can possibly arise in the work group. Next, the members profile their four personality styles (ST, NT, SF, and NF) for use during the five steps of problem management and in their Problem Management Organizations (arranged separately for the strategy–structure track, the reward system track, the radical process track, and so on). The boss and the direct reports in each work group should also discuss their understanding of how assumptional analysis can enable them to define and solve their complex problems, how both inquiring systems (i.e., the Lockean and the Hegelian) are needed during the stages and steps of assumptional analysis, and, finally, how to deduce a new conclusion by integrating the radically different decision trees in their quantum forest.

More specifically, below are the four kinds of questions that the groups throughout the organization are asked to address in order to reunite the boss with his or her direct reports – so they will effectively apply in the workplace what they learned as peer groups during the safe workshop sessions in the first two tracks of the program:

1. Cultural Norms: Now that your group (its peers and the immediate boss) is reuniting at the start of the team track, list all the desired cultural norms of behavior that support long–term success. Review the desired norms that were listed in the culture track discussions (including the group's results from taking the Culture–Gap Survey). After examining your list of *desired norms*, discuss which *actual norms* are still operating in your work group. Now identify the largest culture–gaps that still need to be closed. How does your group plan to close its largest culture–gaps?

2. People Management: What is the most effective people management behavior – concerning how those four personality styles are appreciated (as learned from the Kilmanns Personality Style Instrument) and how such major differences in assimilating information and making decisions can be resolved by using one or more of the five conflict–handling modes, based on the eight key attributes of the situation? Of those agreed–upon behaviors you just listed, which ones are least utilized by your group and, therefore, need to be used more faithfully and more frequently in order to achieve organizational success? What will your work group do to ensure that this desired behavior will be used more regularly and consistently?

3. Problem Management: What is the desirable problem management behavior that will enable your group to achieve organizational success? Consider the material on the five steps – and errors – of problem management. Also consider when to use assumptional analysis in order to minimize the most damaging errors. Finally, consider how to first exaggerate and then resolve alternative perspectives in a Problem Management Organization (PMO), with the use of personality styles and conflict modes. Of those desirable problem management behaviors that you listed, which ones are least utilized by your group and, therefore, need to be used more effectively to achieve long–term organizational success? What will your group now do to make sure this desired behavior will be utilized more regularly and consistently?

4. The All–Purpose Sanctioning System: What sanctions will your work group use to (1) close culture–gaps, (2) foster the development of the most pragmatic PEOPLE management skills, and (3) foster the development of the most pragmatic PROBLEM management skills – which also apply the critical thinking skills that are essential for investigating the TRUTH behind the group's complex problems and conflicts? In particular, what positive or negative sanctions will be delivered when victories or violations occur? How will your group enable each member to break the dysfunctional habits of the past and then do all the things that are necessary for achieving long–term success in the future?

USING A PROCESS OBSERVER DURING ALL GROUP MEETINGS

The diagnostic interviews, along with the survey results from the Kilmann Organizational Conflict Instrument (KOCI), usually reveal that **one of the largest barriers to long-term success is the frustrating experience of attending ineffective group meetings throughout the entire organization.** Often members have been so frustrated by dysfunctional groups, let alone having to attend useless meetings, that they've almost given up on the notion that groups can really be effective. But if they search their collective memories, they can usually remember a few group experiences (perhaps some sports team in high school or college) when the collective mission was accomplished and people felt good about the outcome. Not surprisingly, members typically attribute such group success to mostly luck or leadership – or the group's size and composition. But rarely do group members possess a deep understanding of the fundamental processes that occur during group meetings that determine success or failure.

Many decades ago, I developed the Process Observer Form to help groups improve their process. Below are the key principles that must be followed by every work group at all times:

THE TEN KEY PRINCIPLES OF GROUP PROCESS
1. Planning vs. Doing
2. Assumption Testing
3. Decomposing the Task
4. Task Leadership
5. Group Maintenance
6. Process vs. Content
7. Listening vs. Speaking
8. Supportive Communication
9. Conflict Modes
10. Leadership Styles

I will now expand on the ten key principles of group process, so these guidelines can be deeply understood – and effectively utilized: At the beginning of each group meeting, each member should be fully aware of the objectives of the meeting. Group members should plan their time and determine the priority of their agenda items BEFORE they discuss any subject at length. They should agree to address the most important issues first and the less important issues last. Group members should also plan how each agenda item will be approached and whether it can be subdivided into several manageable pieces (and subgroups), so that a project's complexity does not immobilize them. Naturally, spending a little time planning these matters before proceeding usually saves a lot of time later. As soon as a plan is developed, the assumptions underlying all subsequent discussions should be surfaced – not only to minimize the likelihood of committing serious errors in problem management, but also to reduce the occurrence of any circular, repetitive, and superficial discussions (which might also be based on false assumptions).

Further, the more talkative group members should make a concerted effort to bring the less talkative members into every discussion in order to ensure that all perspectives are heard and all information can be utilized. (This is particularly meaningful if any international members feel shy or hesitant to speak, since the host language is not their native tongue; they might still be trying to figure out the culture and customs of the host country.) Even more to the point, group members should regularly assess whether their cultural norms continue to support new, bizarre, and provocative ideas. All communications should be courteous, thus respecting every person's ego and treating everyone with dignity. Only one member in a meeting should be speaking at any moment; everyone else should be listening very attentively. Instead of a *competitive spirit* (fighting to talk the most and trying to win the final argument), a *collaborative spirit* must be applied on complex problems to make full use of everyone's knowledge for the best outcome. Every now and then, members should take a break from the group discussion on content and inquire about the process: How are we doing as a group? Are we applying the ten key principles and all the skills we learned in the completely integrated program? If not, what should we be doing differently?

When it's time to make sure that all members will actually apply these key principles and be able to improve their group process, it's vital to appoint one member as a Process Observer (PO) at the start of every group meeting. This PO is responsible for monitoring how well the ten key principles guide the group's discussions. At the end of the meeting, using a specially designed Process Observer Form, the PO summarizes what the group did particularly well and in what ways the group fell short. A plan is then formulated regarding what to do differently (hence, better) during the group's next meeting. **Moreover, a different member should be appointed as the PO at the start of the next group meeting. Consequently, during a period of a few months, every group member will have had ample opportunities to develop**

sharp observation skills and practice giving effective feedback. In the future, it will no longer be necessary to appoint a Process Observer; the responsibility for monitoring and improving the group's process will have become shared among all members.

When every group discussion on complex problems reflects such an effective group process, each work group becomes a well-functioning team. If a stranger were to watch such a team in session, he would not be able to tell who's the boss and who are the direct reports. Every individual would be contributing relevant information and expertise as needed: Status distinctions and other irrelevant criteria would not be influencing the way in which important issues were being addressed and then resolved. The physical arrangement of the team members would be round (i.e., holistic) reflecting the equal opportunity that every member would have to participate in all discussions. Before the start of the completely integrated program, the same stranger would not have had any difficulty in correctly identifying the boss during any of the team's meetings: The boss would have been initiating, talking, directing, deciding, and concluding – more than anyone else, on every topic. In some cases, in fact, the boss would have been sitting at the head of a large rectangular (marble) table, in a very comfortable (leather) chair, dictating his pronouncements to his (passive) subordinates.

As shown in Figure 7.2 on the following page, two symbolic portrayals of group process (a rectangle and a circle) capture the kind of transformation that begins with the first two tracks and concludes during the team track.

STEP 2: SENSING AND DEFINING GAPS

In the initial workshops in the team track, two assessment tools are used to help each group identify its most troublesome time-gaps and team-gaps, so action plans can then be derived and implemented to effectively close the GAPS that undermine each group's performance and satisfaction.

FIGURE 7.2
THE TRANSFORMATION DURING THE TEAM TRACK

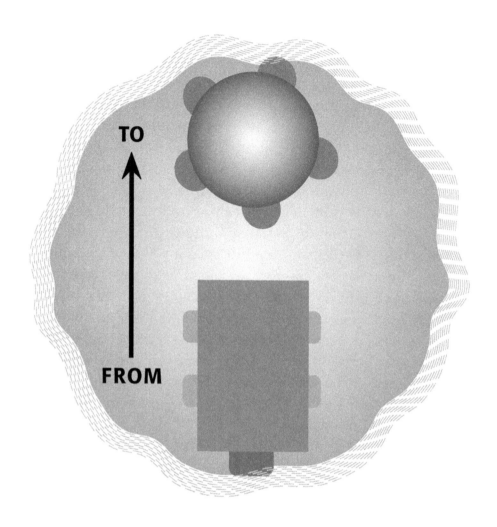

Just like several of the other subjects we've covered in prior chapters of this book (e.g., dysfunctional cultural norms, beliefs in External Control, and hidden assumptions), you first have to see "it" before you can *do* anything about "it." TIME is often taken for granted – like oxygen – yet every member uses it, whether consciously or unconsciously, whether by conscious choice or by habit. **TIME is the great equalizer: We each get 24 hours a day, not a minute more or a minute less. But what do we each do**

with our available TIME? Bottom line: If members cannot make efficient and effective use of their precious TIME, groups won't – and can't – become teams. Period.

Regarding the utilization of time in organizations, there's an important distinction that all members must recognize: **CRISIS management versus TIME management.**

One of the classic ways that a group reveals that it's being run by CRISIS management is when members take on problems as they arise. As such, when a problem is brought to the group's attention, that problem becomes the total focus of all its efforts. **The prime underlying assumption is that the universe presents us with problems in the order of their priority. Once that false assumption has been surfaced, it can immediately be revised to proclaim the TRUTH: Problems do NOT appear in the order of their priority.** Group members must prioritize the importance of all GAPS based on the mission, goals, and objectives of the work group and the organization as a whole.

Another key indicator of CRISIS management is when group members feel they are constantly "putting out fires" – jumping from one problem to the next, but without bringing anything to completion. Decades ago, the members of an organization that were very familiar with my use of "decision trees" for explaining problem management and assumptional analysis actually talked about putting out FOREST FIRES. As a result, **instead of having the opportunity to carefully examine the different decision trees in the quantum forest in order to understand all aspects of a complex problem, these members said they couldn't make use of the decision trees in their forest because their trees were all burning down. Their organization was experienced as being a lot like an out-of-control forest fire – a wildfire!** That's a vivid metaphor for remembering the essence of CRISIS management – which is also characterized by zero planning, no prioritizing, no resting, no reflecting, and no mindfulness about anything.

Here are some additional false assumptions about time that support CRISIS management: If you want group members to get everything done, then make everything the #1 priority. There is considerable slack in group members' jobs, so more work can be added on without negatively affecting the quality or completion of their *other* work. Planning is not work; getting something done (anything) is work. Busyness is the same thing as performance.

The exact opposite of CRISIS management is called TIME management, which requires planning before doing and taking the time to reflect on the complexity of the problem. With TIME management, members rarely have to manage emergencies and surprises; the latter are the exception, not the rule. Indeed, while CRISIS management bypasses the search for different problem definitions (which would be a huge challenge anyway, since all their decision trees are ablaze), TIME management requires that members take the needed time to (1) define problems based on valid assumptions (before selecting a solution) and (2) develop implementation plans based on up–to–date assumptions (before implementing any solution). CRISIS management short–circuits the five steps of problem management (and thus generates one error after another), while TIME management encourages group members to use ALL the material from the first two tracks for the purpose of *minimizing* the five errors of problem management.

What are the most important (true) and certain assumptions that support TIME management? Problems do NOT appear in the order of their importance; they must first be prioritized via strategic goals. Given limited energy, time, and other resources, group members must focus their attention on resolving the most strategically important problems. With little slack in workloads, assigning group members additional work will adversely affect the quality of their other work – if priorities are not adjusted to take that additional work into account. Planning before doing is mandatory for long–term success; busyness is NOT performance, never was and never will be.

IDENTIFYING TIME-GAPS

Kilmanns Time–Gap Survey was developed to assess the tasks and activities that individuals believe they should be spending more time on – or less time on – for the purpose of improving the performance and satisfaction of their internal and external stakeholders. And members can also indicate if they are already spending the right amount of time on those tasks and activities.

To make sure that we assess all the relevant aspects of life in an organization, the Time–Gap Survey purposely includes items that address each formal and informal system in the Complex Hologram. Specifically, the survey presents the respondent with seven tasks and activities for each of the formal and informal systems that pertain to the first five system tracks of quantum transformation: Cultures, Skills, Teams, Strategy–Structures, and Reward Systems. In a later chapter in this book, when we discuss the three process tracks in the completely integrated program, we'll again be especially concerned with TIME: *speeding up* how business processes are described, controlled, and improved. As a result of the last three tracks, customers will receive the products and services they requested even better – and faster – than ever before. Thus, improving TIME management is a vital component of PROCESS management.

As you can see in Figure 7.3, the five system tracks provide a holistic framework for assessing how time is being spent in the pursuit of the organization's goals. In fact, these first five tracks (from the entire series of eight tracks) correspond to the identical five time–gaps assessed by this survey. *A time-gap is defined as the difference between spending the right amount of time on tasks or activities versus spending the wrong amount of time on those same tasks and activities that pertain to any of the five system tracks*.

FIGURE 7.3
DEFINING FIVE TIME-GAPS FOR THE FIVE SYSTEM TRACKS

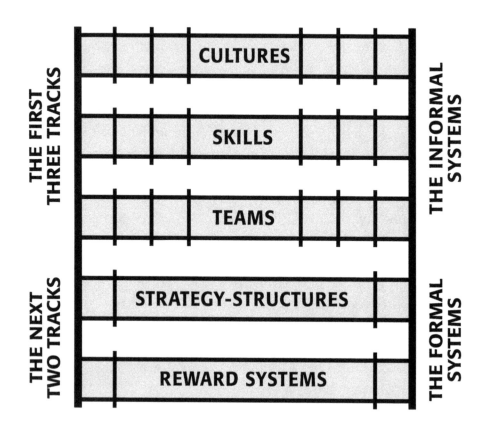

**Spending the Right Amount of Time on
Each System in order to Achieve
Organizational Success**

Cultures: Do you spend time sustaining an adaptive culture, responding to requests from other groups or departments, and encouraging others to forgive previous wrongdoings by moving forward with a clean slate? Or do you, deliberately or not, spend time generating mistrust across departments, conveying doom–and–gloom attitudes, and bearing grudges?

Skills: Do you spend time working to clarify your priorities, planning your workday, and sticking to the most important tasks until you have completed them? Or do you, deliberately or not, spend time working on the wrong priorities, switching from task to task without bringing any task to completion, and saving the important work for another day?

Teams: Do you spend time by sharing your knowledge and expertise with your fellow group members (including your boss), encouraging teamwork, and fostering effective problem-solving efforts? Or do you, deliberately or not, spend time keeping your good ideas to yourself, discouraging the quieter members from participating in the discussion, and publicly agreeing with group decisions even though you really disagree?

Strategy-Structures: Do you spend time seeking to clarify organizational goals, objectives, and procedures with your boss before you pursue your daily work? Or do you, deliberately or not, spend time working on the same old things in the same old way without ever modifying your work priorities – even though organizational goals and objectives have been changing?

Reward Systems: Do you spend time seeking to learn what criteria will be used to review your performance, how the review system works, and what you can do in the meantime to improve your performance for the next cycle? Or do you, deliberately or not, spend time complaining about your organization's reward system – neither trying to understand it nor improve it?

In sum, there are at least five ways that the precious time of members can be diverted from achieving long-term success: (1) not trusting other work groups (Cultures), (2) not using critical thinking skills to prioritize, plan, and do the work (Skills), (3) not cooperating with your group members and your boss in order to resolve important work group problems (Teams), (4) not focusing on the organization's strategic objectives with the right policies and procedures (Strategy-Structures), and (5) not pursuing clear and valid performance criteria that accurately reflect what the organization's internal and external stakeholders need and want (Reward Systems).

By discovering how their precious time is being wasted the same way day after day, individuals and groups can choose to redistribute their time on tasks — from spending the wrong time on the wrong tasks or the wrong time on the right tasks to the right time on the right tasks — and thereby add positive contributions to their organization's long-term success.

Below are the instructions for taking the Kilmanns Time–Gap Survey:

> **For each item below, please select the letter that indicates whether you should be spending less time (L) or more time (M) than you are now in order to increase your contribution to your organization's goals. If you are already spending the right time on the item in question (which could be no time), then select the middle letter (R).**

Here are three items to give you a sense of what's included in the Time–Gap Survey:

1. **I actively foster trust in my organization by speaking very positively and respectfully about other groups and departments;**
2. **I find myself worrying about what salary increase or bonus I will get this year or complaining about what I received last time;**
3. **I meet with my boss to clarify my objectives and priorities (especially after organizational goals or departmental responsibilities have been modified).**

Regarding the results of the Time–Gap Survey, the raw scores on each of the five time-gaps can vary from 0 (the right amount of time is always being spent on that organizational system) to 7 (much more OR much less time should be spent on that system). In terms of interpreting the results, *a score of 3 or higher identifies a significant time-gap.* Such a large gap suggests that a misallocation of time is being spent on one of the five systems tracks: Cultures, Skills, Teams, Strategy–Structures, or Reward Systems. A score of 2 is considered to be a borderline time–gap (i.e., the significance of the gap can go either way), while a score of 1 or 0 suggests an insignificant time–gap. If three (or more) time–gaps are found to be significant according to these guidelines, then a broad–based misallocation of time is currently diverting the group's potential contribution to organizational success.

Figure 7.4 presents the Time–Gap results for a work group of 12 members. Three significant time–gaps are identified for this group. Indeed, all three time–gaps appear in the first three tracks. In this case, the work group is acknowledging that it should be spending more time promoting a healthy culture, making better use of critical thinking skills for prioritizing and planning the work, and managing group discussions and meetings so that all the knowledge and expertise of members is readily available for resolving problems and conflicts.

Regarding the last two tracks to long–term success, however, it appears that the work group is spending the right amount of time clarifying strategic goals and objectives (Strategy–Structures) and ensuring that all members are guided by clear performance criteria and know how the performance appraisal process works (Reward Systems). While this work group seems to be managing the formal systems effectively, it's not fully utilizing its talent and energy: It may know exactly what to do, but the group is being diverted from getting the right things done.

Before I discuss how the largest time–gaps can be addressed in the next steps of problem management, each work group in the team track is also asked to examine *additional* GAPS that will need to be identified and closed. Although the *Kilmanns Time-Gap Survey* examines how members are using – or misusing – their precious time, the *Kilmanns Team-Gap Survey* investigates the actual versus desired functioning in the subunit that is not only about time, but also concerns the additional subjects that were covered during the first two tracks of the completely integrated program.

FIGURE 7.4
AN EXAMPLE OF TIME-GAP RESULTS

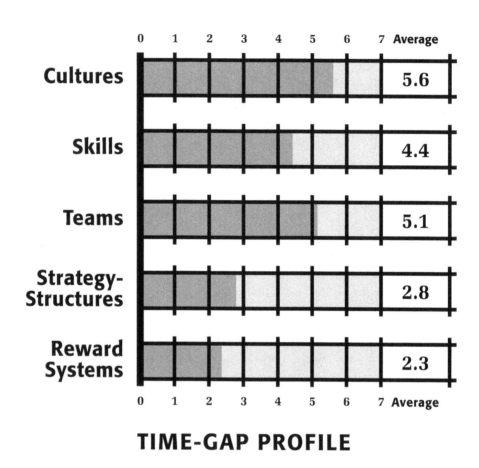

TIME-GAP PROFILE

IDENTIFYING TEAM-GAPS

The members of any group have a great deal of knowledge, expertise, and experience. But will all this available talent in the group actually be used to manage (resolve) business, technical, and organizational problems? Or will all the group's wisdom be wasted? The Kilmanns Team–Gap Survey enables members and work groups to identify what is getting in the way of their daily functioning. *Part 1 of the survey asks all members to indicate the ACTUAL functioning of their group on 24 items. Part 2 asks all members to reveal the DESIRED functioning of their group on those same 24 items.* Naturally, the difference between Part 1 and Part 2 (actual versus desired functioning of the group) will allow each work group to identify its significant team–gaps.

The on–the–job behavior that helps a group accomplish its mission – or, alternatively, what gets in the way of performance and satisfaction – can be organized into four major categories: Cultural Norms, People Management, Problem Management, and Time Management. The latter, of course, is now an integral part of the completely integrated program, ever since the participants took the Time–Gap Survey and then discussed their results.

After each group member has responded to all items on the Team–Gap Survey, each of four scores (one for each of the major categories of group functioning) can range from 0 to 36, since there are 6 items to measure each team–gap, and the difference between actual group functioning in Part 1 and desired group functioning in Part 2 can range from 0 (no difference) to 6 (the difference between 1 and 7 on the scale). As a general guideline for interpreting your results: a score (or average) that's less than 12 suggests an *insignificant team-gap*; a score (or average) between 12 and 24 represents *a significant team-gap*; and a score (or average) greater than 24 represents a *highly significant team-gap*.

Figure 7.5 presents the Team-Gap results for a department that has significant team-gaps in all four categories: Although the team–gaps for Problem Management and Time Management are significant (average scores between 12 and 24), the team–gaps for Cultural Norms as well as for People Management are highly significant (greater than 24). In this case, the entire department – on average – must be having a lot of difficulty in accomplishing its mission. It seems that both problems and time are not being managed efficiently and effectively. In addition, the work units in the department (based on these average scores) are not trusting one another, not adjusting to today's fast–paced world, ignoring attempts to improve their performance, and not striving to learn new methods and approaches (Cultural Norms). Making matters even worse, members are not treating one another with respect

(People Management), which may additionally hamper trust and prevent work groups from managing their time and problems – as a team. Only if these significant team–gaps can be closed will the department be able to utilize all of its talent and experience in the pursuit of long-term success.

FIGURE 7.5
AN EXAMPLE OF TEAM-GAP RESULTS

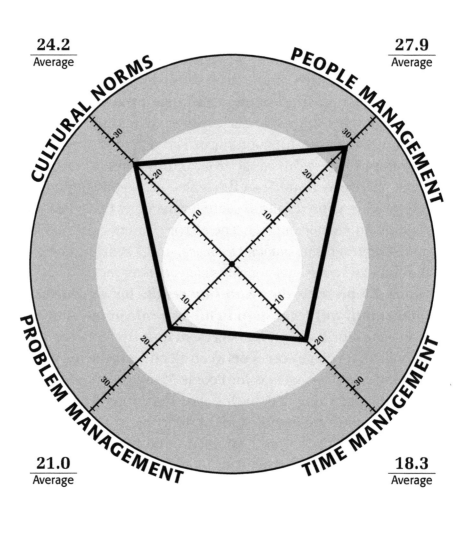

24.2
Average

27.9
Average

21.0
Average

18.3
Average

IDENTIFYING UNIQUE TIME-GAPS AND TEAM-GAPS

Just as we asked each group to identify UNIQUE actual and desired cultural norms that could not be included in the more TYPICAL cultural norms that are shown on the Kilmann–Saxton Culture–Gap Survey, we also encourage work groups to identify UNIQUE time–gaps and team–gaps that aren't included with the TYPICAL items that appear on the Kilmanns Time–Gap Survey and the Kilmanns Team–Gap Survey. As a result, each group is now given the opportunity to identify *additional* GAPS that could not be identified on any standardized instrument.

In a separate room or separate section of a large conference room, each work group is asked to discuss ten probing questions about how well it functions day after day. But before any group discussion begins, one member becomes the Process Observer for the meeting and 10 to 15 minutes are put aside at the end of the meeting so that (a) the PO can provide effective feedback on group process and then (b) the group can discuss what it will do differently during the next group meeting.

1. What is the group's mission? What are the group's objectives?
2. How well is the group accomplishing its mission and objectives?
3. What helps the group in performing its tasks?
4. What hinders the group in performing its tasks?
5. Are group members spending the right amount of time on the right tasks according to the right objectives?
6. Do group members feel that their time is not being spent in the most productive way? How is their time being diverted?

7. Do group members feel that all their knowledge, expertise, and experience are being used? How could their talent be used more extensively and consistently?
8. Are all problems brought out in the open so they can be addressed with all available information and expertise? Why are some problems being avoided?
9. How does the group's profile of personality styles affect the five steps of problem management?
10. Which steps of problem management does the group overemphasize? Which do they underemphasize? Which errors of problem management occur most frequently?

As these important questions about the group's functioning are discussed and debated, key insights that penetrate the inner workings of the group become open for every member to see – which always leads members to sense additional GAPS. At a later step in the process, the group can proceed with defining the root causes of its most troublesome GAPS, so an effective solution can be derived, implemented, and evaluated. If any of the responses to the ten questions suggest a complex problem, however, such as establishing why the group's support services are not being used more extensively throughout the organization – the more elaborate methods for problem management should be applied: Perhaps an assumptional analysis can be conducted by forming several subgroups to debate and then synthesize the underlying assumptions of each problem definition. Each subgroup can be composed of a specialized personality style (ST, NT, SF, or NF) in order to reveal the radically different perspectives – and, hence, different decision trees for this abridged application of a Problem Management Organization (for inside a work group as opposed to across all the subunits in the organization). This simplified use of the PMO helps the group define most of its problems correctly before deriving and implementing solutions.

The responses to the ten questions may suggest problems that not only are complex, but also have ramifications beyond the group's boundaries. Even conducting assumptional analysis within the group would be insufficient in this situation: The full range of expertise and information needed to define the problem would not be entirely available in this analysis, since it resides in other groups in the organization. *The problems that fit this type would be postponed until the interteam building is ready to be undertaken.* Each work group, for now, does the best job it can in identifying both the simple and complex problems that fall under its own domain: UNIQUE time–gaps, UNIQUE team–gaps, and any other troublesome GAPS.

STEP 3: DERIVING SOLUTIONS TO CLOSE GAPS

A lively discussion unfolds when group members consider how to close their identified GAPS: to derive solutions that can enhance channels for success while removing barriers to success. Because deriving solutions is considered a simple task (once the problem has already been defined), group consensus (using the Lockean Inquiring System) is usually sufficient for selecting the solutions to implement.

SOLUTIONS TO OVERCOME THE THREE-DAY WASHOUT EFFECT

At the start of this chapter, I made a big deal about having to face up to the classic problem of *transferring what is learned in a safe workshop into the actual workplace.* Deriving solutions to close the identified GAPS, therefore, must essentially include several methods to ensure that group members (including the boss) will effectively and consistently USE their new knowledge about culture, skills, and teams on their job – every single day. If the "transfer–of–learning problem" is not addressed explicitly, the work group is likely to fall into that useless trap of the *three-day washout effect:* Three days after having learned a new behavior or skill in a relatively safe and secure off-site workshop, it's as if that workshop never took place; when group members are back on the job, it's simply back to business as usual.

One solution that helps to counteract the three-day washout effect is making use of a Process Observer (PO) during EVERY group meeting in the workplace. Indeed, EVERY on-site meeting should begin by assigning the PO and then allotting some time (about 10 to 15 minutes) at the end of the meeting for the PO to report on how well the group applied those ten key principles of effective group process (Planning vs. Doing, Assumption Testing, Decomposing the Task, and so forth) and then to examine what exactly will take place differently the next time the group meets. *Any work group that claims it doesn't need to assign a PO at the start of every group meeting (or doesn't need to discuss the ten key principles of group process) is clearly setting itself up to maximize the three-day washout effect.* Not using a PO at every meeting is thus the clearest sign that the work group has chosen (consciously or unconsciously) to ignore the organization's plan for implementing the completely integrated program to achieve long-term success.

A second solution that helps group members overcome the three-day washout effect is requiring all work groups to discuss what they've been doing differently – in the workplace – since the improvement program was initiated. This most important discussion is greatly facilitated by using my *Work Sheets on Progress Report #1, 2, and 3* (available in my Workbooks for Implementing the Tracks: Volumes I and II).

Setting aside a few hours every month, the members of each group write down (a) what they DID do differently and (b) what they did NOT do differently since the program began, regarding those same topics that were addressed on the Team–Gap Survey: Cultural Norms, People Management, Problem Management, and Time Management.

After each group member has written down what he did and didn't do differently since the start of the program and then, as soon as one member is assigned as the Process Observer (PO) for the meeting, the group discussion proceeds: One member reads his written responses to the other group members and then asks them to comment (provide feedback) regarding what they have observed about his behavior in the workplace: (a) Which of the member's claims about his changed behavior do other members **confirm** have taken place. (b) Which of the member's claims do other members **contradict,** since those claimed behaviors have NOT been witnessed in the workplace? Regarding the latter, the other group members might provide the focal member with this feedback: "Maybe you *intended* to do that differently, or perhaps you *wanted* to do that differently, and maybe you *thought about* doing that differently but, in all honestly, we have never actually observed your claimed behavioral changes in the workplace. The focal member is then asked to write down exactly what claimed behavioral change was confirmed and what claimed behavioral change was contradicted – including any suggestions that were made concerning how he can explicitly demonstrate the desired behavior (and attitudes) in the workplace. In addition, the focal member is asked to write down EXACTLY what he intends to do differently from this moment forward in order to overcome the three–day washout effect.

After each group member has presented his claims of how he has changed his behavior, next received valuable feedback about what was confirmed or contradicted, and then has committed (in writing) to begin doing more things differently in the workplace that others can observe and confirm, the work group schedules the next round of Progress Reports about one month later. Then, in the last 10 to 15 minutes of the current meeting, the PO shares his feedback about how well the group applied each of the ten key principles of group process; the group then discusses what needs to be done better during its next meeting.

About a month later, the group again meets to proceed with the next round of Progress Reports. Before the actual discussion takes place, however, another group member is first assigned as the PO for the meeting. Next, each member, in turn, shares the specific feedback that he received during the last Progress Report and then he reads out loud what he had written down last time, concerning what he planned to do differently – so his changed behavior would be more apparent to his colleagues.

***It's so important to appreciate the ongoing social pressure
that's now being placed on all members to actually CHANGE
THEIR BEHAVIOR in the workplace:*** *Before* beginning the team
track, members might have shared something along these lines:
"I'm willing to change – so long as I do not have to do anything
differently!" But as team building unfolds, especially after a few
monthly meetings on those Progress Reports, members begin to
experience considerable pressure to change their behavior – and
not just their words. After several months of team building, one
now hears this kind of statement: "There is so much pressure to
change: from peers, from our managers, from the consultants,
and from ourselves. I had no idea my colleagues would take me
to task if I didn't apply the key principles in every meeting in a
demonstrable way. I now know why it is so difficult to change
behavior and why all our previous attempts had little chance to
succeed with real behavioral change on the job: ***We had falsely
ASSUMED that members will instantly change their behavior
without the need for any feedback, guidance, or social pressure
from anyone else."***

STEP 4: IMPLEMENTING SOLUTIONS TO CLOSE GAPS

An effective approach to implementation is to subdivide the
work group into several subgroups of two to five members and
give each subgroup responsibility for implementing one or more
of the action plans. A work group of fifteen members may take
the five plans, for example, and assign them to five subgroups.
Either the boss or a member can coordinate this distribution of
assignments. As their derived solutions are being implemented,
each subgroup regularly reports back to the entire group so that
everyone knows what the other subgroups are doing and has an
opportunity to offer suggestions and advice. This kind of sharing
among subgroups allows each member to learn *several* different
approaches for successfully implementing change – rather than
having to learn everything the hard way (as in "reinventing the
wheel"), all on one's own.

***Naturally, the initial plans for implementing solutions will
need to be revised as more is learned about the assumptions
made about each key stakeholder.*** The subgroups, as well as the
entire work group, might find it necessary to brainstorm about
new ways to enhance the implementation of their action plans.
It's important to emphasize that about 10 to 15 minutes should
be set aside at the end of every work group meeting: (1) so the
Process Observer (PO) can present his/her observations of how
well the group applied the ten key principles of group process;
and (2) so all members can then discuss how they will improve
their process during their next meeting. Furthermore, continuing
with those monthly Progress Reports will further stimulate the
implementation process by ensuring that each member's *intention*
to do things differently actually results in *observable* behavioral
changes on the job.

STEP 5: MONITORING AND EVALUATING OUTCOMES

The last step of team building is assessing the outcomes of
the prior four steps to see if the identified time–gaps, team–gaps,
and other identified GAPS have been resolved. If not, then each
step in problem management is thoroughly investigated and the
necessary adjustments are made before any step is done again.
And if new GAPS emerged during the previous cycle of problem
management, those newly identified GAPS are then addressed in
subsequent cycles.

***A few months after the work groups have taken their first
Time-Gap Survey and Team-Gap Survey, and have also gone
through at least once cycle of problem management to close
their largest GAPS, it's worthwhile for group members to take
those two surveys again, score their time-gaps and team-gaps,
and then determine what has improved (smaller GAPS than
before), stayed the same (same sized GAPS), or actually became
worse (larger GAPS than before).*** If you remember, Chapter 5 on
Cultural Management presented a before–and–after comparison
of the Culture–Gap Survey (comparing the four GAPS at the start

of the culture track with their results six to nine months later). Such a quantitative comparison helps pinpoint what additional work still needs to be done to further improve the functioning of every work unit, according to all the key principles and practices of the completely integrated program.

INTERTEAM BUILDING ACROSS WORK GROUPS

Team building works on single parts of the organization, one at a time. Interteam building is necessary because these parts do not make up a simple mechanical system. Rather, the parts of the organization are interconnected at the surface (task assignments) and below the surface (cultural norms, hidden assumptions, and human psyches), which makes for a complex hologram. A work group cannot begin its tasks until it receives certain inputs from other work groups (such as information, materials, services, and other resources), and the value of each group's contributions is determined by how well its output is actually utilized by one or more other subunits (intermediate services or products). Even in the unlikely scenario that a subunit were entirely independent *in a task sense*, each group would still have to be totally cut off from other work units in order to be entirely independent *in a cultural sense*. Members from one work group observe and interact with members of other work groups. They compare, compete, help, and hurt one another. The objective of interteam building is to promote the most functional relationships among work units.

Just as troublemakers must first be identified and counseled before significant progress can be expected with team building activities, sufficient progress with every teambuilding program is first necessary before an interteam process can succeed. **It's just not possible to resolve the problems that divide two or more groups if each group itself is unable to identify and close its own troublesome GAPS and thus resolve its own behavioral problems.** Unless every work group has already benefitted from team building, interteam building will result in finger pointing, scapegoating, and bad behavior. Just as troublemakers tend to project their internal conflicts onto other members, emotionally torn groups also project their mistrust and suspicion onto other groups in the organization. Groups can become cliques fighting over the same issues that troublemakers fight over – except that a group is a much more powerful force than any one person.

Intergroup problems are usually identified when the separate work groups are participating in their teambuilding sessions. As solutions or action plans are being developed, each group delays discussion of certain cross-boundary problems until its internal functioning has improved. Now, however, one group can invite other groups to investigate their intergroup problems together (assuming these other groups are also ready to step beyond their own borders in a healthy, productive manner).

As might seem obvious by now, the five steps of interteam building across work groups parallel the five steps of problem management. Since this chapter has already discussed at length the same steps for team building *within work groups*, the following discussion covers only those aspects of quantum transformation that are unique to managing the kinds of complex problems that flow *across work group boundaries*. Incidentally, by this stage in the improvement program, every work group (without receiving any instructions from the consultants) automatically assigns a PO for every group meeting, so members can continue to improve their group process – meeting after meeting after meeting.

A manageable number of interdependent groups — those that are able and willing to address their mutual problems — are assembled for a one-day workshop. Each group meets in a separate room to prepare a list of perceptions, impressions, and expectations it has for every other group attending the session. Specifically: ***The members in each work group (which includes the boss) list (1) their perceptions of the other groups' mission, objectives, tasks, and responsibilities, (2) their "gut image" of those other groups, and (3) their expectations of how the other groups will describe them.*** If there are four groups attending the workshop, each group prepares three such lists, one for each of the other groups (Blake, Mouton, and Sloma).

When all these lists have been completed (usually in one to three hours), the groups meet back in the community room. One by one, each group makes a formal presentation of its lists to the other groups. Only questions of clarification should be allowed at this time. But all members are encouraged to take extensive notes so they can get ready for the upcoming discussions in the intergroup workshop.

Each work group then meets back in its own room where the members can review their notes, analyze what they discovered, and then decide what they plan to discuss with the other work groups. Several revelations usually emerge during these separate group discussions:

The first revelation takes place when members realize, often for the first time, the radically different perceptions concerning the work domain of every work group. Typically, each group is governed by some formally documented charter, but this charter may be completely out of date. Often responsibilities have been established informally, often implicitly, based on certain critical incidents among the participating work groups. As a result, these conventional understandings are subject to selective memory and other perceptual distortions – depending on which group is questioned. This may seem obvious to the casual observer. To the groups, however, the recognition of these perceptual differences becomes a profound discovery.

The second revelation takes place (and the fun begins) when each work group provides its "gut image" of what it's been like to work with each of the other groups that are attending the workshop. While members can rationalize different perceptions of work domains rather easily, it is tougher to justify their image as empire builders, know-it-alls, kamikazes, disrupters, beggars, sinners, misers, or tightwads. There is often a lot of laughter and much good-hearted humor as vivid gut images are shared and discussed, since those colorful and dramatic gut images always include an "emotional" message that cannot easily be ignored or dismissed. Afterwards, each group must own up to its historical way of relating to the other groups in the organization.

The third revelation concerns the various comparisons that can be made between (a) each group's initial EXPECTATIONS of how it would be seen by the other work groups in the session versus (b) the REALITY of how each group is ACTUALLY being seen by those other groups. A GAP between EXPECTATIONS and REALITY can be shocking: One group may have expected other groups to see it as productive, hardworking, and always helpful to others. But the other work groups may see this focal group as working hard only on the enjoyable projects, being helpful only for certain "favored" groups, and then only helping other groups when there's an immediate payoff. Here the work group has to examine why it might have made such incorrect predictions in judging its public image. Perhaps the group has a glorified image of itself based on how it wants to be seen by others rather than how it really works with others. ***But it soon becomes apparent to each group that without receiving accurate feedback from others, each group is destined to develop a self-serving image of itself that's supported mostly by false assumptions about its actual mission, role, and contributions to long-term success.***

All groups then meet back in a community room to discuss their findings. Many insights usually emerge from such in–depth exchanges. Since both the culture track and the skills track have already made progress (otherwise the team track would not have been initiated), one can expect minimum defensiveness among all the participants as these intergroup discussions proceed. Even if a number of complex problems do not get defined in this first work session, at least everything has been brought out into the open. After a few hours, the members summarize the key points that still divide the groups – the intergroup GAPS that get in the way of interteam cooperation.

Either in the same intergroup workshop or in a subsequent meeting, a community discussion is held to derive solutions and formulate action plans in order to resolve the identified GAPS. If the necessary time and effort are devoted to implementing those action plans in an efficient and effective manner, much progress should occur. Naturally, it's possible that a number of errors in defining problems and in implementing solutions may unfold. If necessary, the process of interteam building might have to travel through the five steps of problem management more than once in order to close the most challenging intergroup GAPS.

CONCLUDING THOUGHTS

When the three components of the team track have had their desired impact on the functioning of the entire organization, the quality of decision making and action taking will be improved: (1) Once all the identified troublemakers have squelched their disruptive behavior, everyone will feel freer to take chances and express opinions. (2) Once each work group has been developed into an effective team, its specific work-related problems will be managed much more successfully than ever before. (3) Once all interconnected groups are inspired to fully cooperate with one another, complex problems that flow across formal boundaries will be managed explicitly – and effectively.

Even if the first three tracks have beautifully achieved their purposes, the formally documented systems have not yet been revitalized – and realigned. Now, however, the organizational members are ready to address the especially complex issues of strategy–structure, reward systems, and process management. We must ensure that all members are working on the right tasks according to the right objectives and are rewarded for doing so.

ALIGNING
STRATEGY–STRUCTURE
THROUGHOUT AN
ORGANIZATION
THE STRATEGY–STRUCTURE TRACK

The first three tracks of the completely integrated program were thoroughly discussed in the previous three chapters in this book. The material on cultures, skills, and teams is very close to home for most people, since the key lessons are very relevant to everyone's personal life, besides being immediately relevant to their work life. Specifically, **all the material in the three prior chapters (tracks) concerns how human beings interact with one another in any social setting:** (1) developing cultural norms that encourage people to be open, candid, and trustworthy during all conversations, as reinforced by an effective sanctioning system to ensure compliance with the desired cultural norms of behavior; (2) learning conflict management skills (i.e., knowing all about those five conflict modes and when to use each mode depending on the eight key attributes that are presently operating), learning people management skills (i.e., knowing about the four different personality styles for assimilating information and then making decisions), learning problem management skills (i.e., knowing all about the five steps and errors of problem management as well as those three stages and steps for assumptional analysis); and (3) learning team management skills (i.e., knowing how to manage troublemakers, and then conduct team building and interteam building), so members can work well with diverse others on all kinds of problems and conflicts – within and across groups.

But the material in this chapter is very different from what was previously presented for the first three tracks of quantum transformation, precisely because strategy-structure addresses the formal systems, which most members experience as being far removed from their daily life at work and at home. Strategy, in fact, is quite abstract, since it asks these challenging questions: Where is this organization headed? What is our strategic plan for the next twenty-five years? Structure is no less abstract, since it asks these far-reaching questions: How should we be organized into divisions, departments, and work units so we have the best chance of achieving our long-term strategic plans? How should we distribute our human, technological, and financial resources into these different subunits – and how do we coordinate these different subunits into a functioning whole?

As typically revealed during the diagnostic stage of quantum transformation, most members in large organizations don't have a clear understanding of their organization's strategic plan (nor how to create it in the first place). Most members also don't have a clear understanding of how that strategic plan must then be fully aligned with the structural design of subunits, including the assignment of resources and authority from the very top of the management hierarchy all the way down to each member's daily job. Moreover, members know even less about HOW to redesign the organization's departments and work groups, let alone how to IMPLEMENT structural change throughout their organization. And because strategy-structure is a highly complex problem, it's not a good idea to treat it as if it were a simple problem that's then delegated to a very specialized function, such as employee development, human resources, or organizational effectiveness.

This widespread lack of knowledge about strategy-structure partially explains why so many members avoid or accommodate their boss or senior managers when it comes to revitalizing the formal strategy-structure documents and standard procedures: *Besides never having had the opportunity to understand what strategy-structure is actually all about, most members silently accept that they don't even have the right to challenge what is*

being done to them from above, since strategy-structure change has traditionally been the prerogative of senior management.

In many organizations today, the top executives instinctively hire outside experts (consultants) to occasionally "dump" a new strategic plan on the membership, which has been referred to as the "seagull model for strategic planning." But it's unlikely that members will understand – or accept – that consultant–driven, top–down, strategic plan. As a result, most members experience strategy–structure as being far outside their line of sight, outside their control, and outside their responsibility.

In this chapter, you'll learn how to thoroughly examine and then revitalize the formal systems of strategy-structure within a Problem Management Organization, so all members WILL HAVE an absolutely clear line of sight between their daily job and the organization's long-term strategic plan — which will be based on accurate, up-to-date assumptions about all the key stakeholders. Eventually, members will be organized into semi-autonomous subunits so they will have immediate access to virtually all the resources they need for completing their piece of the puzzle and, therefore, they'll be able to maximize their contributions to their organization's long-term success. When contemplating any significant changes to the formal systems, we always have to ensure that all the relevant decision trees across the entire quantum forest are completely available for defining strategy–structure problems, deriving viable solutions, and then implementing those solutions throughout the organization.

Many times now, I have stressed the importance of requiring ALL members to participate in the first three tracks of quantum transformation. This requirement is especially essential for ALL senior managers, because their self-identity – their ego – is most often squarely attached to their management position of power and control, squarely attached to their highly specialized area of expertise, and squarely attached to their cherished status–based office assignments. These "psychological attachments" have also been reinforced by a designated box on the organization chart that, depending on the relevant industry, is named something like: Marketing, Finance, Sales, Design, Cardiology, Underwriting, Biology, or Engineering. These long-standing, highly specialized departments are organized around similarly minded colleagues, who share a strong professional identity, all of whom have been working together in that same box, in the same way, for a long time – which further reinforces their common psychological and cultural bonds.

Nevertheless, if there is ever a time when senior managers WILL suspend their ego attachments and office politics in order to see what really can be done to revitalize the formal systems for long-term organizational success, it is after the first three tracks have achieved their purposes: Once an adaptive culture has been developed throughout the organization, once everyone has acquired the special skills for people management, conflict management, and problem management, including the method of assumptional analysis, and once everyone has learned what it takes to become a well-functioning team with diverse others, it becomes feasible to genuinely – and thoroughly – confront one of the most emotional, gut-wrenching, complex, and challenging problems that any organization can face: Are we headed in the right direction and are we properly organized to get there?

As with the previous chapters, I titled this chapter the same as my three-hour recorded course: Aligning Strategy-Structure Throughout an Organization. In that online course, I provide a number of workshop materials to help move the process along in the most productive manner: (1) Work Sheets on Exploring the Strategy-Structure Forest, (2) Work Sheets on Organizing the Strategy-Structure Track, (3) Work Sheets on Closing Strategy-Structure Gaps with Assumptional Analysis, and (4) The Process Observer Form, so every work group can continue to improve its group process, meeting after meeting.

THE ESSENCE OF STRATEGY-STRUCTURE

The term *strategy* often describes top–management's selection of the ENDS (what the organization is attempting to accomplish). But also, by necessity, the term *structure* has evolved to specify the MEANS (how the organization intends to achieve its mission), which is why we rely on that hyphenated term, *strategy-structure*. Two important transitions during the past few decades, however, have significantly challenged the concept of strategy–structure: (1) the evolution to a fast–paced, interconnected, global economy and (2) the evolution toward further self–aware consciousness in people, their organizations, and their institutions. Both of these recent developments require greater member participation and involvement in the formulation as well as the implementation of strategy-structure – because these topics generate very complex problems that can effectively be addressed only by making use of the different minds/brains of an organization's internal (and external) stakeholders.

WHY DO HUMAN BEINGS NEED FORMAL DOCUMENTS?

Right at the start, it's good to review the underlying reasons why all organizational members need *formal documents* – so we know why it's so essential to spend the necessary time and effort implementing the strategy–structure track: hence, getting all the documents right and also realigning them with one another. In fact, if the formal systems do NOT provide all members with the documents they need to guide their daily efforts to long–term success, it matters little if the first three tracks have developed a candid culture, enhanced member skills for defining and solving complex problems, and well–functioning teams throughout the organization. Maybe the members will be so much happier with an effective behavioral infrastructure, especially if they take the lessons and skills learned from the first three tracks and apply them at home or in some other settings. **But if the organization is pursuing outdated goals with obsolete documents, which are based on false assumptions about its key stakeholders, then it's not likely to survive — even if members themselves now interact very effectively with one another.**

To enure you won't forget the underlying reasons for having well-designed and aligned documents, I've found it worthwhile to imagine just how fictional beings on Mars, called Martians, are able to work in THEIR organization in a very different way than we human beings work on Earth. So please indulge me for a moment, even though you might be wondering why we are discussing science fiction in this professional book!

Apparently, "Martians" have very large brains with unlimited storage capacity, which makes it rather easy for them to retain vast amounts of information about their organization and their fellow beings. In addition, Martians can instantly and accurately retrieve all that massive information — much like having a very fast and reliable hard drive or flash drive on a computer. And if their computer brains were not amazing enough, Martians can use mental telepathy to instantly share all this information with all their coworkers. As a result, Martians don't have to ask their supervisors any questions and then wait around for answers. In fact, Martians have no need for any verbal communication. They also don't need to send and receive emails — so they don't need any kind of Internet service.

As such, Martians don't need to have anything written down on paper or have anything shown on a computer screen, such as a strategic plan, an organization chart, or a job description. And because of their perfect access to all relevant information across all Martian brains, even if certain strategy–structure documents were created many years ago, Martians could still retrieve those documents exactly as they were first created, word for word — without error, distortion, or selective recall.

As I'm sure you now realize, the mental and communication capabilities for human beings on Earth are very, very different: Our brains can only store so much information; we may forget what we have heard or read about sometime in the past; and we often, unconsciously or not, choose to remember only what suits us. And we almost always fail at reading other people's minds, since we continually make false assumptions about what others are thinking, including their motives, and what they're about to do. As a result of these cognitive limitations, we must regularly communicate with other people so we can effectively coordinate our efforts, whether with face–to–face conversations or through electronic exchanges.

Bottom line: **To achieve long-term organizational success, human beings need documents that regularly remind them of their organization's vision; documents that specify their work group's objectives; documents that say who has the authority to make certain decisions; documents that stipulate their job priorities and job responsibilities; and documents that specify the organization's standard operating procedures.** Actually, if human organizations took a full inventory of all the documents they've created during just the past few years, including all the emails that are written to clarify, interpret, and remind members of what they must do, I think most people would be shocked at the huge volume of their written documents, text messages, and email communications.

Regardless, we must appreciate these facts of human life: **Our mental capacity for storing accurate information is severely limited. Our memory and retrieval of stored information is faulty and distorted. And we can't read other people's minds.** Until the time comes when our human brains work like Martian brains, our organizations need crystal–clear documents that are up–to–date and based on valid assumptions of all internal and external stakeholders, beginning with the strategic vision of the organization all the way down to the specific job description that is assigned to every member.

An important point to always keep in mind: It would be far better to have NO documents in an organization, rather than to have out-of-date or inaccurate documents that steer members' behavior in the wrong direction. If there were zero documents, especially in a small or medium-sized organization, while there might be a greater amount of chaos, at least people could talk with one another and try to figure out what to do for long-term success. But if the formal documents are dead wrong and people are still being held accountable for the wrong priorities that are mandated in those documents (which might also be backed up by a rigorous performance appraisal system), the organization is much more likely to fail than to succeed. As I've said, in human organizations, **having no documents at all is better than having the wrong documents — but nothing is better than having the right documents.**

ARTICULATING AN ENGAGING STRATEGIC VISION

Now I'd like to emphasize just how crucial it is to create an engaging vision for the organization – ideally, *a strategic vision that deeply connects with each member's heart and soul.* I've read many statements of vision that focus on a desired financial goal, such as earning a particular Return on Investment (ROI) or increasing annual sales by a specified percentage, or gaining a certain percentage of market share, or becoming the Number 1 company in the industry, as measured by sales or using some other quantitative metric. But such monetary-based goals rarely inspire people. In fact, a vision that's couched in financial terms is usually boring, lifeless, and soon forgotten.

In sharp contrast, a strategic vision is much more engaging – and hence ALIVE – when it captures the crucial need that the organization is addressing for its present and future customers; or what inherent value it's adding to the lives of its customers and the lives of its employees; or how the organization is solving a major problem for society; or how the organization is working to ensure the survival of the planet; or how the organization is improving health and happiness around the world. There will be plenty of opportunities to use financial metrics when the vision is later translated into concrete objectives. ***But an organization should never overlook the huge inspirational value of members working for a company that is making a significant (positive) difference in the world.***

During the next chapter on the reward system (Chapter 9), I'll expand on the motivational benefits of developing an engaging vision, since that kind of lofty mission then leads to the creation of inspiring objectives for every single subunit and person in the organization. Moreover, developing inspiring job objectives that faithfully align with the organization's engaging strategic vision then encourages members to ask for – and receive – feedback about how their daily tasks contributes something meaningful to the lives of the organization's clients and customers. Being able to activate that higher–order need to have a positive impact on society is a powerful motivator for participants who've already completed the first three tracks of quantum transformation.

A statement of vision, therefore, should be vital, noble, and engaging, without being trivial, dramatic, or remotely ridiculous. Regarding the latter, it's certainly possible to stretch the vision to the point where employees and other stakeholders don't find it believable, credible, or realistic. To safeguard the possibility of developing a vision that stretches people's sensibilities beyond what seems reasonable, it's probably a good idea to get feedback from internal and external stakeholders so the vision is suitably engaging, without being silly.

MOVING FROM THE ABSTRACT TO THE CONCRETE

Numerous terms have been used to articulate the intended direction of an organization – often called **ends** as distinguished from the **means** of getting there. Some of the many terms used to describe *ends* include dreams, visions, missions, aspirations, ambitions, intentions, expectations, targets, goals, and objectives. The various *means* for accomplishing *ends* include such concepts as structural arrangements of people, tasks, technologies, money, materials, information, and documents (e.g., organization charts, group charters, policies, guidelines, operating procedures, rules, regulations, and job descriptions).

The most abstract expression for *ends* is most likely a **dream**, perhaps best exemplified by Dr. Martin Luther King, Jr.'s famous "I Have a Dream" speech, which he charismatically delivered at the Lincoln Memorial in Washington D.C. in 1963. But his dream (just like any other beautiful dream) must be made very concrete and operational, if that dream will ever become a reality.

For example, an abstract dream can be further translated into a clear vision, purpose, mission, or goal. These four expressions of "ends" become more concrete and operational, especially if we remember John F. Kennedy's 1961 goal of putting a man on the moon by the end of the decade. That goal was absolutely clear and specific, even though the means still had to be determined – and then implemented – for thousands of individuals in scores of organizations and institutions.

For most organizations, formulating a *strategic plan* is so much more concrete and actionable than the other statements of ends, since a strategic plan usually includes all these various elements: an engaging strategic vision, mission, market analysis (including Strengths, Weaknesses, Opportunities, and Threats, as in a SWOT analysis), long-term and short-term objectives – and some action plans. As a consequence of including all these *transformations from the abstract to the concrete*, **an effective strategic plan documents exactly HOW the organization's abstract DREAM and strategic vision have been operationalized into concrete OBJECTIVES.**

The most concrete form of a strategic plan is specifying the *objectives* that must be achieved in the short run, usually in a year or less. Of course, these objectives must be directly aligned with the general vision, purpose, mission, or goal of the organization. Otherwise, achieving the short-term objectives won't contribute to realizing the long-term strategic plan.

However, if an organization documents only its lofty dreams about a far-reaching goal, yet never translates those dreams and goals into a strategic plan, let alone specific structural changes to implement that strategic plan, the organization's intentions will remain in the corporate boardroom – while a business–as–usual paradigm will continue to dominate every member's behavior.

Let's now explore the specific structural *means* by which an organization can achieve its strategic *ends*, which also serves to make this discussion on strategy–structure even more concrete and actionable. ***I have found that focusing on objectives, tasks, and people, and how these are all linked together, provides the most practical framework for examining and then changing the structural design of the organization to support a revised strategic plan.*** Naturally, we must also allocate specific resources to every subunit in the organization, which includes assigning each work group the formal authority to make certain decisions, so the structural documents – the *means* – translate into effective action to achieve the organization's *ends*.

Not only must every member have the necessary documents and resources to do his or her assigned job, but ***each member must also see the link between his daily job and the strategic vision, which is formally defined as a Strategy-Structure Link — or an SST Link for short.*** If the LINK connecting the corporate "dream" to each "job" remains vague, confused, or misleading, then members' priorities – and behavior – will always be off track. Under the latter circumstances, as I noted before, it might be better to have *no* documents, rather than to formulate and implement the *wrong* documents, let alone to have documents that do not show a clear line of sight from each member's job to the organization's dream. In sharp contrast, ***if each person can clearly see the LINK between his or her job and the strategic vision of the organization, then everyone will be able to spend the right amount of time on the right tasks according to the right objectives.*** Allocating effort, time, and other resources in this manner will enable all members to add the most value to customers and other key stakeholders – and thereby achieve the strategic dream, vision, and goal of the organization.

I'd like to remind you of a key concept that I first presented in my Chapter 5 on Culture Management for Organizations. For that chapter, I made the important distinction between a belief in *Internal Control* and a belief in *External Control*. When the culture of the organization (or any subunit) promotes External Control, people feel helpless, since they don't believe that anything they do can make a real difference in their organization. Instead, they believe that whatever happens to them is determined by outside forces. But when self–defeating, collective beliefs in EXTERNAL Control are transformed into desired cultural norms that actively encourage a belief in INTERNAL Control, members eventually realize that their own behavior WILL make a huge difference.

Nevertheless, if the structural design of the organization does NOT provide the clear SST Link between each member's job and the organization's strategic vision, a collective belief in Internal Control cannot, by itself, provide the necessary line of sight. In addition, if members don't have the essential resources and the formal authority at their disposal to accomplish their tasks in an efficient and effective manner, merely *believing* that their actions influence what occurs will not be sufficient to overcome various structural barriers to organizational success.

ARRANGING OBJECTIVES, TASKS, AND PEOPLE

Because of the important role that SST Links play in creating "channels for success," I'll now introduce **the cellular unit of an organization,** which shows the building block for designing an aligned structure to support the strategic vision.

As Figure 8.1 illustrates, the cellular unit of an organization consists of people working on tasks with objectives in mind. A little latter, we'll see that besides people, we'll also add resources and authority to each cellular subunit, so members can, in fact, successfully complete their tasks to achieve their objectives. And if all members see the crystal clear link between achieving their short–term objectives and realizing their organization's strategic vision, then those SST Links will inspire members to contribute to something much larger than themselves.

FIGURE 8.1
THE CELLULAR UNIT OF OBJECTIVES, TASKS, PEOPLE

Objectives, Tasks, People

Figure 8.2 displays a very different kind of organization chart, which, much like a living entity, illustrates the internal growth of an organization by how it can be subdivided into many cellular subunits that become the structural design of an organization – both vertically and horizontally.

FIGURE 8.2

AN ORGANIZATION CHART OF OBJECTIVES, TASKS, PEOPLE

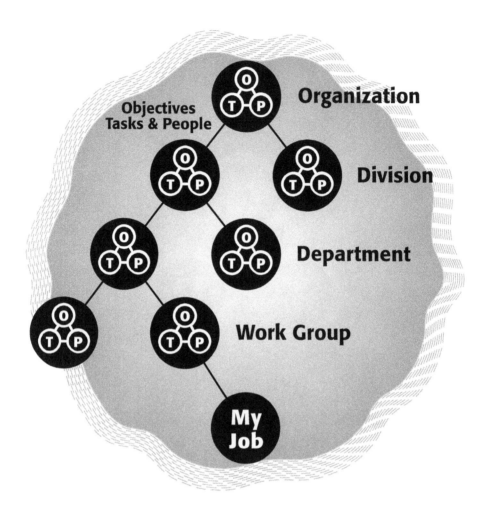

Typically, an organization chart only shows the formal name of every department and work group, such as Marketing, Sales, Design, Engineering, Operations, Accounting, R&D, and so forth. Sometimes an organization chart also shows the assigned tasks to each subunit and, other times, an organization chart identifies the boss or person in charge of each major subunit. But in most cases, the organization chart doesn't show all the people who've been assigned to each subunit, unless it's a small organization.

Rarely, however, does an organization chart include the specific objectives that have been assigned to each subunit – even if the name of the subunit implies a set of objectives. But naming the general business function for a subunit is not the same thing as actually specifying its detailed objectives.

But I'm not suggesting that an organization chart should be so detailed that all the objectives, tasks, and people are shown in every circle or box on the chart. But it's easy enough to illustrate a "big picture" chart on one page, with separate appendices that provide the detailed objectives, tasks, and people for every work unit in the organization. And with the aid of computer software, the SST specification process is not as tedious or cumbersome as it might at first seem. With the proper software, any member can easily access, and then review, any particular SST Links in order to see, quite clearly, how well various subunits are aligned with one another, and how each subunit contributes to the long–term strategic plan – and thereby the structural design of subunits has the potential to realize the organization's strategic vision.

Here are examples of objectives, which cover a timeframe of about one or a few years at the most: (1) to obtain a leadership position in customer service; (2) to improve the quality image of the organization's products/services; (3) to increase the domestic market share; (4) to expand into new international and domestic markets; (5) to lower the per–unit cost of manufacturing and/or providing products to our end customers; and (6) to develop an excellent working environment for all our employees Naturally, I purposely kept these examples pretty general – so most people can get a good idea of how to construct a short–term objective for any organization in any industry.

To achieve the specified objectives, here are examples of the tasks that might need to be performed in various subunits in the organization: (1) designing new products; (2) improving existing products; (3) consolidating databases; (4) preparing budgets; (5) conducting market research studies; (6) responding to customer complaints; (7) developing special sales promotions; (8) pricing new products; and (9) packing and shipping merchandise.

By the way, when I speak of specifying objectives and tasks in each subunit in the organization, especially when I speak of specifying DETAILED objectives and tasks, I don't want to give the impression that each subunit will become overwhelmed with unnecessary "paperwork" or mindless detail. As I'll discuss a little later in this chapter, since each subunit usually faces a different subenvironment and is thus trying to address a different kind of problem (adapting to changes in customer requirements versus complying with federal tax laws), the level of detail for specifying objectives and tasks will vary considerably from one subunit to the next, which, conveniently, fits with the personality style of the members who seek jobs in those specialized subunits. But for the time being, you only need to know that *objectives, tasks, and people must be specified to some degree for the important purpose of aligning all subunits to achieve the strategic vision.*

Here is a list of the prime attributes and skills of the persons who would be best able to perform the subunit's tasks according to their subunit's objectives: personality styles; behavioral styles; conflict management skills, people management skills; problem management skills; team and time management skills; technical skills; business skills; knowledge and expertise in a given field of study; emotional intelligence; and self–aware consciousness. The organization's human resources department is usually entrusted, along with the current (or prospective) managers of the subunit in question, to select or assign members who have the requisite skills and capabilities to successfully perform the tasks to achieve their group's objectives.

DESIGNING SUBUNIT BOUNDARIES

In the previous section of this chapter, I defined the cellular unit of an organization as consisting of specific objectives, tasks, and people. I showed you an organization chart as a vertical and horizontal arrangement of subunits, each of which contains a

SUBSET of objectives, tasks, and people. By establishing crystal clear SST Links among all these cellular subunits, members will have a direct line of sight between their job and the long-term strategic plan – which operationalizes the organization's dream, vision, and mission.

But we have yet to address this challenging question: What is the basis for determining the boundary that is established around each subunit, so each subunit can focus on a particular subset of objectives, tasks, and people? Are there different ways of designing subunit boundaries? And how can you tell whether one way of designing subunit boundaries is better than another? Asked in another way: How does the structural design of subunit boundaries impact on the organization's long-term success?

Consider this bottom-line question: *Are subunit boundaries cast in stone or are they based on outdated assumptions?* As it turns out, the older and larger the organization, and the more its external environment has experienced significant change, *if its subunit boundaries were established many years ago and have remained essentially the same ever since, you can be sure that the current arrangement of objectives, tasks, and people into subunits is based on false assumptions.* And this is exactly why we will make good use of assumptional analysis, within a PMO, to establish a new design of objectives, tasks, and people, which will be based on valid, up-to-date assumptions about the best way to arrange subunits for long-term success in today's world.

But before we get too far ahead of ourselves, we first need to understand the nature of subunit boundaries. On Figure 8.3, for the sake of simplicity, I show only two subunits, even though my comments are applicable to all the subunits on an organization chart. The key question, of course, is how to organize a particular subset of objectives, tasks, and people into ONE subunit, while organizing another subset of objectives, tasks, and people into ANOTHER subunit. Basically: *Where does one subunit end and another subunit begin?*

Figure 8.3 focuses on the all-important connection or channel that exists between any two subunits, which represents whatever materials, services, information, and/or decisions happen to flow across those subunit boundaries. This channel between subunits acknowledges that a boundary is not sealed shut, but is, instead, *a permeable boundary* – which means that tasks, decisions, and actions, and thus even PEOPLE can flow in and out of a subunit's formal boundary.

FIGURE 8.3
THE DESIGN OF SUBUNIT BOUNDARIES

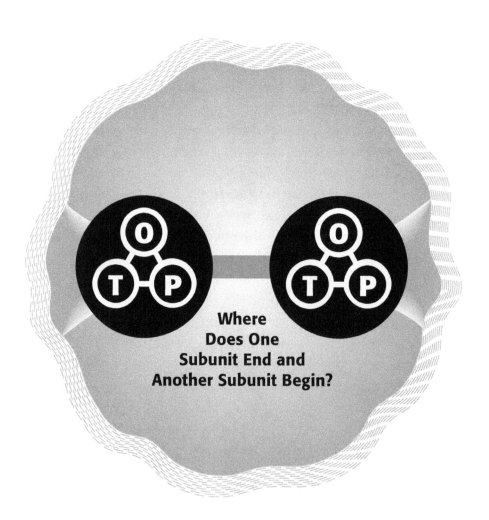

What actually FLOWS between two or more subunits has been referred to as "landing in the white space or open space on the organization chart" or, alternatively, "what falls between the cracks." Managing and coordinating what takes place in this open space entails more communication, more cooperation, and more coordination to get the work done than what would be the case if these decisions and actions could be handled WITHIN the subunits themselves.

FIGURE 8.4

INEFFECTIVE AND INEFFICIENT SUBUNIT BOUNDARIES

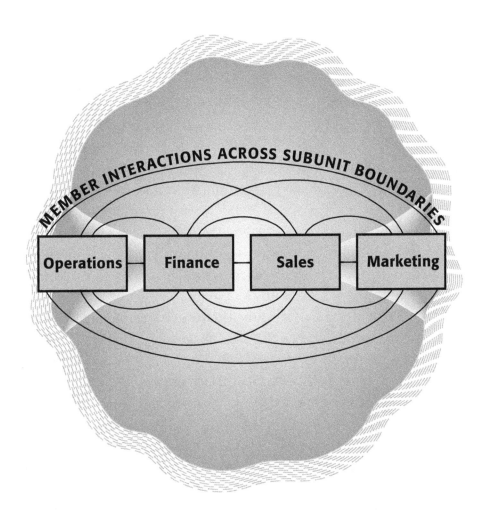

As shown on Figure 8.4, *as much as 80% of member's time is often spent working ACROSS subunit boundaries, while only 20% is spent working WITHIN subunits.* If you think about it, this frequent finding is quite remarkable and begs the question: *Why are members still assigned to these subunits when most of their work must be completed elsewhere?* One indicator that reveals the gross inefficiencies of such antiquated boundaries is when members must, as they claim, "beg, borrow, or steal" from other subunits just to get their own work done, since their own subunit neither has the resources nor the authority to complete the necessary tasks to achieve objectives.

In most organizations, only the subunit's leader or manager has the legitimate authority to help his members get their work done within their own subunit. But when members have to get information or necessary resources from OTHER subunits, their immediate boss simply doesn't have the authority to bring that about. Instead, members have to rely on getting the cooperation from members and managers in those OTHER subunits, which is the primary reason why it's so difficult to get work done across subunit boundaries.

Essentially, the previous figure illustrates all the interactions that might be taking place ACROSS those subunit boundaries – instead of members being able to complete their work WITHIN their own subunit. If "a picture is a thousand words," this telling image demonstrates why the current structural design no longer contains objectives, tasks, and people in an effective manner.

One of the quick-fix solutions that organizations often use to try to overcome such extensive cross-boundary interactions is to establish a number of cross-functional teams. If fact, in the worse cases, MANY cross-functional teams are established and, in fact, many members are assigned to two (or several) cross-functional teams – just to coordinate all the work that no longer fits within the current subunit boundaries. I distinctly remember one such organization where the many members who belonged to several cross-functional teams humorously articulated the folly of how senior management had been attempting to address an outdated structure: For their weekly "Friday Casual Day," these multi-team members wore T-shirts that proclaimed: ***"He who dies with the most teams wins!"***

Naturally, if the first three tracks haven't been implemented, then establishing cross-functional teams cannot possibly lead to the desired results under any set of circumstances: Without the first three tracks, members are prone to protect their fiefdoms at all costs and will probably resist sharing information and other resources with those other subunits – thereby obeying some of the cultural norms that are usually flourishing in dysfunctional organizations: "Don't share information with other groups. Don't trust other groups. Only take care of your own work group."

Incidentally, in that same previous illustration, I make use of the traditionally named subunits in business organizations, since most people can relate to those typical departments. Perhaps "in the old days," when the external environment was simpler and more constant than today, an organization whose subunits were designed around those *business functions* was highly efficient and effective. But as an interconnected environment became the new reality, these traditionally named departments could no longer contain the increasing demands for innovation and the ongoing introductions of new products and services. That's when much more interaction is required across subunit boundaries than ever before: How can we finance new computer-based technologies, which will then change how we manufacture our new products, which we must then market to different customers, which then requires our sales force to learn how to explain the new features of our expanded product line?

As another example of perpetuating the same old boxes on an organization chart, let's examine what goes on in universities: The several departments in the social sciences, as one example, typically include: Psychology, Sociology, Anthropology, Political Science, and Economics. But the social problems in today's world now cut across these specialties, which require cross-boundary educational programs as well as completely integrated solutions. Although several universities have established interdisciplinary departments of one combination or another, in most cases, social problems are still being researched (and thus approached) within the restrictive blinders (decision trees) of each highly specialized department, which makes it very challenging, if not impossible, to resolve today's increasingly chaotic societal problems.

As the marketplace has become more dynamic, complex, and intertwined, structural deficiencies have become quite apparent for essentially all the traditional industries, including healthcare providers, financial services, energy suppliers, food production and delivery, and federal, state, and local governments. Simply put: ***The old subunit boxes on the organization chart, which were designed for yesterday's world, are no longer relevant for success in today's world.***

I'm frequently asked this question: If the familiar boxes on the organization chart, such as Accounting, Design, Engineering, Cardiology, Psychology, Underwriting, Customer Service, Human Resources, Purchasing, etc., will change to something new, what will the new subunits be like and what will they be called? In most cases, novel subunits combine a number of functions that were previously structured into highly specialized departments, which means that considerable activity (member interaction) had fallen between the cracks in that "open space" or "white space" on the organization chart.

One novel, more encompassing department might be called, "Procurement, Logistics, and Distribution," while another novel, more encompassing department might be named, "Marketing, Sales, and Customer Service." But it's important to be wide open to radically different ways of designing new departments, which can differ across organizations and, of course, across industries.

By the way, when I present the material in Chapter 10 on the process improvement tracks, we'll see how ***the strategy-structure***

track should coordinate its mission with the radical process improvement track to help transform the traditional structure that was previously organized by "vertical business functions" into a brand-new structure that is organized for "horizontal business processes." The latter structural design generally does a much better job of effectively containing the necessary member interactions WITHIN subunit boundaries – within new boxes or circles on the organization chart.

In Figure 8.5, we see another kind of quick–fix approach for managing the increasingly busy, open space on the organization chart (before the organization is truly ready to address the root source of its strategy–structure problems). In this example, senior executives keep adding more layers of managers to coordinate all that increasing cross–boundary interaction, which thus adds more vertical boxes on the organization chart for managing all the intergroup conflicts that always arise when so much activity crosses the current subunit boundaries. However, just adding on a few more managers might not be enough to compensate for those outdated, ineffective subunit boundaries: Especially when members are spending more than 80% of their time and effort working across subunit boundaries, top management must then add even MORE layers of managers, so all that cross–boundary activity – and their conflicts – can be more readily addressed and satisfactorily resolved. Nevertheless, ***when members must keep crossing subunit boundaries to perform their tasks for achieving their objectives, executives keep establishing layer upon layer of managers who coordinate other managers who, in turn, coordinate even more managers who, at some point, coordinate THE WORKERS on the very bottom of the hierarchy who are doing the primary work of the organization!*** But this solution is very expensive for the organization and its customers.

FIGURE 8.5
ADDING LAYERS AND LAYERS OF MANAGERS

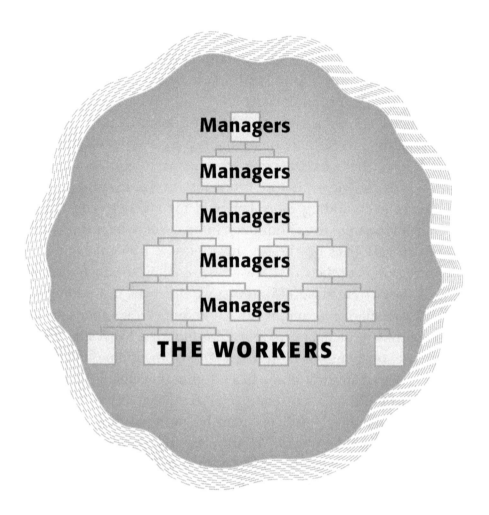

At some point, a critical mass of top executives realizes that implementing various quick-fix solutions (whether establishing cross-functional teams, extra layers of management, or elaborate information and control systems), cannot possibly fix ineffective subunit boundaries. Sometimes, executives come to this grand realization when it is brought to their attention that they have been spending thousands of dollars on teambuilding programs to improve the EXISTING subunits. ***Yet not much of anything has actually improved over time, since all those teambuilding efforts have been applied to the WRONG teams! Why improve the functioning of existing subunits when, in fact, most of the interactions among members still fall between the cracks on the organization chart?***

But before I describe the "PMO process" for revitalizing an organization's strategy–structure by identifying and then closing strategy–structure gaps, I'll first provide a few concepts that will make it easy for you to understand the nature of task flow and what it means to design subunits around different kinds of task flow – so objectives, tasks, and people are aligned for the future.

THREE KINDS OF TASK FLOW

Figure 8.6 illustrates the three kinds of task flow that can take place WITHIN or ACROSS subunit boundaries. James Thompson, in his book, *Organizations in Action*, presented a deceptively simple framework that remains one of the most profound contributions to organization design. Thompson defined three different ways that the performance of one task depends on other tasks, which I chose to symbolize as three different kinds of lines and arrows that interconnect one task to another. On this diagram, I use the terminology of **TASK 1, TASK 2, TASK 3,** and so on, to represent people working on a task in order to achieve an objective.

Pooled task flow, which I symbolize as a dotted line, occurs when two or more people can perform their tasks independently of one another, and then, at some later time in the future, their separate results can be added together, hence *pooled*, to produce useful output. **Sequential task flow,** which I depict as a solid line with a single arrow, occurs when a task needs to be completed by one person BEFORE someone else can complete another task. **Reciprocal task flow,** which I symbolically represent as a solid line with double arrows, occurs when frequent back–and–forth interactions and modifications must take place between two or more people in order to achieve some objective.

FIGURE 8.6
THREE KINDS OF TASK FLOW

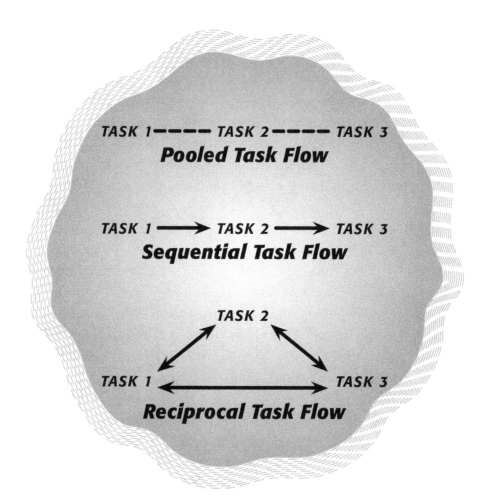

Now that you have a visual image of the three kinds of task flow, I ask you to thoughtfully study and digest Figure 8.7, so you can appreciate two radically different ways to contain objectives, tasks, and people within permeable subunit boundaries.

FIGURE 8.7
TWO WAYS TO DESIGN SUBUNIT BOUNDARIES

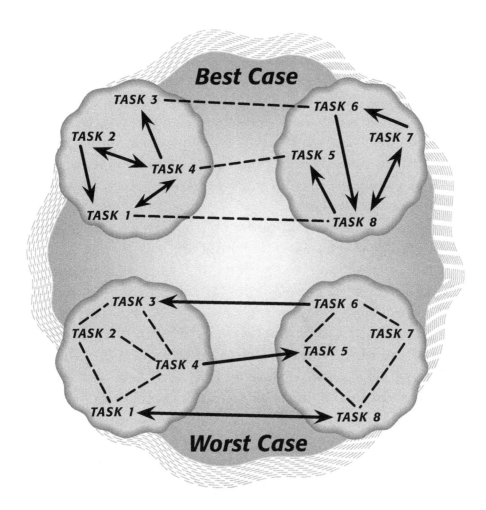

The top portion of this diagram illuminates the BEST way to design subunit boundaries. For the sake of convenience, I rely on just two subunits in order to illustrate this foundational design principle: **Each subunit should be formed to contain, as much**

as possible, the reciprocal and sequential task flow WITHIN its own boundary, thereby allowing only pooled task flow to pass though its boundary to other subunits.

In particular, containing sequential and reciprocal task flow WITHIN boundaries is precisely what enables each work unit to complete its work in the most efficient, effective, and satisfying way possible – since members will have instant and convenient access to all the resources and authority needed to perform their most interdependent tasks. Sometime later, these subunits can easily add together their respective outputs, since mostly pooled task flow now crosses their boundaries – as for the case when two semi–autonomous profit centers *pool* their separate revenues into corporate revenue.

Meanwhile, the bottom portion of that same figure displays the WORST possible way to design subunit boundaries. It again only takes two subunits to reveal the difficulties that arise when reciprocal and sequential task flow is permitted to fall into the white (open) space on an organization chart, while pooled task flow is contained within subunit boundaries. **In this worst-case scenario, members won't be able to get their work done within their assigned subunit – since most of their time and energy must be spent interacting with members in other subunits.**

Containing only pooled task flow within subunits unleashes a structural nightmare, which generates endless frustration and ongoing feelings of helplessness, since members are being held accountable for achieving objectives, yet they're not in control of the tasks that are needed to complete their work – since these tasks are located in someone else's subunit. Such an experience again reinforces members' belief in External Control – since no matter how hard they try, these members cannot overcome these rigid structural barriers to success. Only a significant redesign of subunit boundaries will further encourage members to believe in Internal Control, once they can easily achieve their objectives WITHIN their own subunit.

What is the underlying distinction between the best–case and worst–case structural scenarios? **Each type of task flow differs in** *the cost of managing it — which is primarily determined by the amount of time and effort spent in coordinating interrelated tasks, decisions, problems, conflicts, actions, people, and other resources.* Pooled flows are the least costly to manage, because the outputs of different tasks can be combined at some later time according to standard operating procedures. Sequential flows are more costly to manage than pooled flows, since more time and effort for planning and scheduling are required to make sure the right sequence of activity is taking place. *But reciprocal flows are the most costly to manage, since extensive time and effort must be spent on back-and-forth adjustments among several members as each one influences and is influenced by the other, so they can produce value-added output.*

Let's now investigate why it's less costly to coordinate work when the reciprocal task flow is placed WITHIN as opposed to ACROSS the subunit boundaries. First, WITHIN each work unit, psychological bonds often emerge from members being on the same team and reporting to the same manager, which facilitates cooperation and teamwork, especially with a healthy behavioral infrastructure. Second, WITHIN each work unit, especially when members share the same working space, the everyday physical proximity of the members makes it easy to initiate face-to-face conversations, which is best for resolving complex conflicts and problems. Third, as we learned in Chapter 5 on the culture track, informal peer-group pressure (based on an agreed-upon list of desired cultural norms that are further reinforced by an effective sanctioning system) also makes it much easier for members to influence one another, which includes how their work will be prioritized and coordinated on a daily basis. And fourth, besides these informal systems of personal influence and cultural forces, the reward system (which will be examined in the next chapter) is usually administered WITHIN the subunit, which then allows the manager to explicitly reward (or penalize) her direct reports for performing their tasks for achieving their objectives.

Even though virtual teams can manage their task flow over great physical distances and time zones by making use of group meeting software, having live, face-to-face meetings is still the most effective way to manage highly interdependent task flow, which also tends to deepen the bonds among group members.

Her's an interesting perspective that often gets overlooked in various efforts to redesign organizations for long-term success: Improving performance is never a question of how to minimize, let alone eliminate, reciprocal and sequential task flow. **How the work must be performed in order to achieve objectives dictates a particular kind of task flow.** The only question to address is whether to arrange sequential and reciprocal task flow WITHIN subunit boundaries or to allow that task flow to move ACROSS subunit boundaries, which as we've seen, makes a big difference with respect to effectiveness, efficiency, and satisfaction.

ALIGNING THE ORGANIZATION FOR LONG-TERM SUCCESS

Being in alignment is a matter of making sure that different aspects of a system support one another, encourage one another, reinforce one another, and allow each aspect to provide what it's been purposefully designed to achieve. The opposite, of course, is called *misalignment*, which is when the different aspects of the system get in the way of one another and, thereby, prevent each aspect of the system from fulfilling its intended purpose.

Regarding strategy-structure, a system that specifies where the organization is headed and how it's organized to get there must be aligned in several ways: First, we've already discussed the importance of aligning an organization's strategic vision with its structural design of subunits, so that each member will have a clear line of sight between his daily job and the strategic plan of the organization. Second, we must always do our best to contain reciprocal and sequential task flow within the cellular subunits on the organization chart, which then leaves mostly pooled task flow to "fall between the cracks." By designing subunits in this manner, members will have the resources and the authority to complete their tasks and activities in an efficient and effective manner, without ever wasting their precious time and effort on cross–boundary negotiations – so they can complete their work on time, with satisfying results. Essentially, ***purposely designing subunit boundaries to contain the most costly task flow serves to align members' time and effort with the organization's need for efficiency and effectiveness.***

But there's a third aspect of a strategy–structure system that must be properly aligned to achieve long–term success: ***Once an organization's departments have been designed to contain the costly task flow mostly within boundaries, it becomes readily apparent that each semi-autonomous subunit now faces only a subset of the organization's entire external environment.***

For example, one new, more encompassing subunit might be dedicated to conducting market research in order to discover the needs of *future* customers, and the identical subunit also has the responsibility to create the new products and services to address those futuristic needs. A second, more encompassing department might be responsible for performing a new business process of production, warehousing, sales, logistics, and service for *current* customers and their clients.

The first subunit faces a much more uncertain and complex portion of the organization's external setting, while the second subunit faces a more predicable, certain, and familiar portion of that external environment. As we'll examine in a moment: ***Each different kind of subenvironment must then be aligned with a matching subunit design – in terms of time orientation, the degree of specificity in objectives and tasks, and, whether to design a subunit for creativity or for compliance.*** In addition, we also have to realize that members' different ways of collecting information and making decisions, as nicely captured by those four personality styles (ST, NT, SF, and NF), must also be aligned with the internal design of subunits and their subenvironments.

Figure 8.8 shows how aspects of the strategy–structure system (i.e., four subenvironments, four structural designs, and the four people preferences) must properly align – hence, **FIT** – with one another for long–term organizational success.

FIGURE 8.8
ALIGNING SUBENVIRONMENTS, DESIGNS, AND PEOPLE

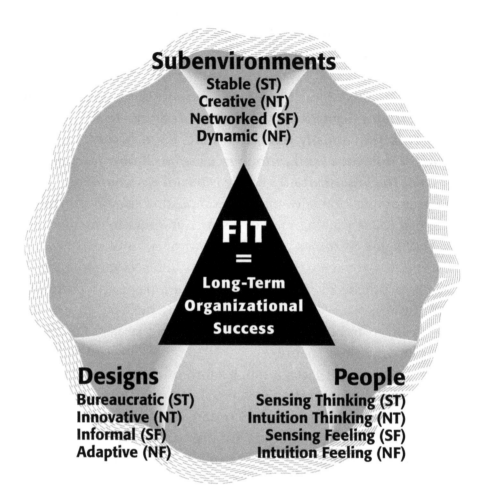

Regarding the four personality preferences that are displayed in Figure 8.8 above, Ian Mitroff, and I have repeatedly found that creating four groups, each based on a different personality style, and then asking each personality–style group to describe its *ideal organization*, produces four very different organization charts, as shown in Figure 8.9.

FIGURE 8.9
FOUR PERSONALITY STYLES AND FOUR IDEAL ORGANIZATIONS

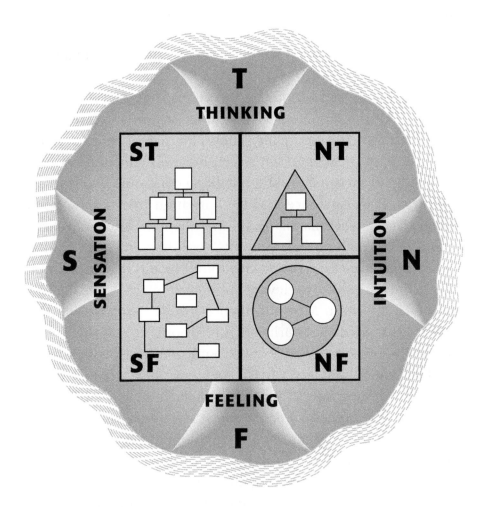

I won't repeat all that I previously presented in Chapter 6 on Critical Thinking Skills, but I would like to remind you that **each personality-style group provides an even more extreme view of an ideal organization than any of its individual members.** It seems that each of the groups invariably reinforces the common personality style of its members and then each group, whether consciously or not, *exaggerates* that mutually shared perspective, which dramatically reveals those striking differences among the four personality–style groups: Thus, the ST group offers an **ST²** version of whatever you ask those group members to describe, whether to draw their ideal organization or how to define and solve a complex problem. Similarly, the NT group offers an **NT²** perspective, and so forth.

In Figure 8.10, I present an abbreviated organization chart of how some of the familiar business functions are often designed very differently. This figure also shows the particular personality style that is most aligned with each business function's way of processing information and then making decisions. Two Harvard professors, Paul Lawrence and Jay Lorsch, in their classic book, *Organization and Environment*, found that the most successful firms had designed each of their subunits very differently, which they termed *differentiation*, so that each subunit would best fit with the unique attributes of its relevant subenvironment. Subsequently, Jay Lorsch and John Morse in their book, *Organizations and Their Members*, extended that earlier theory of organization design to include the personality styles of subunit members, which led to the three–way alignment of (1) subenvironment characteristics, (2) subunit designs, and (3) people preferences.

In sum, the process of *differentiation* is defined as establishing different subunit designs for facing different subenvironments for different people, which allows each subunit to maximize its unique contribution to the organization's strategic vision in the most efficient and effective manner. Although not addressed by the Harvard trio of Lawrence, Lorsch, and Morse, it's much easier for subunits to achieve their objectives when their boundaries contain, as much as possible, reciprocal and sequential task flow, while leaving pooled task flow to fall between the cracks.

FIGURE 8.10
DESIGNING DIFFERENT SUBUNITS WITHIN AN ORGANIZATION

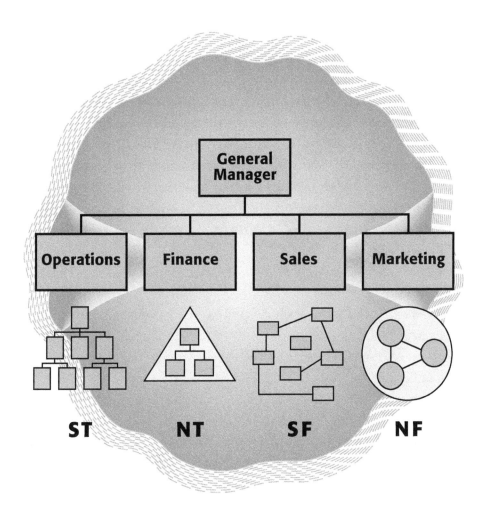

However, given our increasingly interconnected world, there will typically be some amount of reciprocal and sequential task flow that finds its way into the open space on the organization chart. As such, an organization must use a number of *integrative mechanisms* so the work that inadvertently seeps through subunit boundaries can still be completed as efficiently and effectively as possible. Examples of integrative mechanisms include: creating additional management positions; information systems; project teams; task forces; cross-functional teams; coordinating policies and procedures; and various rules and regulations. Basically, **the greater the differentiation among organizational subunits, the more that some integrative mechanisms will also be needed to coordinate these different elements into a fully aligned system of collective action — simply because it takes much more time and effort to resolve conflicts when subunits are composed of different people who naturally have different time orientations and different approaches to certainty, complexity, compliance, and creativity.**

But it's the allocation of resources that officially launches the new strategy–structure into action. The variety of resources that are generally allocated include people; work spaces; equipment, tools, and technologies; information; materials; budgets; support services; and, of course, formal authority to make decisions and take action.

ALIGNING THREE SST INTERFACES

Figure 8.11 reveals how strategy–structure must be deployed at three key interfaces – from the strategic interface, through the structural interface, all the way to the job interface. The **strategic interface** considers how well the organization's dream, vision, and strategic plan have been suitably translated into short–term objectives and tasks. The **structural interface** considers how well the most costly task flows have been assigned WITHIN – rather than ACROSS – subunit boundaries. The **job interface** considers how successfully subunit members are managing their attention to spend the right amount of time on the right tasks according to the right objectives, which will then be accurately appraised and then reinforced through a performance–based reward system (to be discussed in the next chapter in this book).

FIGURE 8.11
ALIGNING THREE INTERFACES FOR LONG-TERM SUCCESS

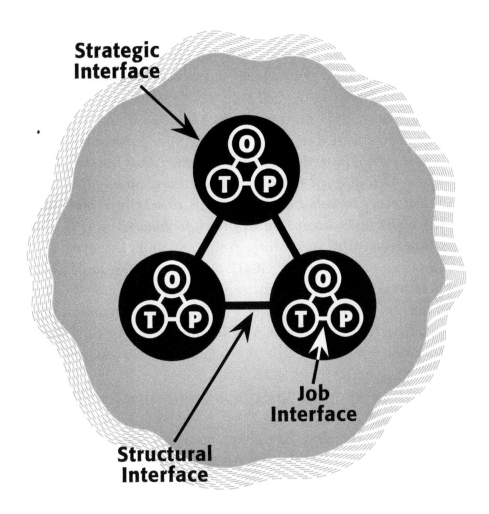

Strategic Interface

Job Interface

Structural Interface

It should be apparent that it's not enough to have two of the three strategy–structure interfaces aligned with one another. *All three interfaces must remain aligned at all times.* If not, it will be most difficult, if not impossible, to achieve long–term success.

Specifically, *if the strategic interface is NOT aligned properly, the remaining two interfaces are inconsequential.* In this case, the structural interface would be allocating the wrong objectives, tasks, and people into subunits – which renders members' time, effort, and skills irrelevant: Efficiency has no meaning unless the right objectives are being pursued and at least partially achieved.

Further, **if the strategic interface IS aligned properly but the structural interface is not, the job interface will result in gross inefficiencies.** In this scenario, members in a subunit would be unable to do their work in an efficient manner, because they are not in immediate control of all the tasks they need to perform in order to achieve their objectives, since some of these tasks have already been assigned to other subunits in the organization.

Lastly, **even if both the strategic interface AND the structural interface ARE aligned properly, each subunit must still make sure that every member is applying his time, effort, and skills on the right tasks according to the right objectives, if the job interface is to fulfill its destiny.** In this situation, however, since members already have the RIGHT objectives, tasks, and people assigned WITHIN their subunit, both effectiveness and efficiency CAN now be accomplished, which will provide all members with great satisfaction since they CAN provide the most value–added contributions to their organization's long–term success.

ESTABLISHING A STRATEGY-STRUCTURE PMO

The fifteen to twenty–five members who are selected for the strategy–structure PMO will represent all the levels, areas, and locations in their organization; they will also have demonstrated leadership during the prior three tracks of the program. Ideally, when the rest of the membership sees the list of persons chosen for the strategy–structure PMO, the response will be: "These are the right people to tackle our strategy–structure problems!"

The **shadow track** (the first PMO that's primarily responsible for scheduling, implementing, and evaluating the improvement program) is also responsible for managing the selection process for establishing this PMO for the strategy–structure track – and the shadow track is later responsible for establishing additional PMOs for the remaining tracks in quantum transformation. Two methods for choosing the participants for these PMOs are most popular: (1) receiving nominations from the membership (and self-nominations as well) or (2) setting up a job posting system whereby members submit a formal "job application" for joining the strategy–structure PMO. Please note: My *Logistics Manual for Implementing the Tracks* provides more detailed procedures as well as sample emails for using either (1) the nomination process or (2) the job–posting process for establishing the several PMOs for the completely integrated program.

Since only fifteen to twenty–five members will be involved in addressing the organization's strategy–structure gaps, **we have to ensure that the entire membership also has the opportunity to learn the same concepts about strategy-structure that the PMO members have received — so EVERYBODY in the organization can actively participate in implementing the strategy-structure solutions that are first derived by the PMO members and then approved by the relevant group of senior executives.**

The usual approach for ensuring that the most up–to–date strategy–structure knowledge is being widely shared throughout the organization is to videotape all the PMO workshops so all members can benefit from the consultants' formal presentations, the C–group debates, and the S–group's resolutions for defining the root causes of strategy–structure gaps, generating solutions, implementing solutions, and evaluating the results. The recorded videos can then be shown to the membership in various public forums – or distributed individually to all members so everyone can watch those workshop videos on their computers or mobile devices at their own convenience.

Once the representative members have been selected for the strategy–structure PMO, they assemble for an inaugural one–day workshop. Initially, some time should be spent on enabling the PMO members to get acquainted with one another (especially since they typically are drawn from different levels, areas, and locations in their organization and, as a result, may never have met one another before). Next, the members list and endorse the desired norms of behavior that will guide all their interactions (as an entire PMO community, in the subsequent C-groups, and then in the S-Groups). The PMO members also agree to a shared sanctioning system (combining the features of the sanctioning systems that they are currently using back in their formal work units in the operational design of the organization). Naturally, the PMO members agree to use a Process Observer (PO) during every group meeting: The Process Observer methodology is one of the best ways to encourage all PMO members not only to sustain – but also to improve – their behavioral infrastructure.

To help you see what's taking place in the strategy–structure PMO, Figure 8.12 reproduces the same figure that I showed you in Chapter 6 when we discussed the formation and functioning of the Problem Management Organization.

Once the PMO members have thoroughly reviewed how to make the best use of what they learned in the first three tracks of quantum transformation, the external consultants introduce the same knowledge about strategy and structure that's contained in this chapter. The goal is to provide all PMO participants with the most up–to–date and useful knowledge about strategy–structure, including how SST Links must be redesigned – and aligned – for those three primary interfaces (i.e., the strategic, structural, and job interfaces) in order to give the organization the best chance for achieving long–term success.

After the PMO participants have devoted some time getting acquainted and learning the core material on strategy–structure, they carefully review the diagnostic results that were presented several months ago (based on the diagnostic interviews with the membership as well as the organization–wide results from the Kilmann Organizational Conflict Instrument). After having been exposed to the latest knowledge for formulating strategic plans and then realigning them with a transformed structural design, the strategy–structure gaps that were previously identified in the diagnostic report become more meaningful. Naturally, additional strategy–structure gaps that emerged since the beginning of the improvement program might be identified, next analyzed, and then closed, as will be done with all other GAPS.

FIGURE 8.12
THE PROBLEM MANAGEMENT ORGANIZATION (PMO)

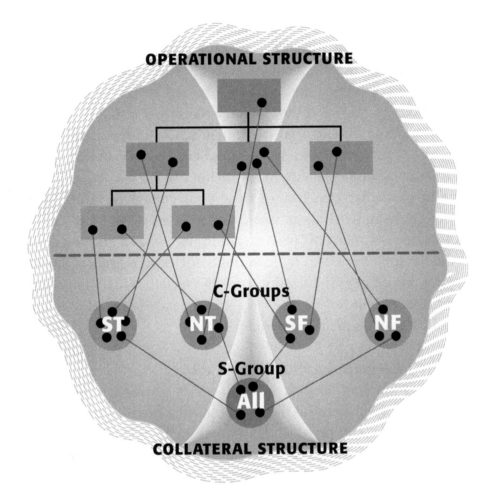

Because of what they learned during the previous tracks, the PMO participants are well aware of the significant consequences that would develop if they committed one (or several) problem management errors: If a defining error were committed while reshaping strategic directions or restructuring resources, then all subsequent attempts at transformation would waste their time. And even if an effective strategic plan and operational structure *have* been formulated, the inherent potential of the organization cannot possibly be activated if an implementing error is then committed. Even though the remaining three errors of problem management could further undermine the overall success of the strategy–structure track, making a defining and/or implementing error is still the most devastating of all.

Nevertheless, I'd still like to mention a certain nuance about Step 1 of problem management: sensing problems. If you recall, a problem is when a gap between "what is" and "what could or should be" breaks a threshold of acceptability. But defining a gap in this manner *assumes* that the initial expectation or aspiration for "what could or should be" has not been reduced or deflated – as a work–around strategy for reducing the size of any existing gap. In particular, one way to close your gaps is to lower your expectations rather than to work harder to bring "what is" closer to a higher standard of "what could or should be," and thus not settle for something less by lowering your expectations or initial aspirations. Some organizations use the term "stretch goals" just so members will not set their sights on easily obtainable – but eventually inadequate – outcomes.

WHAT CAN AND CANNOT BE CHANGED?

For all kinds of reasons, it might not be possible to redesign EVERYTHING concerning the organization's *ends* and *means*, even though that would be ideal. For example, there could be union management contracts that preclude certain changes in how jobs are designed, and certain regulatory agencies might require that designated functions must remain independent and thus intact, so these "oversight departments" can perform their tasks in an objective, professional fashion (i.e., without being integrated with any other departments or subunits). For example, if accounting must keep an arms–length arrangement with the various profit centers (even if there are several strong sequential or reciprocal task flows that will fall between the cracks), the unique criterion of reporting financial results might be more important to honor than abiding by that design criterion of purposefully assigning interdependent task flow into a more encompassing subunit.

But it should be apparent that having to respect too many constraints on the strategy–structure track would then prevent the organization from redesigning its subunit boundaries, which would thus prevent the PMO participants from transforming the identified SST barriers to success into channels for success.

The most pragmatic approach is to simply accept that there will usually be several constraints in the short term that must be respected, which does bring a dose of realism into the PMO process. And yet, enough of the organization's strategy–structure must still be open for change if this track is to support long–term success. Certainly, top management must realize that an overly constrained strategy–structure track will be perceived as a futile exercise. As a result, I usually challenge senior management to constrain the SST process as little as possible, so the participants in the PMO have as much latitude as possible.

During all those instances that I've been actively involved in facilitating the SST process for an organization, I always discuss a number of sensitive issues with the senior executive group – the same group who initiated the completely integrated program in Stage 1 of quantum transformation. I suggest to them that they must be completely forthright and candid regarding what about strategy–structure CAN indeed be changed and what CANNOT be changed, citing good reasons – which do NOT contain even the slightest hint that the motive behind any possible constraint is comfort, convenience, ego, or political expedience. I also ask these senior managers to uncover their assumptions behind any claims that some aspect about strategy–structure should not or cannot be changed, which helps to test whether any constraints are being unconsciously proposed for self–serving reasons.

If you recall, at the center of the Complex Hologram (Figure 1.3 in Chapter 1) is the "social glue" that connects all the systems and processes in every organization: **Culture, Assumptions, and Psyches.** Regarding the latter, we must always address this third dimension of the Big Picture, especially Psyches, not only when we consider how to first identify and then remove the damaging effects of troublemakers (as we discussed in Chapter 7), but we must also address the damaging ego–attachments that managers and members often cling to for convenience, comfort, and safety. Indeed, those ego–attachments, which always seem to fabricate the wrong reasons for doing anything, can seriously undermine the organization's desperately needed strategy–structure change.

In sum, it helps to ease the threat of change by distinguishing the short–term constraints from what CAN be changed sometime in the near future, for example, when the collective bargaining agreements can be modified during those subsequent rounds of union–management negotiations. In any event, **it's essential for senior management to distribute an official statement on the short-term constraints for the strategy-structure track, so that everyone knows, in the most explicit language that's possible, what specific aspects of strategy-structure CAN or CANNOT be changed — for all the RIGHT REASONS.**

PROCEEDING WITH THE PMO ANALYSIS

To be absolutely certain that the organization won't overlook any decision trees in the SST quantum forest (whether the focus is on defining problems or implementing solutions), **it's always good to form four personality-style groups (ST, NT, SF, and NF) when it is time to identify strategy-structure gaps (the most troublesome GAPS that were first identified on the diagnostics report and any new gaps that might have emerged since that time), which is Step 1 in the cycle of problem management.** The PMO then assigns those up–to–date GAPS into two categories, strategy and structure, since the strategy–structure problem will be more manageable if it is approached in those two separate channels for now, *ends* and *means*, even though the means will soon be explicitly designed to achieve those ends.

Typically, the four personality–style C–groups will be actively involved in a few or all of these initial conclusions: (1) the new strategic vision or strategic plan should be _____; (2) the new strategic vision or strategic plan should be implemented in this manner _____; (3) the new subunits should be organized as displayed on this chart_____; (4) the new subunits should be implemented in this manner _____. Naturally, every situation can be different, but most strategy–structure PMOs will conduct between two and four cycles of problem management, which propose and then analyze some very different initial conclusions for defining strategic problems, implementing strategic change, defining structural problems, and then implementing structural change. When this new strategy-structure has been revitalized and aligned, **the SST Links will be — must be — crystal clear to all members in every subunit in the organization.**

Once the four personality–style C-groups have debated and analyzed their four radically different initial conclusions about one of the strategy–structure gaps (and have also had a chance to further investigate and debate the importance and certainty of the key assumptions that underlie each set of initial conclusions), any remaining unresolved issues are assigned to one or more newly formed S-groups. As I suggested in Chapter 6, the use of several S-groups (not just one) is often recommended, so many PMO members will be actively involved in the synthesis process, which also helps to demonstrate the effectiveness of the entire process, since the several S-group presentations always turn out to be very similar, if not identical.

As first presented in Chapter 6, each S-group is composed of one or two members from each of those four personality–style C-groups, **whereby each member also has a balanced profile of conflict-handling modes.** Now that the first three tracks have achieved their purpose, the eight key attributes of the situation (e.g., moderate to low stress, trust, effective communication and listening skills, cultural norms that encourage openness, candor, and integrity, etc.) will allow the use of each of the five conflict modes, as needed. Ideally, PMO members will resolve the most complex and important aspects of strategy and structure on the integrative dimension of the TKI Conflict Model (expanding the size of the pie from compromising to collaborating) – while the less complex and less important topics will be resolved on the distributive dimension of the TKI Conflict Model (by dividing up the fixed pie with a combination of competing, compromising, and accommodating). Only if a previously unresolved issue were determined to be much less important than first thought, would an S–group then use the avoiding mode – so it could focus on *other,* more important, unresolved issues.

No matter which particular aspect of strategy and structure is being subjected to an assumptional analysis in the PMO, each S–group synthesizes a new tree in the strategy–structure forest – one that includes and yet transcends all the wisdom and experience from each of the personality-style C–groups and their exaggerated decision trees and underlying assumptions. Basically, such active participation of the membership in several C–Groups and in one or more S–Groups is precisely why relying on only a few outside strategic planning experts (who represent, at best, only one or two highly specialized decision trees in the quantum forest) cannot possibly provide what the members in a well-functioning PMO can create – and then implement – on their own, since they have already learned all the principles and practices from the first three tracks of quantum transformation.

When all the diverse members of the strategy–structure PMO (1) have completed their assumptional analysis on their initial conclusion and (2) have then deduced a new conclusion on the organization's strategy and structure, as based on their revised assumption matrix, the PMO then presents its strategy–structure recommendations to top management. Please note: Typically, the latter presentation is ceremonial, since several senior executives were purposely included in the PMO in order to make sure that the "powers-that-be" would actively participate – and ultimately support – the PMO's strategy–structure recommendations.

IMPLEMENTING STRATEGY-STRUCTURE CHANGE

The well-seasoned participants in the strategy–structure track now fully realize the absurdity of their attempting to implement change by simply having senior management publicly announce that the new strategy-structure on paper (or on a screen) will be fully operational on a particular date. In actuality, **it's only when members' behavior is guided by the revised strategic direction** *according to the new arrangement of resources will that new structure of subunits and jobs be in effect.* In fact, implementing a structural solution is a complex problem in its own right, since such a massive change involves a difficult adjustment for most members: Disbanding old work groups and forming new ones dramatically modify the distribution of power, friendships, and traditions in the organization. Consequently, management must be sensitive to members' fears and anxieties: "Will I get along with the new people in my subunit? Will I be able to learn the new skills needed to manage people with different backgrounds and personality styles? Will I still be an important asset to this company?" Working through these feelings will ensure a smooth transition to a new way of being.

Just as there are alternative problem definitions that, if not analyzed correctly, will then result in defining errors, alternative approaches for implementing strategy–structure change, if not analyzed properly, will lead to implementing errors. In particular, *implementing solutions that ignore Culture, Assumptions, and Psyches, which is the heart and soul of the Complex Hologram, will limit the benefits of any new formal system.*

At this point in the PMO process, the active participants in the strategy–structure track are asked to devise alternative plans for implementing the revised structure. To ensure that radically different approaches will indeed be considered, the participants again sort themselves into their four personality–style C–groups. The great variety of implementation plans that are discussed in these four groups represent four different "initial conclusions." Each initial implementation plan addresses these fundamental questions: "What is meant by implementation, how long does it take, how does anyone know when it is complete, and is it ever complete?" In their C–groups, the participants next surface and classify their assumptions to provide maximum support for their initial implementation plan. Following a debate of assumptions across all the four C–groups, one or more S–groups are formed to synthesize any remaining differences on assumptions by using, as much as possible, the collaborating mode on the integrative dimension of the TKI Conflict Model – especially since the eight key attributes of the situation should now encourage the use of all five conflict modes, as needed, due to the success of the first three tracks of quantum transformation.

As a result of their thoughtful deliberations, the S–groups often develop a Lockean–based agreement on these synthesized assumptions: (1) Members will experience any strategy–structure change as a potential threat to their self–esteem and self–identity. (2) Members need to know, in advance, what to expect during the process of implementing the revitalized strategy–structure throughout the organization. (3) Members are much more likely to adapt to change if the new situation can be understood as an improved situation from *their* point of view. (4) Members WILL change if sufficient time, support, and developmental activities are provided so they CAN change.

Based on these assumptions, S–groups usually deduce a new conclusion (i.e., a revised implementation plan), which includes the following five ingredients:

First, the switch from the current systems to a revitalized strategy-structure arrangement should proceed gradually (e.g., several months to one year in most cases), so members have the necessary time to adjust – mentally and emotionally – to the new structure that will implement the new strategy. Thus there is a rhythm and pace of change that can be nudged a bit – but should never be rushed. Too much change too quickly results in resistance; too little change too slowly leads to resignation.

Second, during the transition, the active participants in the strategy-structure track should continue to monitor members' experiences and feelings about the new operational structure. As a result of these assessments, information about the process of change can be provided periodically, according to members' needs: (1) What are all the *other* subunits experiencing? (2) What progress is being made across the organization? Honest answers to these questions will help put the human side of the endeavor in a realistic, proper perspective. But if organizational members are uninformed or misinformed, they will assume the worst.

Third, participation should be extensive during the entire process of strategy-structure change, so that members have a chance to understand —and accept — the new strategic focus along with the new structural arrangement of all human and technological resources, along with the formal authority that becomes vested in the new subunits. In particular, every new subunit can regularly meet to further develop its revitalized – and aligned – objectives and tasks into formal charters. These meetings can take place in a collateral arrangement, since most of the members' time and effort is still being spent in the current operational structure. Group members can also be involved in designing new control, budgeting, and information systems (or modifying the current systems) to give them the operating and strategic information they will surely need for effective problem management in their new subunit. (The PMO participants in the strategy-structure track can be involved in designing or adapting the centralized systems for the entire organization.) Furthermore, the members in each subunit can be asked to participate in the design of their jobs. Not surprisingly, ***the more that each job is defined by the same criteria as the design of every subunit — that is, containment of a total piece of work so that Internal Control is augmented — the more that each job will maximize its potential for high performance and great satisfaction.*** In order to realize this potential, each job description should guide the person to spend the right amount of time, on the right tasks, according to the right objectives.

Fourth, developing the right kind of formal documentation for each subunit — both group charters and job descriptions — should be guided by what's expected to achieve success in each case. While there isn't a perfect correlation between personalities and jobs, it's still very useful to match the cognitive strengths of the individual with the information-taking and decision-making requirements of the job.

And fifth, the more that each subunit has changed in terms of different objectives, tasks, and people, the more that certain aspects of the earlier tracks might need to be addressed again.

For example, the members in each newly designed subunit can be assembled for additional meetings to establish the desired cultural norms and the sanctioning system for the new subunit, since each member might have developed a somewhat different approach to culture in her previous subunit. Moreover, special skills training can be arranged to prepare members for their new work situation. Even if each member has already participated in the previous team track, the new structure of members usually requires further discussion on group process in order to develop cohesion, trust, and openness in the new subunit. But in most cases, there's little need for additional interteam building with the new operational structure: The new subunits were purposely designed to be semi-autonomous – linked mostly by pooled task flow – thus minimizing the frequency of intergroup activity.

As a reminder, Figure 8.13 reproduces the same illustration that I first presented to you in Chapter 6, which documents the PMO process side-by-side with the three stages of assumptional analysis. This PMO process might still seem a little complicated or cumbersome, since the various PMO activities usually involve one (or more) cycles of problem management and assumptional analysis, which necessarily include many PMO community-wide discussions, C-group discussions, community debates among the four C-groups, S-group deliberations and, then, the entire PMO community presents its strategy-structure recommendations to top management. I just want to remind you that my three-hour recorded online course, Aligning Strategy-Structure Throughout an Organization, provides you with the professionally designed materials for actively participating in the strategy-structure track in a most comprehensive manner: (1) Work Sheets on Exploring the Strategy-Structure Forest, (2) Work Sheets on Organizing the Strategy-Structure Track, (3) Work Sheets on Closing Strategy-Structure Gaps with Assumptional Analysis, and (4) The Process Observer Form, so each work group can continue to improve its group process, meeting after meeting. All these materials enable the participants in the PMO to thoroughly explore and utilize all the decision trees in their quantum forest.

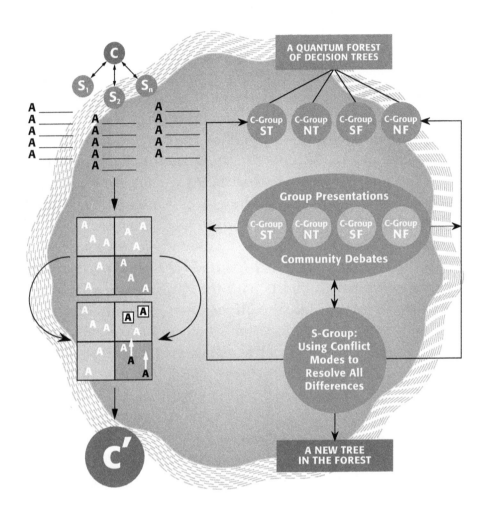

FIGURE 8.13

ASSUMPTIONAL ANALYSIS AND THE PMO PROCESS

As you'll see in the next few chapters, we use the same PMO process to address an organization's reward system gaps and for several other complex problems that are experienced during the last three process tracks of the completely integrated program. So if you aren't yet sure how the PMO process works in practice, you will have a much better idea of how everything works after a few more PMO applications during the next tracks of quantum transformation.

CONCLUDING THOUGHTS

Placing a new structure behind an engaging strategic vision completely aligns the organization's resources (efficiency) in the right direction (effectiveness), which makes members especially happy (satisfaction).

Nevertheless, the participants in the strategy–structure track must still coordinate their efforts with their counterparts in the reward system track, **so organizational members will, in fact, be motivated – inspired – to work on the right tasks according to the right objectives with ALL their energy, skills, abilities, and mind/body/spirit consciousness.** As we will see in the next chapter, while the strategy–structure track is exclusively focused on *alignment*, the reward system track is focused on *motivation*.

But there's still much more to do after implementing the five systems tracks: **The PMO participants in the middle two tracks must coordinate their efforts with the PMO participants in the three process tracks, since not all task flow is equal in terms of contributing to the organization's long-term strategic vision.** During the process tracks, for example, members prioritize the reciprocal and sequential task flow according to what particular tasks and decisions will likely satisfy – as well as delight – the organization's end customers. This highest–priority task flow is named: **business processes.** After learning new tools for process management, members explicitly describe, statistically control, and continuously improve their most *economic value-added business processes* that flow within and across all their subunits.

DESIGNING REWARD SYSTEMS FOR ORGANIZATIONS

THE REWARD SYSTEM TRACK

Organizations offer people a variety of rewards in exchange for the behavior they provide and for the results they produce. All rewards can be categorized into two basic types: intrinsic and extrinsic. **Intrinsic rewards** are those positive feelings a member experiences while performing his job. If the work is meaningful, captivating, and challenging, for example, a member experiences pleasure just by doing what the work entails. **Extrinsic rewards** are those "external things" that are delivered by the organization directly to the member (e.g., salary, bonuses, vacations, benefits, office furnishings, promotions, awards, and so forth).

To receive the intrinsic rewards and extrinsic rewards that are available in an organization, members must provide strategically desirable BEHAVIOR that will subsequently produce accurately measured RESULTS – commonly termed high performance. **All BEHAVIOR and RESULTS that constitute high performance in a quantum organization can conveniently be categorized into the eight tracks:** (1) BEHAVIOR that fosters an adaptive culture, the use of problem management skills, and effective teamwork within and across subunits (culture, skills, and team tracks); (2) BEHAVIOR that contributes to achieving strategic objectives – evaluated by accurate measures of RESULTS (strategy–structure track); (3) BEHAVIOR that administers the agreed–upon reward practices – by measuring subunit and individual performance, distributing equitable rewards based on that performance, and presenting valuable feedback to members so they will improve their performance in the next work cycle (reward system track);

(4) BEHAVIOR that improves "business processes" both within – and across – subunits, based on valid assessments of behavioral contributions and accurate assessments of customer satisfaction (gradual and radical process tracks); and (5) BEHAVIOR that first speeds up the rate of process improvement and then spreads this knowledge throughout the organization (learning process track).

Notice that all these components of high performance are focused almost exclusively on BEHAVIOR and only indirectly on RESULTS, since the desired BEHAVIOR produces the desired RESULTS – so long as members are working on the right tasks according to the right objectives. But as you'll soon discover in the next chapter, all members must also learn how to describe, control, and improve their *value-added business processes*, since this particular task flow produces the most sought–after **RESULTS:** satisfying and delighting the end or final customers who use the organization's products and services. Indeed, after the reciprocal and sequential task flows have, as much as possible, been placed within subunit boundaries, *the members in each subunit then select the most customer-relevant task flow as being their key business processes, which they'll explicitly describe, statistically control, and continuously improve to dramatically improve the RESULTS.* As we will see, not all task flow is equal, so members have to thoughtfully prioritize the task flow in their work group according to which "business processes" are expected to add the most economic value to their organization's customers.

A performance-based reward system that concentrates on assessing and then rewarding the most strategically relevant member BEHAVIOR will produce the desired RESULTS that are essential for sustaining success in today's world. Consider for a moment this likely scenario for a *non*-performance–based reward system: Inherently, the high performers are the most dissatisfied people in an organization, since they don't receive significantly more rewards than the low performers. Yet the low performers are usually the most satisfied members, since they receive almost the same rewards as everyone else, even though they provide *less* desirable BEHAVIOR that produces *less* desirable RESULTS. But the high performers (due to their more effective BEHAVIOR and, consequently, better RESULTS) have more job alternatives than the low performers. As a result, the high performers (the more dissatisfied members with numerous job opportunities) are more inclined to leave the organization, while the low performers (the satisfied ones with few available options) remain behind. This unintended migration of high performers to other organizations neither represents a good human resources strategy nor does it create and maintain long-term success. In contrast, establishing a performance-based reward system not only attracts and retains high performers, but also inspires them to excel.

At this point, it's essential that we appreciate that a quantum organization requires entirely different kinds of formal systems (such as a performance-based reward system) than a Newtonian organization. Figure 9.1 illustrates the timeline that dramatically reveals when the world changed from being fairly predictable to being largely chaotic, which is why the Newtonian organization and its formal systems are totally ineffective in today's world.

On the left side of this timeline, from before the 1950s and into the 1970s, you can see that the Newtonian organization is ideally suited for a highly certain and predictable world, where the distant future is expected to be pretty much the same as the immediate present. For any Newtonian organization, very little time or effort needs to be spent on questioning how strategy and structure should be revised for the future. In fact, doing the same old thing year after year, works especially well for a Newtonian organization that functions mostly within a regulated, domestic marketplace, and thus functions in a familiar environment that's staffed by passive observers and autocratic managers. Not much changes, year by year, in a Newtonian organization.

FIGURE 9.1
USING YESTERDAY'S ORGANIZATION FOR TODAY'S WORLD

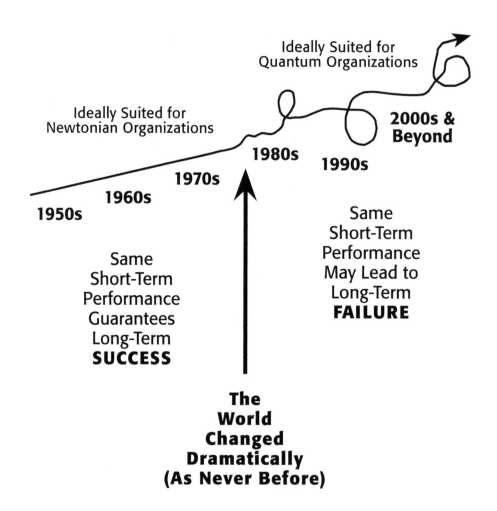

But in the late 1970s and 1980s, as shown on the center of this timeline, the world dramatically changed as never before. In that period of time, we experienced the deregulation of many industries, the political transformation in many nations, and the movement toward a diverse, global economy. And if that weren't enough, we also witnessed the introduction and rapid spread of personal computers in the 1980s and then the Internet provided worldwide interconnectivity to everyone in the 1990s.

As this timeline suggests, starting somewhere in the 1980s, only a quantum organization has the systems, processes, and people for adapting to dynamic complexity. In fact, a quantum organization ASSUMES that the future will bring about exciting new technologies, industries, products, and services, which could unfold in only a few years! In fact, only a quantum organization has the awakened participants, the behavioral infrastructure, the aligned systems, and the learning processes to create tomorrow's brand–new technologies, industries, products and services. Said differently: **In the near future, the quantum organization will lead the way, while the Newtonian organization will be left behind.** Why is this so? Newtonian organizations typically have dysfunctional behavioral infrastructures and misaligned formal systems. And then, to make adapting to changes in the external setting even more challenging, Newtonian organization require their passive members to accept the *top-down, non*-performance based reward system, which typically favors seniority, favoritism, and politics.

In fact, many times in my previous speaking engagements, I took a poll of the attendees who came from many different types of Newtonian organizations: "By a show of hands, how many of you can honestly say that your organization has implemented a well–functioning, performance–based reward system?"

But before anyone could respond, I would summarize these qualifications: "A well–functioning performance–based reward system regularly provides members with specific information on their performance BEHAVIOR and their performance RESULTS (at least monthly discussions). Also provided are suggestions on what members need to do differently in order to improve their performance (at least weekly discussions). And members receive significant rewards for high performance, but they receive only modest or even meager rewards for low performance."

At most, only two or three people in an audience of several hundred would raise their hand to acknowledge that they had a performance–based reward system already in place. The rest of the audience then eagerly wanted to know what companies have employed these fortunate people. The usual response from those two or three lucky ones: "I'm self-employed!"

Let's now consider one of the most perplexing questions that must be answered in the reward system track for creating – and then maintaining – a quantum organization: **What intrinsic and extrinsic rewards will inspire members to demonstrate all the BEHAVIOR and RESULTS that will achieve the organization's engaging strategic vision?** Asked in another way: What reward practices should an organization formulate and then implement in order to achieve – and then maintain – high performance in a fast-paced, highly interconnected, global village?

In this chapter, I'll examine how the Problem Management Organization (PMO) can be used to design a performance-based reward system for satisfying (and delighting) the organization's internal and external stakeholders – short term and long term. Initially, by formally rewarding BEHAVIOR that fosters the new culture, the enhanced skills, and effective teamwork, the reward system will stimulate all those improvements in the behavioral infrastructure. **Subsequently, if all members (both present and future) have good reasons to believe that the BEHAVIOR they provide and the RESULTS they produce will lead to important intrinsic and extrinsic rewards, they'll be inspired to spend the right amount of time on the right tasks according to the right objectives – which is what is required for achieving long-term success in today's world.**

As with the previous chapters, I titled this chapter the same as my four-hour recorded course: Designing Reward Systems for Organizations. In that course, I provide a number of workshop materials to help move the process along in the most productive manner: (1) Work Sheets on Exploring the Reward System Forest, (2) Work Sheets on Organizing the Reward System Track (RST), (3) Work Sheets on Closing Reward System Gaps with Assumptional Analysis and, of course, (4) The Process Observer Form, so every work group can continue to improve its group process, meeting after meeting.

CHAPTER 9

THE ESSENCE OF REWARD SYSTEMS

Without sufficient progress in the four prior tracks, it would be most difficult to develop successful reward practices for the membership. As shown in Figure 9.2, the previous tracks create the necessary pre-conditions for designing and implementing a performance–based reward system – which includes an effective behavioral infrastructure with an aligned strategy–structure.

FIGURE 9.2
THE PRIOR TRACKS AS PREREQUISITES FOR REWARD SYSTEMS

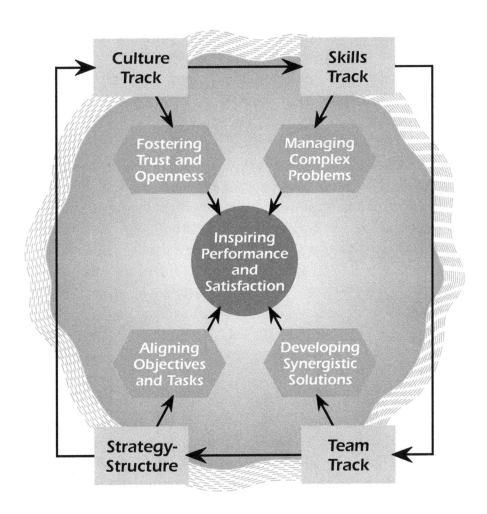

The Effect of Culture on Rewards

Without an adaptive culture that supports trust, openness, and information sharing, members have little reason to believe that achieving high performance today will result in receiving extrinsic rewards tomorrow — let alone that reward practices are honest and fair. In a dysfunctional culture, members believe that rewards are based on favoritism, politics, race, or gender – NOT on performance. Making matters even worse, organizations often keep their members in the dark by NOT giving them the information they need to decide for themselves whether rewards are based on performance – and whether reward practices are fair to all individuals, groups, and larger work units. How does successfully completing the culture track help members decide if it is advantageous for them to work hard (motivation) and to do well (achieve their objectives)?

It appears that a person's decision about how hard and how well to work unfolds from a deliberate thought process – until cultural forces take command. First we examine the situation to determine if there are any extrinsic rewards available that satisfy our reasons for being employed in the organization: **perception of rewards**. If it doesn't appear that available rewards match our **motives** for being employed there, we either leave the situation or do the minimum work to remain as a member until we have a better alternative. But if there *are* rewards that suit our needs or motives, we then determine the probability that we can do what is needed to receive those rewards: **expectancy of effort**. Basically, we examine what the job actually requires from us to do, day in and day out, i.e., **clarity of the job**. We also have to determine whether we actually have the **skills and abilities** to do the work, whether we can control the tasks and decisions that will lead to success, and just how much time and effort we must put forth to achieve high performance. *As long as we have good reasons to believe that desirable rewards will be forthcoming after we've achieved a level of performance that we can control, we WILL apply our best efforts, skills, and abilities on the right tasks according to the right objectives.*

Where do such beliefs about rewards following performance come from? *The formation of beliefs about a reward system is affected more by cultural forces than by some "expected value analysis" conducted by each individual member.* If members do not receive the extrinsic rewards they believe they deserve, the reward system loses credibility. As group members proceed to share these bad experiences with one another, they revise their collective beliefs (i.e., cultural norms) about the reward system: "Don't believe what top management says. In this organization, performance appraisal is the same as personal appraisal." Even if the documents indicate that the distribution of rewards is based on performance, members rely on critical incidents and shared stories when they decide who or what to believe. Consequently, *there may be a big difference — a reward system gap — between what is written on paper and what the membership believes to be the current reward practices. How can this gap be closed? There must be trustworthy information.* If information is not provided, people will surely invent it. This becomes a dangerous situation that almost always results in distortions that negatively affect performance.

Figure 9.3 presents, A Dynamic Model of Performance Cycles, which is based on Porter and Lawler's book, *Managerial Attitudes and Performance.* During a single performance cycle that could last from a few weeks to a year or more depending on the nature of the work, *group members might discover that achieving their objectives is more difficult than they had expected,* perhaps due to the lack of cooperation from other subunits or resulting from other barriers to success that block their best efforts. As you can see from the big feedback loop all around the model, during the next cycle, members then modify their *expectancy of effort:* their estimated probability that they will, in fact, be able to achieve high performance with a particular amount of effort. Naturally, if their expectancy for the next cycle is lowered because they had difficulty in getting the necessary resources during the previous cycle, they'll apply less effort in the next cycle, which produces lower performance, fewer rewards, and less satisfaction.

FIGURE 9.3
A DYNAMIC MODEL OF PERFORMANCE CYCLES

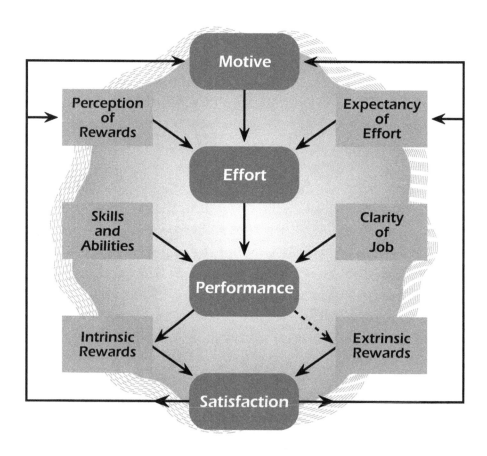

For the next performance cycles, members might continue to lower their expectations about achieving high performance. As a result, they'll put forth even less effort during subsequent cycles, producing lower performance and satisfaction, which creates a vicious cycle over time.

The same dynamic can happen with members' **perceptions of rewards** from one performance cycle to the next: Once a cycle is complete, members consider whether their initial perceptions of available rewards turned out to be accurate: **If members learn** *that there are actually fewer intrinsic and extrinsic rewards available to them than they had initially perceived, they will perceive fewer rewards before the next work cycle begins.*

Predictably, members will then put forth much less effort, which results in lower performance, fewer intrinsic and extrinsic rewards, and even less satisfaction. During the next performance cycles, members might continue to perceive fewer rewards, so they provide even less effort during subsequent cycles, resulting in additional reductions in performance and satisfaction, which further contributes to produce that same vicious cycle.

Notice the particular kind of connection that is highlighted between "Performance" and "Extrinsic Rewards" on the Dynamic Model of Performance Cycles: *That DOTTED LINE is meant to symbolize that not only are extrinsic rewards provided by an external source, but there might also be a time lag between the completion of a performance cycle and the actual receipt of one or more extrinsic rewards.* Perhaps it won't come as any surprise that an extrinsic reward is much more reinforcing – and more satisfying – the sooner it is received and experienced. But the more that time passes before a reward is actually received (such as a cash bonus or an award), the less impact it will have on the member. In the worse case, just consider a member who receives a cash award three years after the very successful completion of a project. Upon receipt, the member says to himself: "I vaguely remember that project. I've completed numerous projects since then." The participants in the reward system track will consider the best timeline for distributing extrinsic rewards, so the reward system will not only encourage high performance, but will also provide the membership with as much satisfaction as possible.

Incidentally, much like pouring salt into an open wound, out of defensiveness from being in an organization that provides few rewards while making it difficult to achieve objectives, members may come to the conclusion that they no longer want what their organization claims to make available to them. By deciding that the organization can no longer fulfill their original reasons for becoming a dutiful member, thereby decreasing the strength of the **motive** that brought them into the situation in the first place, we will witness an additional decline in effort, performance, and satisfaction. With such a vicious cycle, members then do the bare minimum to remain in the organization – until they leave.

On Figure 9.4, I show a simple graph that depicts two kinds of performance cycles: *a GROWTH cycle and a VICIOUS cycle*. On this graph, the Y-axis reflects the level of performance, one cycle after another, depending on the nature of the work for that particular subunit or member. The X-axis shows the TIME that's involved in the sequence of multiple performance cycles.

FIGURE 9.4
GROWTH VERSUS VICIOUS PERFORMANCE CYCLES

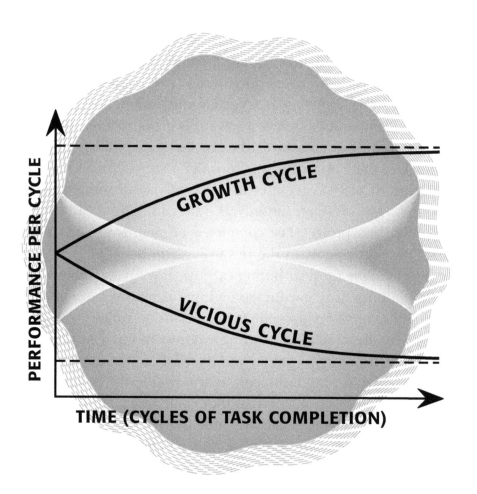

Regardless of what level of analysis is selected (such as an organization, a subunit, or a job) and what timeframe is relevant (one month, six months, or a year), this graph demonstrates the long–term consequences when members adjust their beliefs and perceptions about the reward system, which then directly affects their subsequent effort, performance, and satisfaction.

A vicious cycle emerges when members regularly perceive fewer rewards, reduce their expectations of what might result if they put forth even more effort, or decide they no longer want (motive) what the organization is offering. That dotted line at the bottom of the diagram represents the minimal performance level that must be achieved for either a member or a subunit to remain in the organization.

But it's also possible that a growth cycle might emerge: At first, members might have been somewhat pessimistic about what rewards are available and what it takes to perform well. But cycle after cycle, they are pleasantly surprised to discover that they CAN achieve success by putting forth the right effort on the right tasks according to the right objectives. Members might also discover that there are even more rewards available than they had initially perceived, which convinces members to further modify their perceptions AND expectations in a positive direction — for the benefit of all key stakeholders.

During every subsequent performance cycle, members then put forth more effort, which then results in higher performance, more intrinsic and extrinsic rewards, and greater satisfaction. But such a growth cycle has its limits, too, which is represented by the dotted line on the top portion of the figure: The organization can only grow so much and so quickly, which puts a limit on the amount of extrinsic rewards that can be distributed to members at any time.

It is important to appreciate that Newtonian organizations, with their autocratic, top–down, *non*-performance–based reward systems, are attempting to survive on the lower dotted line with a vicious cycle, which reveals a declining pattern of performance cycles. *But quantum organizations, with their well-functioning performance-based reward systems, still have the best chance of surviving in our chaotic world by functioning in the middle range or even thriving in the upper range of the graph, which represents the membership's sustained level of TREMENDOUS enthusiasm, passion, creativity, and success in one performance cycle after another.*

Now that I've presented the material on performance cycles, let's get back to the key question that powerfully affects whether an organization will experience a growth cycle or a vicious cycle: **Does the current reward system give members the information they need to judge its credibility?** The participants in the reward system track are usually surprised when they realize that crucial information about their own reward system is held in complete secrecy. Although the participants appreciate that many people consider wages and salaries as being personal and confidential, they also recognize that there's a lot of room between complete secrecy and full disclosure. Even if salaries are kept secret, most members would like to know the salary ranges of different jobs, the ranges of cash bonuses, and the average percentage of salary increases, one performance cycle after another.

Moreover, it may be useful to make available – every year – the performance ratings of every subunit, including the ratings of individual members, along with the amount of increases in salaries and bonuses – or at least the percentage change in both. Such information is absolutely vital for determining whether the distribution of extrinsic rewards is based on performance. It is seldom necessary to reveal each member's *actual* salary, however, because that is determined by factors other than performance: the demand and supply conditions for the job at time of entry, education, experience, and the prior levels of performance that have resulted in accumulated increases in base salary.

Porter, Lawler, and Hackman succinctly express the dilemma of secretive versus open reward systems:

"Secrecy about ... pay rates seems to be an accepted practice in many organizations. However, organizations typically do not keep secret how other extrinsic rewards are administered. They do not keep promotions or who gets certain status symbols secret; in fact, they publicize these things. Why then do they keep salaries secret, and what are the effects of keeping them secret? It is usually argued that the pay of individuals is kept secret in order to increase pay satisfaction. Presumably secrecy increases satisfaction because if employees knew what other employees were earning, they would be more dissatisfied with their own pay. This may in fact be true in organizations where the pay system is chaotic and cannot be rationally defended, but it is not clear that it is better to keep pay information secret when it is being well administered. In fact, there is evidence that keeping it secret may increase dissatisfaction and make it more difficult to use it as a motivator." (pages 354–355)

With further discussion on this controversial subject of open versus secretive reward practices, members quickly realize how the culture track has prepared everyone for a more open reward system. Indeed, by the time the membership has progressed to this fifth track, almost all work units have developed norms that encourage the open sharing of information about their complex business problems as well as the financial performance of the organization itself. Extending these norms to the open display of reward system information is not a difficult adjustment in most cases. *Since the culture track has encouraged open information and candid discussions about almost everything else going on, it would be rather hypocritical to keep members in the dark while they decide whether to risk their dedicated efforts for the promise of extrinsic rewards.*

Participants often discover an additional benefit that derives from an OPEN reward system: It helps keep everybody honest! When information is distributed about performance evaluations and the corresponding distribution of extrinsic rewards that are based on those performance appraisals, any gross inequities and questionable reward practices become transparent. *Therefore, all managers will be inclined to administer an OPEN REWARD SYSTEM in a very fair and equitable manner — which further promotes organization-wide trust and thus provides members with additional intrinsic rewards.*

THE EFFECT OF SKILLS ON REWARDS

Regarding the skills track, it would be incredibly difficult to achieve high performance – and thereby receive lots of extrinsic rewards – if members could not address and resolve the many complex problems that come their way. *By being able to surface and revise assumptions behind different problem definitions and implementation plans, members will not only experience intrinsic rewards, but they'll also be able to bypass the problem management errors that would undermine their performance.* Not achieving subunit objectives, for example, could certainly result from having made false assumptions about what suppliers can provide and what customers want. Or deriving a solution to a product or service problem, but then failing to anticipate the customer's particular use of that solution – its implementation – will also fail to achieve the desired results. But if all members are skilled in problem management and assumptional analysis, they will likely prevent such errors before any damage is done.

Conveniently, since members have already learned to choose (and use) each conflict-handling mode effectively depending on the eight key attributes in the situation, they'll be able to resolve the stream of conflicts that inevitably arise during the five steps of problem management, the stages of assumptional analysis, and especially during their participation in a PMO's S-group – when a new conclusion is deduced from the radically different assumptions that were initially surfaced and then debated across the four personality-style C-groups.

THE EFFECT OF TEAMS ON REWARDS

Regarding the team track, participating in a highly effective group process is not only intrinsically satisfying to members; it's also the ideal way to define and solve complex problems. Instead of making use of just one or a few decision trees in the quantum forest, members can explore many divergent viewpoints – and thus see old problems from new perspectives. *But this extensive (and satisfying) use of problem management can only occur if effective group process allows members to take full advantage of all the wisdom and experience in their subunits.* Ironically, when an operational structure is specifically designed to contain the sequential and reciprocal task flows within boundaries, high performance within a subunit is especially dependent on each member providing the BEHAVIOR and RESULTS that's needed by all the other members in the subunit. Such interdependence is conspicuous when one member's output must be combined in a particular sequence with the tasks and activities of the other members in that same subunit, or requires mutual adjustments among subunit members. *Hence, high interdependence among members of the same subunit demands effective group process.* This is one reason why the team track must always precede the strategy–structure track – so highly interdependent members of the new subunits can indeed achieve high performance and then receive both intrinsic and extrinsic rewards.

THE EFFECT OF STRATEGY-STRUCTURE ON REWARDS

The strategy–structure track does a few additional things for the benefit of the reward system track. It should now be evident that the notion of high–performance is basically pointless if the strategic interface has not been addressed. High performance is based on the important assumption that the right objectives are being pursued: to satisfy – and delight – customers and other key stakeholders. As discussed, the painstaking process of using assumptional analysis during the strategy–structure PMO helps ensure that an engaging strategic vision has been developed and then translated into clear, concrete objectives for every subunit and member throughout the organization. In fact, **the strategic, structural, and job interfaces must all be appropriately aligned and effectively implemented in order for members to achieve high performance within their subunits — and then receive all the rewards they desire and deserve.**

Also addressed in the strategy–structure track is the dilemma that extrinsic rewards cannot be correctly distributed according to performance if RESULTS cannot be measured accurately. **An accurate measure — as a numerical score — is composed of two chief qualities: reliability and validity. RELIABILITY concerns whether several independent raters obtain the same number. VALIDITY considers whether the number incorporates the true and complete value of the subunit or individual's contributions to present and future organizational success.**

Often measures are chosen to evaluate each unit's RESULTS with respect to their reliability (number of patents registered or number of customers serviced), not necessarily because those measures assess the right things (economic value added). Thus the ease of finding and then using a reliable measure typically overshadows the special challenges of developing a valid one – which suggests that numerous measures might be rooted in a false assumption: If it can be measured easily, it must be valid.

Participants in the reward system track, drawing from their better understanding of accurate measurement as well as their continuing interaction with participants in the strategy–structure track, now experience this fundamental insight: **When there are many sequential and reciprocal task flows that move between subunit boundaries, it is virtually impossible to establish an accurate measure of RESULTS — one that is reliable as well as valid — except for the organization as a whole** (i.e., profitability, net cash flow, or return on capital). Let's consider the situation in which subunits are structured according to functional specialties:

Every subunit is so interrelated with other subunits that results cannot be measured for any one subunit; each work group's true value to the organization is completely intermingled with its task flows to and from other subunits. Thus each work unit's output may have measurable value ONLY when it is interconnected – sequentially and reciprocally – with the task flow of other units. A research and development (R&D) subunit has limited value, for example, unless its creative outputs are then designed into commercial products by engineering, which next are produced by manufacturing, and which then are sold and distributed to customers by sales.

When several interrelated subunits are formed into a more encompassing unit, however, it is so much easier to construct accurate measures of RESULTS – such as restructuring all the functions that provide one product line into a larger unit, such as a Strategy Business Unit (SBU), which then can be a cash–flow center – as long as the other SBUs remain operationally separate from one another.

Now participants in the reward system track understand how the successful completion of the strategy–structure track sets the stage for the accurate measurement of RESULTS as close to the subunit level as possible – given the dynamics of task flows. The more that an organization is structured to contain the most vital task flows within its subunit boundaries, the more that accurate measures of RESULTS are germane to these semi–autonomous subunits. These valid and reliable assessments of performance outcomes can then be related to extrinsic rewards within each subunit, which can be rationally defended and can therefore be openly shared throughout the organization. Further, the more that each job has been designed to contain an interrelated set of tasks under the *Internal Control* of each member, the more that RESULTS can be accurately measured at the member level (e.g., reductions in process costs and cycle time for a self-contained part of a value-added process) – which also provides the basis for distributing extrinsic rewards to the individual members of each subunit. These "rewards–for–performance" distributions to individual members can be made public within the appropriate sections and departments in the organization – as long as the boundaries of privacy (e.g., individual salaries) are respected.

ESTABLISHING THE REWARD SYSTEM PMO

Assessing every jobholder's BEHAVIOR and RESULTS – and then equitably distributing rewards to members based on these measures – represents a complex problem. Thus another version of the PMO should be used for the reward system track in order to minimize all the errors of problem management, particularly defining and implementing errors. With this purpose in mind, a collateral structure for the reward system PMO can be formed to represent the organization's revitalized strategy–structure. Thus, even if members are still spending most of their time in their old subunits as the new structure of subunits is being implemented, the new reward system should be established for the most recent arrangement of objectives, tasks, and people into subunits.

Once again, it's the shadow track that carefully selects fifteen to twenty-five participants to work on the organization's reward system gaps – a different set of participants from those who are working on the strategy–structure gaps (although a little overlap in membership in both tracks often proves to be very helpful for effectively aligning ALL the formal systems in the organization). As before, the shadow track solicits and reviews: (1) nominations from the membership (also including self-nominations) or (2) job applications for the "positions" in the reward system PMO. The same criteria are used for the selection: The participants should represent all areas, levels, and locations in the organization (in this case, according to the newly designed operational structure); they should exemplify the desired norms and the use of problem management and conflict management skills; they have clout.

As with the previous track, we have to ensure that the rest of the membership has the chance to learn the same instructional materials about reward systems that the PMO members receive, so EVERYONE in the organization can truly appreciate and later successfully implement the particular reward systems solutions that are first derived by the PMO members and then approved by the relevant group of senior management. In this regard, the organization should videotape each PMO session so all members can also learn from the consultants' presentations, the C-group debates, and the S-group resolutions. These recorded videos can then be shown to the membership in various public forums – or distributed separately to members so they can watch the videos at their convenience on their own computers or tablets.

Once the final set of participants have been selected for the reward system PMO, they are brought together for an inaugural one-day workshop, where they can get better acquainted before they dive into the work. Next, the members list and endorse the desired norms of behavior that will guide their discussions (as an entire PMO community, in the initial C-groups, and the eventual S-Groups). The PMO members also agree to a shared sanctioning system. Of course, the PMO participants pledge to use a Process Observer (PO) during every group meeting.

In that initial all-day workshop, the consultants then present material to the PMO participants on such topics as motivation and need theories, intrinsic and extrinsic rewards, reliable and valid measures, behavioral rating scales, open versus secretive reward systems, alternative performance cycles (i.e., growth and vicious cycles), and legal issues in the design and administration of reward systems. In addition, alternative reward systems are presented that combine some of the following distinctions: piece rate versus hourly rate; hourly rate versus salary; skill-based pay versus job-based pay; cash bonuses; gain sharing versus profit sharing; and fixed versus flexible fringe benefits. In most cases, external consultants and human resources specialists instill in the PMO participants the most practical working knowledge on the purpose, design, and functioning of reward systems.

During this first workshop, the participants in the reward system track also review the diagnostic results that were first presented by the external consultants during the second stage of the completely integrated program. The participants uncover new meaning in the gaps that were initially identified during the diagnostics interviews and the survey results from the Kilmann Organizational Conflict Instrument (KOCI).

In the remaining workshops, the participants in the reward system track also meet with their counterparts in the strategy-structure track: Such SST-RST discussions continue during the implementation of the new operational structure and the new reward system. This exchange of "progress reports" (while also making adjustments in strategy–structure and reward systems) helps to ensure that ALL the formal systems in the organization are correctly aligned and thus continually reinforce one another. The PMO participants in the reward system track also maintain two-way communication with the rest of the membership – a process that encourages organization-wide understanding and commitment to all proposed solutions.

FROM NEWTONIAN TO QUANTUM REWARD SYSTEMS

The key question of what really motivates members to high performance (either as individuals or as groups) is deeply rooted in that evolutionary distinction between "passive observers" and "active participants" (let alone, "enlightened participants"), as first illustrated via Figure 1.2 in Chapter 1. For your convenience, I show that same diagram again in Figure 9.5.

An organization that mostly uses external reward practices (such as pay and fringe benefits) in order to PUSH its members to comply with all job assignments and work procedures will surely attract and retain PASSIVE OBSERVERS. Alternatively, an organization that predominantly relies on internal reward practices (e.g., self-designing and self-managing systems) in order to INSPIRE its members toward high performance will attract and retain ACTIVE PARTICIPANTS and ENLIGHTENED PARTICIPANTS. Moreover, an organization that recognizes the amazing potential of human beings (especially their self-aware consciousness) will also inspire its members to bring their heart and soul to bear on all tasks, decisions, problems, and conflicts. Unquestionably, an organization's investment in expanding its members' mind/body/spirit consciousness will attract and retain people who are internally inspired to learn, grow, develop, and evolve – and will give their "all" to a larger purpose.

FIGURE 9.5
THE EVOLUTION OF HUMAN BEINGS

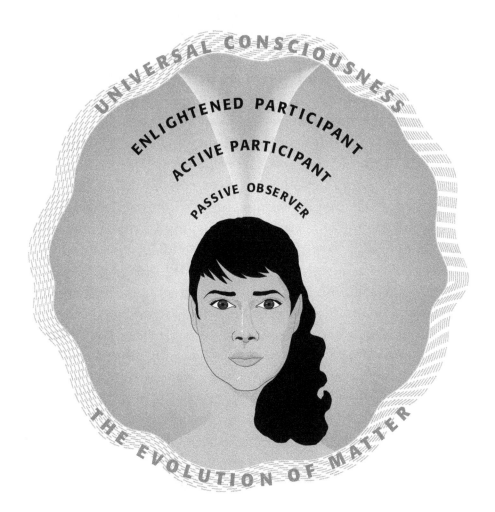

In a Newtonian organization, motivation (which is derived from the Latin word "movere," meaning "to move") is addressed by applying external forces on passive observers — mandates, rules, threats, commands, appeals, and directives spring forth

from bosses and are then imposed on subordinates. Newtonian reward systems also offer money and other extrinsic rewards to externally motivate – *move* – employees to do their very best. But these passive members could not attain high performance even if they tried, since they are obviously constrained and confused by a highly dysfunctional infrastructure and a grossly misaligned strategy–structure. In a Newtonian organization, in fact, the most that one could expect from passive observers is for them to keep doing what *appears* to be the right job.

In a quantum organization, there's a special effort to ignite the internal spark in all members in order to realize the full potential of being human. Typically, a quantum organization first recruits people who desire growthful, participatory, and challenging work settings and who have already developed a threshold of mind/body/spirit consciousness. Since a quantum organization would already have created a healthy behavioral infrastructure, members can enjoy desired cultural behavior and effective sanctioning systems, well–functioning skills for problem management and conflict management, and effective teamwork within as well as across subunits. These features of a quantum organization epitomize the intrinsic rewards that are desired by active participants and enlightened participants.

Further, a quantum organization also provides its members with several opportunities to self–design and self–manage their systems and processes (including their participation in various PMOs). Prior to self–designing the reward system, a quantum organization would already have formulated a new arrangement of subunits, so that every member will be able to clearly see the link between her short–term objectives and the organization's long–term, engaging strategic vision. Furthermore, the principle for creating the new structural arrangement is to contain most of the sequential and reciprocal task flow within – as opposed to between – subunit boundaries, which reinforces the members' self–responsibility, self–identity, and a belief in Internal Control. These opportunities for active participation in designing formal systems provide members with highly prized intrinsic rewards:

meaning, purpose, self-expression, fulfillment, and a legacy for the next generation of an organization's key stakeholders.

Besides these intrinsic rewards that naturally emerge from the behavioral infrastructure and when members are engaged with self-designing and self-managing their formal systems, a quantum organization also distributes extrinsic rewards for achieving strategic objectives. Most convenient for a quantum organization, active participation in managing reward practices transforms extrinsic rewards into additional internal feelings of meaning and purpose. Only when various extrinsic rewards are distributed by outside forces do members experience an external push instead of their own internal pull.

DESIGNING JOBS FOR ACTIVE PARTICIPANTS

As I noted in the previous chapter, revitalizing and realigning strategy–structure involves three interfaces: the strategic interface (translating an abstract strategic vision into concrete objectives and tasks for all the people in the organization), the structural interface (designing subunits to contain the interdependent tasks that must be performed to achieve those objectives), and the job interface (designing jobs to encourage all members to spend the right amount of time on the right tasks according to the right objectives).

The job interface from the strategy-structure track must be coordinated with the reward system track – since it is possible to do more than design jobs whose tasks and activities can be self-controlled by members. Other meaningful job characteristics within each work unit can further motivate members to achieve high performance.

Enabling members to establish their own performance goals, referred to as *participative goal setting* – which would include specifying all the BEHAVIOR and RESULTS that could possibly contribute to long-term success – can intensify the motivational potential of participative job design. The goal–setting process is particularly inspirational when members are encouraged to set their goals far beyond their prior achievements.

Hackman and Oldham developed a practical framework for designing jobs that is perfectly suited for active participants and enlightened participants. ***The activation of three psychological states stimulates self-motivation: experienced meaningfulness, experienced responsibility, and knowledge of results.*** All three internal mental states reside in every individual: (1) the desire for self–expression that makes a major difference in other people's lives, (2) the need to self–control a basic portion of the work that contributes to a useful product or service for others, and (3) the wish for knowing what others actually experience from receiving that product or service. ***The more that a job's key characteristics can be self-designed to satisfy these three profound motives for engaged and empowered behavior, the more that all members will be internally inspired to generate high performance — one work cycle after another.***

According to Hackman and Oldham, there are *five specific job characteristics* that will fully activate those three vital mental states: (1) jobs that embrace a self–contained piece of work that has a coherent theme; (2) jobs that encourage freedom, responsibility, and autonomy while doing the work; (3) jobs that require a great variety of skills for self–expression; (4) jobs that affect the lives and well–being of other people within the organization as well as around the world; and (5) jobs that receive regular and useful feedback about how other people (e.g., end customers) are being affected by the organization's products and services.

The first two characteristics have already been addressed in the strategy–structure track by having contained the sequential and reciprocal task flows within (versus between) self–managing subunits. The last three characteristics provide *additional* qualities that can readily be designed into jobs as the strategy–structure track's concern with the job interface complements the reward track's concern with job motivation. Moreover, the three process tracks (Chapter 10) also offer valuable guidelines for all five job characteristics defined above and therefore must be joined with the two middle tracks through ongoing, cross–track discussions. Specifically, the variety of concepts and tools from total quality management, business process reengineering, and organizational learning are used for improving the value–added processes that satisfy the needs of internal and external customers. In particular, the organization's customers will regularly be asked to provide feedback to group members so they can gradually and radically improve their value–added processes – and subsequently spread that acquired knowledge throughout the organization. Touching other people's lives and receiving feedback about it, while using a great variety of skills and abilities, inspires the self–motivation of active participants and enlightened participants.

With respect to participative goal setting, Locke and Latham have demonstrated that enabling members to set specific goals that support their subunit's objectives increases motivation and performance. Building on the classic technique of management by objectives (MBO), Locke and Latham argue that participative goal setting creates focus, purpose, and meaning. Their research showed that setting goals (1) directs a member's attention to the most important tasks that must be completed – both effectively and efficiently; (2) regulates a member's effort among different tasks – according to their priorities and expected contributions to their goals; (3) increases a member's persistence in working on very difficult tasks (because they are linked to goals) – instead of only completing easy tasks when goals have not been set; and (4) encourages group members to formulate concrete action plans to achieve their goals – which otherwise would have produced impulsive, unfocused, and misguided efforts. Similar to what was advocated for MBO, individual goals must be directly tied to the organization's engaging strategic vision – and should be specific, measurable, time–based, achievable, and somewhat challenging. Specific goals that have roughly a 50% chance of being achieved in a certain time period will certainly be a worthy challenge to active participants: first to develop comprehensive action plans for accomplishing these goals, next to focus their talent, energy, and abilities on implementing their plans and, finally, to persist in their goal–directed efforts even though unforeseen obstacles can interfere with achieving their desired results. Goals that have a greater than 90% chance of success will never inspire members to stretch themselves to the max – since such goals seem easy to attain without putting forth any effort. And goals with less than a 10% likelihood of success will be regarded as unrealistic and disheartening – definitely not challenging.

In sum, all jobs in the organization can be self-designed to incorporate those five characteristics of meaningful jobs and all four benefits of goal setting. By using these two approaches for job design, active participants and enlightened participants will be inspired to contribute everything they have to offer in order to achieve long-term organization's success.

ACCURATELY MEASURING BEHAVIOR

As said before, performance is defined by all the BEHAVIOR and RESULTS that pertain to the eight tracks of the completely integrated program, which acknowledges the seven features of a quantum organization (reviewed in Chapter 1). On the one hand, when measuring RESULTS that appear to be OBJECTIVE (such as net cash flow, sales, market share, profitability, etc.), it is easy to apply well-accepted accounting formulas, rules, and procedures when deriving and then presenting "a number" for subsequent performance reviews and discussions. On the other hand, when measuring BEHAVIOR that appears to be SUBJECTIVE (such as contributions to the behavioral infrastructure), it is difficult to be very precise and derive "a number" that is widely acceptable by accounting or other disciplines. This does not mean we should abandon all assessments of BEHAVIOR; it only means that "soft judgments" will never project the same credibility as "hard facts" (such as productivity, net cash flow, or net income). But measures of BEHAVIOR are nevertheless essential for appraising the true and complete contribution of group members to the short-term objectives that support the organization's strategic vision.

Many types of rating scales have been developed and used to assess member BEHAVIOR. These rating scales have response categories that vary from "poor" to "excellent," from "well below average" to "well above average," or from "strongly disagree" to "strongly agree." Each response on the scale is assigned a number that can then be used for various calculations and discussions. But rating scales also differ in many ways: (1) Who develops the scales? (2) How many response categories are provided for each scale? (3) How behaviorally specific is each response category on the scales? (4) Who responds to these rating scales? (5) How will the responses on these scales (as an average or a total score) be used for performance evaluation and feedback?

One useful approach, called Behaviorally Anchored Rating Scales (BARS), seems to provide the most accurate (reliable and valid) scales for assessing performance BEHAVIOR (Smith and Kendall). Briefly, in response to the above five questions, it's the members themselves, guided by the participants in the reward system track (along with inputs from other stakeholders), who develop their own subunit's rating scales. The group members first determine how finely to distinguish the response categories along each scale (for example, choosing a range of scale numbers from 1 to 5 or 1 to 7). Most important, the members themselves then develop *the specific behavioral descriptions that will correspond to the numbers that are placed on each scale.*

Those detailed descriptions along the scale can help members not only interpret what a given score on that scale really means, but those behavioral anchors also provide a more accurate – and thus confident – basis for providing specific feedback to subunits or individuals in order to help them improve their BEHAVIOR on that particular topic. Without providing specific behavioral anchors, the interpretation of what a particular score on a rating scale means (when only providing a number between "1" and "7", where the former only says "poor" and the latter number only says "excellent") is especially subjective and, as a result, does not suggest exactly what the subunit or person actually needs to do differently during the next performance cycle.

Figure 9.6 presents two items from the Kilmanns Team–Gap Survey. On this figure, you can see the detailed MEANING that defines a score on the two end points as well as the middle point on this Behaviorally Anchored Rating Scale (BARS).

FIGURE 9.6
BEHAVIORALLY ANCHORED RATING SCALES

15. To what extent does your group first define the root causes of its complex problems before it derives solutions and proceeds with action?

1	2	3	4	5	6	7

Faced with virtually any problem, we first discuss different possible solutions and then do our best to implement our chosen solution.

Occasionally, we take a little time to discuss what might be causing the problem. But in most cases, we take our usual approach to fixing what went wrong.

We distinguish simple from complex problems. Then, for the complex ones, we first determine root causes before we proceed further.

16. To what extent does your group analyze its assumptions when it is faced with recurring problems, unresolved differences, and complex situations?

1	2	3	4	5	6	7

We rarely make our assumptions explicit. Usually, we live with unresolved issues and just keep working at things until they somehow get fixed.

Occasionally we analyze our assumptions. But we only do so when all else fails and we can't live with a bad situation much longer.

On all important, complex, and recurring problems, we explicitly analyze our assumptions so we can get right to the heart of the matter.

But who should fill out these Behaviorally Anchored Rating Scales for each group member in an organization? Performance evaluation and feedback seem to be most believable when 360° (full-circle) responses are provided by key suppliers, customers, subunit members, members from other subunits, and any other relevant persons who are able to observe and assess a member's contributions. Given the wide variety of BEHAVIOR that defines performance (what is needed for success across all eight tracks), and given the great variety of meaningful interactions that take place within a quantum organization, full-circle measurement is the most comprehensive approach for appraising the behavior of organizational members.

Naturally, several SUBJECTIVE assessments of BEHAVIOR can be combined with a several OBJECTIVE measures of RESULTS – at different levels of aggregation (e.g., individuals, work groups, departments, divisions, Strategic Business Units, the organization as a whole, and even networks of organizations). Eventually, the **holistic performance formula** that an organization will use for evaluation and feedback must combine the various components of RESULTS and BEHAVIOR. As a result, the holistic performance formula can focus every member's attention on what is required for success: achieving short-term objectives that will eventually materialize the organization's long-term strategic vision.

DIFFERENTIATION AND INTEGRATION IN REWARD SYSTEMS

Once the PMO participants in the reward system track fully appreciate all the foregoing material, they generally agree that a large organization with several divisions in different markets will not be best served by a single, centralized reward system. **While there should be some shared policies and procedures across all subunits — in order to achieve some form of equity and to aid in human resource planning — each subunit may need to have a different reward system to match its unique subenvironment.** The latter is another case of "differentiation," which also pertains to designing the structure of subunits differently to address their different subenvironments with different people preferences for information taking and decision making. However, the more that subunits have self–designed different reward practices, the more that the organization must then use various *integrative mechanisms* in order to coordinate different reward systems into a coherent whole: Greater differentiation requires more integration.

What Can and Cannot Be Changed?

For all kinds of reasons, it might not be possible to redesign EVERYTHING about the organization's current reward system. If any members of the organization are unionized, a special effort should be made to remove the constraints imposed by collective bargaining agreements. If this is not feasible, then some parts of the organization will still be governed by union contracts (even if these include a *non*-performance-based reward system), while other members will be governed by different performance-based reward systems. But the existence of union membership should not preclude the possible option of gaining union/management cooperation, which is quickly becoming the rule rather than the exception in today's global, competitive marketplace.

The most useful approach is to accept that there will always be SOME short–term constraints that must be honored – which does bring a dose of realism into the PMO process; yet enough of the organization's reward system must be open for change if this track is to support long–term success. Identical to what we discussed during the strategy–structure track, top management must realize that an overly constrained reward system track will be viewed as superficial or, worse yet, untenable. As a result, I always challenge senior management to constrain the process as little as possible, so the PMO participants have as much latitude as possible. In any event, **it's essential for top management to develop an official statement on the short-term constraints for the reward system track, so everyone knows what particular aspects of that formal system CAN and CANNOT be changed – for all the RIGHT REASONS.**

Designing the Reward System

Now the participants in the reward system track are asked to devise alternative reward systems for their organization – in the form of general concepts or frameworks, not the detailed reward systems that will be developed in a differentiated form by each subunit. To make sure that a wide variety of approaches will be considered, the fifteen to twenty–five participants in the PMO are divided into their four personality–styles C–groups: NF, NT, ST, and SF. Each C–group begins with an "initial conclusion" for its proposed reward system, based on its unique personality–style tree in the quantum forest. Each initial conclusion answers these same key questions: **What is motivation? What is performance? What is measurement? What is a reward? Lastly, how does the organization motivate high performance with its extrinsic and intrinsic rewards?**

In their four personality–style C–groups, the participants then surface and classify their assumptions in order to support their proposed initial conclusion. Following the debate of assumptions across all the C–groups, one or more S–groups are established to resolve any remaining differences on assumptions, making good use of the five conflict–handling modes, as needed, although the ideal is to primarily use the collaborating mode for resolving the most complex aspects of designing a new reward system.

As a result of all their thoughtful deliberations, the S–groups usually propose these synthesized assumptions:

1. In some ways, people are the same; but in other ways, people are different.
2. People are the same in that their self-worth is based on both *internal criteria* (self-identity, self-confidence, self-perceptions, and ways of looking at life) and *external criteria* (university degrees, job positions, titles, career success, houses, cars, and financial net worth).

3. People are the same in that their work life can be a primary means of satisfying their external criteria for self-worth and can be an important forum for self-expression as well — if their work environment provides the extrinsic and intrinsic rewards they value. Otherwise, people will do the minimum to remain in the organization and will satisfy their needs in other settings.
4. People are different with regard to the extent of their total self-worth (combining both internal and external criteria) and, as a result, they respond quite differently to performance reviews and counseling sessions with their boss or manager.
5. People are different with regard to their need for various extrinsic rewards and the pleasure they experience from various intrinsic rewards.
6. Most people cannot judge the value of extrinsic rewards without making numerous comparisons to other people in similar — and different — situations. Most people can judge the value of intrinsic rewards without making social comparisons — if they feel a high degree of self-worth. Otherwise, they also need to affirm their experiences with others.
7. Most people want to *own* their efforts (the means of production) rather than *rent* themselves to the organization. People differ on what they are willing to risk in order to "own" rather than "rent" their efforts.
8. Most people are reasonable in what they expect to receive from the organization — if they are treated respectfully, sincerely, and honestly, and if they are given the opportunity to understand and influence the key decisions that affect them.
9. Most people begin to take notice of a 5 percent change in bonus or salary, are pleased with a 10

percent change, and are affected deeply by a change greater than 25 percent. The same reactions apply when people become aware of the different percentages that the highest performers versus the lowest performers receive in bonuses and salary changes.

10. Most people greatly appreciate the "little things" in life — a smile, a thank you, a pat on the back — so long as these gestures are genuine.

Based on this set of synthesized assumptions, each S-group deduces a new conclusion in the forest of reward system trees, which generally includes these characteristics: First, the entire organization will be guided by a unified corporate reward policy of measuring performance and distributing rewards to members based on their performance. Usually, this policy includes a more open reward system than previously was the case – so members are provided with the information comparisons that foster the credibility of the new reward system. The policy also expresses a strong commitment to do what it takes to keep the link between each member's performance appraisal and the receipt of rewards absolutely clear. Often, the policy requires that every member's performance rating includes an assessment of both BEHAVIOR and RESULTS, and uses multiple inputs to derive such measures whenever it's possible to do so (e.g., from peers, managers, direct reports, customers, and other key stakeholders). Furthermore, the new reward policy mandates that every manager's performance rating includes how well he or she has conducted performance reviews and counseling sessions.

Second, within this general framework of corporate reward policies, every semi-autonomous subunit in the organization – wholly owned subsidiaries, lines of business, strategic business units, product lines, and profit centers – is encouraged to design a special reward system according to what will lead to success in each case (i.e., what reward practices are expected to FIT with the subunit's particular subenvironment as well as the personality preferences of its members). ***Just as each subunit is encouraged to develop its formal charter, job designs, and desired norms, a participative process is initiated to design a custom-tailored, performance-based reward system.*** The PMO participants in the reward system track will guide this design process – subunit by subunit – so that the entire membership is guided by the same working knowledge of reward systems that the PMO participants themselves have acquired. Nevertheless, human resource experts from either inside or outside the company can be used to ensure that technical guidelines are followed and all legal requirements are met.

Third, while different combinations of reward packages are designed for different subunits, many share similar aspects: The formula that determines a member's overall performance rating might look rather complex on the surface. But closer inspection would reveal that it tries to capture the true and complete value of the group member's short-term and long-term contributions. The performance formula would likely include individual, group, departmental, divisional, and organization-wide assessments of RESULTS – with more weight given to the results that are closest to the jobholder. The performance formula might also include quarterly, annual, and multi-year assessments of BEHAVIOR – with more weight given to the particular behavior that predicts future performance. Management by objectives (MBO) might be used to operationalize the RESULTS aspects of the formula, while Behaviorally Anchored Rating Scales should be used to pinpoint the BEHAVIOR aspects of the formula.

Fourth, so group members will make well-informed decisions on how they can achieve high scores on their formula, they must have access to vital business information (financial, marketing, manufacturing, human resource, and so on) – as supported by proper training and specific guidelines for using this information in a responsible, ethical way. ***Thus, the formal reward system – as supported by control systems, budgeting systems, planning systems, and information systems – plays an integral role in a holographic approach to "performance management."***

And fifth, each subunit offers a wide variety of extrinsic and intrinsic rewards to satisfy different group member's needs and personalities. Typically a cafeteria–style benefit package is given to members so they can match the various health insurance, life insurance, pension plans, and other fringe benefits according to their changing needs. Moreover, various educational and career development programs are included in the package of rewards provided to organizational members. When consistent with the demands of the job, flexible working hours and work–at–home privileges are additional options that might be made available. In some cases, skill–based pay is offered – both to reward those who acquire additional expertise and to develop a multiskilled work force that can adjust quickly to changing circumstances. In other cases, an all–salaried work force is established in order to treat all organizational members as self–reliant professionals. In some situations, employees are offered stock options so they can invest in their own efforts in their own organization.

The range of cash bonuses distributed to members can vary tremendously, depending on the performance formula and the success of both individual and subunit efforts. Annual bonuses are often a convincing incentive in a performance–based reward system, since they can easily range from 0 percent to 100 percent of salary. Spot bonuses, given for a short burst of intense effort or for completing a special project, are excellent reinforcements to the pay–for–performance policy. Increasing member salaries, while clearly desirable for the sake of security, is less effective for inspiring outstanding performance, since increases in salary for one year continue into the future – and rarely do organizations withhold salaries as they withhold bonuses. Finally, all members are encouraged to give one another the simple pleasures in life: warmth, caring, thoughtfulness, appreciation, and kindness.

IMPLEMENTING THE REWARD SYSTEM

While the revised reward system for each semi–autonomous subunit might look impressive on paper and on a laptop screen, the issue, as always, is whether BEHAVIOR in the organization is guided by the documented system. Implementation – translating what's on paper into actual behavior on the job – is a complex problem, especially for a system that's designed to inspire and reward high performance. Once again, the PMO members divide into four personality–style C–groups – which will later transition into one or more S–groups (whereby each S–group is composed of one or two members from the prior C–groups who also have a balanced TKI profile of the five conflict–handling modes).

Each C–group's implementation plan for the revised reward system becomes its "initial conclusion," which is then the basis for a thorough assumptional analysis and the subsequent debate across all four C–groups. Not surprisingly, the "new conclusion" that the S–groups deduce for implementing the revised reward system is usually similar to what was derived for implementing the organization's new operational structure, as discussed in the last chapter: The process takes time (perhaps several months to a year), and group members' feelings about the process should be monitored regularly. Further, extensive participation should be encouraged so that improvements in the new reward system are developed – and accepted – by the membership. Personality style differences should also be taken into account throughout the implementation process.

The key issue to consider in implementing the new reward system is the quality of each member/manager relationship – especially when the "boss" officially presents the results of the performance appraisal to his "direct report" and then counsels him or her on what to do differently during the next work cycle. *To maintain a quality interaction between these two unequal partners, it's necessary to distinguish the evaluative component (i.e., when performance ratings, bonuses, and salary changes are officially delivered to the group member) from the learning component (i.e., when feedback is given on how behavior and results can be improved).* While these two components usually are discussed together in the same meeting, they really need to be handled in separate meetings and to be separated in time as well. In most situations, a "subordinate" being appraised by a "superior" raises sensitive questions and can trigger underlying anxieties about one's self-worth – particularly since our society judges people according to the work they do and how well they perform. According to Allenbaugh:

> "Performance appraisal systems are often used to accomplish two conflicting objectives: determining the rewards an individual will receive and providing counseling and feedback for purposes of improvement and development. These goals call for different discussion emphasis and can have different effects on the employee. When the performance evaluation is used in determining the rewards an individual will receive, employees have a reason for defending their performance and presenting themselves in the best possible light. Under such circumstances, they are likely to give invalid data about themselves in order to look good. As such, the performance appraisal serves neither purpose well." (pages 22–23)

The PMO participants in the reward system track usually recommend that each subunit manager meet with his or her work group to discuss how the two types of discussions can be designed – and also scheduled – to address the organization's requirements as well as the needs of its members. What will be expected in both reward system meetings should be spelled out in advance, so the members will know how to prepare for them, mentally and emotionally.

Regarding **performance reviews,** these meetings should be scheduled according to the particular rhythm and cycle of work in each subunit. While it's often convenient for an organization to establish one review each year, this plan may not be desirable if divisions, departments, and work groups have different types of objectives with different completion cycles. In a dynamic work setting, it might be best to review performance more frequently.

If several performance cycles take place in a year, holding only annual reviews means that opportunities are missed to modify performance form one cycle to the next. Instead, a subunit might establish these agreements: The boss will meet with each group member once a month to review performance results, while the formal performance review will take place every six months; any member, upon request, can see her file; any member can request an appeals procedure, without any negative consequences, if she disagrees with the results of her full performance review.

Regarding **counseling sessions,** the manager and her direct reports usually agree to hold frequent face-to-face discussions to clarify expectations, identify blocks, suggest improvements, and give lots of encouragement. These discussions focus on culture, assumptions, skills, behavior, attitudes and, of course, teamwork. Often these barriers to success have been identified during the previous performance review. The idea is to provide a constant stream of support and feedback so that members can improve their performance – in terms of efficiency (the proper allocation of time on tasks) and effectiveness (completing the right tasks according to the right objectives). Thus a subunit might establish these agreements: Each group member can arrange a counseling session with his immediately boss whenever he wants additional feedback and discussion. If the boss believes that a subordinate needs some more help, he would suggest that they sit down and discuss "how things are going." But it's totally up to the member to decide when that counseling session should take place.

IMPROVING REWARD PRACTICES

After the first round of implementing new reward practices throughout the organization, the mission shifts to *improving* job design, enhancing intrinsic and extrinsic rewards, measurement, evaluation, and feedback – thus improving all aspects of reward practices within each subunit. The PMO participants can survey subunit members on their motivational experiences and study results for performance trends. Subunit by subunit comparisons with regard to motivation and performance will likely suggest numerous opportunities to improve actual reward practices – or their implementation.

It is also essential to establish how performance formulas can be adjusted in any work unit – to improve both reliability and validity. Furthermore, there should be a simple procedure that allows for negotiation and change in a formula – not as an excuse for failing to achieve a realistic and attainable goal, but as an acknowledgment of dynamic complexity.

At some point, the participants in the reward system track should reexamine the progress made in the previous tracks and recommend improvements, since the behavioral infrastructure and alignment of strategy-structure significantly influence the organization's reward policies and practices, the experience of intrinsic rewards, and the distribution of extrinsic rewards.

CONCLUDING THOUGHTS

The participants in both the strategy–structure track and the reward system track will join together to ensure that all formal systems are appropriately aligned and functioning as intended. This ideal scenario is evident when all subunit members have internalized a crystal–clear message of what specific BEHAVIOR and RESULTS are needed for long–term success.

The participants in these two middle tracks also interact with their counterparts in the next three process tracks of quantum transformation – since the organization's systems and processes are so highly interrelated: Processes (as a sequence of tasks and decisions) become value–added when they directly contribute to the organization's strategic vision; value–added processes (hence, task flows) take place within and across subunit boundaries; and value–added processes will be self–managed successfully only if members receive the intrinsic and extrinsic rewards they desire and deserve.

What interconnects the active participants across all eight tracks is the means to improve the behavioral infrastructure, the formal systems, and business and learning processes better

and faster than any other organization in the world. Such a engaging strategic vision may be the ultimate stretch goal for every quantum organization. Achieving this vision, however, means that process management must be completely integrated with the organization's behavioral infrastructure and its formal and informal systems.

IMPROVING
PROCESS MANAGEMENT
FOR ORGANIZATIONS

THE GRADUAL, RADICAL, AND
LEARNING PROCESS TRACKS

Up to this point, all members have been actively involved in the first three tracks of quantum transformation for the purpose of establishing a healthy behavioral infrastructure. In addition, a select group of fifteen to twenty-five members, representing all areas, levels, and locations in the organization, has been actively involved in a Problem Management Organization (PMO) for the special mission of revitalizing and realigning strategy–structure. Meanwhile, another group of fifteen to twenty five members has been actively involved in another PMO so they can redesign and then implement a well-functioning, performance–based reward system for their organization and its subunits.

Based on what has already taken place, all members are now primed to participate in the ***gradual process improvement track*** from within their current arrangement of work groups – which includes their immediate boss. If you recall, each boss and his or her direct reports have already been united in the team track so open and candid conversations, effective problem management, probing assumptional analysis, and flexible conflict management can take place whenever each boss meets with his direct reports. ***But it will be much easier, safer, and secure for members to first learn how to describe, control, and improve processes WITHIN their current work groups before they attempt to manage the more challenging processes that still flow ACROSS the existing subunits in the organization.***

But after sufficient progress has been achieved in the gradual process track, the shadow track establishes several PMOs for the **radical process track,** so groups of carefully selected participants can then use their newly learned process tools to address those cross–boundary processes. Specifically, ***working closely with the PMO in the strategy-structure track, the PMO participants in the radical process track will be able to restructure the current subunits that were previously designed according to specialized business functions into reformulated process-based subunits — so the organization is in the best position to achieve long-term success in today's increasingly turbulent world.***

Regarding the last track, **the learning process track**, another PMO is formed so that active and enlightened participants can describe, control, and improve the learning processes that will enable their organization to achieve gradual and radical process improvement in the future – in half the time as before.

Incidentally, the reason I present the last three tracks in one chapter is because each of the three process improvement tracks involves describing, controlling, and improving the business and learning processes that flow within and across the organization's systems – and thus the last three tracks share many of the same tools and techniques. Even though the three process tracks are intended to be implemented in the specified sequence (one at a time), I believe that *learning* the material that pertains to all three process tracks in one integrated chapter is the most efficient and effective way to proceed. Essentially, whether the focus is within groups or between groups, or whether the focus is on business processes or learning processes, the various tools and techniques for improving processes represent a unified discipline that's now known as: Process Management.

The popular name for the material presented in the gradual process track was initially known as: Total Quality Management (or TQM for short). With regard to the radical process track, the popular name for this approach to dramatic improvement was initially called: Business Process Reengineering (or BPR for short).

Yet the material in the learning process track is still referred to as Organizational Learning (OL), even though it's sometimes called: Knowledge Management.

It's a real shame, however, that these three particular process approaches developed a bad reputation in the 1980s and 1990s because of the high failure rate of implementing these programs in hundreds if not thousands of organizations. In fact, the failure rate for TQM, BPR, and OL has been reported to be anywhere from 70% to 90%. Because of these disappointing results, these improvement efforts of past decades were dismissed as passing fads and are rarely discussed in the media today, except in terms of process improvement in general.

The high failure rates for implementing TQM, BPR, and OL primarily resulted from disregarding ineffective infrastructures and misaligned systems, as opposed to any inherent flaws in the process tools themselves. Basically, "the baby was thrown out with the dirty bathwater," which discourages organizations from again trying to implement these valuable concepts and tools. But by purposely using more neutral terms, such as gradual process, radical process, and learning process improvement, and, then, by investigating process management within that larger context of behavioral infrastructures and formal systems, as highlighted on the Complex Hologram along with the eight tracks, perhaps the excellent concepts and tools from TQM and Reengineering can still be used as first intended. Yet any effort at organization-wide improvement that does not first rectify ineffective infrastructures and misaligned systems is also doomed to failure and, therefore, will eventually become just another passing management fad.

Similar to the prior chapters, I titled this chapter the same as my four-hour recorded course: Improving Process Management for Organizations. In that online course, I also provide workshop materials to implement process management: (1) Work Sheets on Describing Processes, (2) Work Sheets on Controlling Processes, (3) Work Sheets on Improving Processes, and (4) Work Sheets on Managing Complex Processes.

The Essence of Process Management

Most people can see the immediate result of their efforts – especially when that result is packaged into a concrete product that's delivered to someone else. That same experience applies as well to a service that's provided to a customer or client. What is less obvious, however, is seeing the **intangible process** that was used to produce the **tangible result** – since the process remains subtle, silent, and hidden (if not unconscious), as if the person's brain stayed on autopilot while getting something done. In the past, organizations that introduced Total Quality Management (TQM) soon discovered that **formal educational sessions were necessary for all members to become consciously aware of the implicit processes they use to produce explicit results.**

Recall the previous chapters in which you learned the many benefits of discussing cultural norms, implicit assumptions, and group process. By talking about these topics out loud, what was once unconscious or habitual became open for inspection and thus available for improvement. The same kind of illumination occurs when a work group learns to make its processes explicit. In fact, by conducting open discussions about processes in a safe workshop setting, members suddenly realize that **the process of doing something might be more important than the results, since the PROCESS actually determines the RESULTS** in much the same way that BEHAVIOR determines the RESULTS (as we discussed in the prior chapter about the reward system track). With regard to the prime benefit of process management: **If all active participants continuously improve their PROCESSES, the RESULTS will continuously improve.**

In Figure 10.1, I present the **PROCESS CELL**, which captures the foundation of the process approach for achieving long-term success. A process is defined as a sequence of tasks and decisions that take place over time – which includes first receiving **Inputs (I)** from suppliers and then delivering **Outputs (O)** to customers. All activity in an organization is intended to be a **Value-Added Process (P)** for customers as well as other key stakeholders. On the one hand, if a group receives certain inputs from its suppliers and then hands off those same exact items to its customers, the work group has not added any value to its outputs. On the other hand, *if a group performs particular tasks and makes certain decisions on the various inputs it receives from its suppliers, which DOES indeed result in material and/or informational contributions to the product or service that its customers want or need, the group has then performed a value-added process.*

FIGURE 10.1
DEFINING A PROCESS CELL

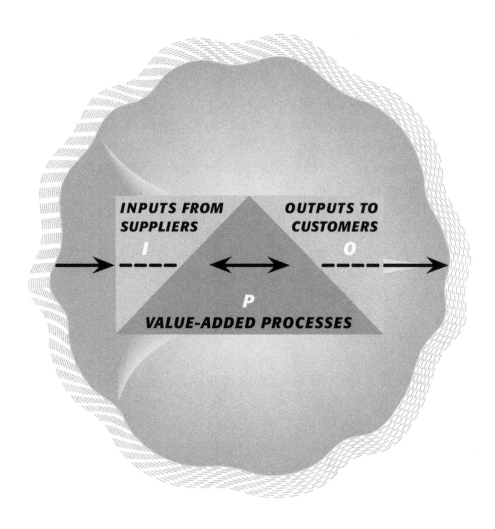

INPUTS FROM
SUPPLIERS

OUTPUTS TO
CUSTOMERS

I

O

P

VALUE-ADDED PROCESSES

Let's define the **suppliers** to the process cell. Given the nature of your job, whatever you need before you can perform certain tasks and make certain decisions, by definition, comes from one or more suppliers – whether you need more information, tools, equipment, guidelines, instructions, or advice to complete your job. But it's important to distinguish the supplier who's another member of your organization, an **INTERNAL supplier,** from a supplier who's a member of another organization, which we call an **EXTERNAL supplier.** Usually, members only think of outside vendors as their suppliers, even though most of what they must receive before they can get their daily work done actually comes from other members in their group or from other departments in the same organization.

It is also helpful to make the same kinds of distinctions for **customers,** who can be other members or other departments in your organization or the final, end customer in another part of the world who wants to purchase your company's products or services. *All group members must appreciate that whomever receives something from them should be regarded as a highly valued customer, whether that person is next door or is located on the other side of the planet.*

As shown on Figure 10.2, building on the basic process cell, we can now connect members (and work units) together into a **PROCESS CHAIN** – according to the outputs they *hand off* to one another down the line. Further, three kinds of feedback provide opportunities to revise/modify the work being done so that the end customer is completely satisfied: (1) each person can actively encourage customer feedback in order to know what customers need and want; (2) each person can explicitly define what quality inputs are then needed from suppliers – so that every processes can add value all down the chain; (3) each person in the chain can measure the quality of his or her own work and make the necessary mid–course corrections – BEFORE any output is given (handed off) to someone else. Keep these two sayings in mind, for they will help you appreciate the PROCESS CHAIN: *Garbage in, garbage out; a chain is no stronger than its weakest link.*

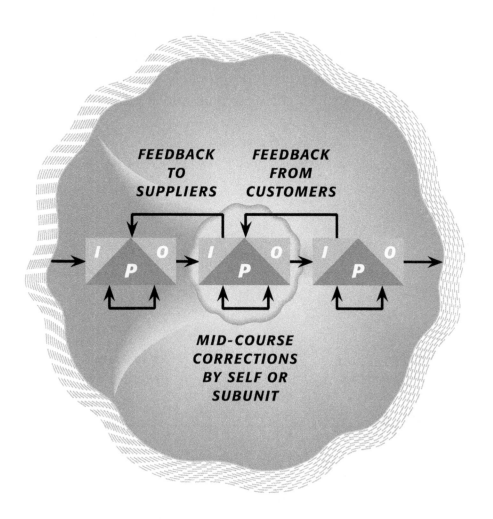

FIGURE 10.2
DEFINING A PROCESS CHAIN

In Figure 10.3, we expand the PROCESS CHAIN far beyond a few group members or subunits in an organization. **The center circle now includes all the value-added processes throughout the organization itself, while the process cells to the left of the organization reveal the upstream supply chain of EXTERNAL SUPPLIERS, while the process cells shown on the right side of the organization reveal all the EXTERNAL CUSTOMERS that make use of the organizations products and services.** From this diagram, you can therefore see the flow of work all the way from upstream processes to the downstream processes, including the midstream processes inside the organization. At the same time, the small circle in the middle of the diagram and the larger circle that entirely surrounds the process chain are meant to indicate that processes go **FULL CIRCLE *from womb to tomb***, beginning with an initial customer need to ultimately satisfying that same need through an explicit chain of value–added processes.

FIGURE 10.3
SEEING AN ORGANIZATION'S ENTIRE PROCESS CHAIN

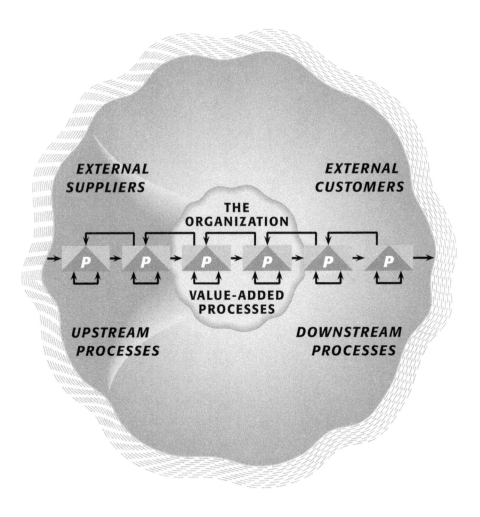

CHAPTER 10

Figure 10.4 summarizes the costs of not managing processes well or simply leaving them implicit. Here you can see that there are no feedback loops or mid-course corrections that would help in providing customers exactly what they need, when they need it. In the worst cases, making errors **upstream** (as when suppliers provide deficient materials through deficient methods) wind up creating challenging problems **downstream** (when internal and external customers receive defective products and poor service).

FIGURE 10.4
THE COSTS OF POOR PROCESS

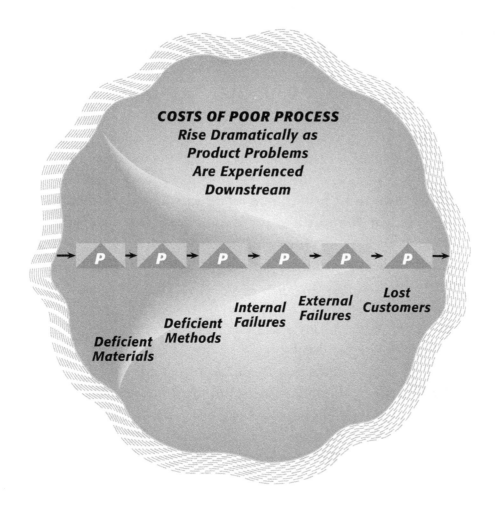

Providing such inferior products and services results in lost customers who subsequently choose to purchase their products or services from another organization. To appreciate the costs of poor process, organizations try to estimate the lost revenues they incur for every lost customer. When that estimate for each lost customer is several hundreds of dollars, let alone thousands of dollars, members soon become convinced that they must now manage their processes more explicitly and effectively.

The out-of-date assumption: It takes more time and money to provide better and better products and services. That scenario only can happen when an organization decides to improve the quality of its products by hiring tens or hundreds of inspectors to check its outputs BEFORE delivering them to the customer – which includes hiring additional inspectors to assess whether all the *other* inspectors are effectively performing their jobs! But the point is soon reached where the costs of detecting and correcting errors downstream develop into a very large percentage of sales. But simply eliminating all those inspectors will not resolve the problem, since poor quality will then be passed on to customers.

Figure 10.5 shows the other side of the equation: the benefits of good process. **Now the process cells are drawn with all the feedback loops and mid-course corrections intact, which helps ensure that high-quality materials and accurate information will be produced upstream, that all value-added processes are performed midstream and, most important, that high-quality outputs are sent downstream to the final customers.** Basically, better managing processes upstream will better satisfy customers downstream: Just consider the benefits from shorter work cycles, less waste, lower production costs, reduced inventory, delighted customers and, perhaps best of all, more customers!

Here is the up-to-date assumption that is rooted in current reality: If a process is addressed upfront – upstream – because of the customer and supplier feedback as well as mid-course corrections that can quickly catch errors before anything is sent

downstream, better process costs much less in the long run:
Downstream inspectors are no longer needed and customers
receive exactly what they want! While it's easier to measure the
costs of poor process as opposed to the *benefits* of good process,
it's still worthwhile to estimate just what the organization gains
by improving processes, especially gaining more customers and
increasing market share.

FIGURE 10.5
THE BENEFITS OF GOOD PROCESS

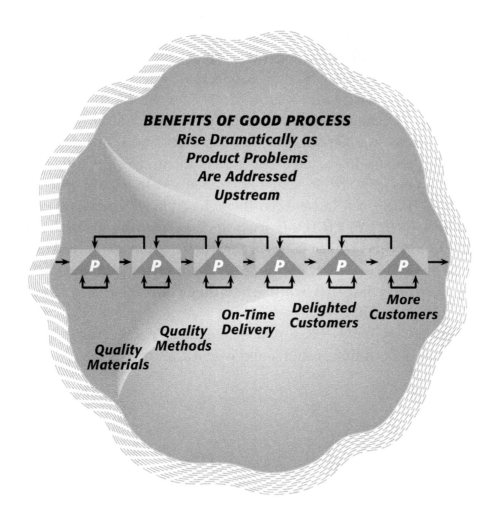

As discussed in Chapter 7 (regarding the team track), TIME is the most limited resource that, ironically, is freely available to all persons and organizations. Yet, how well time is managed has a huge impact on whether subunits can achieve their short-term objectives. Indeed, completing tasks and decisions on time is far better than not completing those activities until sometime after the due date, which can be as bad as not completing them at all. *It should not be surprising that process management is most concerned about CYCLE TIME: the time it takes to complete a set of tasks and decisions, which is largely based on the explicit or implicit design of the process itself — and how consistently members use that process as the standard operating procedure for achieving their short-term objectives.*

Figure 10.6 illustrates how time affects the flow of tasks and decisions throughout the PROCESS CHAIN, which, in this case, reveals **slow cycle time.** As you can see on this illustration, the processes in the chain are left implicit – so they do not include feedback to suppliers or feedback from customers, nor do they include self-feedback for the members themselves. In addition, the process cells are elongated horizontally with a lot of space – hence, TIME – left in between them. In all likelihood, *everyone in this PROCESS CHAIN is wasting time waiting around for the inputs they need to perform their piece of the work. And the end or final customers are certainly losing their patience with not getting what they want when they want it.* In fact, when processes are not explicitly described, statistically controlled, and continuously improved, suppliers, members, and customers are wasting a lot of time, waiting and waiting, for this or that.

FIGURE 10.6
SLOW CYCLE TIME

SLOW CYCLE TIME
*Is Caused by
Not Describing,
Controlling, and
Improving Processes*

Figure 10.7 illustrates just the opposite result: **fast cycle time.** By managing processes explicitly, and making considerable use of feedback loops – upstream, midstream, and downstream – the distance between the process cells has been shrunk to nothing and the final customers get exactly what they want when they want it. Not surprisingly, fast cycle time is highly correlated with the benefits of good process – just as slow cycle time is highly correlated with the costs of poor process.

FIGURE 10.7
FAST CYCLE TIME

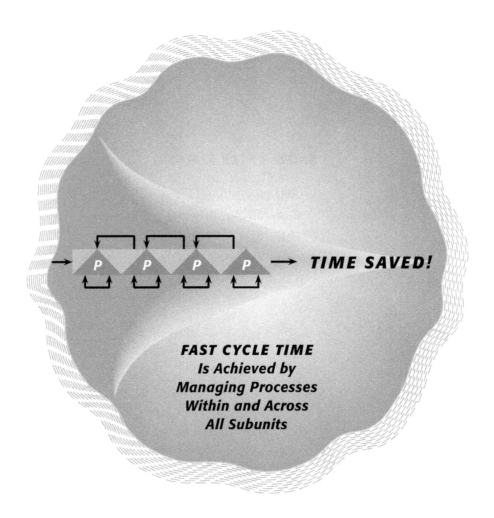

TIME SAVED!

FAST CYCLE TIME
Is Achieved by
Managing Processes
Within and Across
All Subunits

Figure 10.8 highlights another important concept in process management, which has been called: **Just-in-Time**. In particular, *a PROCESS CHAIN of receiving inputs from suppliers Just-in-Time to use those inputs and also providing quality outputs to customers Just-in-Time for them to make instant use of those outputs is the epitome of process management.* Basically, when members can manage all their processes Just–in–Time, that's the key indicator that they're highly skilled in process management.

FIGURE 10.8

JUST-IN-TIME PROCESS MANAGEMENT

Fast Cycle Times Can Be Achieved If All Subunits Know What They Need When They Need It and Receive It from Internal and External Suppliers on Time

Results in Delivering High-Quality Products and Services at Low Cost in a Short Time, Which Delights All Internal and External Customers

To reinforce the key principle, it's very costly for members to be waiting around to receive the right inputs in order to proceed with their value–added processes. To deal with such a situation, subunits often build up their inventory **Just-in-Case** they do not receive from their suppliers exactly what they need when they need it. Alternatively, it would be far more effective, efficient, and satisfying if members would be spending all their precious time on performing value–added tasks and decisions that allow them to deliver their high–quality outputs **Just-in-Time** to internal and external customers and other key stakeholders.

Regarding the accumulation of inventory (as a hedge against poor process management), **Just-in-Case inventory** takes added time and cost to maintain warehouses, which includes the time for first storing materials and later retrieving materials, simply because suppliers don't deliver materials and information just when they are needed. In other situations, **members purposely duplicate tasks and activities** so they don't have to depend on other subunits to provide the necessary inputs on a timely basis. But there is a significant unintended consequence of purposely duplicating activities, choosing to hoard resources, or excessively warehousing inventory:

All these *just-in-case* strategies for adapting to poorly managed processes serve to keep problems out of sight and out of mind, which significantly increases the costs of providing products and services to customers. In contrast, *if members are motivated to reduce inventory levels, eliminate hoarding behavior, and stop the duplication of tasks and activities, the organization is then forced to manage its processes most explicitly and efficiently — up and down the process chain — and to thus make absolutely sure that suppliers provide the necessary inputs just when they are needed for the organization's value-added processes.* In fact, organizations that are experienced at process management only use external suppliers that manage their *own* processes explicitly and successfully, up and down their own process chains. Note: When producing products, it's easiest to pinpoint inventory as accumulated materials, work in process, or finished goods. When services are provided, however, inventory can be viewed as any nontangible buffer (for example, text messages, phone messages, or emails that have piled up and have not been addressed).

THE GRADUAL PROCESS TRACK

With this general background on the process cell, the process chain, the costs and the benefits of good process management, slow and fast cycle time, Just-in-Time, and excessive inventory, all organizational members are now ready to attend a series of one-day workshops for the gradual process track – so they can learn the essential tools and techniques for process management. Incidentally, as organizations transition into the last three tracks of quantum transformation, they might reformulate their prior strategic vision to especially emphasize customer *delight* and not just customer satisfaction: **We are actively involved people who are continuously improving processes to delight present and future customers by greatly exceeding their expectations with better and better products and services.** It is apparent that many organizations can *satisfy* their customers, but are losing them to competitors who provide products or services that mesmerize people by anticipating their needs and then quickly responding to special requests with exceptional flexibility. Such experiences generate **customer DELIGHT** and not just customer satisfaction.

Regarding the tools and techniques for process management, in Step 1, Describing Processes, you'll learn how to make your value-added processes absolutely explicit by drawing flowcharts of the inputs, tasks, decisions, and outputs that represent your high-priority task flows. Then, in Step 2, Controlling Processes, you'll learn to apply the standard statistical tools in order to get those value-added processes under control. I'll use a few simple diagrams so you can easily visualize on-target performance with random variation without your having to make any statistical calculations. Lastly, in Step 3, Improving Processes, you'll learn the benefits of benchmarking processes, so you and your work group can then set world-class performance goals. Incidentally,

I'll present those three steps for value-added processes that are currently taking place *within* subunits, which is the prime target for gradual process improvement – since that's the easiest and safest environment to initially learn those tools and techniques. And then, after we have thoroughly reviewed the key principles and practices of describing, controlling, and improving processes *within* work groups, we'll then focus our attention on the more complex processes of radical process improvement and learning process improvement, which cut across subunit boundaries.

By the way, I use the same language in these discussions that we previously used for "systemic barriers to success" (during the first five tracks) to now refer to the "process barriers to success" (in these last three tracks), specifically: **Description Barriers** that promote confusing, redundant, inefficient, and non–value-added processes, **Control Barriers** that always prevent processes from performing as intended, and **Improvement Barriers** that prevent processes from hitting better targets with less variation.

STEP 1: DESCRIBING PROCESSES

One of the most illuminating events is when the members of a work group first observe their implicit processes face-to-face. It's one thing for group members to discuss how they get their work done – using the usual terms in their vocabulary. But it's quite another thing for them to draw a flowchart of their tasks and decisions – including the inputs they receive from suppliers and the outputs they deliver to customers. On some occasions, I ask each group member to draw a detailed flowchart of his/her work – individually – before all members share their process descriptions with one another in a group meeting. But when the sharing begins, the differences among members – who are trying to accomplish the same goals in presumably the same way – are quite alarming. Openly seeing and discussing these flowcharts, however, enables the group to investigate the reasons *why* each member is performing that value-added processes so differently.

DRAWING FLOWCHARTS *encourages members to clarify, simplify, and streamline processes – leading to a more efficient*

and effective sequence of tasks and decisions – which is more likely to delight customers. And then **USING FLOWCHARTS** as the standard operating procedure for determining which specific steps should be performed, and in what designated sequence, enables members to add value to the whole process chain in a reliable and consistent manner – no matter who in the group is performing that process for the customer on any given day, at any given time. As shown on Figure 10.9, I encourage everyone to use these *standard symbols for drawing flowcharts*.

FIGURE 10.9
STANDARD SYMBOLS FOR DRAWING FLOWCHARTS

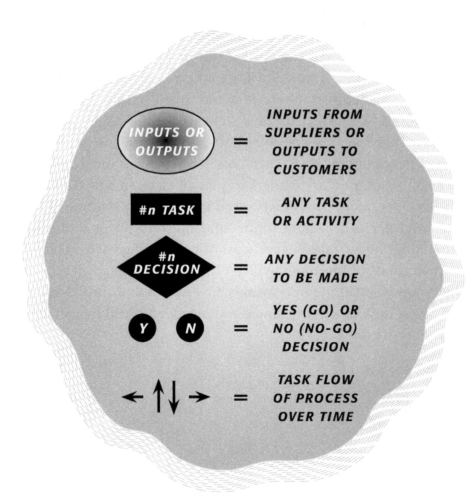

Using those standard flowchart symbols serves to establish a common language (and procedures) for describing processes. Inputs from suppliers and outputs to customers are displayed as **ovals**; tasks are shown as **rectangles** and are numbered as well; decisions (as clear checkpoints for possibly making mid–course corrections) are shown as **diamonds** with yes and no **circles** (or go and no–go loops) that can move backwards to the previous step or forward to the next step in the sequence – depending on the outcome of the decision. And numerous **arrows** are used to indicate the specified sequence of tasks and decisions as well as the direction of go/no–go loops. *If all members consistently use these standard symbols when they flowchart their work, it will be much easier managing processes within each work group, let alone managing processes across work group boundaries.* Note: These symbols for drawing flowcharts were established by the American National Standards Institute (ANSI).

On Figure 10.10, I now illustrate an eight–step flowchart that uses those standard symbols. In actual work settings, of course, there would be many additional steps in a value–added process. Sometimes, while drawing flowcharts, it's worthwhile to include comments right next to the symbols – especially if the definition or meaning of any task or decision is not clear. In some cases, a "process dictionary" can be prepared that formally defines all the tasks and decisions – and inputs and outputs – alphabetically. Estimating the actual time and cost of performing each step and then calculating the totals will be most meaningful later, once the group has had the opportunity to streamline its process so it can assess how much time and cost have been saved by using its revised process.

FIGURE 10.10
USING STANDARD SYMBOLS FOR DRAWING FLOWCHARTS

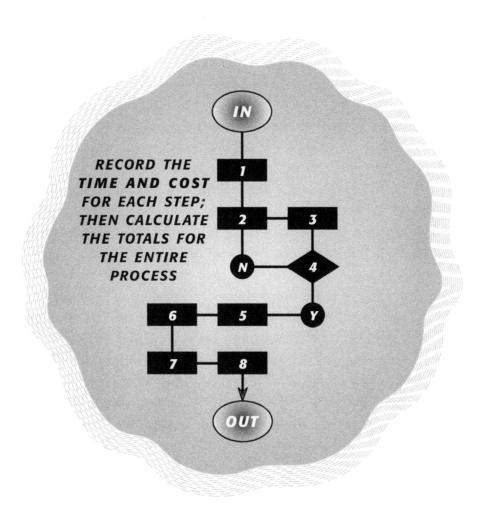

Distinguishing Three Types of Value-Added Processes

This is the time to introduce an eye–catching approach for making flowcharts even more informative for group members – which distinguishes among three different kinds of value–added activities: **Customer Value-Added (CVA)** activities are tasks and decisions that your customers would very gladly pay for. Most customers, for example, would refuse to pay for the preparation of an organization's income taxes or what they would define as unnecessary paperwork. They only want to pay for activities that directly give them exactly what they want. To be clear: In most cases, CVA refers to the final or end customer who is external to the organization, as usually noted in the organization's strategic vision and strategic plans.

But in order to remain in business, each organization is still required (whether by law or by social pressure) to satisfy OTHER stakeholders besides the end customer. But the objective is to do only what's essential to satisfy these other stakeholders, so scarce resources are not diverted away from the organization's strategic vision: to delight the end customer. As such, **Other Value-Added (OVA)** activities are tasks and decisions that other stakeholders (e.g., stockholders, regulatory agencies, and local communities) require the organization to provide. No organization, however, can afford to divert its limited resources to any **No Value-Added (NVA)** activities that no customer desires to pay for, and no other stakeholder requires the organization to provide.

On Figure 10.11, I display the same eight–step flowchart as before, except that I now distinguish the value (or lack thereof) of each step in the process. *I show the background of each CVA step in BLACK to emphasize its value-added activity for the end customer. Meanwhile, I present the background of every OVA step in GRAY to signify its moderate value-added activity for other stakeholders. Lastly, I show the background of each NVA step in WHITE to suggest its no value-added activity for any internal or external stakeholder.*

FIGURE 10.11
A FLOWCHART WITH CVA, OVA, AND NVA ACTIVITIES

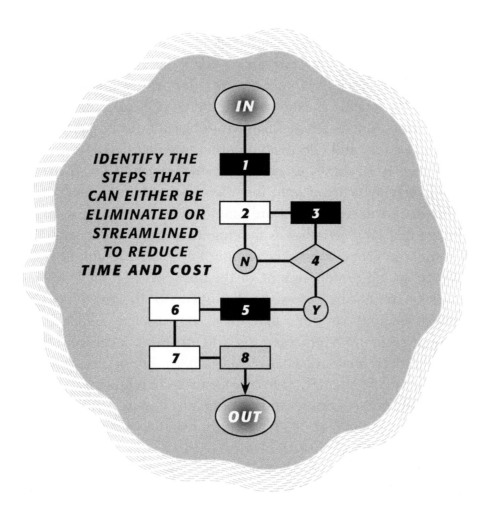

If you draw each symbol with a background "color" of black, gray, or white, it'll be rather easy to quickly identify which tasks and decisions should be streamlined (CVA and OVA) and which tasks and decisions should be eliminated (NVA). As processes are streamlined, they will likely reduce cycle time, process costs, and inventory levels – which will be a big win–win outcome for the organization and its stakeholders. By showing the estimated time and cost next to each step in the process (and adding the totals) provides the key information for members to learn how they are wasting their time and resources on tasks and decisions that no one wants (as shown in a white background). Furthermore, since some activities are for *other* stakeholders, perhaps these can be minimized – since the final customer does not want to pay for these requirements (as shown with a gray background). But the most value-added activities (shown in black) must be performed both efficiently and effectively in order to delight all customers.

Figure 10.12 shows several **additional symbols for drawing flowcharts,** which can help members recognize different kinds of tasks and decisions that are often habitual – and thus taken for granted. Any activities as moving items from one location to another, or group members waiting endlessly for inputs from another group or department, or the boss checking on someone else's job, or storing excess supplies *just-in-case* the group doesn't receive its inputs on time, all of these activities may significantly increase cycle times, process costs, and inventory levels, and thus result in decreased customer satisfaction. An important question is whether customers want to pay for these activities, or whether other stakeholders can require the organization to perform these tasks, or when, in fact, NO ONE really wants members to spend their time in these particular ways.

In many cases, NVA tasks are an outgrowth of prior attempts to control the membership – probably due to mistrust. In other cases, NVA tasks are the outdated leftovers from all prior quick fixes, work-arounds, and patch-up jobs that were used to solve problems that now, apparently, no longer exist – yet their traces remain. But it's now time to see these NVA tasks face to face, so they can be examined – and eliminated.

FIGURE 10.12

ADDITIONAL SYMBOLS FOR DRAWING FLOWCHARTS

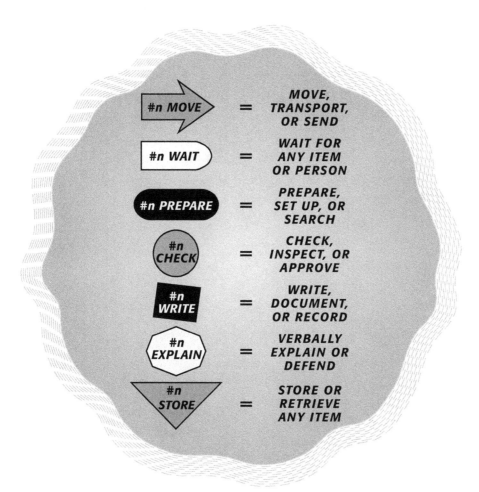

Figure 10.13 is a flowchart of that same eight-step process, which not only reveals a finer discrimination of each kind of task and decision, but also shows how group members have assessed the particular value-added quality of each step in the process.

A value–added assessment of any task or decision (whether CVA, OVA, or NVA) should not be based on the time or the cost of completing the work. Instead, value should strictly be based on what your customers and other stakeholders want, regardless of how much time it might take or how much it might cost for you (or anyone else) to provide it. Sometime later, you and your work group will have the opportunity to reduce cycle times and process costs in Step 3 of process management, which is known as Improving Processes.

FIGURE 10.13
USING ADDITIONAL SYMBOLS FOR DRAWING FLOWCHARTS

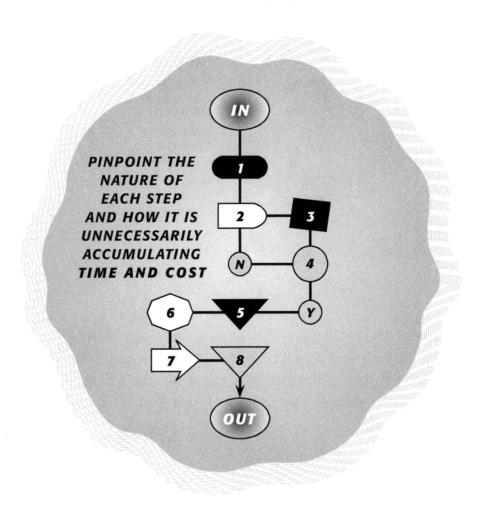

CHAPTER 10

Figure 10.14 illustrates how subunit members were able to streamline their original eight-step process into a new four-step process by eliminating all the NVA activities (Steps 2, 6, and 7) and removing one of the OVA tasks (Step 8). The new flowchart shows a revamped process that now focuses on CVA tasks and decisions to the delight of the final customer. Once this revised process has been performed for a number of cycles, it will be worthwhile to reassess the average time and cost of every step, and then compare these averages to the previous assessments.

FIGURE 10.14
DESCRIBING THE NEW STREAMLINED PROCESS

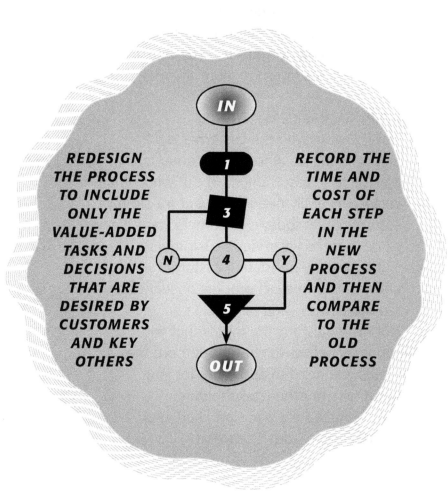

Identifying and Removing Description Barriers

Below are the kinds of Description Barriers that must first be identified and then removed to fully activate – and effectively use – the streamlined process. In essence, this list summarizes just what occurs when processes are not discussed or described in the group: ***These Description Barriers make it very difficult for group members to add value for end customers and others.*** Only by removing these barriers can work groups proceed to control and then improve their CVA processes. Incidentally, for the time being, the focus is exclusively on identifying and then removing the hidden Description Barriers, which strictly means that group members must make the very best use of all existing "factors of production" (i.e., resources) that have been officially allocated to subunit. A little later in the gradual process track, when the focus changes to improving those described processes, members will be able to reduce cycle time and process cost by changing the "factors of production" that determine their results.

Description Barriers
- Not knowing who the customer is;
- Not agreeing on who the customer is;
- Making false assumptions about what your customers really need and want (or simply assuming that today's customers want the same thing as yesterday's customers);
- Not accurately translating customer needs and wants into exact product or service requirements – and targets;
- Not distinguishing the inputs that your suppliers deliver to your group from the inputs you need to add value for your customers or other stakeholders;
- Not having an explicit, simplified, and efficient value-added process;

- Not having sufficient decision points (yes-or-no quality checks) throughout the process — so you can make the necessary mid-course corrections;
- Not agreeing on the value-added process that must be used by all group members, at all times, except for agreed-upon special circumstances.

As a result of flowcharting a value–added process, members discover that they do not exactly agree on who their customer is, since they never talked about that before. In the past, members simply performed their tasks, day after day, just as they were taught to do.

As might be expected, once group members have identified one or more conflicts with respect to (1) who the customer is and (2) what that customer really wants (whether it's an internal or external customer), members use one or more of the five conflict modes to resolve their differences. However, since everything the group does hinges on having an accurate, shared understanding of their customers' most important needs and wants, it would be best for the members to make use of the collaborating mode on the integrative dimension of the TKI Conflict Model – to ensure that every member understands all aspects of their customers' needs and wants in the same exact manner.

As members continue to identify their Description Barriers, another revelation usually occurs when **members acknowledge that without being up to date (and accurate) about what their customers need or want, it would be difficult, if not impossible, to specify what exact inputs the group needs from its internal and external suppliers.** And even if group members were crystal clear about their customers' needs and were able to specify the exact inputs they need from suppliers in order to proceed with their process, they would still have to add several decision points during the process so they could make the necessary mid–course corrections before delivering a product to their customers.

Regardless, *even if members have designed a value-added process that's based on updated assumptions about customer needs and supplier inputs, if every group member doesn't USE that process exactly as described, all the work that went into redesigning that process would be a total waste of time, energy, and money.*

Why would members NOT follow the described processes as their standard operating procedures? They misunderstand them, don't know about them, have not been trained to follow them, were trained to do them differently, do not have the tools and equipment – or the time – to do them, or someone told them to do the procedures differently. There are many more reasons NOT to follow the standard operating procedures than to do what's essential for delighting customers and other key stakeholders.

But once the actual Description Barriers have been accurately identified and thoroughly debated, members can then remove those identified barriers in one cycle of problem management – so long as they do not commit a defining or implementing error along the way.

THE GENERIC STEPS FOR DESCRIBING PROCESSES

Step 1: Pick a Core Value–Added Process to Examine. Consider some of the tasks that your work group performs on a recurring basis: at least several times a day or certainly several times every week. (Do not select tasks that are only performed every now and then.) If this is the first time your work unit will be describing a process, pick one that is not too complicated, but don't pick one that is rather simple – for example, receiving an email, reading it, writing back, and so forth. *Select a process that you perform frequently, your group can control, is CORE to your work group's mission and to the success of your organization, needs to be improved, and isn't too complicated.* Once your work group has learned the knack of describing processes, you can then apply this skill to a more complex process.

Step 2: Assess Customer Needs. Recognizing that there's no substitute for conducting market research (whether through surveys about customer needs and wants or by paying special attention to what your customers suggest to you), list what your group believes to be the most important needs of end customers regarding the process you have picked to examine. You'll find it advantageous to make your assumptions about your customer's needs explicit – particularly the relative certainty of your most important assumptions: from 50% (i.e., highly uncertain) to 100% (i.e., completely certain). Of course, *it's essential for you to collect data on your most important and uncertain assumptions, so your assessments of customer needs are indeed accurate!*

Step 3: Translate Customer Needs into Clear Targets. Regarding the particular process you picked to examine, given your assessment of customer needs along with an assessment of your most-important assumptions, pinpoint the specific *targets* that you must achieve in order to delight all your external and internal customers. Consider **what** they need, **when** they need it, **where** it should be delivered, and **how** you'll deliver it to them. Then translate each target into a number (for example, respond to each customer within 24 hours versus "as soon as possible"). Numbers will help members assess how well they are actually achieving their targets, as the focus later switches to controlling processes and then to improving processes. *But don't forget to verify your proposed targets with your customers!*

Step 4: Stipulate Supplier Inputs. What exactly do you need from internal and external suppliers in order to proceed with your work on the process you picked to examine? Consider these items: information, materials, tools, instructions, forms, and any intermediate products or services to which your work group adds value. Although you don't always receive these inputs just when you need them, specify the ideal: **what** you need, **when** you need it, **where** it should be delivered, and **how** it should be delivered to you – so you can proceed with your value–added process. Again, use numbers to stipulate your inputs. *But do not forget to verify your proposed numbers with your suppliers!*

Step 5: Flowchart the Ideal Process. Using those standard symbols (and the additional symbols), your group members can now draw a flowchart that shows the *ideal* way their value–added process should be performed in order to delight their customers and satisfy other key stakeholders. *Be sure to include several decision points (steps) for making mid-course corrections. And be absolutely sure to distinguish each and every task and decision as being CVA, OVA, or NVA.*

Step 6: Flowchart the Actual Process. At this point, your group should draw a flowchart to describe the *actual* process by which the work is now being done. Be sure to distinguish each and every task and decision as being CVA, OVA, or NVA. *Knowing the value (or lack thereof) of every step in your process will then help you streamline your process to be value-added for your customers and for your other key stakeholders.*

Step 7: Close the GAP. If there's a significant GAP between the ideal process and the actual process, continue with the steps of problem management: defining root causes (hence, identifying Description Barriers) and subsequently choosing solutions that are expected to remove those same Description Barriers. But no matter how well a new, revised process has been captured by a flowchart on paper or onscreen, *your group must still implement – hence use – this revised process as its standard operating procedure.*

Step 2: Controlling Processes

Once your value–added process has been described (and any significant GAPS between the actual and the ideal flowchart have been closed), the next step is to determine how well your group members are performing that revised, streamlined process in the workplace. In this section, I'll introduce several new concepts – and tools – to see if your work group is hitting its targets with random variation.

The prime reason for translating customer needs into targets, as numbers, is to be able to MEASURE (rather than guess) how well you are doing. Collecting data is a key tool for assessing if your process is under control and, if it's not, for doing something about it. The reason I stressed describing a process that occurs frequently (a few times every day or week) is so you can collect sufficient data to make your decisions with greater confidence, rather than basing your assessments on just one or two unique experiences with the process. If you and your group had chosen to describe a process that occurs only once or twice, a flowchart (done by all group members) can be a helpful planning tool, but it won't be possible to know whether that infrequent process is actually under control.

Is your group performing its value-added process reliably and consistently, day after day, which delights your internal and external customers or, alternatively, are your customers mostly dissatisfied since what they receive doesn't consistently meet their needs and expectations?

On Figure 10.15, I introduce the metaphor of **target practice** as a way of presenting some important statistical concepts in an intuitive, easy-to-understand manner. In particular, I define the center of the target – the bull's-eye – as the needs and wants of the end customer. **The primary goal in providing any product or service is to hit the bull's-eye, as perceived by the customer.** At times, customers can be rather vague about what they need or want. They say things as: "Give me quality, make it reliable, and be very nice about it." It is thus necessary to pinpoint just what customers actually want so you can determine if their needs are being met – what I call, "setting your sights."

The 10-point scale of vertical numbers in the middle of this target pinpoints exactly what the end customer needs or wants. Of course, any scale can be used in place of 1 to 10. But for now, we'll get used to setting our sights on a number on this target that, if obtained, would result in customer delight. As you might have noticed, this metaphor is a bit modified from the usual one for target practice (whether using darts or arrows). For one thing, I drew a horizontal line through the middle of the target, so the numbers above the bull's-eye represent different targets than the numbers below the bull's-eye. In addition, usually the bulls-eye is given the highest number (10), with the numbers decreasing as the circles move away from the center of the target. But for our purposes here, it's useful to show the scale as going from 1 to 10, from the bottom of the target to the top of the target.

FIGURE 10.15
DEFINING THE TARGET AND SETTING YOUR SIGHTS

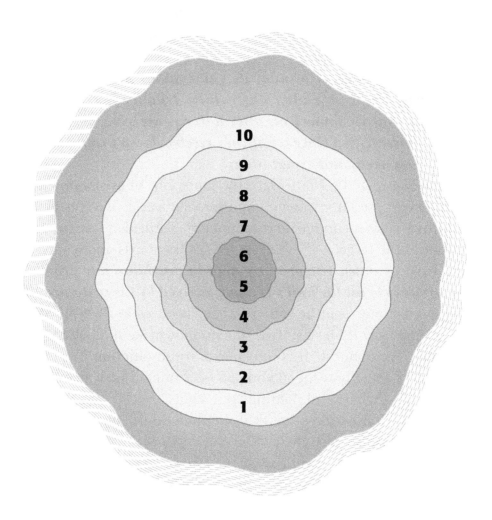

Let's now consider the case of a customer who always expects to receive delivery of a custom product within five to six hours after having ordered it. As shown in Figure 10.16, each white dot at the center of the target represents a "hit" for the customer at a different point in time. The concentration of white dots on the bull's-eye suggests perfect on-target performance: Every "hit" is within customer specifications, which thereby meets or exceeds customer expectations.

FIGURE 10.16
PERFECTLY ON-TARGET PERFORMANCE

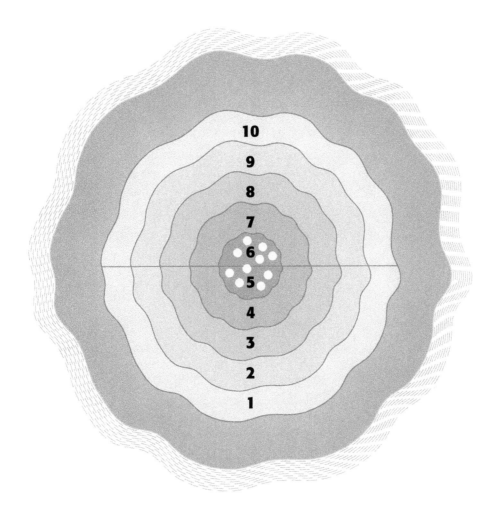

On Figure 10.17, we see the opposite result: **This distribution of hits (white dots) demonstrates inconsistent performance:** A customer cannot depend on the performance of this product or service from one moment to the next. On any day at any time, just about anything can and will happen – other than what is desired. As such, the performance of the process is clearly out of control and must therefore be corrected. If not, these customers are likely to purchase the product or service from someone else.

FIGURE 10.17
COMPLETELY OFF-TARGET PERFORMANCE

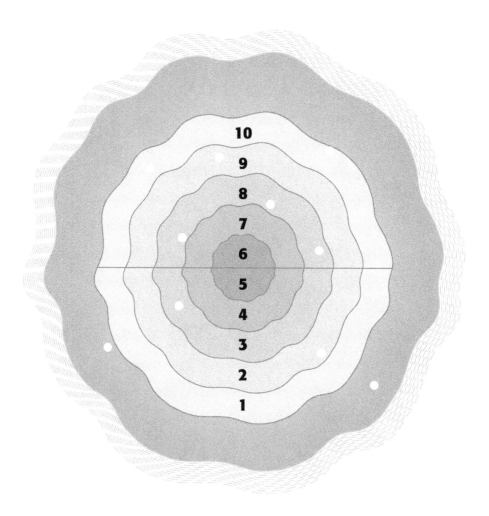

As shown on Figure 10.18, somewhere in between perfectly on-target and completely off-target performance, we experience what is **NORMAL:** Many hits at the center – with a few misses on other regions of the target. In a world where little, if anything, can be totally explained, predicted, and controlled (or measured with perfect precision), there will always be *some normal variation* in providing any product or service to customers. Imperfections result in *normal random variation* around the target.

FIGURE 10.18
NORMAL RANDOM VARIATION AROUND THE TARGET

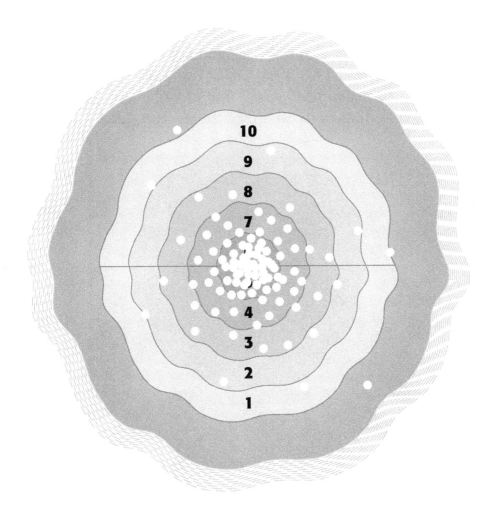

Actually, there is a key principle to remember at all times: No matter how careful and precise a member's effort, all processes are affected by "random variables" that can't be fully controlled: random variations in weather conditions; random variations in tools, machines, and materials; random variations in knowledge; variations in motivation; variations in cognitive, emotional, and behavioral skills; and the complex interplay of all combinations of these various causes of normal variation.

As Figure 10.18 implies, **it's necessary to collect many data points in order to know, with considerable certainty, whether your process is either UNDER CONTROL or OUT OF CONTROL.** When only a few data points are available, it's hard to know if those few hits are due to luck – or if the process is something a customer can really count on, again and again. On Figure 10.19, the pattern of hits on the target can be rearranged to reveal what is called a normal distribution of data points. **When the process is under control, the hits reveal the classic "bell-shaped" curve.**

FIGURE 10.19
FROM TARGET PRACTICE TO A NORMAL DISTRIBUTION

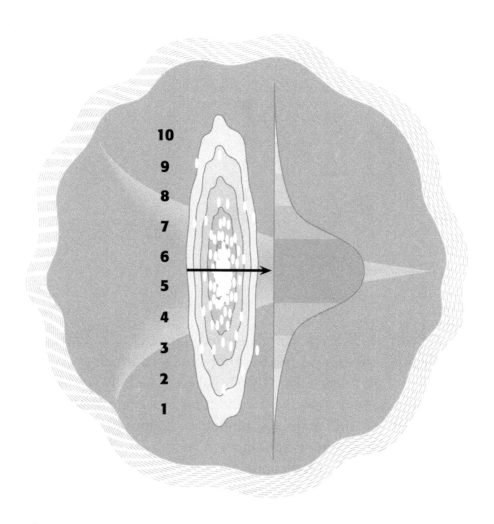

More specifically, on Figure 10.20, you can see exactly how the data points create that bell–shaped curve, as we transfer the hits on the target directly onto a statistical distribution of data points. We have seen this bell–shaped curve before: The Lockean Inquiring System, if you recall, focuses on the middle section of the normal distribution, what members can easily endorse, while the ends of the normal distribution are dismissed as irrelevant. Meanwhile, the Hegelian Inquiry System focuses on the extreme end points and ignores the middle of the normal distribution.

FIGURE 10.20
THE BELL-SHAPED CURVE OF A NORMAL DISTRIBUTION

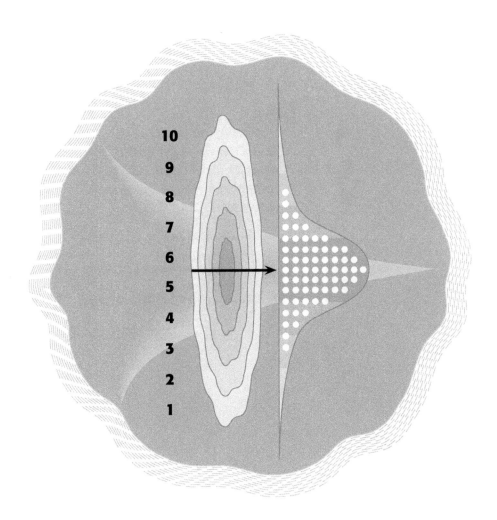

The Key Parameters of a Normal Distribution

The five terms listed on Figure 10.21 will be used frequently as we examine how to control processes. Our focus, however, is on understanding the core concepts – not on making statistical calculations or analyzing actual samples of data. As suggested in this diagram, **VARIATION** is the actual spread of data points (or hits) around the target. Shortly, I'll say more about each of these five key terms and plotting data points, so group members can discover if their processes are on–target with normal variation.

FIGURE 10.21
THE KEY PARAMETERS OF A NORMAL DISTRIBUTION

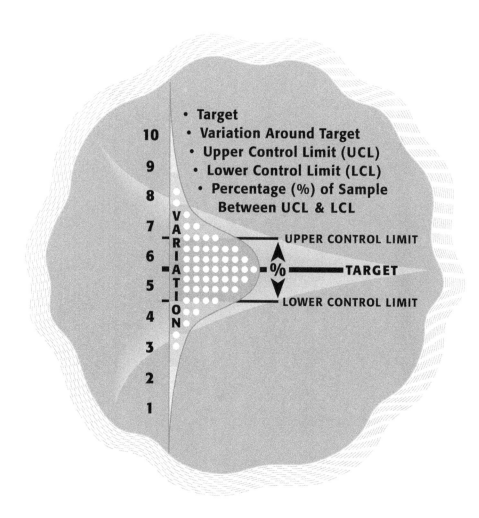

As you can see on Figure 10.22, an important attribute of a normal distribution is the actual percentage of data points that fall within the **Upper Control Limit (UCL)** and the **Lower Control Limit (LCL)** – depending on the "bands" of the distribution. The first band is always defined as one "standard deviation" around the mean/average of the distribution. The second band is two standard deviations around the mean, and so forth. ***Virtually all efforts at managing processes focus on the third band of the distribution for SENSING if a process is out of control.***

FIGURE 10.22
INSIDE THE THIRD BAND OF A NORMAL DISTRIBUTION

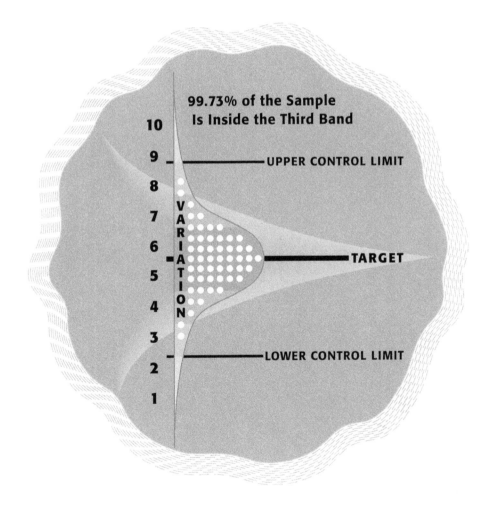

Practically speaking: If data points hit the target outside the third band more than 1% of the time, the process is identified as being out of control. If that were the case, the steps of problem management would then be used to define *why* the process is out of control and *what* can then be done about it. Figure 10.23 is a reminder that collecting data occurs one moment after another. While I initially showed you how the hits were arranged inside a normal distribution, **this diagram shows the actual sequence of data points along the dimension of TIME.**

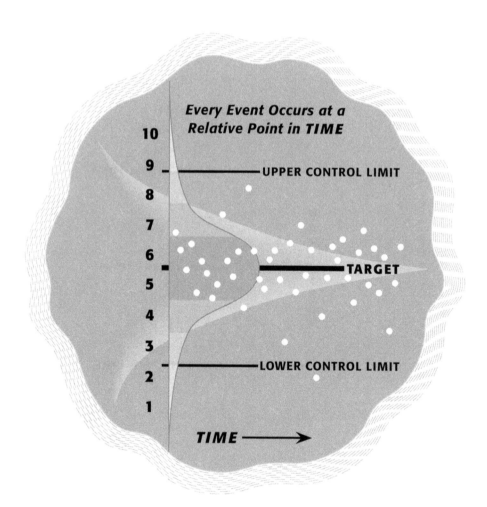

FIGURE 10.23
A TIME-BASED DISTRIBUTION OF DATA POINTS

How to Interpret a Process Control Chart

Figure 10.24 illustrates one of the most used tools of process management: **The Process Control Chart**. However, when only a few calculations are made to determine the UCL and the LCL, the graph is named a run chart. While it's easy to get carried away with making statistical calculations, a *value-added perspective* should always be taken: **Are the time and effort to make the statistical calculations worth the gain in precision?** A lot can be learned from graphing simple "run charts."

FIGURE 10.24
A Process Control Chart

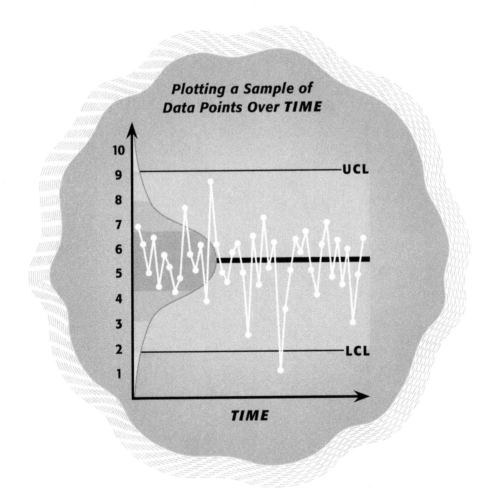

Regarding the Process Control Chart on Figure 10.25, just by eye-balling the distribution of data points, you can see that this process is out of control – what we previously called completely off-target. Notice the many data points that fall beyond the third band of the distribution – well beyond both the UCL and the LCL. **_Because the distribution of data points does NOT look like a bell-shaped curve, this process is surely out of control. But we can now do something about it: by first identifying the control barriers and then removing them._**

FIGURE 10.25
OUT OF CONTROL

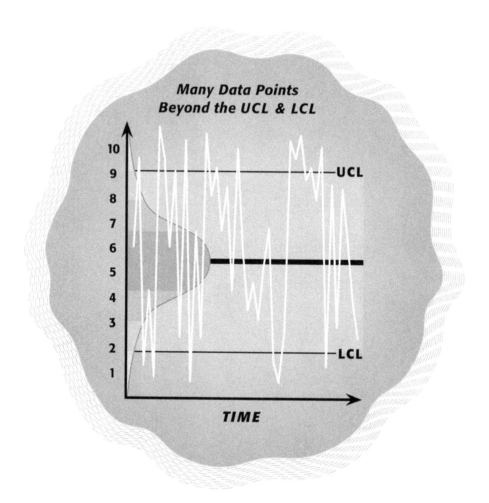

Figure 10.26 identifies two kinds of aberrations on a Process Control Chart, which also signal that a process is out of control. With practice, group members can learn to distinguish normal random variation from a trend or spike that is non-random in appearance. In fact, it's not difficult to identify *when* these trends and spikes took place, since the chart pinpoints the exact time when things went wrong – and thus who was working at that time and what else might've been going on at that time, which also could have undermined the performance of this process.

FIGURE 10.26
NON-RANDOM TRENDS AND SPIKES

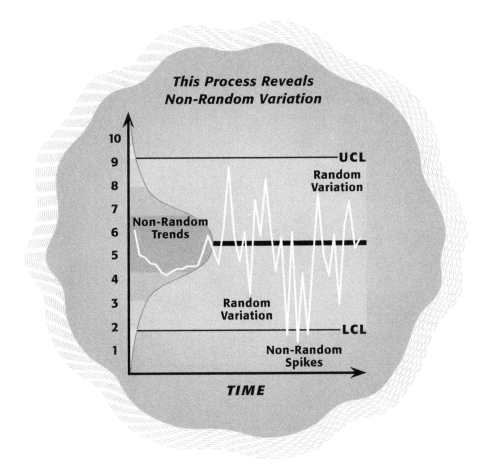

Figure 10.27 reveals the desired transition – from a process that was initially out of control to one that is now under control. Customers will now receive what they want when they want it – between the two control limits – no matter who performs the process. The challenge: If a process is out of control (hence, a problem has been sensed), define the root cause of the problem (identify the Control Barriers), and then continue with the next steps of problem management. If zero errors occur, this process will be under control in one cycle of problem management.

FIGURE 10.27
FROM OUT OF CONTROL TO UNDER CONTROL

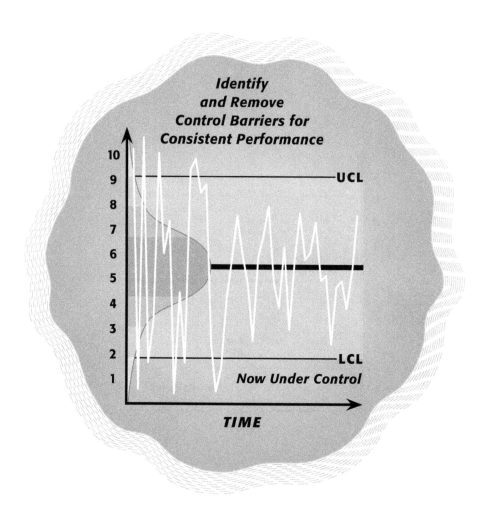

On Figure 10.28, I introduce a key principle that helps group members appreciate **the close relationship between controlling processes and improving processes.** Any process that is under statistical control (i.e., normal variation within the UCL and LCL) may not, however, be within the specification limits defined by the customer's **Upper Specification Limit (USL)** and the **Lower Specification Limit (LSL).** The process shown in this figure is not presently capable of consistently meeting customer needs. This under–control process is therefore a **non-capable process**.

FIGURE 10.28
A NON-CAPABLE PROCESS THAT DISAPPOINTS CUSTOMERS

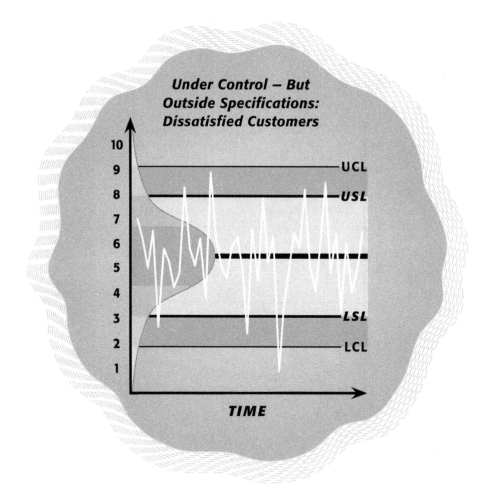

Notice that a number of points on this Process Control Chart are **outside** the customer's Upper Specification Limit (USL) and the Lower Specification Limit (LSL), even though more than 99% of the data points are **inside** the Upper Control Limit (UCL) and the Lower Control Limit (LCL). *Let us now see what a capable process actually looks like — as shown in Figure 10.29. The end customer, as before, wants a quality feature to range between 3 and 8, with 5.5 as the target. The improved process is now able to deliver — and does so consistently, again and again!*

FIGURE 10.29
A CAPABLE PROCESS THAT DELIGHTS CUSTOMERS

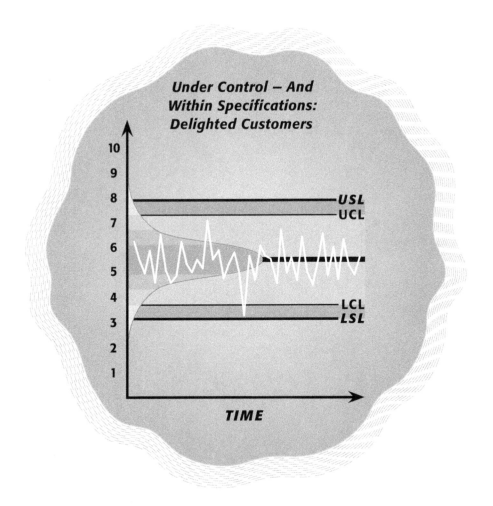

IDENTIFYING AND REMOVING CONTROL BARRIERS

I will now be more specific about what is actually meant by Control Barriers. As background, we always have to be open to the possibility that various GAPS in the behavioral infrastructure (culture–gaps, time–gaps, and team–gaps) or the formal systems (strategy–structure gaps and reward system gaps) might still be undermining this process – even though all members in the organization have actively participated in the first three tracks of quantum transformation and some of these members have been participating in the two PMOs for those middle two tracks. Aside from such GAPS that still need to be closed, let's consider some of the *root causes* that would prevent a value–added process from taking place as intended.

One possible root cause of a Control Barrier is the persistence of some Description Barriers that I discussed earlier. Specifically, **it should be apparent that a process would be out of control if members do not use their flowchart as the standard operating procedure to follow at all times in all situations.** In addition, another root cause that emerges from a flowchart concerns the decision points or check points in the process, as illustrated by those diamonds with "yes–and–no circles" that either return the process to a previous step or propel the process forward to the next step. In most cases, these explicit decision points are there to encourage members to monitor the quality of their work so, if necessary, they can make various mid–course corrections – and thus catch errors, defects, false assumptions, or other deficiencies before their outputs are delivered downstream to their internal and external customers. **Yet, when a process is frequently out of control, perhaps additional decision points should be added to the flowchart so group members have more opportunities to use self-feedback — which will signal them to transform that out-of-control process into an under-control process.**

Another Control Barrier would be operating if members were not making the best use of all the resources needed to perform the process. In other words, **by not applying members' efforts and skills on the right tasks according to the right objectives —**

and not having easy access to the required tools, technologies, materials, information, personnel, and policies for performing those tasks – processes become out of control very quickly.

Lastly, a Control Barrier would also be apparent if members have not been properly trained to perform their work – let alone if they have been trained to do something *besides* what's clearly specified in the latest flowchart. In many situations, in fact, **an ineffective or nonexistent training program is the PRIME root cause behind many out-of-control processes.**

You might be wondering why there's some overlap between the previous discussion on Description Barriers and this current discussion on Control Barriers. It seems that significant process improvement can be achieved merely by streamlining tasks and decisions in a flowchart and then ensuring that group members actually use this flowchart as their standard operating procedure, which might include adding on more decision steps for making mid–course corrections, training members to perform each step efficiently and effectively, and encouraging members to use all available resources for performing each step in the process. **All these process improvements can be achieved during that first step of DESCRIBING PROCESSES – without making a single statistical calculation for CONTROLLING PROCESSES.**

But even greater process improvement can be achieved by taking the next steps in process management: collecting data, making statistical calculations, and then using Process Control Charts to bring all processes under statistical control. Statistical process control thus enables group members to see – *much more precisely and convincingly* – if dutifully following the steps in their flowchart, making the necessary mid–course corrections, training employees, using all available resources to perform each process, and so forth, allows their value–added processes to function as intended. Bottom line: **Some organizations will be content with the gains they can achieve from explicitly describing their most value-added processes and then removing Description Barriers. Other organizations will want to add even more value to what they will hand off to their internal and external customers by**

removing any identified Control Barriers and thus statistically controlling their value-added processes within three bands of a normal distribution.

THE GENERIC STEPS FOR CONTROLLING PROCESSES

Step 1: Develop or Obtain Valid Measures. To conduct the next steps of process management, it is necessary to measure how the process behaves as your group proceeds to perform the tasks and make the decisions that are described in your process. Consider all the ways of counting how often something happens and how others experience your tasks and decisions – such as your customers. Valid measures in many cases include: (1) cycle time – how long it takes for your work group to complete the process; (2) process cost – how much it costs your organization to complete the process; (3) inventory levels – how much extra or excess materials you have to keep in stock due to unreliable processes; (4) errors, defects, or failures; and (5) customer delight.

Step 2: Collect Sufficient Data. Once you have selected or developed the measures that fit your process, your group must formulate a plan to collect data through repeated work cycles. Since you were asked to pick a process that takes place at least several times a week or several times a day, it shouldn't take long to collect sufficient data to plot a Process Control Chart. Caution: Do not restrict the data collection to just one person, at one time of the day, for only one customer. Be sure to collect data across the entire range of operating conditions for your process.

Step 3: Plot Process Control Charts. As previously shown on Figure 10.24, plot the data points on a Process Control Chart. Define your scales (vertical and horizontal axes) to contain the full range of data points during the entire time period. In case you wish to actually calculate the Upper Control Limit (UCL) and the Lower Control Limit (LCL), see: Amsden's book on *Statistical Process Control,* which will also explain when it's essential to plot *sub-groups of data points* (instead of only plotting each data point separately) in order to make sure that your process will display a NORMAL bell–shaped curve when it's under control.

Step 4: Examine Variation Around the Targets. Review your Process Control Chart for abnormal non–random variation (trends and spikes) suggesting that the process is out of control. You can determine if a trend or spike is random or non–random either intuitively or statistically. **Using intuition** is invaluable in detecting – by eye – the persistence of a trend or spike that is unlikely to be a chance occurrence. And it is also rather easy to detect if too many data points (well beyond 1% of your sample) are outside your estimates of the UCL and LCL on you Process Control Chart. For now, we will continue to rely on *intuition* for sensing if your process is out of control.

Step 5: Use the Steps of Problem Management to First Identify and Then Remove Control Barriers. If the analysis of variation around any target reveals that your process is out of control, the steps of problem management can be performed to identify the root cause of the GAP (which involves one or more of those identified Control Barriers), derive solutions, implement solutions, and evaluate results.

STEP 3: IMPROVING PROCESSES

The performance of group members is primarily determined by the design of their value–added process (including the effect of their surrounding systems), but is also affected by the random variation of equipment, materials, methods, people, information, and the interplay of these different "factors of production," also known as the "available resources." *But once the process is under control, group members cannot improve the target or reduce the variation around the target – if they neither improve the underlying process nor enhance the resources that are used in the process.*

As members become more and more proficient at describing and controlling their value–added processes, they often *become increasingly frustrated by resource constraints, especially when their under-control processes are STILL not capable of meeting customer specifications.* To repeat: During the first two steps of process management, group members must make effective use of whatever resources the organization has previously allocated to their subunit, group, and job. The best that members can do under these circumstances is to continue applying the assigned resources to their streamlined processes, while they keep those processes under statistical control.

Now, however, with the shift to improving processes, almost nothing is considered as fixed, let alone sacred. On the contrary, *each work group is expected to achieve better targets with less variation by changing the various resources that determine — cause — how the process behaves when it is under control.* The only real constraints stem from short–term resource limitations (or allocations) that a work group cannot persuade management to change, at least not for the time being.

Figure 10.30 illustrates what a Process Control Chart reveals when a process is improved over time by changing the resources that are used in the process. Here we see that the original target was 6 with the Upper Control Limit (UCL) of 10.5 and the Lower Control Limit (LCL) of 2, which thus creates a range of 8.5 units between those two statistical control limits.

As you can see, this process was initially under control. But then the customer wanted better service. In fact, the customer's specification was a target of 5 with an Upper Specification Limit (USL) of 7.5 and a Lower Specification Limit (LSL) of 2.5, which produces the range of 5 between those two specification limits. (The range, by the way, is a convenient estimate of variation.) If the group could accomplish this process improvement, the target would be reduced from 6 down to 5, which amounts to a 17% improvement, while the range around that better target would be reduced by 3.5, which amounts to a 41% improvement.

However, members need additional or modified resources to achieve an improvement in the target as well as a reduction in the variation around the target: *By providing better and faster technology, additional members, better materials, more timely information, more supportive policies, and more efficient flows (and locations) of people and other resources, group members will be able achieve their more ambitious goals and objectives.*

FIGURE 10.30

IMPROVING A VALUE-ADDED PROCESS

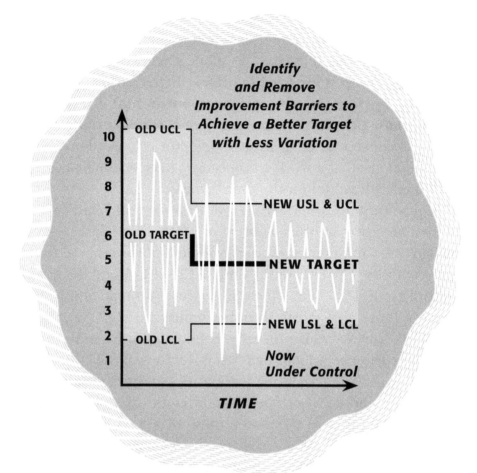

As additional resources are made available to the group, the new target will eventually be achieved. But first, the improved process will likely be out of control: Members first have to learn how to use the additional resources in an efficient and effective manner, because there's usually a steep learning curve to master. For example, if employees are added to the group, they must first be properly trained and they must then practice going through the various steps in the process – before they'll be up to speed with the more experienced members in the group. But in time, by first identifying and then removing the Control Barriers, the improved process will eventually be under control.

IDENTIFYING AND REMOVING IMPROVEMENT BARRIERS

Let's now consider six major categories of resources that are needed to perform – and then improve – a value-added process: people, technology, materials, information, policies, and flows (of people, things, and other resources). **When one or more of these resources are holding back a group's efforts to further improve its under-control processes, the identified resource limitations are called: Improvement Barriers.**

People: Examine how each group member's behavior, skills, traits, abilities, and mind/body/spirit consciousness affect your value-added process. *But first try to improve the human resources you already have in place (training current members), before you and your group even consider acquiring new resources (hiring new employees).*

Technology: Examine how computers, machines, tools, and equipment affect your process – any kind of mechanical and/or electronic device that extends you abilities to perform the tasks and decisions in your designated process. *If you have not yet learned how to improve the use of your old technology, however, what makes you think that it'll be any easier to use newer, more sophisticated technology?*

Materials: Examine how the quality of all the materials that you regularly receive from your internal and external suppliers affects your value-added process. Maybe now is a good time for your group to work with your suppliers in order to encourage them to provide high-quality inputs (on time) that achieve better targets with less variation.

Information: Examine how the kind, quality, and timing of information (and reports) affect your process. In particular, not having instant access to information about process costs, cycle times, defects, errors, inventory levels, and customer satisfaction is, in essence, another Improvement Barrier that typically stems from an out-of-date information system, which might implicitly be supported by a number of false assumptions.

Policies: Examine how various organization's policies (e.g., procedures, rules, and regulations) regularly affect your process. When asked about a particular policy, members might remark: "They're never going to change that approval process! It's been in place since the beginning of time!" Nevertheless, by explicitly questioning the underlying assumptions behind any restrictive policy that prevents your group from improving its value-added process, it's often possible to show senior management the folly of maintaining those outdated rules and regulations that nobody really wants or needs.

Flows: Examine how the location and flows of people, things and other resources affect your value-added process. I encourage you and your group to think about what travels through your organization, which includes people, materials, and information, which immediately affects how members perform their process. Indeed, some groups find it useful to flowchart how human and physical capital moves around from here to there – which can significantly affect your cycle times, process costs, and inventory levels. Bottom line: Your group needs to have immediate access to all kinds of resources, and getting these resources to WHERE they are needed, exactly WHEN they are needed, usually enables members to improve their process.

The Generic Steps for Improving Processes

Step 1: Benchmark Best Practices. It's so easy to fall into the trap of believing that no one else does it better than you and your group. Very often, in fact, the most fascinating approaches to your selected process are already occurring in work units in different organizations, industries, and nations. Hopefully, your group has already established desired norms that encourage all members to learn from other people and organizations: It's not only more efficient (instead of "reinventing the wheel"), but it's also more effective (since "two heads are better than one"). Note: The outdated cultural norm of "it wasn't invented here – so we can't and won't use it" is strikingly universal. Actually, it's hard to find a subunit or organization that hasn't had to confront this malfunction. But in a dynamic, interconnected, global economy, isolating yourself is not productive or psychologically healthy. Probably the best way NOT to get caught in your own trap is to make use of assumptional analysis. Most often, it is only a few out-of-date, hidden assumptions that can prevent your group from seeing the value of different approaches that were, in fact, "invented" by other subunits or other organizations.

Essentially, benchmarking encourages members to discover how others have addressed the same resource constraints with their value-added processes and have, in fact, already succeeded at identifying and removing those same Improvement Barriers – whether their resource constraints involved people, technology, information, materials, polices, or flows of all these resources. Finding the appropriate organizations to benchmark can take considerable time and effort – especially finding organizations that will readily share their practices with you and your group. But a special market developed many years ago to address this need: One of the first organizations to provide a benchmarking service is called the International Benchmarking Clearinghouse in Houston, Texas.

Keep in mind that there might be corporate policies and legal requirements concerning what can be shared between different organizations. First learn about these guidelines and restrictions before you contact other organizations to exchange information. While most people enjoy sharing their work with others, it does take time for them to show you their processes. This is time away from *their* CVA activities! Therefore, consider what you can offer others in exchange for your learning opportunity – so they can also benefit from your benchmarking projects.

Step 2: Establish World-Class Performance Goals. Once you've collected sufficient data to determine the size of the GAP between your value-added process and how others perform it, consider what's possible to achieve within the next year (broken down into a few intervals of three, six, nine, and twelve months). In as much detail as possible, establish world-class performance goals and their associated short-term objectives: What is your work group striving to accomplish – by what date, as assessed by whom, and based on which measures?

Step 3: Identify Improvement Barriers. Use the method of assumptional analysis as well as various statistical tools (e.g., Process Control Charts) to uncover the variety of Improvement Barriers that are preventing your work group from achieving its world–class performance goals. Once your group has thoroughly analyzed the various differences between your process and how others do it better, itemize what your group has learned about each identified Improvement Barrier and any remaining GAPS from the first three tracks that could still be operating (such as culture–gaps, skills gaps, and so forth). Surface and analyze your assumptions about what can, and cannot, be done differently, according to whom (stakeholders), and what your work group is able and willing to do differently – to close your process GAPS. Also, analyze your assumptions about what additional resources can be obtained or developed in order to improve your process. To resolve the many process conflicts that usually emerge from such discussions, be sure to use the conflict–handling modes that best fit the key attributes of the situation.

Step 4: Remove Improvement Barriers. Proceed with the next several steps of problem management (deriving solutions, implementing solutions, and then evaluating outcomes) so your work group can remove those identified Improvement Barriers and, thereby, achieve your world–class performance goals.

Step 5: Describe the Improved Process. Use the standard and additional symbols (including those background "colors" of black, gray, and white to indicate CVA, OVA, and NVA activities, respectively) so your group can describe (flowchart) the *improved* value–added process.

Step 6: Control the Improved Process. Once your work group has described that improved process, you need to collect data in order to see if it's under control. In case it is not, you'll then have to identify and remove Control Barriers – making use of problem management, assumptional analysis and, of course, conflict management, time management, team management, etc.

Step 7: Continue Improving the Process. Once you have been able to get your improved process under control, to what extent have you achieved your world-class performance goals? What new performance goals will inspire you to achieve an even higher standard of customer satisfaction – and delight? Do you need to conduct another round of benchmarking?

THE RADICAL PROCESS TRACK

We can now transition from gradual process improvement to radical process improvement. For one thing, benchmarking the most value-added processes within your work group might have revealed that gradual process improvement is not sufficient to achieve your world-class performance goals. Or it might be that previous efforts at gradual improvement have already achieved the limits of what's possible from managing processes WITHIN your work group – given the available resources. As a result, *any additional improvement now requires huge structural change across the traditional boundaries in your organization, which also includes modifying or adding even more resources to those longer process chains.*

There are two pre-conditions that must be established before an organization can successfully switch from gradual to radical process improvement:

The first pre-condition for radical process improvement is that organization-wide teamwork must be firmly established BEFORE attempting to proceed with radical change across the boundaries. It's one thing to develop trust and cooperation with your immediate colleagues inside your own work group for the purpose of improving your value-added processes. But it's quite another thing to gain that same level of trust and cooperation with members who come from OTHER subunits that represent OTHER functional areas, specialties, and disciplines. Once again, it's so important that the team track precedes the process tracks, but it's especially important that the first three tracks precede the initiation of any kind of radical change.

The second pre-condition for radical process improvement requires that members must already have become proficient at describing, controlling, and improving processes within their function-based subunit. Why is this so? Understanding human nature suggests that it would be more difficult to acquire these process management skills at the same time that members are trying to achieve (and absorb) massive change. Not surprisingly, it is much easier to learn something new under more relaxed conditions. Identical to the stated reasons for implementing the team track before proceeding with the strategy–structure track, existing work units will always be the most efficient and effective environment in which to develop the essential skills for gradual process improvement – and then to spread this new wisdom all around the organization. *Having established this foundation in process management skills, group members will be better able to understand (and accept) the particular reasons why certain cross-boundary processes must now be restructured into more encompassing horizontal work units — even if this means that numerous work units might be eliminated in which members have already taken the time and effort to describe, control, and improve their within-group, value-added processes.*

BUSINESS PROCESSES AND MANAGEMENT PROCESSES

Let's now distinguish two types of cross–boundary processes that are explicitly addressed during the radical process track: The first type of cross–business process is named, *business processes, which are primarily focused on Customer Value-Added (CVA) tasks and decisions*. Such business processes will likely include some OVA activities, since other stakeholders (such as the federal government, regulatory agencies, or trade unions) always pose some requirements on the organization. *But the main thrust of a business process is to delight the end customer.* Examples of business processes are as follows: Customer Request to Delivery; Customer Services; Manufacturing, Packaging, and Distribution; Enterprise Logistics; Partnering with Suppliers; and New Product Development. From these examples, you can probably tell that end customers would gladly pay for these tasks and decisions, since these business processes determine whether customers will receive exactly what they want, exactly when they want it.

The second type of cross-boundary process is usually called, ***management processes, which are primarily focused on Other Value-Added (OVA) tasks and decisions.*** Management processes are designed to streamline how the organization is managed, so these OVA activities primarily concern *internal* stakeholders who are managing the enterprise. As a result, management processes address such essential, behind-the-scenes tasks and decisions as planning, organizing, staffing, coordinating, reporting, budgeting, and so forth. ***Thus the main thrust of a management process is to satisfy key stakeholders OTHER than the customer.*** Examples of management processes include: Developing, Deploying, and Updating the Strategic Plans; Creating New Strategic Alliances; Allocating Resources Across Business Processes; Integrating the Differentiated Subunits; Improving the Behavioral Infrastructure; and Measuring and Rewarding Organization–Wide Performance. End customers, however, don't want to pay for these particular tasks and decisions since these activities don't immediately add value to the products or services that they wish to receive.

INTEGRATING STRUCTURE WITH PROCESS MANAGEMENT

There is a strong interconnection between strategy-structure and all three process improvement tracks: Redesigning processes within and across work groups assumes a particular strategy and structure: (1) where an organization is headed and (2) how it is organized into subunits to get there. Modifying the strategy of the organization has immediate implications for every business and management process, since strategy dictates what is meant not only by Customer Value–Added (CVA) activities, but also by Other Value–Added (OVA) activities. And modifying the structure of an organization changes the definition of what processes flow within – and across – subunits, since structure *defines* subunits, which includes their formal boundaries. Once again, we see the strong interrelationships among all eight tracks.

Recall the three kinds of task flow that can take place either WITHIN or ACROSS subunit boundaries. Pooled task flow is the easiest and least costly to manage: sequential and reciprocal task flow, however, require more time and energy to coordinate. In other words, handling sequential and reciprocal task flow adds to cycle time and process cost. As a result, containing sequential and reciprocal task flow WITHIN boundaries is precisely what enables each subunit to complete its work in the most efficient, effective, and satisfying manner possible – since members will have immediate access to the resources and authority needed to perform their most interdependent tasks. Sometime later, these subunits can easily add together their respective outputs, since mostly pooled task flow now crosses their formal boundaries.

Figure 10.31 translates the language of the strategy–structure track into the concepts for process management. Basically, task flow is just another way of describing the value–added processes that flow within and across work units. **This illuminating figure shows how the containment of task flow is exactly what brings value-added processes directly under the INTERNAL CONTROL of the members in every subunit.** The essence of radical process improvement is designing subunits around business processes, which, of course, begins with that flow of **inputs** from external and internal suppliers and then ends with the subsequent flow of **outputs** to internal and external customers: womb to tomb.

A self-managed, semi-autonomous group can more easily describe, control, and improve those processes since mid-course corrections are easier to manage (each group member becomes his or her own customer) than coordinating and responding to feedback between customers and suppliers who are located in other subunits in the same organization. By seeing the striking similarity between task flows and business processes, it becomes possible to design subunits that not only contain the costly task flows within subunit boundaries, but those semi–autonomous subunits also offer members the opportunity to describe, control, and improve their value–added business processes in the most efficient, effective, and satisfying manner.

FIGURE 10.31
STRATEGY-STRUCTURE MEETS PROCESS MANAGEMENT

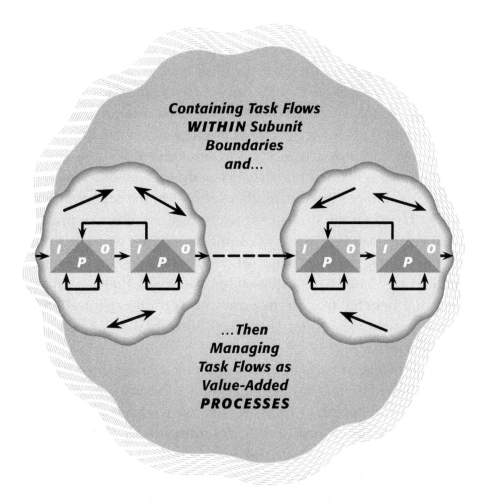

DESIGNING SUBUNITS AROUND FUNCTIONS OR PROCESSES

I will now address one of the most misunderstood questions about radical process improvement: ***Should subunit boundaries be organized around business functions or business processes?***

As I mentioned several times now, most organizations today are still structured into functions, specializations, or disciplines, which do not directly focus on delighting the end customer. The traditional boxes on a Newtonian organization chart are named for a well-developed area of expertise, for example: Accounting, Design, Engineering, Sales, Marketing, Operations, Production, R&D, Underwriting, Human Resources, Purchasing, and so forth. Even when a subunit is named Sales or Customer Service, the members in these business functions still have their hands tied, since they have little control over the design of the product or service itself, nor do they have control over their organization's delivery services to customers, since these business functions are assigned to *other* specialized departments. For example, it's often challenging for Sales or Service to promise customers that they'll receive certain products or services on a given day, at a certain time – since scheduling or delivery is up to someone else, who reports to another boss in another subunit in the organization.

But based on the strategy–structure concept of containing the most costly task flow within subunit boundaries along with the process management principle of directly focusing on delighting the end customer with value-added processes, there are many potential benefits from transforming a vertical organization of functional empires into a revitalized horizontal organization of business processes.

I'll now take you on a pictorial journey so you can clearly see the transformation of the organization's subunits from business functions into business processes. After we complete this journey of the **Newtonian House** and the **Quantum House**, I'll provide a useful example to illustrate just how a cross-boundary process can be radically improved when functional walls are eliminated, and, as a result, a much longer process chain can be contained within a single, more encompassing, process-based subunit.

THE NEWTONIAN HOUSE

Figure 10.32 illustrates what I playfully call the "Newtonian House," as based on our prior discussions about the Newtonian organization. For convenience sake, I show only three traditional functional specialties: Operations, Marketing, and Sales. But you can substitute other specialties that pertain to your organization or industry – whether it's an auto dealership or a university.

FIGURE 10.32
DESIGNING VERTICAL SUBUNITS FOR BUSINESS FUNCTIONS

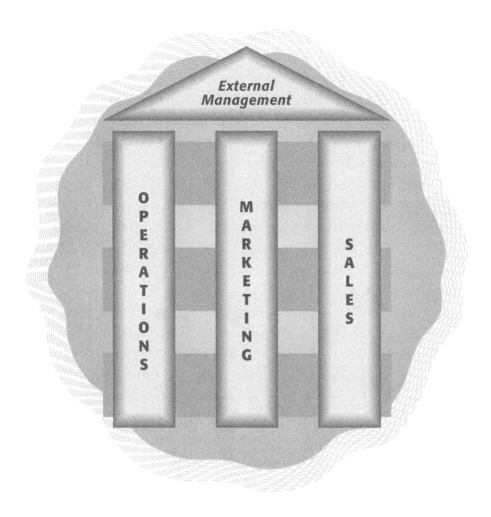

This figure shows three tall **vertical structures** – which takes each subunit a lot of (excess) time and effort to gain the needed cooperation from the other specialized departments. People have used terms like empires, silos, chimneys, fiefdoms, and fortresses to capture the usual rigid focus on pleasing the boss "upstairs" rather than pleasing customers "out there." Notice the pyramid shape on the top of the Newtonian House, which represents the traditional pyramid organization that is controlled by a slew of managers, who report to other managers – all of whom remain largely removed from the day–to–day activities that take place in their organization, which is why I purposely selected the label, **External Management**, to refer to the Newtonian pyramid.

Also notice the long horizontal bars in the background that lie in between those tall vertical bars, which represent what falls between the cracks or what is passed over the walls. It's essential to know that these often overlooked areas of "empty space" are precisely what tends to boost cycle time and process cost in a vertical organization. **Yet this so-called "empty space" between the vertical silos is anything but empty.** Indeed, no matter how well each specialized function performs its activities, the entire organization still can't perform to its potential – since the costly task flow between the vertical structures continually negate the dedicated efforts of these isolated functions. So let's take a closer look at what's actually inside these tall vertical structures in this Newtonian House.

In Figure 10.33, you can see the sequential and reciprocal task flow that's within each of the tall vertical silos, each representing a business function (Operations, Marketing, Sales, etc.). For the time being, group members in each subunit only focus on their own specialty. However, we can see the start of gradual process improvement within these functional departments, as members begin viewing task flow in process terms: arranging their work into a continuous flow of tasks and decisions – which they can subsequently describe explicitly by drawing a flowchart of their value–added processes. **But notice the arrangement of task flow is moving vertically, up and down the hierarchy, focusing only on what the boss or manager needs or wants – NOT focusing on what the end customer needs or wants.**

FIGURE 10.33
TASK FLOW WITHIN TALL VERTICAL SILOS

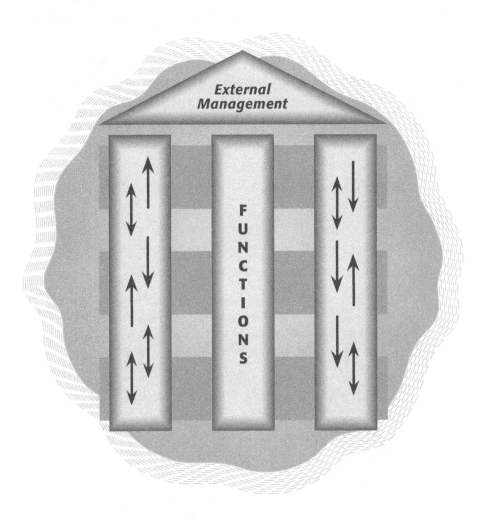

On Figure 10.34, you can see that the vertically arranged task flow within each department has now been developed into an explicit process chain, based on the specialized knowledge of the members in that subunit. But, once again, the focus is satisfying senior managers up the hierarchy – who externally control the members below. As you might expect, satisfaction also flows to the top of the hierarchy, since senior managers are usually most pleased with their role in the organization – while the members at the bottom of the hierarchy are usually the most dissatisfied.

FIGURE 10.34
GRADUAL PROCESS IMPROVEMENT WITHIN TALL VERTICAL SILOS

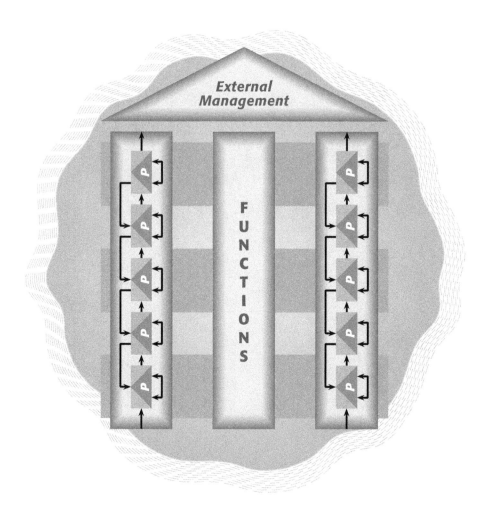

On Figure 10.35, let's reflect on the often overlooked "open space" or "white space" on an organization chart, which is what boosts cycle time and process cost in a vertical organization. In fact, the more that costly task flow falls into the open space on these horizontal bars, the more that members will be limited in how effectively they can gradually improve all their value-added processes, since the formal authority and resources to redesign these processes have already been allocated to other functional departments in the organization.

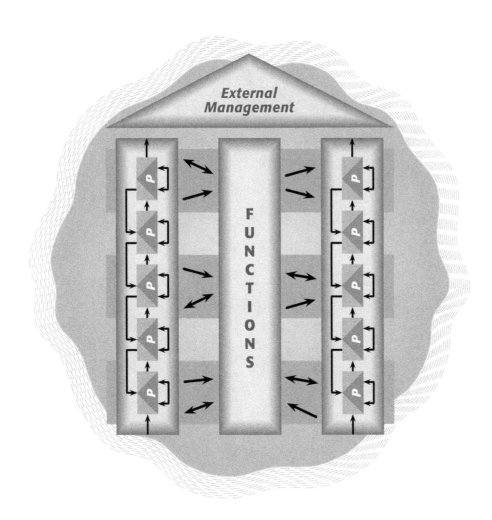

FIGURE 10.35
THE FILLED SPACE BETWEEN TALL VERTICAL SILOS

Figure 10.36 shows that External Management often relies on cross–functional teams to address all the excessive task flow that cuts across the organization's specialized, vertical departments. As a result, many members will be assigned to one, if not more, cross–functional teams for the purpose of describing, controlling, and improving all this cross–boundary task flow. If just a few such teams are used, this patch–up solution may be effective. But when more interdependent task flow fills those horizontal bars, many cross–functional teams must be established.

FIGURE 10.36
USING CROSS-FUNCTIONAL TEAMS TO MANAGE TASK FLOW

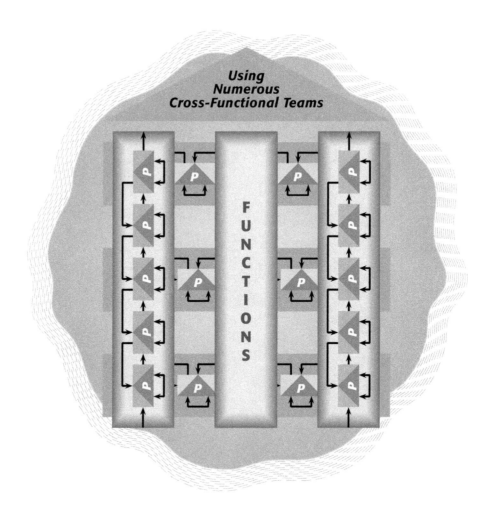

Even for organizations that have already implemented the first three tracks, it's only human nature for members to be more loyal to their back–home work group than to the other members on a cross–functional team, since people tend to be more loyal to the members of their own family than to different people in the neighborhood. Further, the managers in functional departments usually administer the reward system for their direct reports – who are only rewarded for performance that's directly relevant to that particular functional department. Most often, member participation on cross–functional teams doesn't even count when it comes to the reward system that's administered within each functional department. As a result, ***while cross-functional teams might look great on paper, they usually do not work well in practice, because psychological and cultural bonds, physical proximity, and the administration of the reward system all make it easier and quicker to address problems and conflicts WITHIN established work units, rather than addressing such challenges with members who come from other departments.***

Even though cross–functional teams can easily be assembled to manage the processes that flow across subunit boundaries, cycle times and process costs increase dramatically by members having to go back and forth across subunit boundaries. ***Instead of producing increased cycle time and process costs from using numerous cross-functional teams to compensate for a deficient structural design, it is probably best for organizations to take a serious look at rearranging members and all other resources into horizontal business processes — which takes our pictorial journey into the realm of radical process improvement.***

THE QUANTUM HOUSE

Figure 10.37 illustrates the Quantum House: Self–managing, semi–autonomous subunits replace the authority and top–down control of External Management over the members below. The horizontal bars that were in the background of the Newtonian House now move to the foreground, since the Quantum House designs subunits around the HORIZONTAL business processes.

In these new horizontal subunits, group members are provided with the necessary authority – and resources – to control most of the task flow for that much longer PROCESS CHAIN than was previously the case when these same members were assigned to specialized, vertical subunits. As a result, **members are now able to self-manage their own work without first having to get the necessary approval up and down the hierarchy from External Management. Nor do members have to waste their time and energy constantly crisscrossing those rigid vertical silos.**

FIGURE 10.37
DESIGNING HORIZONTAL SUBUNITS FOR BUSINESS PROCESSES

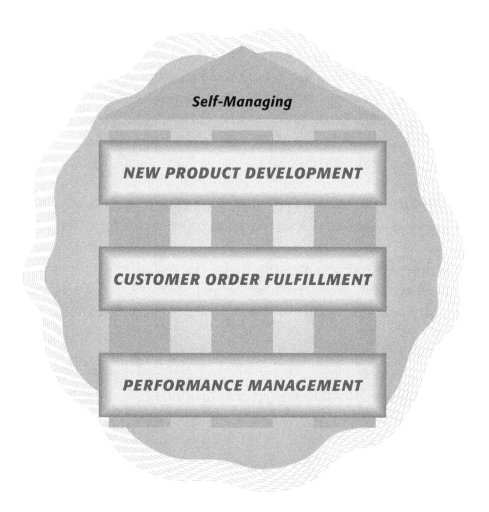

In the previous figure, the Quantum House makes use of two business processes: (1) New Product Development (which spans the business functions of Marketing, R&D, Design, Finance, and Operations) and (2) Customer Order Fulfillment (which spans the business functions of Sales, Customer Service, and Delivery of Products and Services). But to add a little spice to this example, I also add a management process: (3) Performance Management (which might integrate Strategic Planning, Allocating Resources, Budgeting, Accounting, and Human Resources).

FIGURE 10.38
TASK FLOW WITHIN HORIZONTAL SUBUNITS

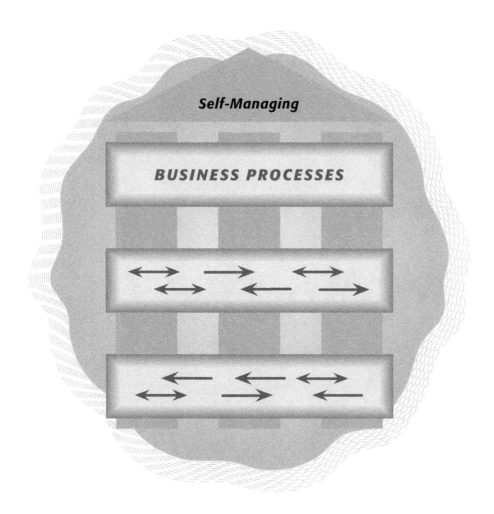

On Figure 10.38 on the previous page, you can see that the reciprocal and sequential task flows in this Quantum House are now primarily contained inside the larger, more encompassing horizontal work units. Many of these task flows had previously fallen between those cracks in the antiquated Newtonian House. Most important, **the direction of the task flow in the Quantum House is now horizontal, which thus flows directly toward the end or final customer — instead of up the hierarchy to External Management.**

FIGURE 10.39
RADICAL PROCESS IMPROVEMENT

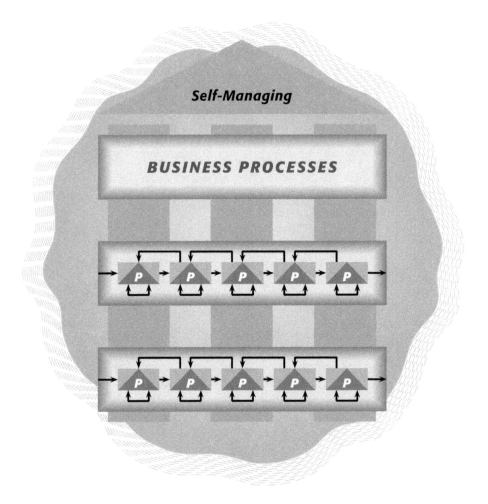

As you can discern from Figure 10.39, group members in the horizontal organization have now translated the reciprocal and sequential task flows into value–added processes, which can then be explicitly described, statistically controlled, and continually improved. As a result, this Quantum House has achieved radical improvement, since members are now able to wrap their arms around a much longer process chain with much more authority and resources than they previously had in their vertical, highly specialized, functional departments.

FIGURE 10.40
THE FILLED SPACE BETWEEN LONG HORIZONTAL HIGHWAYS

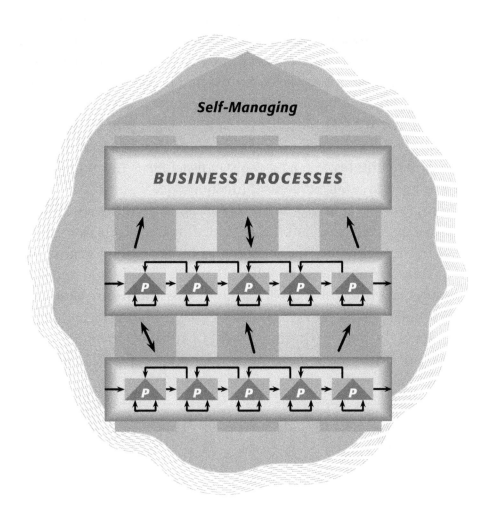

But as the previous Figure 10.40 reveals, there'll always be SOME interdependent task flow that falls between the cracks, since arranging the complex activities in today's world can never be perfectly and completely contained within subunits with any kind of structural design. As such, this horizontal organization still has some "open space" that must be addressed in those tall vertical bars in the background. While names such as silos or chimneys have been used to nickname the functional subunits in a Newtonian organization, the process-based subunits of a horizontal organization might be nicknamed highways, tunnels, or bridges, implying that even semi-autonomous subunits have SOME interdependent task flow across their boundaries.

Figure 10.41 concludes our pictorial journey that addresses the fundamental question that I posed earlier: ***Should subunits be organized around business functions or business processes?*** On this figure, it is apparent that any costly tasks flow that now falls between the horizontal subunits can be explicitly described, statistically controlled, and continuously improved by forming a few – not many – cross-process teams. A ***cross-process team*** is a group of members who represent two or more process-based, horizontal subunits versus a *cross-functional team* that represents two or more specialized vertical functions.

This evolved quantum organization directly addresses: (1) the most strategically relevant, value-added business processes that have been assigned to the horizontal subunits in the foreground and (2) the cross-process task flow that falls into the old vertical business functions in the background. This ***Quantum House*** – which builds on all previous tracks of quantum transformation – represents the very best arrangement of systems, processes, and people for achieving long-term success in an imperfect, chaotic, and complex world.

FIGURE 10.41
THE PROCESS-BASED QUANTUM ORGANIZATION

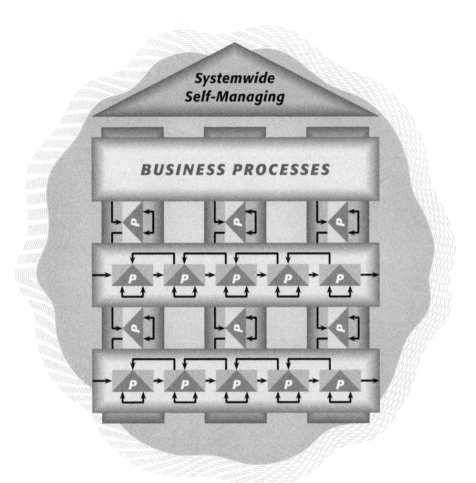

Organizing PMOs for the Radical Process Track

Let's now consider the PROCESS Management Organization, which is another type of PROBLEM Management Organization. *While the PROBLEM Management Organization concentrates on addressing complex problems, the PROCESS Management Organization focuses on complex processes.* It should come as no surprise that we use a PMO for radical process improvement. The fifteen to twenty-five participants who'll be assigned to the PMO's four personality-style C-groups (which can also include external suppliers and customers) can then surface, classify, and debate the assumptions behind four radically different ways of designing a business or management process. After the intensive community debates, one or more S-groups are formed with one or two members from each personality-style C-group, who also have developed a balanced use of the five conflict modes. The mission for each S-group, of course, is to resolve the remaining unresolved assumptions in order to deduce a new conclusion. The first new tree in the quantum forest will reveal the structural design of the new horizontal organization; the second new tree will provide the implementation plan for formally establishing that new horizontal organization – ideally, without any of the vertical walls that typically interfere with long-term success in today's world.

In my four-hour recorded course on this subject, Improving Process Management for Organizations, you'll receive a 38-page document: Work Sheets on Managing Complex Processes. Such extensive materials enable the PMOs in the radical process track to establish the most effective quantum organization.

An Example of Radical Process Improvement

Starting with Figure 10.42, I'll now present the core concepts of radical process improvement. Take the case of four functional departments that are structured into a tall vertical organization: Sales, Credit, Manufacturing, and Shipping. These four subunits are all involved when a customer places an order. Yet not one subunit, by itself, can manage all the task flow.

FIGURE 10.42

AN EXAMPLE OF RADICAL PROCESS IMPROVEMENT

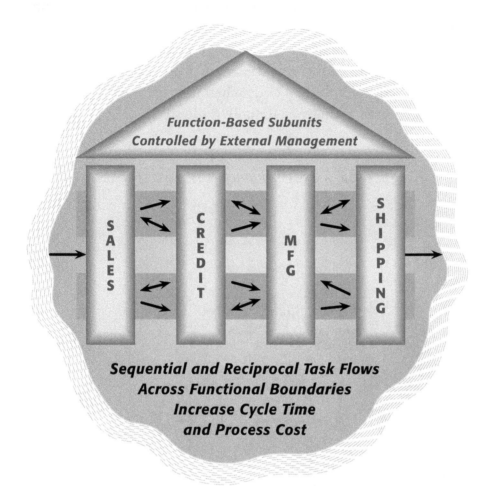

Although numerous cross-functional teams can help manage all the sequential and reciprocal task flow that falls between the cracks, the extra time and effort to work across the walls of these traditional silos significantly increases cycle times, process costs, inventory levels, and customer dissatisfaction.

Once members have established (1) an effective behavioral infrastructure by having actively participated in those first three tracks of quantum transformation, (2) two effective PMOs for the strategy–structure track and reward system track, and (3) a few rounds of gradual process improvement within their functional areas, a Process Management Organization (PMO) is formed of a few representatives from each of those four vertical departments, including a few senior managers, suppliers, and customers.

As shown on Figure 10.43, the PMO members have described the complex, cross–functional business process that starts with a customer request and then ends when the customer receives the product or service that was initially requested.

FIGURE 10.43
DESCRIBING A CROSS-FUNCTIONAL BUSINESS PROCESS

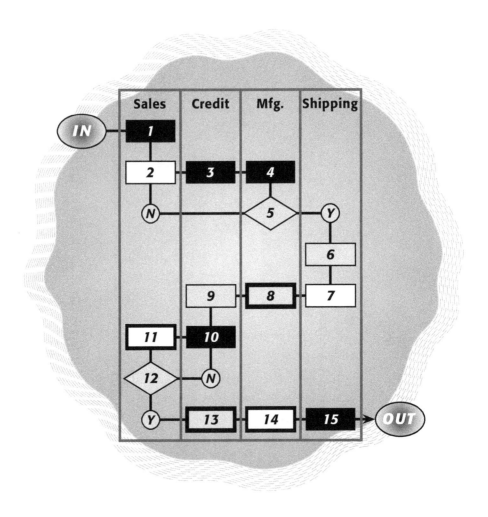

The tall vertical lines pinpoint the boundaries – the walls – that typically divide the functional subunits in an organization. On that same figure, notice that the tasks and decisions of this process are distinguished according to the three types: Customer Value–Added (shown in black), Other Value–Added (displayed in gray), and No Value–Added (depicted in white).

Now I introduce a new symbol that's especially useful when flowcharting cross–boundary processes: ***a thick line around a task or decision signals duplication*** – a common symptom of vertical functional subunits that don't communicate, collaborate, or trust one another. Basically, as a hedge against not receiving inputs just when they're needed, subunits accumulate *just-in-case* inventory by wasting time and effort on completing those tasks themselves, rather than waiting endlessly to receive those same materials or information *just-in-time* from other departments in the organization. ***But once a cross-boundary process has been described on a flowchart, it will be rather easy to eliminate the No-Value-Added (NVA) duplicated tasks and decisions that were propelled by a silo-based culture of "we'll do it ourselves!"***

On Figure 10.44, you can see that the tall vertical lines that had previously divided the four function–based subunits have all been eliminated. Now, a much longer process chain can be radically improved without being constrained by any functional department hoarding resources that other units need for process improvement. What were initially fragmented business functions that focused only on a small portion of the entire process chain have been assigned to one horizontal, business–process subunit, which is named, ***The Order fulfillment Process.*** Now, instead of negotiating across kingdoms, fiefdoms, turfs, and chimneys, one all–encompassing, semi–autonomous, horizontal process enables psychological bonds among group members – as supported by their desired cultural norms and effective sanctioning systems – to manage the most costly task flow from beginning to end, as a closed loop. ***This empowered, process-based subunit will have the authority – and the resources – to manage a long process chain in an efficient, effective, and satisfying manner.***

FIGURE 10.44

RESTRUCTURING BOUNDARIES AROUND A BUSINESS PROCESS

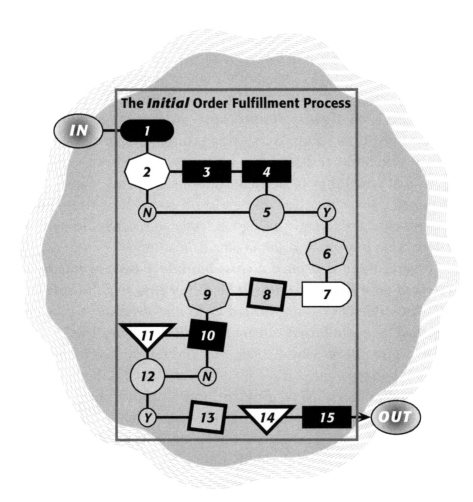

This flowchart of "The *Initial* Order Fulfillment Process" also makes use of those additional symbols that distinguish different kinds of tasks and decisions. Specifically, this description of the entire process chain reveals the No Value–Added (NVA) activities that involve members having to explain something before action can be taken, having to check with other subunits before certain decisions can be made, having to explain why something has to be done a certain way, then having to wait around for approval, next having to write a report that's being duplicated in another department, followed by further explaining and defending, and then having to store some material that is already being stored at another location in another subunit (as indicated by the thick border on this duplicated task), and so forth.

Those additional symbols make it very easy for members to clearly see that many of the steps in their business process are NVA and OVA activities, but NOT Customer Value-Added tasks and decisions. As you can determine from those black symbols, CVA activities involve only 5 steps in this 15–step process chain. The PMO members of The Order Fulfillment Process, however, can now proceed to streamline this process and then redescribe it for the members in the new horizontal organization to use as their standard operating procedure.

Figure 10.45 shows the NEW, streamlined, Order Fulfillment Process, which was developed by eliminating all NVA activities while minimizing OVA activities. *All the remaining CVA tasks and decisions can now be managed within one encompassing subunit that readily communicates with external customers, quickly initiates their orders, seamlessly brings their orders to completion, and then rapidly delivers these finished products or services to the right customers at the right time.* As long as this radical change in structure and process is effectively reinforced – and rewarded – by the new performance–based reward system, members will be inspired to do their very best, one work cycle after another, thus sustaining a *growth cycle*.

As you can see at the bottom of the figure, there will always be some "leftover" task flow that falls between the cracks of a horizontal organization, which can then be coordinated with a *few* cross–process teams. Nevertheless, the old Newtonian House of tall, vertical, function–based subunits has been transformed into a Quantum House of horizontal structures of process–based subunits, which will now statistically control and continuously improve their business and management processes.

FIGURE 10.45
REMOVING DESCRIPTION BARRIERS

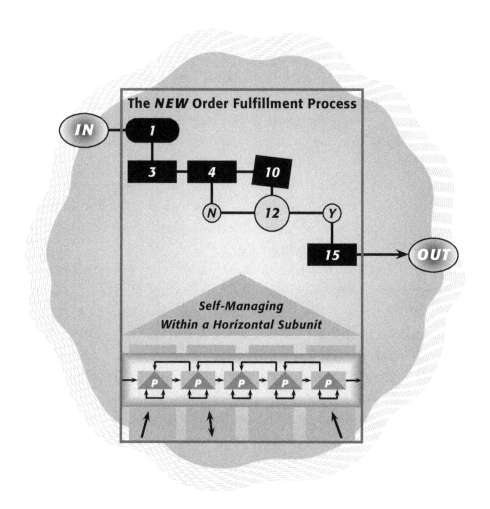

THE LEARNING PROCESS TRACK

Peter Senge's book, *The Fifth Discipline*, which was published in 1991, is often credited with stimulating the surge of interest in organizational learning. Based on numerous research studies on systems thinking at Massachusetts Institute of Technology (MIT), Senge defined learning organizations in this way:

Learning Organizations are "organizations where people continually expand their capacity to create the results they truly desire, where collective aspiration is set free, and where people are continually learning how to learn together." (page 1)

Soon after Senge's book appeared, David Garvin, a professor at the Harvard Business School, while admiring the inspirational quality of Senge's definition of organizational learning, criticized Senge's work for its vagueness. Garvin insisted that **we must be more specific about what organizational learning means, how to measure it, and how to manage it — what he called the three Ms — if organizations are to derive economic value from this novel approach to long-term success.** Garvin officially provided his own definition: "A learning organization is an organization skilled at creating, acquiring, and transferring knowledge, and at modifying its behavior to reflect new knowledge and insights." (page 80) Garvin's definition says what organizational learning is intended to produce: **better knowledge for better action.**

Ikujiro Nonaka, a Japanese professor who received his Ph.D. degree at the University of California at Berkeley, took a similar approach with his theory of the **knowledge-creating company**. Nonaka noted that knowledge creation involves transforming what is now *implicit* (such as an idea that hasn't been discussed or shared) into something *explicit* – by expressing, documenting, and then sharing this knowledge widely in an organization. **An continual cycle of moving back and forth between IMPLICIT IDEAS and EXPLICIT KNOWLEDGE thus defines the flow for creating useful knowledge.**

As you've seen throughout this chapter, at the very start of process management, we recognize an *implicit* flow of tasks and decisions that are mostly habitual and unconscious – and then make these tasks and decisions *explicit* in the form of a flowchart. In fact, throughout the completely integrated program, whether the discussion is about cultural norms, hidden assumptions, or group process, **we always uncover something that's IMPLICIT**

and then make it EXPLICIT, so it can be discussed and debated within a work group, and then, if necessary, it can be improved through knowledge–based action.

But what is knowledge? Two types of knowledge have been proposed: **Declarative knowledge** is a conceptual understanding of systems, dynamics, relationships, events, and facts (knowing why, knowing about, or knowing that something else is about to happen) – whether or not you can *do* anything with this type of knowledge. **Procedural knowledge** is having the skill to actually do something, mentally or physically (knowing how) – whether or not you *understand* what you're doing. **Integrating declarative with procedural knowledge offers the best of both worlds, thus providing the "whys" behind the "hows" for informed decision making, action taking, and learning across all organizational, industry, and national boundaries.** (Take note of the subtitle of this book!)

But where is knowledge located? Organizations make some of their declarative and procedural knowledge explicit and then store it electronically or on paper (as policies, procedures, and processes). **But most of the knowledge acquired and used for organizational tasks and decisions turns out to be located in the minds of individuals.** Interestingly, cognitive psychologists (e.g., Leahey and Harris) believe that each person's knowledge is stored as categories and interrelationships as networks (schemas) in his or her mind. And, it's especially interesting to know that two types of mental schemas have been proposed: **declarative schemas** are mental networks of meaning for understanding the "whys," and **procedural schemas** are mental networks of action for performing the "hows." Thus, those two types of knowledge, declarative and procedural, perfectly match those two types of schemas in a human being's mind.

But there's another relevant parallel in the study of learning, knowledge, and mental schemas. In particular, there are a couple of methods for improving a person's mental schemas: The first approach is known as **GRADUALLY restructuring schemas** – by adding several new categories or changing some relationships among those categories. The second approach is referred to as **RADICALLY restructuring schemas** – by changing schemas as a whole and their relationship with other whole schemas. As such, to enhance individual and organizational learning, **we must be able to describe, control, and improve all the declarative and procedural schemas in every person's mind — both gradually and radically.** Isn't that amazing! The way we improve our work processes in organizations with those recurring cycles of gradual and radical process improvement perfectly parallels that way in which we can improve the declarative and procedural schemas in our mind.

But where is the mind located? The classic debate still rages whether the organic brain contains all of a person's mind and consciousness, or if the brain is a conduit for the collective mind that exists "out there" somewhere in the holographic universe (as we'll discuss in the next chapter on Expanding Consciousness). Nevertheless, explorations of the human brain with the latest imaging technologies reveal that the brain's organic structures and biochemical networks store both the long-term memory and the short-term memory of our declarative and procedural knowledge. Specifically, the cerebral cortex and the cerebellum amass long-term – **implicit** – memory in our automatic neural networks. The hippocampus and the surrounding cortical tissues can use conscious, short-term – **explicit** – memory to accurately retrieve those schemas from our long-term memory, next use these schemas to collect data, make decisions, or take action, and then gradually or radically restructure these schemas before they are stored back into long-term memory.

Suffice it to say that the effective functioning of a quantum – learning – organization nicely parallels the dynamic functioning of neural networks in the brain and networks of meaning and action in the mind. To succeed, **a quantum organization must function as a collective brain that has continual access to both its declarative and procedural schemas — and can restructure those schemas gradually and radically as needed.** Developing a collective mind/brain of shared schemas represents the essence of creating, storing, retrieving, and using knowledge within and across all the boundaries in a quantum organization.

Recognizing the mental and neurological processes that allow individuals to learn makes it so much easier to understand the corresponding organizational processes by which knowledge is being acquired, distributed, interpreted, and used. In particular, everything we've learned to date about describing, controlling, and improving processes within and across subunits can now be applied not only for gradually and radically improving learning processes in organizations, but also for gradually and radically improving the learning processes that are flowing inside every member's mind/brain.

I offer this definition for establishing learning organizations: *Learning organizations explicitly describe, statistically control, and continuously improve the processes by which knowledge is obtained, interpreted, stored, retrieved, and used — within and across all subunits — in order to delight customers and satisfy other key stakeholders.*

THE GENERIC STEPS FOR THE LEARNING PROCESS TRACK

There are a few steps involved for using the tools of process management for describing, controlling, and improving learning processes:

1. Members learn the necessary skills for gradual and radical process improvement;
2. Members describe the processes by which they obtain and use knowledge for gradually and radically improving their performance;
3. Members bring their learning processes under control;
4. Members improve their learning processes — so they can obtain and use knowledge better and faster during every subsequent performance cycle.

Notice that the first step is learning the skills for gradual and radical process improvement. As you might imagine, **it is much easier for members to initially learn how to make their WORK tasks and decisions explicit in a flowchart, before they tackle the more subtle and unfamiliar processes by which they create declarative and procedural KNOWLEDGE.** But once members have gone through a few rounds of improving processes, both within and across subunits, they are then ready to uncover the unconscious steps they go through as they learn something new and then translate their rather **implicit experiences** into **explicit knowledge** that can be shared – and used – with other members throughout the organization.

THE LEARNING IMPERATIVE AND THE HALF-LIFE PRINCIPLE

I will state the **Learning Imperative** in the extreme so you'll never forget it: **If organizations do not learn how to obtain and use knowledge better – and faster – in our highly competitive global marketplace, and if organizations don't translate what they learn into radically improved systems, processes, people, products, and services – they will die.** As a result, it's imperative that members radically improve their learning processes, since how organizations create – and use – knowledge will ultimately determine whether they survive, let alone thrive.

Bottom line: Learning may be the most unique ability that distinguishes human beings from all other animals. We create organizations to provide what individuals on their own can't do. If we can renew organizations with the capacity to learn that is far beyond individual capabilities, our organizations will be able to reach beyond the stars. It all begins and ends with learning. In fact, one way of viewing the eighth track is to consider the seven prior tracks as establishing the necessary systems, processes, and people for creating organizations that can learn better and faster, year after year, which benefits all living beings and the planet itself.

I'll conclude this section with Ray Stata's "Half-Life Principle for Organizational Learning." He proposed that the key indicator for effective institutionalized – collective – learning is **when an organization can complete a complex project, with the same or better quality, in half the time than it took before.**

ESTABLISHING A PMO FOR THE LEARNING PROCESS TRACK

The shadow track establishes another Process Management Organization (PMO) that is composed of fifteen to twenty-five members who represent most or all of the subunits in the newly emerging quantum organization. This PMO's exclusive mission is to describe, control, and improve the learning processes that flow within and across the boundaries. Capturing value-added knowledge and making it immediately available in customized forms for all subunits in the organization – the primary goal of organizational learning – is aided by various software programs for knowledge management. As this PMO learns how to manage knowledge better and faster, a *quantum organization* can reduce the time it takes to improve its behavioral infrastructures, formal systems, and business ventures the next time around. Being able to perform these complex projects in half the time as before is the underlying goal of the learning process track. And if any subunit is faced with a perplexing problem, it can quickly learn if that same problem has already been addressed by the other subunits in their organization. In addition, a subunit might also contact other organizations in other industries – to learn more.

CONCLUDING THOUGHTS

Gradual process improvement initially takes place within the boundaries of subunits that were previously organized as highly specialized, functional departments. The overall structure of the organization is considered as fixed, at least for the moment. But this temporary constraint serves to provide a safe and familiar environment for members to learn the basic principles and tools for process management.

Radical process improvement, however, takes very little for granted. While Reengineering has often focused on information technology, the essence of this process track is challenging the implicit assumptions behind old structural arrangements. As a result, previously designed vertical subunits that were organized according to specialized *functional areas* can now be transformed into new horizontal subunits that are structured for performing *business processes* for the end customer.

Learning process improvement is being self-reflective: How did we improve all aspects of our organization (as represented by all the interconnected systems, processes, and people in the Complex Hologram) – and how can we do this work better and faster during the following cycles of quantum transformation? This same learning perspective can also be used for enhancing behavioral infrastructures, aligning formal systems, speeding up process management, and resolving complex business decisions, problems, and conflicts.

"Take a deep breath ... you're about to go deeper and farther than ever before: Your authentic self will soon begin awakening and expanding its consciousness, even if your ego doesn't think it's a good idea."

Ralph Kilmann, 2021

EXPANDING
CONSCIOUSNESS IN
ORGANIZATIONS

RESOLVING YOUR FOUR INNER CONFLICTS

This chapter could have been positioned as the very first one, since the theme of self–aware consciousness permeates through every aspect of creating a quantum organization. However, I've often found that people first need to be exposed to the theory and methods of the completely integrated program while only being provided with a few glimpses of the consciousness that's essential for activating the potential of their new organization. Otherwise, people might be "scared away" by being immediately challenged with what's lurking INSIDE of themselves (which is often taboo to discuss in the workplace), because our society has conditioned its citizens to focus on organizational problems and conflicts that are OUTSIDE their skin–encapsulated psyches.

In this chapter, we'll first acknowledge the major revolutions that have affected human society, beginning with the Big Bang about 14 billion years ago, and then followed by one revolution after another until the present time – when we find ourselves at the advent of the Consciousness Revolution. Next I'll review the stages through which a person's mind/body/spirit consciousness develops and expands. It seems that academics and practitioners have discovered the same general progression of consciousness, even if they focus on different aspects of human behavior, such as mental and moral development, the expression of emotional energies, and numerous approaches for healing and becoming whole. Then I will discuss the waves of subtle energy that radiate both INSIDE and OUTSIDE our physical body, which form two types of sacred boundaries: temporal and spatial boundaries.

In four sequential sections, you'll then have the opportunity to learn all about the four foundational – INNER – conflicts that emerge during the progression from one stage of consciousness to another. I'll address each foundational conflict, one by one, making use of the TKI Conflict Model: (1) Are you a physical body OR are you an energy body? (2) Are you governed by your ego OR are you governed by your soul? (3) Is your inner self separate from your surrounding systems OR are your systems an integral component of your inner self? (4) Have you healed your primal relationships OR are you doomed to squander your unique gifts since your wounded boundaries have never fully healed? **How you resolve these four INNER conflicts (whether on the protective, distributive, or integrative dimension on the TKI Conflict Model) then determines how well you'll be able to resolve all your OUTER conflicts.**

I'd like to share a curious thing I've learned from delivering this material to numerous audiences in many workshop settings: There is a *mysterious magic*, as I call it, that takes place when you experience any serious presentation about ego, soul, and mind/body/spirit consciousness. It's as if your authentic self is always hungry to discover itself and to learn about its full potential. **The mysterious magic that you will likely experience is that your authentic self will soon begin awakening and expanding its consciousness, even if your ego doesn't think it's a good idea!**

What I'm saying is that by just reading this chapter, you're destined to benefit from my material on consciousness, whether you like it or not. I do not think I'm being particularly arrogant here. I am simply reporting what I have experienced myself and what other people have expressed to me, time and again: *Your consciousness is eager to evolve – and will do so – even on an unconscious level!* So, bottom line: Plan on having a meaningful and profound experience while reading this chapter. I assure you: *You and your life will never again be the same!*

Just as I have done for the earlier chapters, I have given this chapter the same, identical title as my six-hour recorded course:

Expanding Consciousness in Organizations. That online course includes a rather intriguing exercise that asks you, in just a few sentences, to contemplate: (1) What does your ***ego*** want for you (regarding such concerns as safety, security, stability, love, value, worth, achievement, power, glory, and longevity)? (2) What does your ***soul*** require of you (regarding your special gifts, service to other souls, living your dreams, and honoring Spirit)? If you've never done a reflective exercise like this before, be prepared for some eye-opening and life-changing experiences.

Before I proceed, let's first put this chapter's comprehensive discussion on consciousness into the Big Picture: Recall the social glue (the third dimension), which gives the Big Picture its depth: Culture, Assumptions, and Psyches. We last discussed Psyches in Chapter 7, when I introduced the psychodynamics of managing troublemakers. In this chapter, however, we take the Psyche to its deepest level yet by explicitly investigating the psychodynamics of mind/body/spirit consciousness.

THE EXPLOSION AND EVOLUTION OF CONSCIOUSNESS

Below is a list of several mega revolutions that have occurred since the very beginning of time – as we know it. Most scholars agree on the profound significance of these several revolutions, which determined how life and society have unfolded on Planet Earth. One could also include the various political revolutions, such as the American Revolution in 1776, but I wanted to confine this list of major revolutions to the prime transformations that have shaped our human society (Peter Russell, page 10).

- **The Physical Revolution** — 14,000,000,000 years ago
- **The Biological Revolution** — 3,000,000,000 years ago
- **The Agricultural Revolution** — 10,000 years ago
- **The Industrial Revolution** — 200 years ago
- **The Information Revolution** — 20 years ago
- **The Consciousness Revolution** — NOW!

The Physical Revolution, also referred to as the BIG BANG, took place about 14 billion years ago, which set energy, matter, and light into motion. Whether there were previous universes before ours, or whether there are parallel universes (also known as multiverses), will remain a subject of debate among scientists until some empirical evidence is discovered that confirms things one way or another.

The Biological Revolution, also called, LIFE, began on earth about 3 billion years ago, whether it started in a warm swamp with all the right chemicals and energies mixed together, or if life on this planet originated somewhere else, such as on Mars, and was subsequently transported on an asteroid to Planet Earth, as some scientists have suggested (along with some trace evidence that supports their "science–fiction–type" hypothesis). Sometime later, *The Agricultural Revolution, followed by The Industrial Revolution* emerged due to several inventions and innovations in organizations, tools, and machines.

Then in the 1990s, only a few decades ago, *The Information Revolution* moved to the forefront, primarily based on the rapid growth of personal computers with quick and easy access to the World Wide Web, which interconnected thousands of millions of people across the globe – at the click of a button. And right now, as some scholars have suggested, we are at the dawn of *The Consciousness Revolution*, propelled by the many people who now have the wherewithal to contemplate their spiritual unity with everyone and everything on the planet. In the past several years, there has been an accelerated increase in the number of books, movies, and TV programs that explore self–improvement, spiritual awareness, the evolution of the cosmos, and discussions about "what it all means" and what's the future for our society.

Once the Big Bang set everything in motion, and once the human species evolved on Earth, every subsequent revolution has been a quantum leap, a dramatic discontinuity, as well as a paradigm shift in how people survive – and thrive – on this planet. As the physical universe and as life continued to evolve, people have been able to create many extensions of themselves, including all kinds of tools, machines, and equipment in order to overcome their physical, biological, and social limitations. **It is most important to appreciate that by using such technological extensions, people have been able to accomplish more WITH others than they could possible accomplish on their own. Such is the impact of organizations, tools, machines, technologies, information, and mind/body/spirit consciousness for enabling society to overcome the inherent limitations of individuals.**

But whether or not you concur with the six revolutions that I've chosen to pinpoint, **the key point is to recognize the rapid acceleration of paradigm shifts that has been taking place since the Big Bang.** Indeed, many millennia ago, it took a few hundred years before humans developed the next innovation that radically changed how they mastered their environment, improved their health and wellbeing, or fundamentally changed how they got things done. Certain groundbreaking inventions – such as the "creation" of fire, the wheel, or the computer – then enabled the development of the next generation of technologies. Such a **positive feedback loop,** when one invention provides the technology that inspires and enables the creation of additional inventions (and subsequent innovations), is what generates the acceleration of these paradigm shifts.

Eventually, revolutions took only decades to emerge, then a few years, and now revolutions seem to take only a few months to materialize in the marketplace, which further extends human capabilities in unimaginable ways. In fact, the instant worldwide connections that are made possible by our mobile devices (e.g., smartphones and tablets) have fostered a collective mindset that unifies humanity as has never happened before. The perennial principle – perhaps the perennial hope – that "we are one" has recently become the new social reality, which has conveniently propelled the Consciousness Revolution to the forefront of our attention. Pinpointing the next revolution is anyone's guess but, in all likelihood, it's only a few months or a few weeks away!

Figure 11.1 shows a graph of the increasing pace of change, invention, and innovation as a function of time, which highlights the acceleration of our major revolutions. Although this graph is not drawn to scale, you can see that the curve rises very rapidly as it approaches the extreme right side of the graph, called an **asymptote,** where the pace of change in society goes to infinity. For more discussion on this topic and the graph that illustrates the pace of change with the major revolutions, see Peter Russell's book, *Waking Up in Time* (especially pages 9–10).

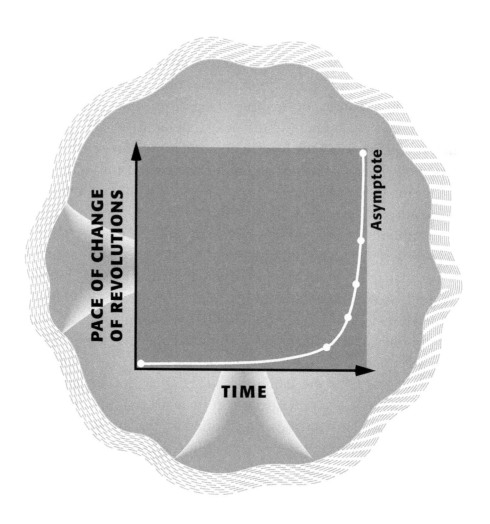

FIGURE 11.1
THE ACCELERATING PACE OF CHANGE

In all likelihood, however, the next revolution that's rapidly approaching this asymptote would not be of a physical nature, since that would defy the physical laws of time and space, which remain dictated by Newtonian science and quantum physics. But transformations in consciousness could possibly take place that rapidly, since consciousness has no physical boundaries in time and space. Moreover, consciousness seems to generate what has been called, synchronicity (manifesting actual events across the planet with mere conscious intention), time travel to the past (or the future) on guided journeys, as well as remote energy healing across time and space. Such a trend in expanding and deploying consciousness is, of course, mostly conjecture at this point, but it does suggest that the human species might soon experience it's biggest surprise yet, as we learn to harness our consciousness in ways that have only been entertained in science fiction, but have yet to be taken seriously in science and organizations.

THE ESSENCE OF CONSCIOUSNESS

The essence of **mind consciousness** is realizing that you've been culturally indoctrinated to see, think, feel, and behave in a certain way – based on your upbringing in a particular family, community, school, religious organization, and the surrounding culture from your geographical region and your country. Some of what you learned in your childhood and adolescence is very functional for your personal life and work life. Yet other beliefs, thoughts, feelings, and behaviors that you have unconsciously acquired in your youth are quite dysfunctional for adult living, which severely limits your happiness, joy, meaning, and the gifts you can provide to others. *Becoming aware of what works for you, and what doesn't, is the first important step in claiming full responsibility for becoming the person you are destined (or choose) to be.*

But a profound question then arises: "How do I break out of my dysfunctional patterns (now that I've become aware of them) and replace them with more effective and satisfying approaches to living my life?" Asking this reflective question is the province of the mind – and your mind can surely make a lot of headway in modifying your limiting beliefs, your false assumptions, and the relationship you have with your inner self, which will then allow you to change how you see, think, feel, and behave in all settings in your life. But, as it turns out, the mind can only do so much, since your habitual ways of being are also embedded in your body, which includes your brain, central nervous system, and your connective tissues and cells.

That's where **body consciousness** comes into play. No matter how many self-help books you've read, how many years of talk therapy you've endured, or how many group discussions you've had about the desire to change your unconsciously conditioned approach to life, *your habitual ways of living are thoroughly ingrained in your neural networks and all the other cellular structures in your body. So to break your patterns, habits, and cultural brainwashing, your physical body has to release those stored tension patterns and then replace them with functional flowing energy, wisdom, and new experiences.* Said differently, learning how to FEEL the sensations in your body and how to pay special attention to your body's many signs and signals – all of which we call **somatic awareness** – will make it a lot easier for you to translate your mind's genuine intentions for change into living your life in altogether new ways. Indeed, enhancing your somatic awareness will prepare your essence for becoming more than your mind and your body.

That's where **spirit consciousness** comes into play. It seems that the primary source of all wisdom, creativity, insight, and inspiration actually derives from outside of you, what C. G. Jung referred to as the Collective Unconscious. All past, present, and future knowledge and experience reside in that undifferentiated, collective, and universal reservoir of human potential. The only question is how to RETRIEVE all that knowledge and experience that's far beyond what has been called, your "skin–encapsulated ego." *Once you've significantly expanded your mind and body consciousness, by making use of various modalities that help you connect to a higher source, you'll be able to channel, hence download, that divine intelligence and then you'll be able to use all that wisdom and experience in your daily life.*

Spirit consciousness isn't organized religion, although some religious experiences are excellent examples of connecting to a higher source of intelligence and wisdom. Spirit consciousness enables a much broader perspective without having to espouse any dogma about the origin of life, or having to wear any special clothing, or having to attend any religious services, or having to read religious texts and scriptures. Spirit consciousness is beyond any organized religion or philosophy of life. In its simplest form, *spirit consciousness merely suggests that we're more than our mind and our body, and each of us can potentially have access to that collective reservoir of universal wisdom.*

A PARTICULAR SEQUENCE FOR EXPANDING CONSCIOUSNESS

I would now like to emphasize that a particular sequence for expanding consciousness seems to be the most effective way to proceed, although *ANY* sequence for enhancing self–awareness is much better than doing nothing at all. From my experience, *I have found that a threshold of mind consciousness is usually necessary BEFORE you will have the strength and fortitude to explore what is stored and stuck in your body, since it takes a lot of courage to feel the pain of past traumas. And then, once a threshold of mind AND body consciousness has been realized, it will be much easier to open yourself up — to be able to see yourself as more than your mind and your body — which will then allow you to download the divine wisdom that resides in the Collective Unconscious.*

Recall that particular sequence of eight tracks: To transform organizations, we first establish an effective informal system of culture, skills, and teams (which is somewhat analogous to the mind of the organization); next we revitalize the formal systems of strategy, structure, and rewards (which is somewhat analogous to the body of the organization); and then, built on that base, we can then improve the value-added processes that flow among all those informal and formal systems (which thus is analogous to the spiritual unity that interconnects all pieces and parts of the organization). **With that same philosophy of doing "first things first," mind consciousness strengthens the ego for taking the next courageous steps into the unknown; body consciousness allows subtle energies to gather and flow at will; and then spirit consciousness enables people to truly know their larger self and thereby have immediate access to universal wisdom. Or to paraphrase what has been proclaimed by others: Once you've become a SOMEBODY, you then have the ego strength to become a NOBODY, but with access to EVERYBODY.**

MODALITIES FOR EXPANDING CONSCIOUSNESS

Figure 11.2 shows a person who's in the stage on his journey where he can examine the reflective questions, as shown by the double-arrow halo that's right above his head: "Who am I? Why was I born? What am I here to do?" By actively participating in a sequence of mind/body/spirit modalities, he arrives at the point where he experiences himself as much beyond his mind and his body. In the process, he's eventually connects with the Collective Unconscious that surrounds his existence. In this diagram, take note of the **Arc of Consciousness** that emerges and radiates from the top of this head, which we'll later recognize as coming from his crown chakra.

While the term, *spiritual enlightenment*, has been used with little understanding of what it really means, let's just say that spiritual enlightenment is the somatic realization (directly experienced in the body and not just conceptualized in the mind) that you ARE, in fact, united with everyone and everything that ever was, exists now, and will emerge in the future – and that you actually FEEL this epiphany in the deepest core of your being.

FIGURE 11.2
THE EVOLUTION OF MATTER TO SPIRITUAL ENLIGHTENMENT

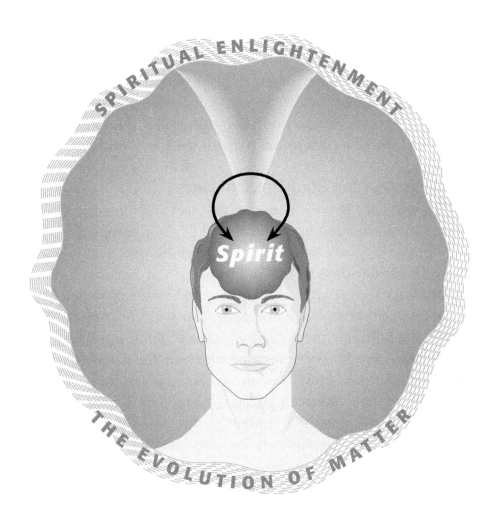

MODALITIES FOR MIND CONSCIOUSNESS

Now I'll list some modalities that can help you expand your mind consciousness: self–help books; diaries and journal writing; psychology courses; coaching or counseling sessions; sensitivity training groups (T–groups); psychotherapy; psychoanalysis; and group therapy.

But even if you read some self-help books or keep a personal diary, or even if you are participating in one form of talk therapy or another, you are using your MIND to learn (1) what patterns of thought, feeling, and behavior (which you learned years ago) are still very functional for your adult life today versus (2) which of your habitual patterns interfere with your happiness, which includes all your relationships and your vocation. Modalities for mind consciousness, by definition, do not explore what is stored and thereby stuck in your body. Remember this: *If an unhealthy pattern is stuck in your mind, it's also stuck in your body.*

MODALITIES FOR BODY CONSCIOUSNESS

I'll now suggest several modalities that can help you expand body consciousness: Yoga, Tai Chi, and Qigong; aerobic exercise (running, biking, swimming, dancing); Holotropic Breathwork; Network Spinal Analysis (NSA); Pulsor Crystal Healing; Rolfing and massage; Feldenkrais techniques; and Somatic Experiencing.

In all likelihood, you're not as familiar with these modalities as you are with our previous discussion of mind modalities. *In the Western world, we've focused more on the mind than on the body.* Our educational system, in fact, starting from the first grade and concluding with college or graduate school, focuses almost entirely on reading, studying, and discussing intellectual topics – which are deliberately kept distinct and separate from taking physical education classes in the school's gymnasium.

Besides our traditional physical education that is mainly about staying fit and playing sports, there are no mainstream university courses on somatic awareness and various kinds of bodywork. It appears that the body is off limits in most formal educational programs, which thus ignores the body's sensations, emotions, and signals. Even psychology courses concentrate on the theories and concepts of human behavior; they don't help you consider (let alone investigate) what your body is saying to you through its sensations, aches, and ailments.

In the Western world, people have been hearing more about Hatha Yoga, Tai Chi, and Qigong – primarily for the purpose of reducing stress and increasing mental focus and energy, but NOT in terms of becoming more connected to the cosmos by paying greater attention to the physical sensations in your body. And while people are pretty much aware of different kinds of aerobic exercise, these physical activities are primarily undertaken as a means for losing weight and staying physically fit, but NOT in terms of exploring the tension patterns in the body – and what they mean for your journey to wholeness.

Research suggests, in fact, that except for elite athletes, most people *dissociate* from their body while they're participating in an aerobic exercise (by listening to a digital music player, watching TV, or reading a magazine while riding on a stationary bike). In contrast, if you were to use an aerobic exercise for the purpose of expanding your body consciousness, you'd have to *associate* with exactly what's going on in your body during that activity, The same basic principle applies if you're receiving any kind of massage at a health spa: Do you *dissociate* by thinking of other things, or do you *associate* with the sensations in your body and what they are telling you about your dysfunctional patterns of conditioned behavior?

The other modalities I mentioned about body consciousness are unfamiliar to most people, which only reinforces the point that body consciousness is mostly undeveloped and generally ignored in our Western society. At this time, I won't summarize what each of these unfamiliar modalities can do for the body, since that would sidetrack us into more intellectual discussions, which is NOT what body consciousness is all about. Instead, I encourage you to search the Internet for information about the purposes and procedures for these various modalities: But you really have to directly experience them for yourself and not just read about them. There is a big difference between discussing an intellectual topic and listening to your body.

Keep in mind that any body modality, often simply referred to as *bodywork*, cannot possibly substitute for what we learn from mind modalities. Just as mind consciousness does not focus on body consciousness, the reverse is also true: **If you're living life with limiting beliefs, false assumptions, and/or self-defeating judgments about your self-worth and self-esteem, bodywork won't be able to revise those dysfunctional mental images you have of yourself.** That's exactly why a sequence of mind AND body modalities is needed for expanding human consciousness, which, of course, will then propel you to participate in additional modalities to continue your journey for becoming fully human.

MODALITIES FOR SPIRIT CONSCIOUSNESS

Once you've made some progress with expanding your mind and body consciousness, here are some possible modalities that can help you expand spirit consciousness: praying and chanting; singing and dancing; Epstein's Somato Respiratory Integration; Transcendental Meditation (TM); Vipassana meditation; Holosync meditation; third–eye meditation; Deeksha blessings; and hikes along majestic rivers, canyons, valleys, and mountains.

The first modality is familiar to most people, especially since prayer is practiced in all the mainstream religions. But ancient and folk religions also made use of chanting, dancing, drawings, and breathing techniques in order to enter a non–ordinary state of consciousness, which then allows people to connect with the divine source in the universe.

Many people have been exposed to some kind of meditation, since this modality has been included in some popular books, movies, and TV programs. And while meditation has often been recommended to reduce stress and tension, this modality can also be used for intimately connecting with the field of Universal Consciousness that is much beyond your mind and your body. In its basic form, meditation is exclusively focusing on one single thing, whether it's only the sensation of air flowing through your nostrils, a candle, a chant, a word, a sound, or a favorite song. And whenever your focus wanders from that one single thing –

and it surely will – you just bring your attention right back to your focal point (without rendering any negative judgment) and continue your dedicated concentration. After you've learned how to meditate for an extended period of time, say several hours of focusing on one single thing only, it'll be easy to return to that meditative state in a shorter period of time.

As I recommended before, search the Internet for any of the listed spirit modalities that are unfamiliar to you, so you have a better idea of what they can offer you – so long as you remind yourself that *reading* about these spirit modalities isn't the same thing as actually *using* them!

Regardless of which modalities you use to expand your spirit consciousness, and thereby your intimate connection with the divine intelligence in the universe, ***if you only pursue modalities for spirit consciousness, you will not be resolving the limiting beliefs that might still be ruminating in your mind and you won't be healing the tension patterns that might still be stuck in your body.*** Expanding consciousness does seem to require all three kinds of modalities – mind, body, and spirit – which are most effective to utilize in the prescribed sequence.

If you've already participated in some of these mind/body/ spirit modalities, do you discuss your experiences with other organizational members? In most cases, I find that people keep these "personal" experiences to themselves, since they view the organization's cultural norms as discouraging any discussion on this topic. There might be stories about someone who took part in psychotherapy, shared their experience, and was then viewed by his colleagues as crazy – or worse. Such widely shared stories then prevent other members from revealing similar "personal" experiences to their colleagues. So often, I've found that people are truly enthusiastic about what they learn about themselves *outside* their job, but there's a cultural norm in the workplace that says: "Don't take the chance of sharing your newfound wisdom with others. It's not worth the risk." Everyone then loses out on the organization's culture that silently discourages its members from sharing their adventures in expanding consciousness.

However, as long as the consciousness topic is not explicitly examined until AFTER the organization has developed a healthy behavioral infrastructure (which, once again, partly explains why I'm presenting this chapter now and NOT at the very beginning of this book), members will indeed benefit from conversations that encourage them to transform from a passive observer to an active participant and, ultimately, to an enlightened participant, by making use of one or more mind/body/spirit modalities and then bringing those experiences directly into the workplace.

Ordinary and Non-Ordinary States of Consciousness

Psychotherapy, also called talk therapy, can only access what you can retrieve from your biographical life – usually beginning from your first memory when you were between three and five years old. A few people can recall events that happened when they were one or two years old, while others can only remember events that happened several years later. Indeed, painful events are often suppressed by the mind, although they might still be accessible through hypnosis – or from analyzing your dreams. Yet it's important to realize that psychotherapy assumes that you can directly recall the influential events in your childhood that have significantly contributed to some dysfunctional pattern of thinking, feeling, and behaving; and psychotherapy also assumes that those disturbing experiences can be completely resolved by simply talking them through with a licensed practitioner. While mind consciousness can be expanded through various schools of psychotherapy, there's a lot more to consciousness than what the mind can recall, starting from those early years in your life.

On Figure 11.3, I reveal Stan Grof's theory of the Holotropic Universe. "Holotropic" means moving toward wholeness, which is exactly what expanding consciousness is really all about. Grof also created a unique modality, **Holotropic Breathwork**, which allows anyone to access the non–local information and energy in the Holographic Universe by transporting a person in his usual state of ordinary consciousness into a deeply heightened state of non–ordinary consciousness.

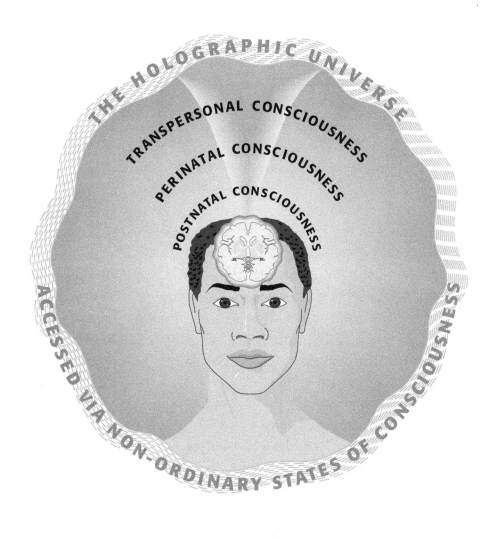

FIGURE 11.3
THE HOLOGRAPHIC UNIVERSE

Let's start by distinguishing an *ordinary* state of consciousness from a *non*-ordinary state of consciousness. **Being in an ordinary state consciousness** is when you're focused on the here and now, your present situation, and what you can easily recall from your biographical life – without using psychoactive drugs or another mind–altering substance. Most people have a relatively easy time being in that customary, ordinary state of consciousness: It is so automatic and familiar that we don't even think about it.

Being in a non-ordinary state of consciousness, however, is quite unusual for many people. Grof learned that members of ancient tribes used breathing, chanting, dancing, drawing, and psychoactive herbs so they could transport their awareness into another state of existence, which then enabled them to connect with Universal Consciousness – past, present, and future.

Grof then realized that the source of physical, sexual, mental, and emotional distress might stem from another time and place, NOT just from a person's biographic life. As a psychiatrist, Grof was able to heal distress and disease by helping people reprocess the underlying source of their ailments in a non–ordinary state of consciousness, often retrieving and then releasing the horrors that an *ancestor* had experienced many generations before or the trauma that was experienced during the ordeal of *childbirth*.

Let's take a penetrating look at the focal person in that same illustration of the Holographic Universe. You can see the symbol of the brain, which includes the person's mind and his ego. Right above his head, and thus closest to his everyday functioning, is the memory of his biographical life, which Grof calls: **Postnatal Consciousness**: the awareness of what happened to that person sometime *after* his birth.

Moving further away from the person's everyday life, he now enters a non–ordinary state of consciousness – so he can travel back in time to his experiences just before or right after his birth, which includes conception through the birth process. Grof refers to this particular non–ordinary state as, **Perinatal Consciousness:** the prefix "peri" means "near" or "surrounding" something or, in this case, the time near or surrounding childbirth.

Surprising or not, many of our biggest fears and challenges, which includes our habitual patterns of dysfunctional thoughts, emotions, and behavior, are experienced just before and during birth. Since these powerful events in the womb can't be recalled from memory in any ordinary state of consciousness, it is most useful that traumas in the perinatal stage in life can be assessed (and can be released) in a non–ordinary state of consciousness. My impression is that at least 50% of worldwide participants in

Grof's Holotropic Breathwork revisit their birth trauma if they are on a dedicated path of healing and becoming whole.

As we travel even further away from ordinary consciousness, we can experience transpersonal events in a non–ordinary state of consciousness. *The transpersonal realm often includes your ancestors, past lives, archetypes, mythical creatures, and plants, animals, and other individuals that exist currently, lived many years ago, or might be alive in the future. As you can surmise, transpersonal consciousness stretches the Western Mind more than any other form of consciousness, since it defies the laws of space-time, which are rooted in the Western world's worship of science, such as Newtonian physics, Einstein's relativity theory, and quantum mechanics.*

As that previous illustration suggests, it is only by entering a non–ordinary state of consciousness that we can experience the Holographic Universe "up close and personal" – where all past, present, and future wisdom resides and blends together into a "woven fabric of everyone and everything." With the advent of the Consciousness Revolution, just think what creativity, insight, inspiration, invention, and innovation can be brought into the workplace if all organizations would actively encourage – and inspire – their members to access divine intelligence from the Holographic Universe (what Carl. G. Jung named the Collective Unconscious).

FOUR STAGE MODELS FOR EXPANDING CONSCIOUSNESS

I have described how people can make use of various mind/body/spirit modalities for evolving from a passive observer to an active participant and, finally, to an enlightened participant. Many scholars have further arranged this progression of human evolution into several ever–expanding *STAGES* of consciousness, where *each unique stage involves different mental and moral perspectives, different energies that radiate outward from the physical body, and different possibilities for healing and thus becoming whole.*

Shortly, we'll see how a person's stage of consciousness is the primary factor that determines how she attempts to resolve her four foundational – INNER – conflicts, which then shape how she attempts to approach all the OUTER conflicts in her life. **By understanding these several models of human consciousness, you'll better understand what motivates human behavior in both family settings and organizational settings – far beyond what is explained by conventional views of social psychology and organizational behavior.**

While there are several stage models of consciousness that have been developed during the past centuries, and even though they each use different words and labels, there tends to be many more similarities than there are differences. I'll review four such stage models, which is more than sufficient to give you a sense of the usual progression from a passive observer all the way to an enlightened participant. Nevertheless, these four models also reveal the striking similarity among them, although each focuses on a somewhat different aspect of human consciousness. I have chosen to highlight Ken Wilber's, David Hawkins', and Donald Epstein's writings on the stages of human consciousness, as well as the ancient Hindu, Tantric, and yogic traditions of identifying the major energy points – the seven chakras – that manifest a person's energy body in contrast to his physical body.

Let's consider a profound "dual dynamic" that is purposely utilized in each of those stage models of human consciousness: **INCLUDING and TRANSCENDING**. We never leave a prior stage of development behind by completely ridding ourselves of what we've previously learned and experienced. We always INCLUDE all that we have experienced before, since we are, by nature, a hologram of the universe. But we must then TRANSCEND what we experienced previously, since that allows us to expand our perspectives, energies, and dedication to healing and becoming fully human.

The path of human development can best be represented as a **spiral**, which does move upward over time through a series of stages, phases, or steps – but NEVER in a linear fashion. People have their ups and downs, and they may regress to an earlier stage of development, which gives them the opportunity to work through some unresolved issue. Occasionally, however, people remain stuck at an earlier stage of development for quite some time. But by making use of various mind/body/spirit modalities, such as talk therapy, Holotropic Breathwork, and various types of meditation, people can release what was previously stuck in their mind and body, which then allows them to spiral onward and upward toward spiritual enlightenment.

WILBER'S STAGES OF MENTAL AND MORAL DEVELOPMENT

Figure 11.4 presents an image that represents Ken Wilber's stages of human consciousness. Notice the person with a symbol for her brain, which contains her mind and her ego, as well as the Arc of Consciousness that radiates from the top of her head, which represents her intimate connection with the Holographic Universe and the Collective Unconscious.

I'll now address each of Wilber's four stages: The egocentric perspective is when you consider yourself as the center of the universe: everything revolves around you and you have a hard time seeing that other individuals could possible have a different worldview. Indeed, if others DO have a different point of view, an egocentric person will probably judge them as either wrong or misguided. **In the egocentric stage, you automatically see yourself as human and everyone else as an object, and all such objects should be treated accordingly.** At an early age and stage of development, most children are naturally egocentric – every conversation is in terms of I, me, and mine – and these young children can't even conceive of, let alone have compassion for, a different social reality.

The ethnocentric perspective changes the focus to your peer group, which is usually defined as your family, community, race, religion, political affiliation, work organization, sports team, and the like. **In the ethnocentric stage, you now think in terms of what's best for YOUR group, but anyone OUTSIDE your group can be treated as an object – not as a fellow human being.**

FIGURE 11.4
WILBER'S STAGES OF DEVELOPMENT

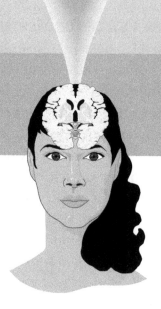

- **Spiritcentric**
- **Worldcentric**
- **Ethnocentric**
- **Egocentric**

Many people never evolve past an ethnocentric perspective, and every problem or conflict is approached as "us versus them," whether in their community, in their place of work, or between nations. The ***dark shade of gray*** in the background of both the egocentric stage and the ethnocentric stage represents the lowest (darkest) emotions and energies of human development (such as shame, fear, anger, grief, and pride), which will definitely limit a person's capacity to resolve her four foundational conflicts in a manner that leads to sustained bliss, success, and wellbeing.

The worldcentric perspective **includes** the prior ethnocentric and egocentric stages, but **transcends** them to respect all people and groups on the planet. *In the extreme worldcentric stage, the person now sees every challenge, problem, and conflict from the perspective of how any proposed solution will affect humanity as a whole, across all distinctions of nationality, race, religion, and politics.* A person at the worldcentric stage of development feels a genuine responsibility for every living being: If people on the other side of the globe are suffering from a disease (e.g., AIDS in Africa), the identical compassion for resolving that affliction is experienced as if the same event had happened to *his* family members or best friends. A **medium shade of gray** is used as the background for the worldcentric stage in order to represent the transformation from a conditioned mind to a self–aware adult, who, with courage, is now prepared to be a responsible citizen in human society.

The spiritcentric perspective **includes** the three prior stages of human development, but **transcends** them to embrace not just courage, but also to radiate love, joy, peace, and compassion for everyone and everything. *In the extreme spiritcentric stage, a person deeply FEELS the unity among all sentient beings and the physical universe in every cell in her body and thus fully embraces the entire cosmos.* Although few people have attained spiritual enlightenment, this stage of development is potentially available to every human being who's actively participating in a sequence of mind/body/spirit modalities. I use a **light shade of gray** for the background of the spiritcentric stage to represent a spiritual connection with the divine intelligence – LIGHT – that comprises the entire universe.

Figure 11.5 revisits the modified rendition of the TKI Conflict Model that I first presented in Chapter 2. But instead of using assertiveness and cooperativeness to define five conflict modes, I recast those two underlying dimensions in order to explore a certain conflict, presented as a polarity: Either This – Or That. *We can therefore use the TKI Conflict Model to depict any polarity or dialectic: In the OUTER world, we can depict what Person A*

wants versus what Person B wants. In your INNER world, you can investigate what your ego desires versus what your soul requires. Or you can examine the foundational conflict of your surrounding systems versus your inner self. Using the "either this or that" distinction gives the TKI Conflict Model enhanced power to analyze ANY outer or inner conflict using the same terms. In this diagram, I investigate the foundational – INNER – conflict of whether you are a physical body OR an energy body.

FIGURE 11.5
WILBER'S STAGES ON THE TKI CONFLICT MODEL

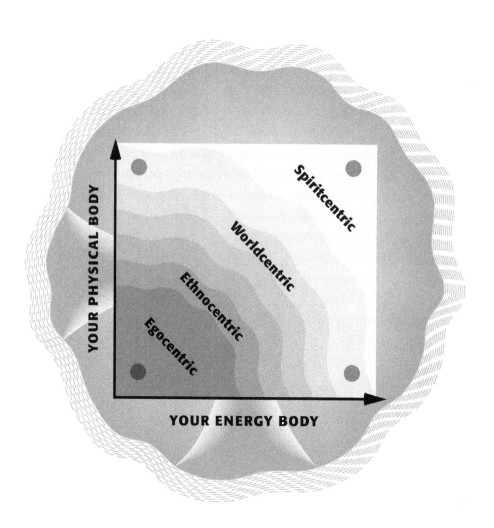

The main point of this figure is to show how Wilber's stages of mental and moral development can be mapped onto the TKI Conflict Model: The egocentric stage of "I, me, mine" is placed by the protective dimension on the bottom left of the diagram; the ethnocentric stage of "us versus them" is then placed near the distributive dimension; while the worldcentric and spiritcentric stages of "we are all in this together" is shown moving up the integrative dimension on the top–right side of the diagram.

As we'll discuss, the propagation of shades from dark gray to light gray represents the quantum waves of subtle energy that radiate from within people and spread outward. These radiating emotions and energies greatly affect how people see, experience, and address their INNER and OUTER conflicts.

HAWKINS' STAGES OF EMOTIONAL ENERGIES

Figure 11.6 presents David Hawkins' stage model of human consciousness. He focused on the particular **emotional energies** that express a person's stage of consciousness. Shown in a dark shade of gray, the lowest energies are shame, guilt, apathy, grief, fear, etc., which Hawkins refers to as **Ego Force,** which is quite similar to Wilber's egocentric stage of human development.

As you can surmise, all those dark energies, taken as whole, present a very different feeling than the emotional energies that are listed in the medium gray zone. In fact, Hawkins emphasizes that **courage is the beginning of empowerment: taking charge of your life by including — and transcending — your habitual behavior.** Addressing your conflicts or problems with courage, neutrality, willingness, acceptance, and/or reason will obviously produce different outcomes than approaching the challenges in your life with those lower energies in the dark gray zone.

FIGURE 11.6
HAWKINS' STAGES OF EMOTIONAL ENERGIES

- Enlightenment (700–1000)
- Peace (600)
- Joy (540)
- Love (500)
- Reason (400)
- Acceptance (350)
- Willingness (310)
- Neutrality (250)
- **Courage (200)**
- Pride (175)
- Anger (150)
- Desire (125)
- Fear (100)
- Grief (75)
- Apathy (50)
- Guilt (30)
- Shame (20)

As a person's development continues to unfold, he then has the potential to radiate the **Spirit Power** of love, joy, peace, and compassion (i.e., enlightenment), as expressed on that light gray background. These highest – and brightest – emotional energies are similar to Wilber's spiritcentric stage of development.

Hawkins used a logarithmic scale to position one emotional energy relative to the other emotional energies. The number in parentheses specifies what Hawkins assigned to that emotional energy. Essentially, those higher energies, due to that logarithmic scale, will always dominate those lower energies – which is why

Spirit Power overcomes Ego Force. In a moment, I'll say more about what happens when a person who's radiating the highest energies interacts with persons who are experiencing the middle or lower energies on this scale of human consciousness.

Figure 11.7 shows each of Hawkins' energies plotted on the TKI Conflict Model, beginning with shame at the bottom of the protective dimension, through courage alongside the distributive dimension, and then positioning the energies of love, joy, peace, and light (enlightenment) on the integrative dimension.

FIGURE 11.7
HAWKINS' STAGES ON THE TKI CONFLICT MODEL

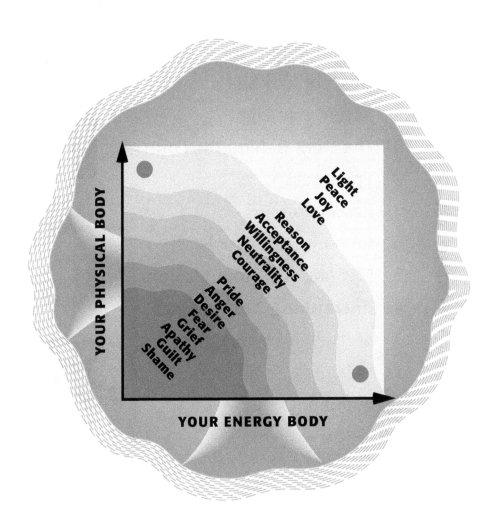

Epstein's Stages of Healing and Becoming Whole

We will now review another stage model for examining the development and evolution of human consciousness. As shown in Figure 11.8, Donald Epstein arranged the spiral progression of consciousness into his 12 stages of healing and becoming whole, which are then sorted into three categories, **Discover, Transform, and Awaken.** These broad categories of healing conveniently fit those same three background zones of dark gray, medium gray, and light gray.

FIGURE 11.8
EPSTEIN'S STAGES OF HEALING

AWAKEN	
	12. Community
	11. Descent into Self
	10. Ascent into Light
	9. The Light Behind the Form
	8. Emptiness

TRANSFORM	
	7. Resolution
	6. Preparing for Resolution
	5. Merging with Your Illusions
	4. Reclaiming Your Power

DISCOVER	
	3. Stuck in a Perspective
	2. Polarities
	1. Suffering

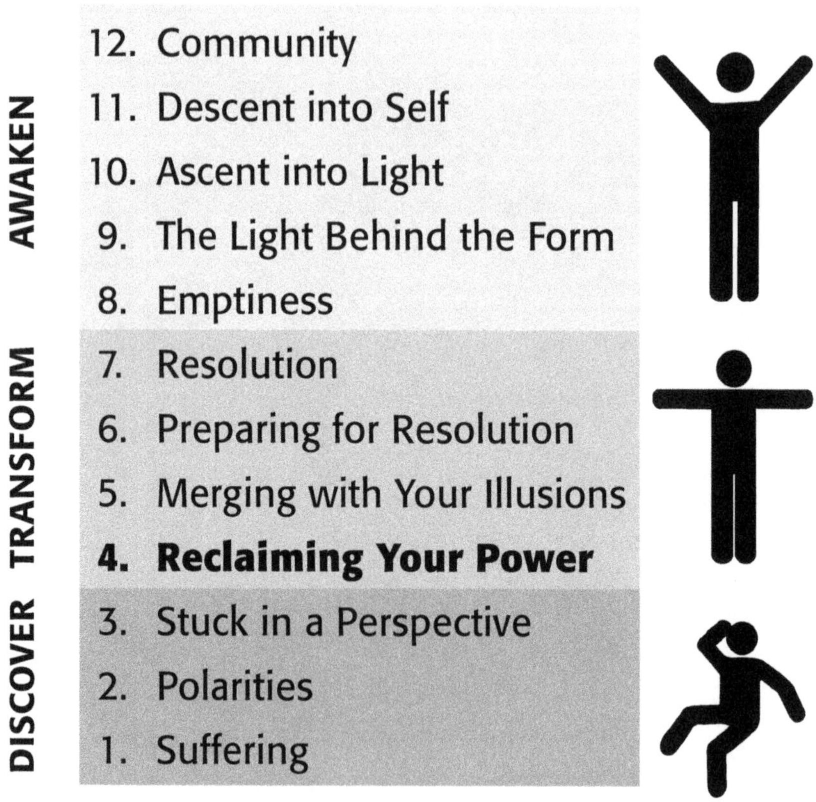

In the dark gray zone (Discover) a person's journey to healing and wholeness begins with **suffering**, which is when the person feels helpless and hopeless, and sees no way out of his pain and despair. The next stage of healing, **polarities,** captures his wish that someone else (or any other external source) will rescue him, maybe a spouse, a therapist, a teacher, or a minister (or a magical treatment or miracle cure). In the third stage of healing, **stuck in a perspective**, he realizes that he's been repeating a pattern that has locked him into his suffering, while he has been longing for someone else to save him. But at least the individual has now DISCOVERED his pattern, which is the first step to breaking it.

The medium gray zone (Transform) begins with **reclaiming your power**, which is identical to Hawkins' emotional energy of courage. Now the person transforms his perspective by **merging, preparing for resolution, and then resolving** the illusions and polarities in his life: thus including – and transcending – all his stories and challenging experiences in his past, which opens the door to living an AWAKENED life.

The light gray zone (Awaken) unfolds as the person becomes more comfortable with uncertainty, referred to as **emptiness,** or simply not knowing what is coming next – but firmly believing that something wonderful IS about to happen. The person then experiences the **Arc of Consciousness, seeing the light and then ascending into the light,** which then connects him to Universal Consciousness and thus allows his soul to awaken to its divine purpose. This person then **descends back into his evolved self, having included – and transcended – each prior stage, so he can joyfully give his greatest gifts to a diverse community of human beings.**

Epstein's three lower stages of healing have the same feeling and thought pattern as Hawkins' lowest energies and emotions (e.g., shame, grief, and anger). Epstein's higher stages of healing suggest a similar feeling and mental quality as Hawkins' higher energies (e.g., love, joy, peace, and compassion). At the same time, the lower stages reflect Wilber's egocentric stage of mental and moral development, while the highest stages of healing suggest spiritcentric development. Once again, there is a strong overlap among the different stage models of human consciousness.

To further highlight the various distinctions among Discover, Transform, and Awaken, I have positioned a relevant stick figure next to each gray zone in order to represent its essence: First, at the bottom of the progression, next to a dark gray background, we have an individual who's suffering: "Oh woe is me!" Second, in the middle of the progression, right next to a medium gray background, we see a person who's empowered to take charge of his journey to wholeness: He is now ready to fly! And third, in the top of the progression alongside that light gray background, we have a person who throws his arms up in the air to express his supreme joy, a lot like sprinters do just when they cross the finish line. Apparently, raising your arms way above your head, which energetically activates the **Arc of Consciousness,** enables human beings to connect with the Holographic Universe.

On Figure 11.9, we again use these same three stick figures to reinforce those three major categories of human development, as Epstein's 12 stages of healing are positioned on the TKI Conflict Model. As before, the stages of healing begin at the base of the protective dimension with Stage One: Suffering. Beginning with the Stage Four, Reclaiming Your Power, you're now able to cope with problems and conflicts by moving back and forth along the distributive dimension, which enables you to combine various aspects of any either/or debate into a workable solution (at least for the time being). *And then, at some point in the future when you are ready, you can include and transcend your mind and body, and thereby connect with Universal Consciousness, which will allow you to heal yourself with a synergistic, enlightened solution to whatever challenges you're facing — instead of your passively waiting around for someone else to save you with a new relationship, drug, or treatment plan.*

FIGURE 11.9
EPSTEIN'S STAGES ON THE TKI CONFLICT MODEL

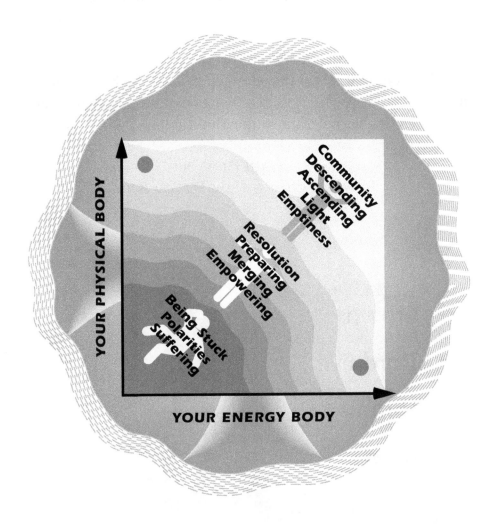

CHAKRA ENERGIES FOR HUMAN CONSCIOUSNESS

While not a stage model as such, the seven central chakras in the human body also suggest a progression from the lower/root energies to the higher/enlightened realm of human experience – based on the Hindu, Tantric, and Yogic traditions in India. Figure 11.10 reveals the same three categories (e.g., Discover, Transform, and Awaken) that reveal the seven chakras of the human body. In addition, our yogi reveals exactly where the seven chakras are located along the centerline of the physical body.

FIGURE 11.10
THE ENERGY CHAKRAS IN THE PHYSICAL BODY

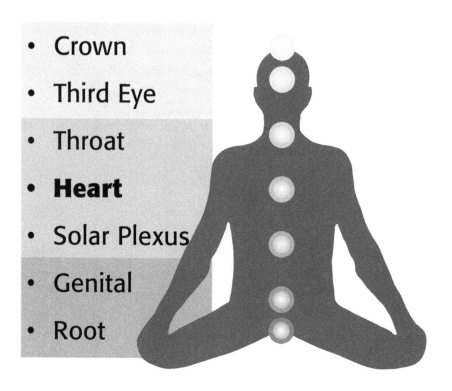

- Crown
- Third Eye
- Throat
- **Heart**
- Solar Plexus
- Genital
- Root

The seven chakras provide every person with the life–giving energy to his surrounding organs and connective tissue, which suggests the important interface between the energy body and the physical body. As we'll see, instead of your being EITHER a physical body OR an energy body, you can express yourself as BOTH, for the best of both worlds.

Figure 11.11 shows the seven chakras positioned onto the TKI Conflict Model – revealing those same radiating fields of human consciousness, shown in shades of gray (from dark to light).

FIGURE 11.11
THE SEVEN CHAKRAS ON THE TKI CONFLICT MODEL

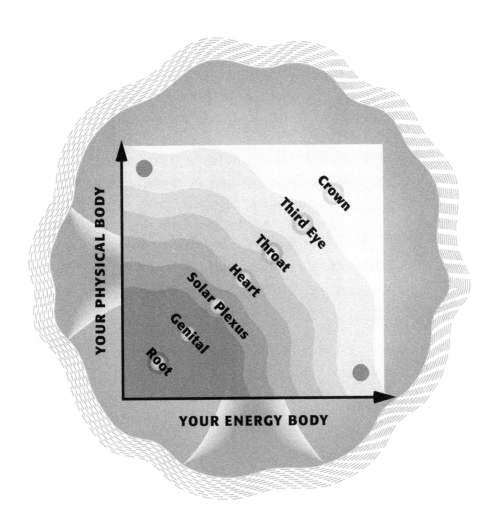

As you might expect by now, the root chakra is at the base of the protective dimension, the heart chakra is positioned on the distributive dimension, and the third eye chakra and the crown chakras move up the integrative dimension. Now, the question of whether you are either a physical body OR an energy body is especially relevant to whether you acknowledge the existence of subtle energy – as portrayed by the seven chakras in the human body – or if you can only recognize the purely physical nature of your being.

THE SACRED BOUNDARIES AND THEIR ENERGY FIELDS

Figure 11.12 further integrates the seven chakras that reside *inside* the energy body with the corresponding energy fields that radiate *outside* the physical body. With regard to this integration (which includes and transcends all that we have discussed to this point), we can now investigate how those internal and external energies actually create a sacred arrangement of time–based and space–based boundaries, which will help you establish healthy – conscious – relationships in all settings in your life.

Indeed, most of the dysfunctional behavioral patterns that you experience in life, including all varieties of mental and/or emotional challenges, derive from someone having violating your sacred boundaries or, in the reverse scenario, from your having violating another individual's sacred boundaries. But by becoming aware of your temporal and spatial boundaries, how to maintain them in a secure and satisfying manner, and how to honor OTHER people's sacred boundaries, you'll be able spend most of your time, energy, and talent on addressing the most important and challenging problems in the world, instead of being mentally distracted and emotionally drained by having to struggle with ineffective boundaries at home and at work.

FIGURE 11.12
INTERNAL AND EXTERNAL FIELDS OF SUBTLE ENERGY

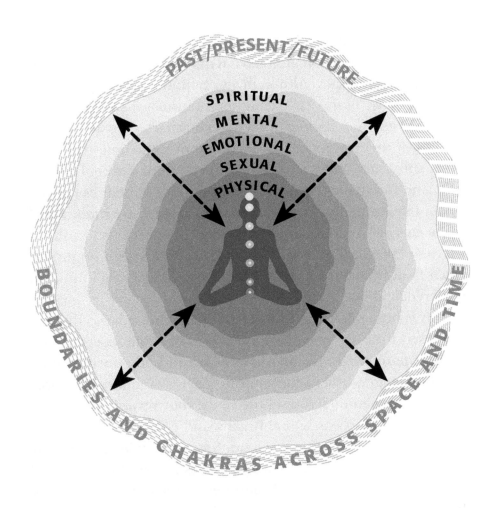

THE FIVE SPATIAL BOUNDARIES

Let's examine those five sacred spatial boundaries: physical, sexual, emotional, mental, and spiritual boundaries. Picture these spatial boundaries – as concentric oblong spheres – surrounding the gross shape of a human body.

I first learned about boundaries as a psychological concept, since practicing psychologists have written most of the books on managing boundaries. Although the boundary concept helped me make sense of my early childhood traumas, I still wondered if boundaries were entirely a mental construct, a figment of the mind, or if there were, in fact, made up of something real, with actual substance. But not until I learned about external energy fields and internal chakras did I realize that boundaries are not just an intellectual concept: **Boundaries, in fact, are made up of subtle energy!** And it is a person's stage of consciousness that'll determine the TYPE of subtle energy that forms each boundary, which then influences exactly how that boundary will function in everyday life.

This is how I now view those five spatial boundaries that are composed from various quantum waves of subtle energy: Your **physical boundaries** include your face and body (including all your organs and other biochemical systems) and a comfortable physical space around your entire body. Your **sexual boundaries** include not only your sexual organs and erogenous zones, but also your sexual identity. Your **emotional boundaries** are how you feel about anything or anyone – especially how you feel about yourself. Your **mental boundaries** relate to your beliefs, thoughts, assumptions, opinions, and judgments, especially the various thoughts and judgments you have about yourself, which necessarily include your ego's needs, wants, and desires. Lastly, your **spiritual boundaries** include your potential to experience being one with Universal Consciousness. At the individual level, your spiritual boundaries also include your soul's purpose: Why you were born into human form and what you are here to do.

If you're conscious of your sacred boundaries, you'll notice when another person crosses what shouldn't be crossed: your

body, your sexuality, your feelings, your beliefs, or your reason for being. To get a sense of your physical boundaries, remember a time when another person – a stranger, for example – came up to you and stood so close to you (either in your face or in your space) that you felt very uncomfortable. You might have taken a few steps away from that intruder in order to establish a more comfortable physical space between the two of you. Your other spatial boundaries operate pretty much in the same way, except that these other boundaries are more subtle than physical, since they have to do with intentions, innuendos, feelings, thoughts, or spiritual beliefs.

Imagine what would result from teaching young children that they're entitled to their own physical, sexual, emotional, mental, and spiritual boundaries — and that no one, not even their parents, should violate their sacred boundaries. Besides from being afforded a *Bill of Rights*, therefore, every child is also granted a *Magna Carta of Sacred Boundaries*. With this entitlement, every child would be taught that he has the right to his body, his sexuality, his feelings, his beliefs, his own destiny, and a spiritual connection to everyone and everything in the cosmos.

I'm talking here about what it means to be fully human – and the ethical respect of the physical, sexual, emotional, mental, and spiritual boundaries that surround all living beings. **When a person's boundary system is functioning well, it's that person herself who decides what flows in and out of each boundary. Other people's touches, emotions, beliefs, and judgments would be ignored, deflected, or absorbed: The choice would entirely be determined by the person herself, assuming she is fully aware, confident, and effective at managing her sacred boundaries.**

THE TWO TEMPORAL BOUNDARIES

As boundary–damaged children grow to become adults, they not only have a hard time establishing and maintaining spatial boundaries between themselves and other people, but they're also unable to establish a clear boundary between the past and the present. As such, their boundary violations from the past are unconsciously projected onto any present situation. Sadly, **not distinguishing the past/present boundary prevents you from authentically interacting with the person who's right in front of you; instead, you inadvertently treat that individual in the present just as you would treat those people who violated you in the past.** For the purpose of maintaining mental health and long-term wellbeing, it's crucial to know the difference between now – and back then.

Boundary-damaged adults also have difficulty establishing a boundary between the present and the future. They assume that no boundary can be formed between now and sometime later. **Yet for a human being, it is possible to create a present/future boundary in order to "jump into the future" by seeing yourself five or ten years from now and then imagining, perhaps in a non-ordinary state of consciousness, what life would be like if you continued doing what you're now doing.** Once you have a good sense of what this future might be like, you can return to the present, back to an ordinary state of consciousness, and then change your attitudes, beliefs, and behavior so you can create a more desirable future for yourself and others.

Essentially, it will be most difficult to improve what you are doing in the present unless you recognize the regrets that you'll likely suffer sometime in the future – if you continue down the same path with no thought or feeling about where you're going. When you're behaving unconsciously with ill-defined temporal boundaries, **being stuck in the present will surely prevent you from being happy in the future.**

ACCESSING INFORMATION FROM MORPHOGENETIC FIELDS

Figure 11.13 portrays Rupert Sheldrake's paradigm-breaking contribution to our understanding of biology, life, and energy fields. In his seminal book, *A Science of Life*, Sheldrake argued that the information that's provided in a living being's genetic code is insufficient to inform different cells how to perform their unique function. Sheldrake believed that **living beings must therefore be receiving the vital information for their biological growth**

***and development from OUTSIDE their body — from invisible,
subtle energy fields, which he called: Morphogenetic Fields.***

Another aspect of Sheldrake's morphogenetic fields is that
they reinforce a double–arrow exchange between living beings
and those external fields of energy: Let us define **INVOLUTION**
as the process of *downloading* existing information from the field
to the person (which explains one aspect of that double arrow),
while **EVOLUTION** is *uploading* your knowledge to that external
field (which explains the other side of that double arrow),

FIGURE 11.13
SHELDRAKE'S MORPHOGENETIC FIELDS

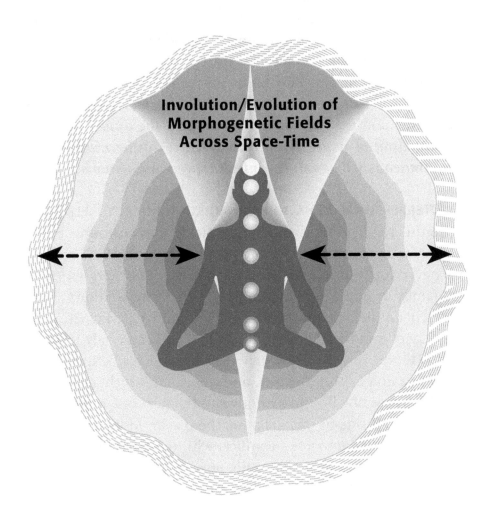

When an animal or person learns to do something better and faster than before (such as a rat learning to run a maze or a child learning to ride a bicycle), that new information gets uploaded into the external morphogenetic field, which then makes it easier for all other members of the same species to download that same information and knowledge so they can do that activity (or process) even better and faster than before. It's most profound to realize that the path of evolution may be much more affected by the information that is automatically (or purposefully) uploaded into the morphogenetic field and later downloaded to other people, in contrast to the slow and local process of face-to-face interactions – let alone the much slower process of Darwinian natural selection of the genetic code.

The Information Revolution has already demonstrated how information on a smartphone can be uploaded to a global server and then downloaded to another user at the speed of light. But with the Consciousness Revolution, instead of being constrained by physical technologies that are limited by the constraints of space–time and the constant speed of light, *the uploading and downloading of what living beings learn can be transmitted instantaneously through the infinite speed of consciousness.*

INTERPERSONAL BEHAVIOR AS RADIATING ENERGY FIELDS

Figure 11.14 presents the energy fields that surround every interaction between two or more people. Try to recall this image whenever you're trying to resolve conflicts with others, whether in a family or in a work environment. Ordinarily, we don't sense these energy fields with our five senses. But by participating in a variety of mind/body/spirit modalities, you can easily learn to PERCEIVE the energy fields that swirl around you – since each field has a unique tone, texture, and color to it, which allows you to FEEL where one boundary ends and the next one begins.

On the left side of this diagram, there is an individual who's suffering, so he approaches conflicts with the lowest (dark gray) emotional energies of shame, guilt, apathy, grief, anger, fear, and so on, as radiated through his root and genital chakras.

FIGURE 11.14
PEOPLE INTERACTING WITHIN ENERGY FIELDS

The person who is positioned at the bottom of this figure is in the empowerment stage of healing and is addressing all his interactions with the middle (medium gray) emotional energies, notably courage, neutrality, willingness, acceptance, and reason, as radiated through his solar plexus, heart, and throat chakras.

Yet the person on the top portion of this illustration is in the higher stages of healing and becoming whole, connecting his inner light with Universal Consciousness – which then results in his interacting with others via the highest (light gray) emotional energies that radiate through his third eye and crown chakras: love, joy, peace, and compassion.

Do remember the size and shading of these three radiating fields and – as a result of the interactions among these three people – how their fields overlap and influence one another. As I've mentioned previously, David Hawkins' research consistently showed that the light gray energies always seemed to dominate the medium gray energies, and both were able to dominate the dark gray energies – due to the logarithmic relationship among these emotional energies. Based on these energetic dynamics, ***it's always a good idea to include at least one person in a group who's radiating those highest emotional energies, which will create the essential inspiration for all members present in the situation to approach their important and complex conflicts on the integrative dimension on the TKI Conflict Model.***

On Figure 11.15, I propose the ideal scenario for both your personal life and your work life: Here we see that each person in the situation is radiating the highest emotional energies, and is thus able to see every conflict and problem with all the wisdom that is contained in the Holographic Universe. Encouraging such interpersonal behavior would allow all members to bring their whole being – mind, body, and spirit – into the dialogue, which would make it possible to derive the most creative, innovative, inspiring, and effective solutions for whatever concerns them – whether at home or at work.

But radiating an enlightened stage of consciousness for two or more interacting people can only be attained, I believe, if their surrounding systems have actively encouraged them to expand their mind/body/spirit consciousness.

FIGURE 11.15
PEOPLE INTERACTING WITH THE HIGHEST ENERGIES

After we examine the four foundational – INNER – conflicts that must be addressed on the path to spiritual enlightenment, we will return to the challenge of transforming an organization's systems and processes not only to inspire members to take the necessary steps to expand their own consciousness, but also to bring that expanded consciousness into the workplace – so all conflicts and problems will be approached at a highest levels of human consciousness.

THE FOUR FOUNDATIONAL — INNER — CONFLICTS

For the next four sections, I'll use the TKI Conflict Model to help you pick which of those five conflict-handling modes, and which diagonal dimensions, will help you resolve each of your four foundational – INNER –conflicts:

1. Are you a physical body OR an energy body?
2. Are you governed by your ego OR your soul?
3. Is your self (as some combination or synthesis of your ego and your soul) separate from your surrounding systems OR are your systems an integral part of who you are?
4. Given the progress you've made in resolving the inner conflicts among your ego, soul, and systems that exist within your physical AND energy body, are you now ready to resolve your primal relationships? OR have you, de facto, chosen to spend the remainder of your life being emotionally drained and mentally distracted by your wounded spatial and temporal boundaries?

By the way, I purposely present these four inner conflicts as EITHER/OR choices in order to prepare for a dialectical debate on the TKI Model's distributive dimension. By actively exploring the extreme portions of the quantum forest, we are more likely to develop a deeper understanding of ourselves (knowing the roots that underlie all the relevant trees in the forest), which will allow us to continue our progression to wholeness and harmony with the Holographic Universe. In fact, as we'll see, each of the four foundational – INNER – conflicts can easily be expanded into something much larger in scope, which will allow us to use the collaborating mode on the integrative dimensions (so long as the key attributes of the conflict situation already encourage the use of that conflict-handling mode). ***Ideally, each EITHER/OR inner conflict can be resolved in a way that integrates BOTH aspects of each foundational conflict. In so doing, you'll evolve toward greater WHOLENESS, since you'll able to function as BOTH a physical body AND an energy body, as you integrate BOTH your ego AND your soul into a whole self, as you then integrate BOTH your self AND your surrounding systems into one dynamic conduit for healing your primal relationships.***

1. ARE YOU A PHYSICAL BODY OR AN ENERGY BODY?

Quite purposely, I've already provided a lot of background on the question of whether you're a physical body OR an energy body: We learned that every stage of consciousness radiates a different emotional energy that arises from the physical body. And the range of emotional energies (starting from shame all the way up the scale to compassion) are fueled by the subtle energy that's expressed by the internal chakras – those internal energy vortices that are positioned along the centerline of the physical body. Further, the external morphogenetic fields, which provide the essential information for both cellular growth and for the evolution of human consciousness, also seem to perform their "action at a distance" through those same energy points within the physical body. Even the sacred boundaries of subtle energy that surround each person, which serve to establish a safe and secure environment for family and work relationships, seem to be composed of quantum waves that radiate outward from the physical body.

As shown Figure 11.16, I purposely modified the labels for the five conflict modes, since the language for discussing INNER conflicts is somewhat different from discussing interpersonal or systems conflicts. Specifically, if you select the competing mode for seeing yourself as being a physical body and not an energy body, this kind of language could imply there is some sort of "competition" going on within yourself. Instead, I think it's more appropriate to suggest that you are simply **maintaining** a view about something, such as primarily being a physical body. But if you stop maintaining that point of view, you're then **conceding** that you're an energy body. Likewise, it might be more precise to say that you might be **combining** particular aspects of being a physical body with particular aspects of being an energy body (when you feel energy flowing through your spine), rather than suggesting that you might have "compromised" your position.

FIGURE 11.16
YOUR PHYSICAL OR ENERGY BODY ON THE TKI MODEL

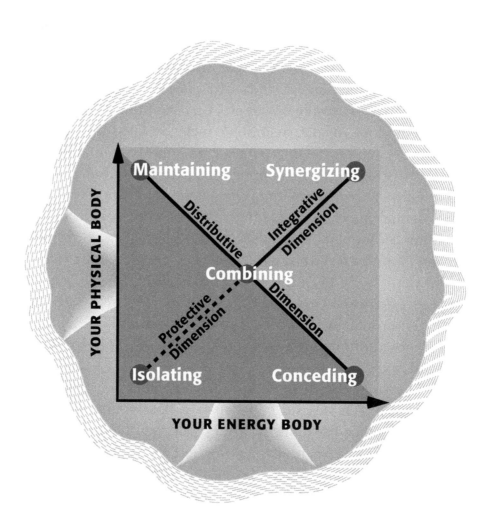

Those renamed conflict modes (maintaining, combining, and conceding) will constitute the distributive (either/or) dimension of conflict management. Similarly, I also modified the names of the remaining two modes on the standard TKI Conflict Model: avoiding now means **isolating** yourself from such a discussion about your inner being, which can help to protect yourself from engaging in such a probing (possibly threatening) introspection. Meanwhile, the collaborating mode is modified to **synergizing** in order to acknowledge the potential for deriving an expanded and completely integrated solution that's always possible when moving up the integrative dimension.

Let's now proceed with using the TKI model to address this first foundational conflict. In Figure 11.17, we see a person in the suffering stage of healing, who is so wrapped up in his despair and feelings of helplessness and hopelessness that he can't even consider the question of whether he is a physical body – OR an energy body: His egocentric life on the protective dimension is entirely focused on surviving day after day. **It's likely that his subtle energy is stuck in his root and genital chakras, and he's thus radiating the lowest emotional energies of shame, guilt, apathy, grief, and fear.** The stick figure reveals a "small" person, one who has not been able to realize his power and capacity for being fully human.

By primarily radiating the subtle energy in his lower chakras, the individual shown on the TKI Conflict Model is inadvertently preventing his higher chakras from nourishing the neighboring organs and cellular structures in his physical body, which makes him more vulnerable to a disease process. In a sense, by isolating himself from his true nature, he might find himself chasing the symptoms of his discomfort, distress, and disease with one failed remedy after another – instead of squarely addressing the root cause of his situation: **He's not addressing his true nature and he's not developing a more encompassing perspective of what comprises his existence.**

FIGURE 11.17
YOUR PHYSICAL OR ENERGY BODY ON THE PROTECTIVE DIMENSION

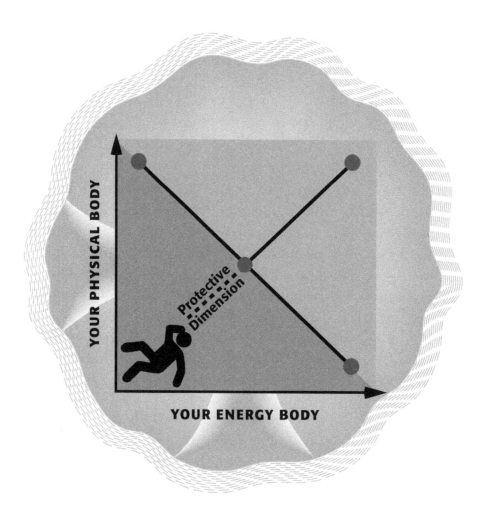

On Figure 11.18, see what happens when an inner dialogue proceeds on the question of whether "you're a physical body or an energy body," which moves the conflict up to the distributive dimension. **The image of this person has been expanded from a small person who had been stuck in the suffering stage to now being a much larger person (yogi) who's reclaimed his power during the TRANSFORM stage of healing, and thus reflects on his life with an ethnocentric, if not a worldcentric perspective.**

FIGURE 11.18
YOUR PHYSICAL OR ENERGY BODY ON THE DISTRIBUTIVE DIMENSION

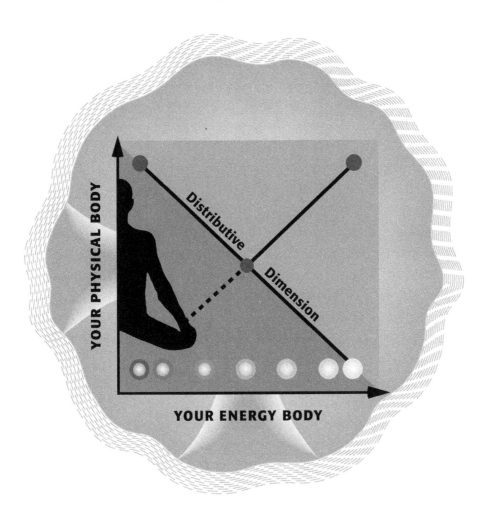

The larger person in the above illustration now radiates the middle energies of courage, neutrality, willingness, acceptance, and reason through his solar plexus, heart, and throat chakras. Viewing this inner conflict in either/or terms not only includes but also transcends this person's prior suffering on the protective dimension. Indeed, on the left side of the TKI model, the yogi is shown in stark black to signify his purely physical nature, while on the bottom of the model, I represent his energy body as the centerline of the seven life-nourishing chakras. Nevertheless, our yogi is fragmented – polarized – on the distributive dimension because his physical body remains split from his energy body – and he hasn't yet explored how his duality can become whole. As this person continues to explore his true nature by actively participating in mind/body/spirit modalities, he might develop a workable answer to his either/or question, which COMBINES some features of being a physical body with some features of being an energy body. But our yogi is not yet ready for a more encompassing solution to his inner conflict.

On Figure 11.19, we see what happens when a person is able to generate those highest emotional energies of love, joy, peace, and compassion with his third eye and crown chakras: *Our yogi is now able to transcend to the AWAKEN stage of healing by experiencing emptiness and seeing the light that connects him to Universal Consciousness. By also experiencing the full ascent into light and then the descent back into his larger self, he'll witness the perpetual cycle of EVOLUTION and INVOLUTION, which is what gives him instant access to the morphogenetic fields within the Holographic Universe.* At this moment in time, every option for healing and becoming whole is entirely open to him, including all the wisdom of humanity – past, present, and future. *By being able to ascend the integrative dimension, our yogi becomes a synergistic manifestation of the physical universe AND the energy universe, all integrated via Universal Consciousness* – which is illustrated by the centerline of chakras that shows the formerly stark physical body decorated with all his chakra energies.

The initial question of whether he is a physical body OR an energy body dissolves into nothingness: Such a distinction, like all other human-made, conceptual distinctions, is, in the end, artificial. Wholeness, oneness, unity, and synergy eradicate such distinctions, which enable our yogi to proceed with his joyful journey through life by radiating a spiritcentric perspective in all matters, which includes how he will now approach all his other inner and outer conflicts.

FIGURE 11.19

YOUR PHYSICAL *AND* ENERGY BODY ON THE INTEGRATIVE DIMENSION

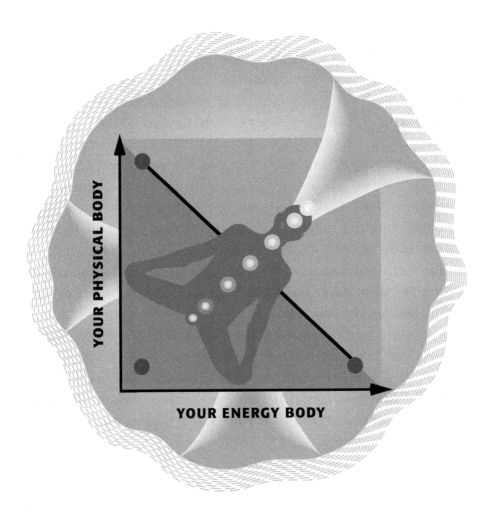

2. ARE YOU GOVERNED BY YOUR EGO OR YOUR SOUL?

We will now explore the inner conflict of ego/soul: Which of these two "voices" will guide *what* you do in life – and *how* you do it? I've found that even if people don't believe they have an ego (let alone a soul), having them ponder two vastly different perspectives about their needs or desires will still expand their consciousness. As before, we'll use of the TKI Conflict Model to see the different ways in which your ego/soul conflicts can be approached and then resolved.

It seems that we receive many messages that suggest how we should be living our life – which arrive from family members, friends, neighbors, colleagues, children, and strangers. We then INTERNALIZE some of these outside voices and take them on as our own. As a result, some of these **outside voices** become our **inside voices,** which then suggest how we should be living our life. Naturally, we might also download the messages from the Holographic Universe, Collective Unconscious, morphogenetic fields, or however we acknowledge Universal Consciousness, and then those NON–ORDINARY voices might tell us why we were born and what we're here to do. As you might expect, **whenever we are contemplating some decision or action, there could be many conflicted voices in our head giving us mixed signals as to how we should live our life.** It's no wonder that many people feel misguided or confused!

There are numerous ways to sort the types of messages we receive, concerning what decisions we should make and what actions we should take. For me, **most of these "inner voices" can be sorted into two very different perspectives: What does your EGO want for you? What does your SOUL require you to do?**

Even after having simplified the inner voices into these two categories, the answers to those two questions still generate a lot of conflict, if not a tug of war, since your ego's desires are often completely at odds with your soul's purpose. Which brings us to the prime question: How do you resolve the conflict of whether your ego or your soul should govern your decisions and actions?

Before we make use of the TKI Conflict Model to answer this question, it's important to clarify what I mean by ego and soul, since these two words are often used without specifying what they really mean, which leads to all sorts of misunderstandings. When I speak of **EGO,** I'm not in any way applying a Freudian perspective or relying on the many endless academic nuances of this rather complex concept. Rather, I use this term to represent the mind's approach for deciding what is vital and desirable for living life, as strictly perceived through MENTAL subtle energies. Furthermore, when I use the term **SOUL,** I'm not referring to any religious persuasion, although the term, soul, has a long history in theology. Instead, I use this term to represent a holographic approach to what's vital and desirable for a person's direction in life, as viewed through SPIRITUAL subtle energies. No particular knowledge of psychology or theology is needed to see that ego and soul are intended to be entirely neutral in meaning, even though the ego and soul perspectives provide people with two very different criteria for making decisions and taking actions in their personal life and in their work life.

Let's explore the essence of what constitutes an ego-driven life: focuses on self-image, safety, security, survival, and success; radiates those lower emotional energies of fear, pride, anger, desire, grief, and guilt; stands ready to defend self and all prior decisions and actions; feels especially good about successes but feels bad about failures; grasps for pleasure and possessions; runs from pain and loss; seeks power, control, influence, fame, attention, and immortality. As you can see, most of these items again suggest that the ego radiates the lower emotional energies of human consciousness that derive from the lower chakras, as best captured by Wilber's egocentric stage of mental and moral development. The ego is a mental construct of the mind within the brain, which is why I've previously used the popular phrase: the skin–encapsulated ego.

Let's explore the very essence of a soul-driven life: focuses on a divine calling; radiates the higher energies/emotions of love, joy, peace, and compassion; experiences life as lessons to learn across several lifetimes; encounters literature, art, dance, and music as connections with Spirit; serves others and the planet; sees life as actively participating in the continued expansion of consciousness; everyone/everything is already divine, perfect, and unfolding. As you read through this list, you can tell that the messages from the soul radiate the emotional energies that arise from the third eye and crown chakras, and thus represent

Wilber's spiritcentric stage of development. You can also surmise that the soul connects each person to the Holographic Universe, which potentially enables every person to download and upload the key lessons for living life from the past, present, and future. The soul views life as actively participating in the evolution of consciousness, which, to me, also means that the soul must fulfill the primary reason for the person having being born into form, since every person's life is meant to fulfill a unique piece of the universal puzzle.

Hopefully, my two paragraphs on what the ego desires and what the soul requires makes it easy for you to appreciate the very different criteria that each "inner voice" offers for how you should life your life, whether at home or at work.

On Figure 11.20, I present how the inner conflict of your ego versus your soul can be viewed on the protective dimension on the TKI Conflict Model. On this figure, you can see the portrait of a woman who has isolated herself from the question of whether her ego or soul governs her life. ***Since she is living at a lower stage of consciousness (suffering, being controlled by external polarities, or feeling stuck in a perspective), she'll have little inclination to explore her ego's desires and her soul's purpose.*** Her life is driven by habit, cultural rules, and the dictates of *other* people. Thus, she's living a much smaller life than she's capable of living, as portrayed by that very small head on the protective dimension. In all likelihood, NEITHER her ego NOR her soul is governing her life. Instead, she feels quite helpless and hopeless. Indeed, she doesn't even have the wherewithal to question her existence, let alone to find a way out of her unhappy dilemma. And yet, she's now ready to DISCOVER that she's been repeating a dysfunctional pattern.

FIGURE 11.20

YOUR EGO OR YOUR SOUL ON THE PROTECTIVE DIMENSION

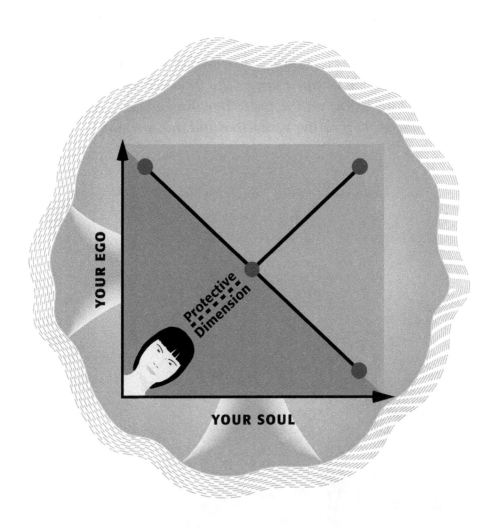

On Figure 11.21, we see that the same woman has grown in her capacity to examine her ego's needs and her soul's purpose, as symbolized by the larger figures on the conflict management space. However, her image is split: Her SELF on the distributive dimension is divided into two pieces (ego and soul), each with a different plea for direction. ***Such either/or thinking, of course, provides her with a much larger life than when she had been isolated (and stuck) on the protective dimension — which had only allowed for a rather restrictive and unconscious life.***

FIGURE 11.21
YOUR EGO OR YOUR SOUL ON THE DISTRIBUTIVE DIMENSION

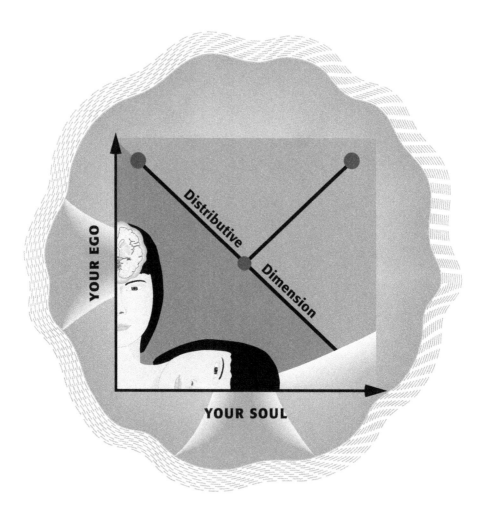

But even being on the distributive dimension does not offer her with all that she has the potential to be. Regardless, the process of TRANSFORM has at least begun: Her ego (the mind/brain that's positioned on the left side of the diagram) and her soul (connecting through her radiating "Arc of Consciousness" to the Holographic Universe that's positioned on the bottom right side of the diagram) are wide open for reflection: "Do I follow the dictates of my ego's desires OR my soul's purpose?"

Consider the either/or solutions that will surely occur on the distributive dimension: If the ego wins the argument or conflict, the soul loses. The person will remain off course and eventually experience frustration, dissatisfaction, and disease. But if the soul wins the argument, the ego loses. In the latter case, the person will lose her will to achieve what her mind desires, which will also result in frustration, dissatisfaction, and disease – but for different reasons. Given that she's debating her inner conflict on the distributive dimension, at least the path to wholeness has been initiated, probably because she's now being able to radiate the emotional energy of **courage** through her heart chakra.

Various spiritual writings have suggested that you must first destroy your ego if you want to realize enlightenment – while other spiritual writings suggest that you should *honor* your soul after you have discarded your ego. **But why would you want to destroy or discard any part of you that has served you well on your unique path to wholeness? Quite the contrary, I believe that we'd be much happier and more resourceful if we were to develop greater self-acceptance and self-love for ALL that we were in the past, are now in the present, and will surely be in the future.** That's why I endorse the philosophy that views the evolution to a higher stage of consciousness as including AND transcending all those previous stages of consciousness, whether the interest is about mental and moral development, emotional energies, or the twelve stages of healing. **Rather than destroying or discarding any aspect of ourselves (whether our ego, soul, or anything else), we always have the option to SYNERGIZE our fragmented parts into a whole person.**

As shown on Figure 11.22, this woman is now able to enter the AWAKEN stage on the integrative dimension, since she's now able to radiate the highest emotional energies through her third eye and crown chakras: love, joy, peace, and compassion. At this point, the dilemma of whether her ego or her soul governs her life moves up the integrative dimension, which allows the either/or paradox to expand into a unified answer to her fundamental question: ***She thus discovers that her ego and soul are equally relevant to her life, so she can now derive a synergistic solution.***

FIGURE 11.22
YOUR EGO AND YOUR SOUL ON THE INTEGRATIVE DIMENSION

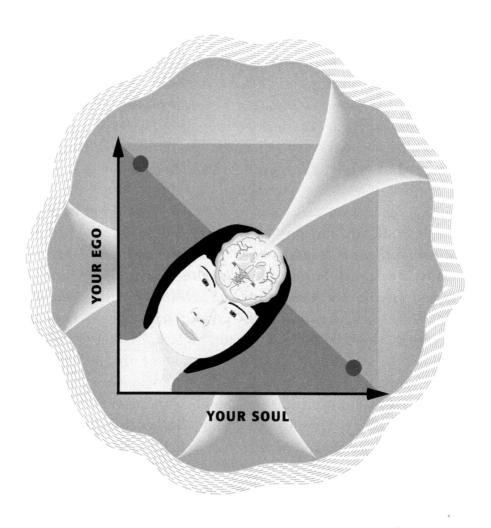

CHAPTER 11

Moreover, the woman can now be shown as a much larger person on the TKI Conflict Model, since she embodies not only her ego within her mind/brain, but she also embodies the Arc of Consciousness that gives her access to the Holographic Universe. With her ego's desires and her soul's purpose fully aligned and harmonized, her journey to wholeness will likely express more joy and happiness.

3. Is Your Self Separate OR Fused with Your Systems?

We're ready to investigate the third of the four foundational conflicts, which has the potential to alter your relationship with your surrounding systems.

By **SYSTEMS,** I specifically refer to the Complex Hologram, which I first presented in Chapter 1 (Figure 1.3). By **SELF,** I mean a particular combination or synthesis of your ego and your soul (as already addressed through the prior inner conflict). The third inner conflict can be stated as follows: Do you consider your self as being separate from your surrounding systems OR is your self integrated – fused – with those surrounding systems? How you actually resolve this inner conflict then affects: (a) whether you blame your systems for interfering with your life or (b) whether you take complete responsible for transforming your systems to support you and all others.

Even after a person has synergized her physical/energy body conflict as well as synthesized her ego/soul conflict, the tendency still persists to view her expanded self as completely INSIDE her mind/brain and body. Perhaps Western society's primary focus on **the individual instead of the collective** has conditioned us to automatically view the self within that outer layer of skin, so even a synthesis of ego and soul, which necessarily recognizes a person's intimate union with the Holographic Universe has, in fact, only broadened a person's "skin-encapsulated ego" to her "skin-encapsulated ego and soul."

This inner conflict of SELF versus SYSTEMS challenges the self-identity of anyone who does not yet grasp the unity of the Holographic Universe. However, as soon as you recognize the

holographic nature of the universe, can anything be separate from who you are? This profound question then suggests this follow-up question: "Who is responsible for transforming your surrounding systems to propel the continued development and evolution of human consciousness?" This is the perfect place to remind you of the William Blake's quote that I presented at the very start of this book: **"I must create a system or be enslaved by another man's."**

The Complex Hologram illuminates the particular systems and processes that will enslave you and further condition your behavior unless you awaken to a higher stage of consciousness, take full responsibility for your organization's forces and forms, and then actively participate in redesigning your surrounding systems to better serve your ego, your soul, and all other internal and external stakeholders.

Always keep this key principle in mind: **About 80% of what determines behavior and results in an organization is shaped by its systems and processes, while only 20% is determined by individual preferences and skills. That 80/20 Ratio is reason enough to take Blake's quote seriously and for you to be very diligent in addressing the question of whether you're separate from your surrounding systems, or whether your surrounding systems are an integral part of who you are.**

On Figure 11.23, you can see that small image of a woman who's once again stuck at the base of the protective dimension. By now, it should be readily apparent to you what perspective of mental and moral development, what emotional energy, what stage of healing, and what activated chakras prevent her from exploring the question of whether her ego/soul is separate from OR an integral part of her surrounding systems. You also know, at the lower stages of consciousness, people aren't likely to face this complex conflict: They're too busy just trying to survive.

FIGURE 11.23
YOUR SELF OR YOUR SYSTEMS ON THE PROTECTIVE DIMENSION

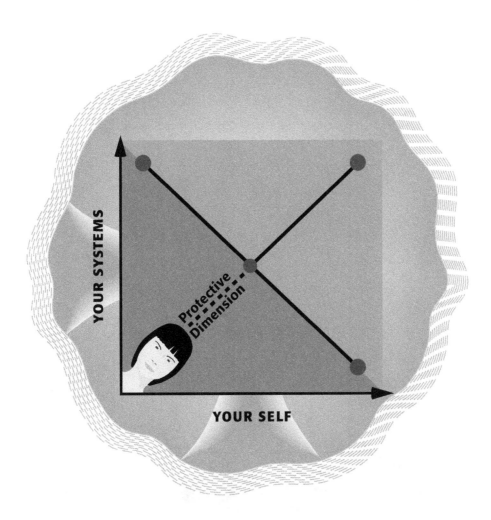

On Figure 11.24, we can see that same woman, but she's now represented with a larger image, since she's been able to move up to the distributive dimension and so she's ready to have an inner dialogue on this foundational conflict. On the bottom of the TKI model, she's already developed a combination (perhaps a synthesis) of her ego's desires (depicted by the symbolic image of her mind/brain) and her soul's purpose (represented by the Arc of Consciousness from her crown chakra to the Holographic Universe). And yet, she still views her systems as being outside of herself, as shown by the split image of her surrounding systems (represented by that familiar symbol of the Complex Hologram) on the left side of the distributive dimension. By deriving a good combination of her self and her systems, she's making progress.

FIGURE 11.24
YOUR SELF OR YOUR SYSTEMS ON THE DISTRIBUTIVE DIMENSION

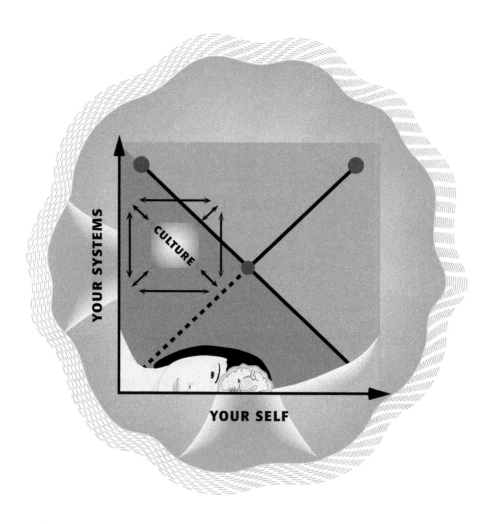

In particular, the person in the figure has begun addressing the third foundational conflict, which might eventually help her evolve to a broader definition of her self-identity – one that will COMBINE some select aspects of her surrounding systems, such as a strong attachment to her work group, but will not include ALL features of her surrounding systems, especially if she still views her organization's strategy, structure, rewards, and culture as outside of her self-identity and, therefore, as someone else's responsibility. Take note: You should already know what specific stages of human consciousness (mental and moral development, emotional energies, stages of healing and becoming whole, and internal chakras) tend to keep this person's inner dialogue going back and forth along the distributive dimension.

On Figure 11.25, you can see that this same woman has just moved up the integrative dimension, which now allows her to synthesize her ego, her soul, and her systems into one holistic view of who she is and what she's here to do – all fused into an integrated physical/energy body. As this woman synthesizes her third foundational – inner – conflict, her surrounding systems become a prime feature of her connection with the Holographic Universe. Consequently, **when this woman considers how she can take better care of her own health and happiness, she'll also consider how she can improve her surrounding systems and processes.**

FIGURE 11.25
YOUR SELF AND YOUR SYSTEMS ON THE INTEGRATIVE DIMENSION

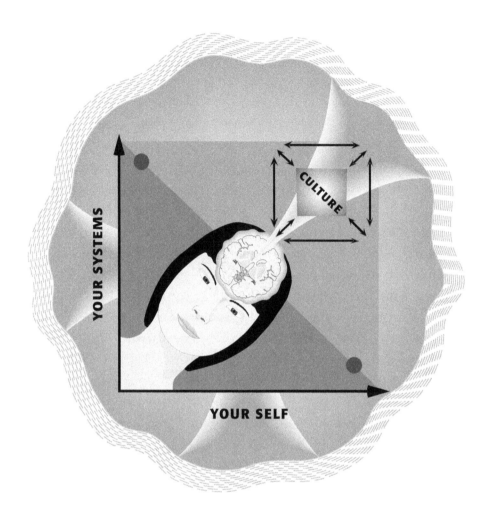

4. HAVE YOU RESOLVED YOUR PRIMAL RELATIONSHIPS?

If you've now been able to develop a more integrated SELF (synergizing your ego, soul, and systems), you will then have the inner foundation for resolving your primal relationships. If such a foundation has NOT yet been established, any attempt at confronting your most troublesome relationships in the past is not likely to succeed.

What is the primary purpose of attempting to resolve your primal relationships? *If you've not found peace with your most significant relationships in the past (i.e., parents, guardians, siblings, relatives, trusted others, and strangers), your energy, passion, and focus will not be available to you in the present. But by engaging in a process to resolve those primal conflicts, you will then be able to regain your lost energy, passion, and focus, and then bring that more engaging behavior into your personal life and work life.*

Although you might consider whether it would be better to first resolve your primal relationships BEFORE the other inner conflicts are addressed, I assure you: To directly face your worst demons takes more courage and fortitude than what's needed to address any of the other foundational conflicts. *It might not be ideal or perfect, but first synergizing your physical body with your energy body, your ego with your soul, and your self with your surrounding systems — will give you the necessary inner strength to face your worst fears and your painful wounds.*

Keep this in mind: A person's wounded SPATIAL boundaries usually accompany ineffective TEMPORAL boundaries. Basically, *a wounded person has a hard time being at ease with certain people in the present if they unconsciously remind him of his early traumas, which can produce a strong defensive reaction in the present.* Such a defensive reaction is really being directed to his perpetrators in the past – not the actual people whom he happens to be interacting with in the present. Of course, those people in the present situation don't know that, so they'll surely wonder why they're being treated unjustly.

Living with wounded spatial boundaries therefore leads to ineffective PAST/present boundaries. And those same wounded spatial boundaries also make for ineffective present/FUTURE boundaries. If a person is constantly being drained by having to safeguard his wounded boundaries, he has neither the peace of mind nor the required energy to spend time visualizing what his life would be like in five or 10 years from now if he continues to approach people and problems as he's now doing.

And because he's not able – or not inclined – to enter into a non–ordinary state of consciousness (so he can get a glimpse of the long–term consequences of his present behavior), he's also not able to bring what he would have learned in the future back into the present so he could adjust his current behavior for the purpose of creating a better future for himself, his family, and his organization. **Wounded spatial and temporal boundaries thus make it tough for a person to realize his destiny, regardless of how well he's developed a synergized solution to his first three foundational conflicts.**

So how can past traumas be healed if people have such a tough time facing and confronting their wounded boundaries? It's become evident to me that unresolved conflicts from the past (which led to one person becoming the victim whose boundaries were severely violated, while the other person was viewed as the perpetrator who violated the other person's boundaries) can be reframed as two people having very different versions of what happened and who did what to whom. Said differently: **Each person who participated in the "primal relationship" believes that he knows the TRUTH of what happened between them, although each person's version of what actually took place is different: The two people are thus in conflict over the truth!**

Although there are many different ways to talk about old wounds, demons, and bad behavior, the reframing of violated boundaries into an interpersonal conflict over the TRUTH about what happened often enables the two people to proceed with the healing process – once they accept the basic premise that a "conflict about truth," just like any other interpersonal conflict, is something that can be approached with one or more of the five conflict–handling modes – with each mode leading to different opportunities for healing boundaries and becoming whole.

Rarely can we know what really happened between the two people a long time ago – even if there were a video recording of those past events. Any such recording of an interpersonal scene is selectively focused on only one camera angle, while ignoring all other vantage points of the same exact scene.

It's also good to realize that our mind and memory work in the same way: We remember events as if we had originally seen them through the lens of a camcorder, deciding on what aspect in the scene to digitally record or store into long-term memory – and what aspects of the scene to ignore. Therefore, **when we use a camera, or retrieve a memory, we decide what's showcased in the foreground and what's relegated to the background.**

It's also been determined that eyewitness accounts of what took place way back when can vary tremendously, based on the unique perspective and unconscious agenda of each observer, especially if time has elapsed, say years or even decades, since the original event occurred. *A person's memory is always based on selective recall to support his self-identity and self-esteem. I say all this to suitably emphasize that knowing the truth of what happened between two people is a very subjective matter, even when having access to video recordings and eyewitnesses. As a result, the conflict between every person's version of the truth is based more on a subjective psychological reality than on an objective physical reality, which means there is always a wide-open space, hence, a CONFLICT MANAGEMENT SPACE, for negotiating the truth of some past event.*

I'd like to be absolutely clear on this very important caveat: Consider a past event in which an adult victimized an innocent child. In this situation, the truth of what happened in the past is strictly one-sided, with no justification for trying to negotiate a different version of what took place between those two people. But even in this extreme scenario, the innocent child, who's now an adult, may still have a distorted version of that bad event, including the supposed reasons for the abuse, which only makes the open wounds worse and more difficult to heal.

Of course, there might also have been a one-sided violation between two grown adults that leaves little or zero room for a revised story of what actually happened. Regardless, it's a good idea to address boundary violations as soon as possible, before additional time and selective memory make the original event even more traumatic, intractable, and unresolvable.

Here's the key point: Once we reframe a primal relationship that created wounded boundaries into an interpersonal conflict over two versions of the truth between two people, whether the violation was one-sided or not, we can ask these two questions: (1) What are the different ways to resolve this conflict? (2) What are the consequences, short term and long term, for attempting to resolve the conflict in one way or another?

THE STAGES FOR RESOLVING PRIMAL RELATIONSHIPS

Figure 11.26 summarizes the nine stages for resolving primal relationships, which was especially created to show how ***Stage 0 significantly affects all the remaining stages — through those quantum waves of subtle energy that determine how the two people will interact with one another.*** As shown by those light gray radiating waves, which provide the superhighway across all the subsequent stages of resolution, the more that one or both persons are approaching the other with the highest emotional energies, the more likely that they will negotiate a synergistic version of what happened between them. Although we'll spend the most time discussing Stage 3, Negotiating a Joint Version of Reality, since it is the most neglected stage in the process, there are a number of stages BEFORE any negotiations should begin and there are several important stages AFTER the two people have developed a workable solution (some combination of their different versions of the truth) or a fully synthesized resolution of what might have happened between them.

Although there are valid reasons for this particular sequence of nine stages, progress will usually be non-linear — just as we learned about those four stage models of human consciousness that we covered earlier in this chapter. As a result, there can be a back-and-forth movement among these nine stages.

FIGURE 11.26
THE NINE STAGES FOR RESOLVING PRIMAL RELATIONSHIPS

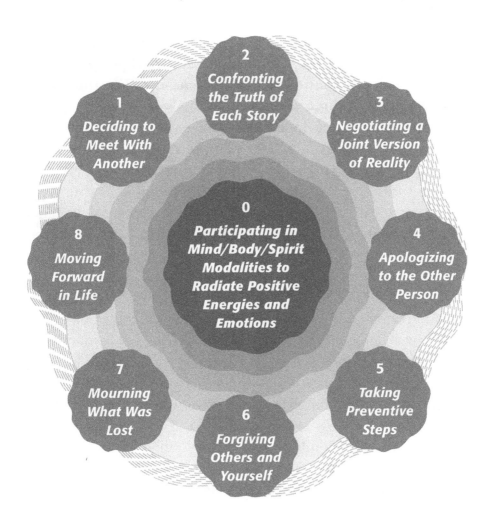

Stage 0 has a huge impact on the remaining eight stages for achieving resolution, which is why I used the designation "0" to emphasize its fundamental nature. ***The field of subtle energies surrounding the people not only determines which approach they'll use for negotiating the truth between them, but also determines whether they might use a spiritual perspective on the integrative dimension to first include, and then transcend, their wounded boundaries.*** This Stage 0 also impacts the mood and tone of all interactions (e.g., compassion versus anger) and whether forgiveness can be given and received, despite the past hurt between the two people in the situation.

Stage 1 in the process includes your thoughts and feelings regarding which of your boundaries have been most violated by other people. Of those violations, which ones can be resolved without interacting with the person involved versus which ones require a live conversation?

For you to make the best decision, it usually helps to discuss what happened with trusted friends and/or an expert therapist. But if the relationship has survived and involves your family of origin (parents, siblings, or other caretakers), there are benefits from meeting face to face (before the person is no longer alive), as long as you take the necessary steps to protect yourself from being further harmed. Also, if you expect to have regular contact with this person, it's often best – long term – to pursue a live resolution: One of the prime advantages of a live conversation (versus an imagined discussion during a therapy session) is that an actual dialogue can provide you with a different perspective and a lot more information than was available to you when you were much younger and when you had to rely on your rather undeveloped mental abilities to make sense of a frightening and painful experience.

But if you infrequently come into contact with the person who harmed you, or if you have valid reasons to believe (from your previous efforts at resolution) that a productive dialogue cannot take place, it might be best to resolve the relationship on your own. From my experience, ***if you're attuned to the subtle*** *sensations in your body, you'll know which resolutions must take place in a live meeting and which ones can be resolved on your own.* Besides, whatever you decide, you can always change your mind later. Essentially, Stage 1 is meant to get the process started by selecting which boundary violation by which person, if resolved with a live dialogue, would make a big difference in reclaiming your drained energy, mental focus, and battered self.

Stage 2 involves setting up an in-person meeting to discuss the boundary violations that allegedly occurred, either recently or, in most cases, a long time ago. A fair amount of **courage** is usually required to propose such a confrontational meeting in our society, where the prevailing culture generally discourages discussing hurtful and violent behavior. As I noted in a previous section in this chapter, **at least one person in the relationship must radiate positive emotional energies for both persons to have a chance at healing their wounds.** Yet it also helps if the first meeting to address past wounds has been carefully planned in advance, with an agenda and a readiness on the part of both persons to minimize their defensiveness. But it's not unusual for spontaneity to spring forth, whereby the two people just happen to be in the right place at the right time and in the right mood when the topic magically appears and the dialogue unfolds.

For some boundary violations, it may take many years before one person has the courage to raise the topic, set up a meeting, and confront the other individual. After the fact, here's a typical response: "I wish I would have confronted him years before. We wasted so much time and heartache by avoiding the topic." And yet, here's another typical response: "What was I thinking? I can't believe I brought up the topic and thought we could resolve it. I'll never try that again!"

In advance, of course, it's difficult – if not impossible – to know how the two people will respond to such a confrontation. And that's exactly why a good dose of courage is required – **the COURAGE to risk a bad experience for a worthwhile purpose by confronting another person with a potentially threatening, but highly therapeutic topic.**

Stage 3 proceeds after the two people have already shared their versions of the truth with one another: the different stories of what happened between them in the past, including who did what to whom – and for what reason or purpose. In most cases, it's a question of convenient memory: Each person remembers the events to protect his ego from shame, blame, and guilt, and to guard against the chance of experiencing one more threat to his self–identity. *That's why it is so important for one or both persons to radiate the highest – the most positive – energies of human consciousness: to soothe the shame, anger, pride, and fear while expressing love, joy, peace, and compassion.*

During this third stage, each person chooses, consciously or unconsciously, which conflict mode to use for negotiating the truth of what actually happened. *If both people are interacting within that middle range of energies and emotions (courage, willingness, and reason), they will then negotiate truth along the distributive dimension (e.g., maintaining, conceding, and combining). But if one or both of them are radiating a positive energy field (love, joy, peace, and compassion), they are more likely to resolve truth along the integrative dimension – thus moving from combining to synergizing.* Although the mode of isolating oneself from the other person seems rather irrelevant (especially since both are meeting, confronting, and negotiating with one another), it's not usual for discussions to break down. But if a positive energy field surrounds the two individuals, it's unlikely they will use the isolating mode for very long.

Stage 4 of resolution must, obviously, be based on a shared understanding of what took place and why. If an agreement on TRUTH has been developed on the distributive dimension and is based on one person having violated the other, then a genuine apology can be sincerely voiced by the perpetrator and accepted by the victim. But if the maintaining mode (along with the lower emotional energies) was used to *force* an agreement on the truth, then any apology, no matter how it's delivered, is still unlikely to be accepted by the other person.

Bottom line: If an agreement on truth has been won through battle, any apology is utterly meaningless and will fall on deaf ears. However, **when an agreement on truth has been resolved on the integrative dimension (somewhere between combining and synergizing), each person can fully apologize to the other, since they both recognize that each of them has contributed to one another's pain and suffering.**

Stage 5 provides the necessary progression from apology to forgiveness. Essentially, **an apology is more likely to be accepted if it includes a plan to make sure that the previously violated boundaries are now safe from further harm.** In cases when the violation took place in childhood, the immediate adult situation guarantees everyone's safety: The former child can now assert and safeguard his boundaries. Thus no further plan for action is needed, unless it would be healing for the prior victim to know, traveling back in time, how the same situation would have been handled differently – with today's consciousness as opposed to yesterday's blindness.

Stage 6 of resolution can be easy or difficult – depending on the mind/body/spirit consciousness of the people involved in the situation. At the one extreme is the oft-cited claim: "If I can't forget, I can't forgive." Or, stated in its converse form: "I'll forgive when I can forget." While we should never minimize the pain of a severe boundary violation (e.g., involving physical boundaries, such as childhood beatings, or sexual boundaries, such as rape), **if there's no forgivingness, there's no healing.** Instead, various masks or addictions are used to avoid the misery of living with a damaged self. **Rather than live with such pain, the healthier option is to find a way to forgive through an internal dialogue and/or a live meeting.** Naturally, a live meeting might not be possible or would create more harm by replaying the violation. But with mind/body/spirit modalities, it is also possible to view the identical situation from a higher stage of consciousness (from the integrative dimension) and to then greet every person (even those who've harmed us) with love, joy, peace, and compassion.

Stage 7 recognizes that both people have been living with decreased energy and diffused focus, whether from having their sacred boundaries violated or from feeling guilty from having caused so much pain and damage to another person. *Mourning is an emotional process for deeply feeling the sadness, rather than defending against it by claiming, "I'm already over it," or by denying that anything bad ever happened. In fact, the more the two people can feel what they've lost, the sooner the mourning period will end so a happier life can begin.*

I truly appreciate, however, that people often prefer to bypass the mourning stage, because they want to quickly resolve the conflict – and thus not feel the pain of what they lost. But if the seventh stage has not been successfully addressed, that skipped stage of mourning will surely prevent the persons from healing their wounds and thus transcending their previous perspectives and stories.

Stage 8 of resolution is about redefining – and reforming – the sacred boundaries that were previously violated: to replace what was previously lost with a more solid and secure container, and thus a stronger sense of self.

Once mourning has successfully passed and those previously wounded boundaries have begun to heal, a tremendous relief is experienced, a release of stuck energy, whereby each person now feels lighter, younger, more at peace, and more optimistic about life. *It's only after this powerful experience of relief and release that people can truly appreciate how previously living with an unresolved primal relationship had been continually draining their energy and distracting their mind. With clear boundaries, a stronger sense of self, and more positive emotional energies, each person can now move forward in life – by living his soul's purpose, as supported by his healthy ego, while revitalizing his surrounding systems.*

Often, after having resolved a difficult relationship, another unresolved relationship springs forth. The healing process then cycles back, one more time, to Stage 0, and then proceeds with Stage 1, deciding to meet with another person, and so forth.

STAGE 3: NEGOTIATING A JOINT VERSION OF REALITY

Let's spend a little more time discussing Stage 3, the critical turning point in the process of resolution – since there must be some agreement on the TRUTH (i.e., a joint version of reality) of what violations happened in the past before any real progress can be made on the remaining stages of resolution.

Figure 11.27 displays what might've been going on between the two people before either of them had the courage to set up a meeting to process their past pain.

FIGURE 11.27
YOUR TRUTH OR MY TRUTH ON THE PROTECTIVE DIMENSION

As you can see, the TKI Conflict Model uses the stick figures for "suffering" to show two people stuck in the past and unable to move forward. Radiating those lowest emotional energies of shame and anger, etc., each desperately clings to a self-serving account of what happened between them. Moreover, we see the two people positioned at the base of the protective dimension and, symbolically, **turning their backs on one another.** If two people are so stuck on suffering, there's little hope for resolution, as their energy, time, and talent are wasted on self-protection, defensive reactions, and one addiction after another.

But eventually, as displayed on Figure 11.28, the two people have found the requisite **courage** to move up to the distributive dimension, even though they still remain in conflict over whose version of the truth is correct. Thus, the negotiation over reality remains polarized (as an either/or exchange on the topic), but at least they are talking! After a little while, the two people might be able to develop a joint solution by each conceding something to the other person's story and thus COMBINING a few pieces of their separate stories into a modified version of what took place in the past – which can bring *some* peace, but not *all* the peace that's potentially available to both of them.

Incidentally, if the boundary violation that occurred between the two people was one-sided in the distant past, involving, for example, an innocent child and a caretaker, it's rather easy to arrive at a solution, once the older person concedes that he had inappropriately used his power and position to take advantage of the innocent trust that the child had placed in her caretaker's hands. With a shared understanding of what had happened in the past, the two of them can then move forward in the process, instead of BOTH of them continuing to live with guilt, shame, grief, and sorrow.

FIGURE 11.28
YOUR TRUTH OR MY TRUTH ON THE DISTRIBUTIVE DIMENSION

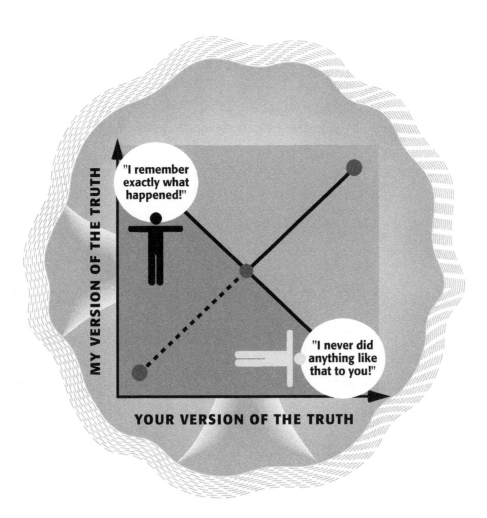

As celebrated on Figure 11.29, the two people have now been able to transition up the integrative dimension by radiating the higher emotional energies through their higher chakras – surely having benefitted from mind/body/spirit modalities (Stage 0). Now their hearts and minds are open to creating a solution that will lead to happiness, instead of only achieving a rather meager revision of their separate stories of what happened and why. As a result of an open, candid, and compassionate dialogue, the two persons agree on an expanded version of their prior stories.

FIGURE 11.29
YOUR TRUTH AND MY TRUTH ON THE INTEGRATIVE DIMENSION

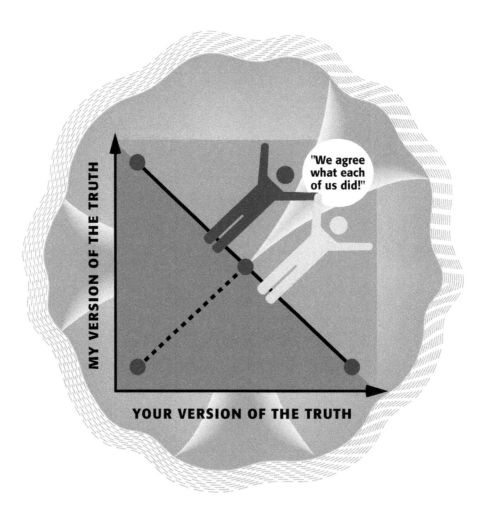

Addictive Behavior to Numb Your Body from Pain

When a person cannot muster the courage (or any of those other middle energies) to address his wounded boundaries and unresolved primal relationships, he might get himself hooked (consciously or not) on one addiction or another – so he won't have to face the heartaches in his life. There are so many ways that people can trick themselves into thinking that everything is well, while they do their best to bury their pain and misery.

Based on the prevalence of addiction in our society, I want to say more about this rather extreme instance of FLIGHT, when, in essence, a person literally flees from the feelings in his body, besides fleeing from the fears in his mind. The extreme form of fleeing – which is rarely a mindful decision made under peaceful conditions – involves obsessively engaging in any activity that numbs the person from his pain and anguish.

It's important to realize that becoming addicted to something is the opposite of trying to enhance your somatic awareness and improve your body consciousness. Somatic awareness enables you to vividly FEEL the sensations, stories, and tensions in your body; becoming addicted to something dramatically REDUCES your capacity to feel what's going on inside you.

There are many types of addictions, besides the classic ones of numbing yourself with alcohol or drugs. Sometimes, in fact, people can be quite creative in finding new ways of numbing their body, while their family members and friends, for example, continue to admire the inordinate hours they spend at work or how they remain compulsively engaged in a seemingly useful activity. Meanwhile, the addicted persons are so exhausted from all their intentional busyness that they can't even think clearly and they can't take care of all the OTHER responsibilities in life, like taking care of themselves and their loved ones.

I want to call your attention to what is probably the most insidious addiction in all human society, since it's the easiest one to embrace and the hardest one to detect: Living out your life, day after day, while you haven't yet resolved your primal relationships. This addiction causes so much suffering across

the globe, that I consider it "a resolution crisis for humanity."
Indeed, this resolution crisis is probably the root cause of all
other addictions. But by addressing the source — the resolution
crisis — I believe it's possible to prevent ourselves from getting
involved with one or more of those tempting addictions in life!

However, without satisfactorily addressing and resolving the
first three inner conflicts, I think it is unlikely that people will
become aware that they are staying insanely busy, or numbing
their body in other ways – just so they never have to face their
past demons and wounded boundaries. Instead, **by addressing**
the four inner conflicts in the proposed sequence, more people
will be eager to expand their consciousness, satisfy their ego,
fulfill their soul, take full responsibility for their surrounding
systems, and heal their wounded boundaries.

EXPANDING CONSCIOUSNESS IN THE WORKPLACE

In Chapter 1, I spent some time describing an unpublished
study that randomly assigned 30 students to participate in one
of two types of organization: a PYRAMID organization and a
CIRCLE organization. After a few work cycles, two students (one
student was initially working in the circle organization while the
second student had been working in the pyramid organization)
switched membership. Again, after a few more work cycles, a
different two students traded places. Eventually, all the original
students from the pyramid organization were now working for
the circle organization, and vice versa. Although the members
had completely shifted between the PYRAMID and the CIRCLE,
the prevailing system of organization still ruled how the work
got done. This experiment vividly demonstrated the influence
of the system over its individual members (the 80/20 rule). But
how do we decipher whether the PYRAMID or the CIRCLE will
ultimately create the best system of organization?

Before I say more about the pyramid/circle conflict, I want to
share with you how my own thinking has evolved on the matter
of endorsing the Newtonian (pyramid) organization versus the

quantum (circle) organization. Back in the 1990s, as I was writing my book, *Quantum Organizations*, I considered transformation as moving AWAY from the Newtonian organization while moving TOWARD the quantum organization. Implicit in all my previous writings was that the Newtonian organization was undeniably out of date and, for all practical purposes, should be discarded. As an analogy, it was pretty much the same line of thinking as if I had argued that we should discard the ego and focus only on the soul.

During the first decade of the new millennium, however, as I further examined the stage models of human consciousness, I realized that a more enlightened approach had to first include – and then transcend – what came before, as I've emphasized at several points in this chapter. But at this point, I'd like to direct your attention to why I'm purposely creating a striking dialectic between the pyramid organization and the circle organization: **I want to create an open dialogue and debate, so we can discover an entirely NEW system of organization, one that will include and transcend both the pyramid organization AND the circle organization, which I now realize is far more synergistic than simply picking one system and not the other. In fact, having to choose only one organizational system will usually result in discarding the pyramid organization and endorsing the circle organization.** We can do much better than simply sticking with the either/or distinction on the distributive dimension – just as I've demonstrated with each of the four inner conflicts.

Let's proceed: Figure 11.30 shows the pyramid/circle conflict on the protective dimension, which is the case when members are routinely discouraged from bringing their mind/body/spirit consciousness into the workplace. As such, we can imagine how the established, traditional, pyramid system that's positioned at the bottom of the protective dimension continues to enslave its members: **Everyone in a Newtonian organization is radiating the lowest level of consciousness without any encouragement or opportunity to investigate "what those external systems are doing to us and what we can do about it."**

FIGURE 11.30
THE PYRAMID OR THE CIRCLE ON THE PROTECTIVE DIMENSION

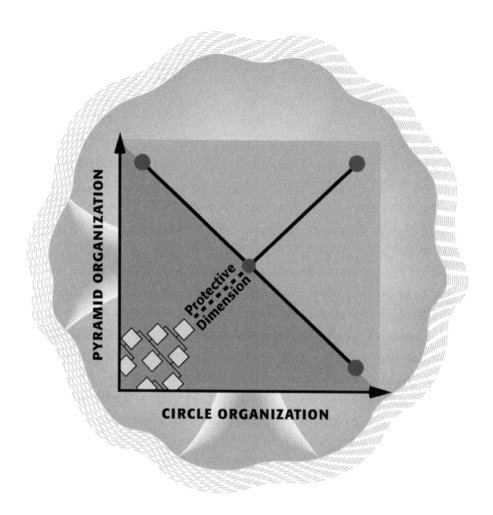

On Figure 11.31, we can see that the managers and members of the pyramid organization have been able to radiate enough **courage** to question whether their surrounding systems (i.e., a pyramid, Newtonian organization, as shown on the top–left side of the diagram) OR a novel arrangement of systems, processes, and people (i.e., a circle, quantum organization, as shown on the bottom–right portion of the figure) could significantly improve their performance and satisfaction.

FIGURE 11.31

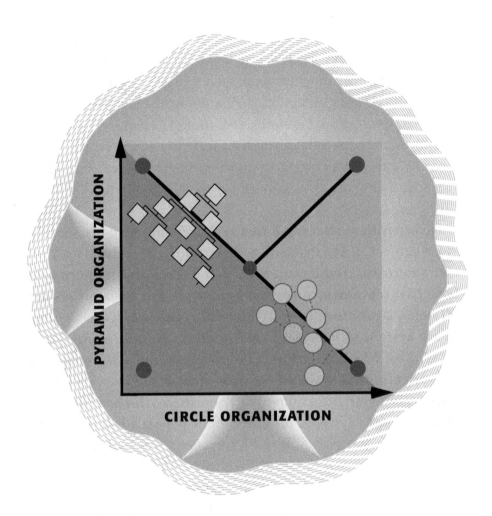

Although the debate remains either/or for the time being, at least it's now possible for the members to COMBINE some attributes of the pyramid organization with certain attributes of the circle organization.

Top managers often fabricate a pyramid/circle combination by delayering the rather tall vertical hierarchy into fewer layers of management positions and then consolidating several of the small work units into large departments. This solution has been called: restructuring. This partial resolution *does* streamline the old system into fewer hierarchical levels and departments, which often results in faster decisions and thus greater efficiencies. But the restructuring, which combines some aspects of the pyramid organization with several aspects of the circle organization, is usually decided and implemented in a top–down manner, and thus treats the membership as passive observers – not as active participants or enlightened participants. And remember that all the *other* organizational systems, including strategy, rewards, and the culture, have remained pretty much the same, which tends to render the restructuring as more cosmetic than substantive, since members continue to perform most of their work exactly as they did before.

Meanwhile, such a top-down restructuring also ignores the whole subject of consciousness: Essentially, members see that some structural change can be realized, (even if it was brought about in a top-down, superficial manner), but their minds are still being conditioned by a Newtonian culture and a defunct reward system that prevent the members from providing any meaningful involvement in self-designing and self-managing their surrounding systems. As such, members experience their surrounding systems as separate from their self-identity, as the design of those systems remains other people's responsibility. This either/or mindset only serves to reconfirm that the system enslaves its members while, at the same time, they do their best to squelch their negative emotional energies.

Figure 11.32 shows how to go beyond the either/or conflict of whether to retain the pyramid organization OR to self–design a circle organization. By moving up the integrative dimension, we can participate in a still more promising dialogue: **How can we create a NEW system of organization that includes — and transcends — BOTH the pyramid system AND the circle system into an even more compelling self-identity of who we are as individuals, which includes every one of us being completely integrated with all our surrounding systems?** Just asking this question shows the value of resolving the four INNER conflicts.

FIGURE 11.32

THE PYRAMID AND THE CIRCLE ON THE INTEGRATIVE DIMENSION

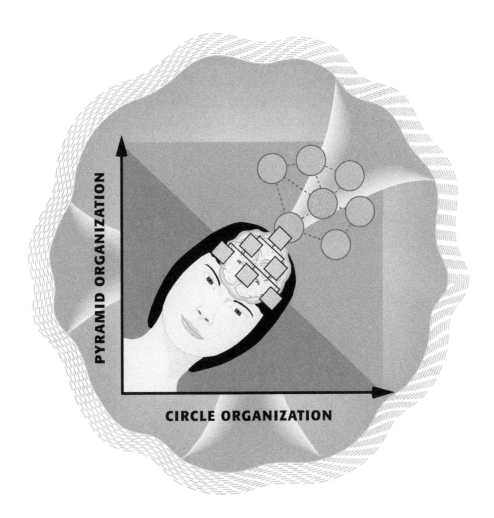

Naturally, we need to examine exactly what this new system of organization is all about, and then, of course, we must take the necessary action steps to bring it to life. For the moment, see that **I've positioned the pyramid organization on the person's mind/brain, while I have positioned the circle organization on the "Arc of Consciousness" that links her crown chakra to the Holographic Universe. These artistic decisions were guided by a synergistic solution: As we will see, a pyramid organization**

is ideally suited to satisfy the ego's needs and wants, while a circle organization is ideally suited to fulfill the soul's purpose.

On Figure 11.33, I present a modified image of the Problem Management Organization, which is the name I've given to the PMO arrangement that integrates the old pyramid system with the new circle system. The dotted line running across the middle of this illustration temporarily divides the two components of this NEW organization: The top of the PMO taps the ego's needs, while the bottom of the PMO is attuned to the soul's purpose.

FIGURE 11.33
CREATING THE PROBLEM MANAGEMENT ORGANIZATION

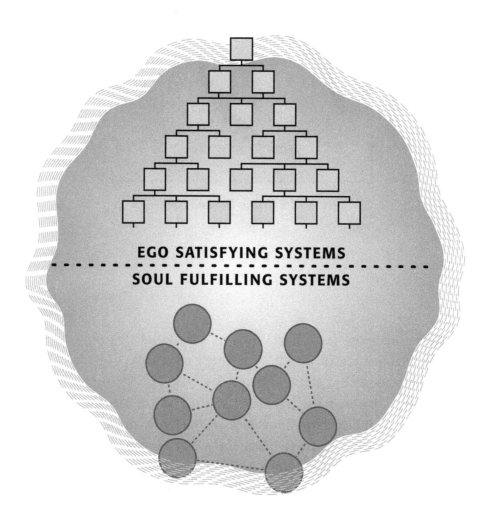

The PMO's pyramid system is especially designed to satisfy the ego's desires for safety, security, survival, success, power, control, influence, fame, attention, and longevity — at least to the extent that these experiences can be sustained in today's dynamic, turbulent marketplace. The PMO's circle system will focus on every member's divine calling, which includes serving other internal and external stakeholders, as well as the planet as a whole, and will thus enable the members to radiate love, joy, peace, and compassion during all their interactions while they address their organization's problems and conflicts.

Previously, the traditional Newtonian organization kept its members stuck in the lower stages of healing, thereby radiating the lower emotional energies of consciousness. Now, however, the pyramid side of the PMO will encourage members to satisfy their ego's desires by providing a safer, more secure, and a more trustworthy environment, including a clear career path up the corporate latter, which will certainly satisfy the ego's desires for achievement, advancement, and holding leadership positions.

The circle portion of the PMO will provide what no other organization to date has offered: an opportunity for members to be fully human, surrounded by a healthy setting to express their divine calling on a regular basis. By allowing members to self-design and self-manage not only the circle system but also the pyramid system, the PMO will inspire members to express their synergized self-identity, which would integrate their ego's desires, their soul purpose, and their surrounding systems – all within a synergized physical/energy body. And even better, by encouraging all members to resolve their primal relationships, every person, whether functioning in the pyramid or the circle potion of the PMO, will be fully present with his coworkers and all other stakeholders, instead of having his energy drained and distracted by still reacting to past perpetrators and unresolved traumas. *The PMO thus offers the best of both worlds, which can only be achieved with a completely integrated program of quantum transformation.*

On Figure 11.34, I re-emphasize just how essential it is for members to resolve their four foundational – INNER – conflicts. Even if the first three conflicts have been resolved, just imagine the dysfunctional conversations within the circle organization if members regularly projected all their past, unresolved traumas onto one another. In sharp contrast, **by having already healed their spatial and temporal boundaries (i.e., by resolving their primal relationships), members are more likely to participate in TRANSCENDENT DIALOGUE.**

FIGURE 11.34
THE PMO AND THE FOUR INNER CONFLICTS

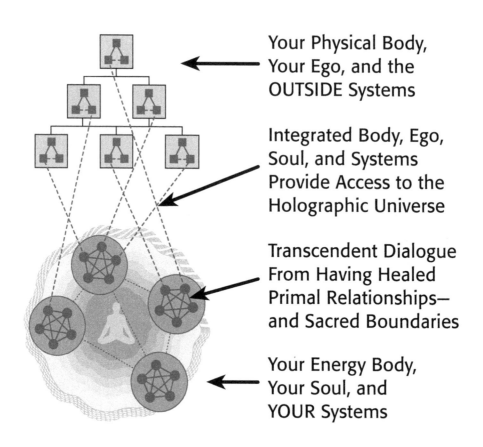

Your Physical Body, Your Ego, and the OUTSIDE Systems

Integrated Body, Ego, Soul, and Systems Provide Access to the Holographic Universe

Transcendent Dialogue From Having Healed Primal Relationships— and Sacred Boundaries

Your Energy Body, Your Soul, and YOUR Systems

Can you even imagine what it would be like if members could discuss an intractable problem while they were all in a non-ordinary state of consciousness? As a team, they'd be able to download insights, information, and experiences — past, present, and future — and infuse that holographic wisdom into a most creative dialogue on any complex problem or conflict.

Lastly, I would like to clarify a very important dynamic that becomes possible only when the fourth foundational conflict has been suitably resolved: **Unless people are at peace with the past, unless they have healed their wounded boundaries, unless they can clearly know the difference between the person in front of them versus the people who violated them in the past, unless they can "jump into the future" and investigate the long-term consequences of their current behavior so they can then return to the present and make the necessary mid-course corrections — basically, unless people have been able to actualize all these growthful qualities, it's difficult to imagine how any team of diverse experts could use their collective, holographic wisdom for deriving synergistic solutions for long-term success.**

People have heard about those unique cases of INDIVIDUAL geniuses – people who have somehow found their own unique means to download inputs from the Holographic Universe, such as a Wolfgang Amadeus Mozart, a Vincent van Gough, an Albert Einstein, and a Carl Gustav Jung. **Yet, if we can bring expanded consciousness into our organizations, instead of waiting for an individual genius to create the next invention or innovation, we'd experience many more quantum leaps forward than ever imagined — which, essentially, is what can be predicted as the Consciousness Revolution approaches the asymptote of infinite change that I graphed at the beginning of this chapter.**

Even though the "separate" individuals who are connected to the Holographic Universe will continue to provide us with their artistic, scientific, and technological breakthroughs, **I'm sure that such individual-based inspirations are wholly insufficient for healing the plethora of complex, messy, chaotic problems that increasingly threaten the quality of life for the peoples of the**

world. To paraphrase Albert Einstein: In the end, it takes NEW systems of organization that are functioning at a higher stage of consciousness to resolve the problems that were created by our OLD institutions that were functioning at a much lower stage of human consciousness.

CONCLUDING THOUGHTS

If an organization were to make a substantial investment in helping its members further expand their consciousness so they could radiate the highest emotional energies of love, joy, peace, and compassion, not only could they develop synergistic solutions for their four foundational conflicts, but they could also use their third eye and crown chakras to download great insights and wisdom from the Holographic Universe — which WOULD BE far more creative and integrative than they could possible derive on their own, as "separate" individuals. If such mind/body/spirit consciousness were infused into the circle side of the Problem Management Organization, the sky's the limit. OR, even more amazing, **Universal Consciousness is the limit.**

I recommend that organizations heavily invest in expanding the consciousness of ALL their members, so it's more likely that every work group will eventually have at least one person who radiates the highest spiritual energies. That one person in every group becomes "the informal leader in expanded consciousness," which will enable the organization to produce amazing results – precisely because that person in every group will have already resolved his four foundational conflicts. If more than one person in every group radiates those highest energies of consciousness, **the more the merrier!**

TWENTY
CRITICAL SUCCESS
FACTORS

CREATING A QUANTUM ORGANIZATION

I've used a particular sequence of eight tracks to provide a completely integrated program of quantum transformation. But there is nothing magical about the digit 8. Another number of tracks, trails, paths, or avenues could also have been suggested for helping members create a quantum organization. Whether any program for change or transformation actually achieves its potential results, however, depends on several Critical Success Factors that must be addressed, whether there are twelve steps, nine stages, four paths, or eight tracks to long–term success.

More specifically, following the recommended sequence that begins with group members *first* working together to develop a healthy behavioral infrastructure (culture, skills, and teamwork) BEFORE they revitalize their organization's formal systems is a Critical Success Factor that must be honored, regardless of the rhetoric of an n–path program. Next, asking group members to work together to renew their organization's strategy, structure, and reward systems BEFORE they attempt to reduce the cycle time of their value–added processes is another Critical Success Factor that must be honored, regardless of what specific labels are used to examine and debate an organization's ends, means, and incentives. In this concluding chapter, therefore, while I'll continue to make use of the eight tracks (since that language is most familiar to me), all members must effectively apply these twenty Critical Success Factors (CSF: #1 to CSF: #20) – under any and all circumstances – if they wish to create a true quantum organization, no matter the number of paths, tracks, or trails.

CSF #1: A "critical mass" of senior executives should be well versed in all principles and practices of the program — including the antiquated qualities of a Newtonian organization versus the emerging features of a quantum organization, the eight tracks and their prescribed sequence, the five stages of quantum transformation, and these Critical Success Factors.

The top executives in a Newtonian organization (sometimes referred to as the "powers-that-be"), must become fully aware of all the many ways in which a completely integrated program is fundamentally different from the infamous quick-fix approaches that were repeatedly implemented in the past, precisely because those narrowly focused approaches never succeeded in bringing about the desired change, improvement, or transformation. The senior executives should also be fully informed about the whys and hows of implementing the noted sequence of eight tracks and what is required of their commitment, time, and resources throughout the entire program.

Ideally, the top executives should never be subjected to any huge surprises during the implementation of the improvement program. In fact, perhaps the best indicator of having provided all the relevant information up front to a critical mass of senior managers is when not one of them could ever say: "Why didn't I know about this beforehand?"

CSF #2: Senior managers must agree on what specific behavior and attitudes will express their active support for the improvement program versus what specific behavior and attitudes will send the kind of signs and signals that will kill the program.

There is a popular dynamic in Newtonian organizations that passive observers look to their superiors to learn if they're really serious about their latest decision or an improvement program. Indeed, if senior managers are only giving "lip service" to their support of an improvement program, members will soon learn to focus on other, more important activities. ***Since many senior managers may be particularly unaware that subtle aspects of their behavior are sending mixed signals to the membership, managers often need coaching on their verbal and nonverbal communication.*** Indeed, when managers are consciously aware of how other people read them, it becomes an act of sabotage to continue sending those signs and signals that undermine the success of the program. In most cases, it's worthwhile to provide that same education on verbal and nonverbal communication skills to the entire membership.

> CSF #3: All managers' performance appraisals should include an assessment of the extent and quality of their involvement and support of the completely integrated program.

If senior managers are genuine about following through on quantum transformation, they should use the reward system to reinforce and reward their active involvement in the program – even if the formal system will be revised sometime later. In one organization, at the beginning of the program, it was publicly announced to the membership that 25% of the annual bonuses of all managerial personnel would be based on their genuine support and involvement in creating a quantum organization. If that announced percentage had been only 5% or 10%, this new policy would not have had a big effect on members. And a 5% or 10% bonus might not have had much impact on the managers either. ***But a bonus of 25% delivered a resounding, organization-wide message to all managers and supervisors: If you are not actively involved throughout the improvement program, it's going to cost you dearly.***

At that moment, no one had any idea as to how the concept of "active involvement" would be determined or measured. But a strong signal was sent nonetheless: Of utmost importance, the members now sensed that something very different was about to happen with *this* latest improvement program – as compared to all the previous attempts at organizational change that were always silent on how the formal reward system could or would be used to stimulate the improvement effort.

> **CSF #4: Changes in key management positions should be made to actively support the principles and practices of the completely integrated program.**

During the length of an improvement program – especially the eight tracks that will probably proceed for a few years – key managers come and go. Sometimes, some of the senior managers who had spearheaded the program leave the organization (or are transferred to some other location) for all kinds of credible reasons. What members agonize about, however, is simply this: "Who's going to replace these key managers?" Consider the early stages of the program: Changes in top management personnel can have an adverse effect on the continuation and success of quantum transformation. *A strong signal to send the members is to replace these managers with those who clearly have the abilities and the determination to become actively involved in supporting the improvement process and thus setting the best example for everyone else.*

But if management positions are staffed with replacements who have the opposite behavior and attitudes, the success of the program could be seriously jeopardized – first, by the members who take those staffing decisions as a prime signal that senior management doesn't know what it's doing (or is not genuinely interested in seeing the program through); second, by the actual damage that's caused by the new managers when they thwart members' efforts to improve their organization. All managerial decisions and actions, therefore, must always be in sync with the principles and practices of the program.

> **CSF #5: Outside experts must conduct a comprehensive, organization-wide diagnosis of the dysfunctions in systems and processes; all organizational members then receive a formal presentation of the diagnostic report, so they can**

understand its findings and further discuss the next steps for addressing its recommendations.

It is essential to obtain a comprehensive, in–depth diagnosis of the organization's deficient informal systems (the first three tracks), misdirected and misaligned formal systems (the middle two tracks), and inefficient and implicit processes (the last three tracks) because two questions arise, again and again: (1) Why are we implementing this program? (2) Is this program really that important – in comparison to the other business and technical challenges that we have to address right now? If the diagnostic report is well done, it offers a probing analysis of the tangled web of dysfunctions that will continue to undermine all efforts at resolving the organization's business and technical problems, especially the complex problems and processes that flow across subunit boundaries, which usually account for the majority of problems that organizations face in today's turbulent economy.

Ironically, one way to tell if expert consultants conducted the diagnostic interviews and prepared the diagnostic report with the purpose of moving the organization into action is if an open dialogue of the diagnostic report evokes pain among senior executives. A valid, insightful, and penetrating diagnosis is not an easy thing to absorb, for example, when it's brightly projected on a large screen in a darkened room. Just imagine a large auditorium where these cultural norms, which have never before been spoken or written down, are officially presented to senior management: "When things go wrong, punish and blame others; ridicule members from other groups and departments; if you don't trust other departments to give you what you need, duplicate their work; don't trust senior managers' motives, they lie; don't trust members' commitment, they loaf; don't speak to those who arrived from 'the merger', which took place ten years ago; don't be the bearer of bad news or you will be shot on the spot; don't disagree with your managers in public – since any such disagreements will be held against you; talk a lot about the need to change, but don't do anything differently."

Even such an intriguing list of actual cultural norms doesn't convey the profound and probing analysis that can be provided in a comprehensive, insightful, and candid diagnostic report, one that identifies all the potential barriers and channels to success that are highlighted in the Complex Hologram (shown in Figure 1.3 in Chapter 1). But this essential point must be made: ***Such a probing diagnostic report always answers those two recurring questions about the program. In essence, it's the dysfunctions in the organization's systems and processes that justify "why we are implementing this improvement program" and "why we won't be able to accomplish much of anything else that's crucial and complex unless we remove the identified barriers to success."*** Sometime later, for purposes of evaluating the results of transformation, it is usually worthwhile to conduct another diagnosis (including a few before–and–after surveys of systems conflicts, culture–gaps, time–gaps, team–gaps, etc.) to discover if the previous dysfunctions in systems and processes, which were identified at the outset, have been eliminated by implementing the completely integrated program.

CSF #6: A steering committee (representing all levels, areas, and locations in the organization) is assigned primary responsibility for the program's success.

Responsibility for scheduling and implementing the program and then evaluating its results is not assigned to consultants nor assigned to some staff group. Instead, the top managers form a committee of about fifteen to twenty–five members, called the **shadow track**, which operates parallel to (in the shadow of) all eight tracks. The shadow track is given the prime responsibility for the success of the program. Its members – comprising senior executives and other managers and members who represent all levels, areas, and locations in the organization – are thoughtfully selected after a nomination process (or a job–posting procedure) has provided a very diverse applicant pool for membership on the shadow track. ***Basically, the members of the shadow track meet regularly to monitor the impact of the program on the functioning of the organization and to discover and/or invent additional methods for effectively implementing the program.*** The shadow track also orchestrates the process for selecting the participants for the several Problem Management Organizations that are established in the later tracks of the program.

> CSF #7: Since process improvement creates excess capacity, an ethical and compassionate plan to redeploy and/or divest human resources should be developed to gain economic efficiency for the organization along with greater financial returns for internal and external stakeholders.

The gradual process track (Total Quality Management) and the radical process track (Business Process Reengineering) both assume that an improved process will lead to improved financial results. But such a premise should not be taken solely on faith. Just consider the case in which an organization achieves a 100% reduction in cycle time and a 50% reduction in process costs by eliminating many No Value–Added (NVA) activities and, thereby, reducing the active involvement of several members who had been performing those unnecessary steps in the old process. Are those members just standing around and not doing anything? If they are NOT redeployed to other value–added activities (e.g., expanding the customer base for current products and services or inventing new products and services for future customers), then their employment should be terminated (divested) – but always compassionately. But if underutilized members remain on the payroll (and thus are neither redeployed nor divested), the organization cannot gain significant financial returns from its success at gradual and radical process improvement. ***Failing to redeploy or divest the idle capacity that results from process improvement, therefore, makes it impossible to realize all the potential economic value of quantum transformation.***

Before an organization attempts to make major system and process changes, the shadow track develops a plan that outlines the corporate-wide policies and procedures for addressing the excess capacity (i.e., human resources) that results from process improvement. More specifically, the Shadow Track's plan should include how resources will be redeployed to take full advantage of excess capacity (thereby creating additional economic value) and how any remaining idle capacity will be removed to reduce operating expenses (which will also improve financial returns). Developing such a plan well in advance of radically improving systems and processes and then sharing it with the membership may not only avoid very painful decisions (such as layoffs), but also serve to establish fair procedures in case such unpopular decisions prove necessary. Consequently, a good knowledge of economic value–added is essential: to understand the reasons for managing excess capacity proactively – and compassionately.

CSF #8: All members should be required to attend all workshop sessions (tracks 1, 2, 3, 6, and 8) and should be fairly represented on all Problem Management Organizations (tracks 4, 5, 7 and 8).

It would be especially nice if all members acknowledged that transformation is vital for organizational survival and success – and knew they had to significantly change their familiar ways of seeing, thinking, feeling, and behaving. So often, however, most people believe that it's the *other people* who need to change their ways. Moreover, change triggers the risk of embarrassment and failure, and sometimes evokes pain or, at the very least, some inconvenience in having to do customary things in new ways. When invited to experience uncertainty, loss, and/or discomfort voluntarily, most people will likely say, "no thank you" (or wait for everyone else to change BEFORE they would even consider going through the process themselves). Therefore, it is essential to *require* all members to participate in the program – to attend all workshop sessions (which requires one day every month on average) and possibly participate in one or more PMOs in the later tracks of quantum transformation (about five to ten hours a week for a few months). Top executives may have to modify members' other job responsibilities, of course, so they are not overwhelmed with too much work. ***But if transformation has a high priority (as it must if it's to succeed), it should not only be required for everyone, but also must take priority over some other projects.*** Voluntary participation in such an improvement program will only be forthcoming *after* organizational members have already transitioned from being passive observers to their becoming active participants and then enlightened participants.

I recall one organization that seriously questioned whether to make the monthly, one-day workshops (tracks 1, 2, 3, 6, and 8) required for all members and, further, whether to schedule these workshops as often as every month for that entire year. Senior managers continued to vacillate over whether they could add all this extra work onto the organization. I reminded them of the diagnostic report: It had identified significant dysfunctions in systems and processes that, in essence, made it very difficult to accomplish their work. Yet, those senior managers continued to complain: "One day a month for all members is just too much time! Couldn't we make the program voluntary and schedule it on the last Saturday of every other month?"

I then asked the senior managers to list the ways in which they currently waste their time now – called, time wasters – and to calculate how much time they waste every month. Their own lists of time wasters totally shocked them; in fact, they actually recreated many of the findings from the diagnostic report! They also estimated that they waste between three to five days every month because of the various dysfunctions in their behavioral infrastructure, the formal systems, and their business processes. As a result of this simple exercise about time management, the senior managers came to the obvious conclusion that investing in the required one-day workshop per month for every member in the organization would soon recover the three to five days a month that they were now being wasted in various ways. This critical mass of slowly awakening managers promptly decided to proceed with what they now viewed as an essential investment (with required member participation in monthly workshops) in implementing a completely integrated program in a successful AND timely manner.

> ### CSF #9: All members should attend monthly workshop sessions in their intact — natural — work groups.

The primary danger for most off-site educational programs is that the skills and new knowledge learned in a comfortable workshop setting will not transfer back to the actual workplace. I call this common experience the ***three-day washout effect:*** In as little as three days after participants have returned from that safe workshop to their daily job, it is as if the workshop never, ever occurred! Even when they ask their bosses to modify how something is done, as based on what was learned at the most recent workshop, members are often faced with: "Get back to work. We'll talk about it later." But "later" never comes. Instead, it's back to business as usual. However, if what's learned in a workshop is NOT transferred back to the job, there's little hope of transforming an organization – or even a single work group.

One way to counteract the three-day washout effect is for members to attend off-site workshops with their intact, natural work units. ***If the instructional material is learned as a group, it's more likely to be used as a group – if for no other reason that members can remind one another of what was learned and also give one another emotional support for trying to do things differently and much better than before.*** Another way to eliminate the infamous three-day washout effect is to conduct the workshops on a recurring basis – month after month after month – to reinforce what is being learned and applied on the job. Nothing that is complex (and new) can possibly be learned and put to use in just one workshop session.

CSF #10: Homework should be assigned to all work groups every month during the first three tracks in order to continue the learning process back in the workplace; every work group should complete its monthly homework assignment on time and then email their written responses to the facilitators before the next workshop.

A series of monthly, one–day workshops with intact, natural work groups is essential to establish – and then sustain – the social momentum of ongoing improvement. A difficulty arises, however, if members do not continue working on the change process in between those monthly workshops. ***To overcome the propensity to talk transformation during the one-day, off-site workshop but then revert back to "business as usual" for the rest of their time in the workplace, each workshop ends with a homework assignment: All intact work units are required to complete, back on the job, the various exercises and group discussions that began during the most recent workshop.*** And by documenting – putting in writing – what was learned from doing those monthly homework assignments, work groups can move ahead in a very efficient and effective manner, instead of wondering: "Tell me again. What were those cultural norms and implicit assumptions we analyzed during the last session?" And while doing the homework, members begin talking about many other things: "What did you do about that problem you had? It would help me to know." As such, members experience various by–products from doing homework assignments – captured by this slogan: "It hurts, but it works!"

CSF #11: A team of dedicated professionals should manage the many logistical aspects of the program in an efficient and effective manner.

Scheduling and then implementing the eight tracks can be a logistical nightmare if the process of transformation has not been planned, organized, and managed with extra-special care and extreme attention to detail. **Besides scheduling members for different tracks, workshops, and sections, there are numerous types of materials to distribute to the right members at the right time.** Furthermore, managing conference facilities for the workshops is a major responsibility in its own right – especially since many things can go wrong (traffic, food service, computer equipment, weather, and so forth). Even if the workshops are held via a virtual platform, there are still many logistical details to manage, so the right work unit can meet at the right time and are provided with clear instructions on how to learn the most from the many activities in the improvement program.

Even an improvement program for a few hundred members requires a full-time **Logistics Coordinator** as well as a part-time assistant. Programs that involve thousands of members would always need an entire **Logistics Team**: a coordinator with a few subgroups to focus on maintaining a database of all members, managing audiovisual equipment, keeping workshop materials up to date and ready for distribution at the right time and place, providing clerical assistance, and more. **The prime mission of the Logistics Team is to enable members to focus on learning, rather than complaining about the workshop materials, the food, the coffee, the temperature in the room, etc.** Incidentally, I published a 166-page, *Logistics Manual*, based on my experience in implementing the tracks in many organizations over several decades, which gave me the opportunity to learn how to manage all the behind-the-scenes activities from incredibly competent and dedicated Logistics Coordinators and Logistics Teams.

CSF #12: All members should learn the identical language, concepts, tools, and techniques from the program, which is enabled by the consistent use of expert facilitators and workshop materials.

When hundreds or thousands of members are participating in quantum transformation, due to logistical demands, there will be many sections of work units attending monthly workshops (approximately fifty to one-hundred participants per session). Consistency in what is learned during these workshops is vital, since members from different groups will be working together on numerous cross-boundary teams (plus several PMOs during later tracks in the program) and, subsequently, may be assigned to new subunits (after rearranging their business processes into a horizontal organization). ***If there is great variation in what different work groups learn, it'll be much more challenging to solve all the cross-boundary problems and conflicts, which necessarily require a common language as well as a mutual understanding of how to use complex skills and techniques, such as assumptional analysis.***

Furthermore, if there is a perception that some sections of members are assigned *better* – and not just *different* – facilitators, presentations, and materials, bad feelings of mistrust, inequity, and frustration might spread, thereby reinforcing the particular dysfunctions that the program is striving to remedy. But using equivalent materials for all sections of members, using the same facilitator for each workshop session (or effectively coordinating the presentations of different facilitators across many workshop sections), and monitoring possible inconsistency problems from one session to another (and making adjustments, as necessary, to improve consistency) will help group members receive the identical concepts, techniques, knowledge, and principles – and perceive this to be so.

CSF #13: All members should be encouraged to continually enhance their self-aware consciousness by first surfacing and then discussing their cultural norms, implicit assumptions, and group process; thereafter, all members should be encouraged to resolve their four foundational – inner – conflicts, so they can continue to expand their mind/body/spirit consciousness.

During the completely integrated program, members should frequently – and genuinely – be encouraged to expand their mind/body/spirit consciousness. In the beginning, all members attend the all-day, monthly workshops for the first three tracks, where they are asked to examine their own behavior, attitudes, beliefs, and assumptions, which they might not have ever done before. If organizational members become thoroughly involved in these discussions (as encouraged by their managers), they will likely gain the threshold of self-aware consciousness in order to make that switch from passive observers to active participants. Afterwards, members should be encouraged to further develop themselves by participating in mind/body/spirit modalities that will enable them to include and transcend each of the various stages in the evolution of consciousness. The results of all this dedicated work for integrating ego, soul, systems, and primal relationships, all inside a synergized physical/energy body, will then enable all members to live a healthier, happier, and more meaningful life – which not only benefits them personally, but also contributes to the long-term success of their organization, their planet, and the entire universe.

> CSF #14: Each work group should self-design as well as self-manage its own sanctioning system in order to celebrate victories and penalize violations during the process of quantum transformation.

It's not until the fifth track – the reward system track – that formal incentives will be available to all members for behaving according to all the principles and practices of the completely integrated program. Before the reward system is redesigned and then implemented, however, an *informal* reward system should be developed and utilized within every work unit. **Essentially, if there are no penalties for continuing in the old ways and no rewards for engaging in more effective behavior, why would anyone want to change?**

During the early sessions in the culture track, each work unit is asked to create an effective sanctioning system that monitors and enforces the skills and behavior learned in the workshops. Specifically, each work group is asked to reach a consensus on what exactly will be done to a member whenever he or she acts out dysfunctional behavior (referred to as a violation) or engages in effective behavior (referred to as a victory). As long as such an informal reward system is ethical and legal, every work group can be encouraged to be as innovative as possible in rewarding desired behavior while penalizing outmoded habits. Ironically, those group members who claim they don't need such a "silly" sanctioning system are usually the first ones to be sanctioned!

CSF #15: Work groups should use a Process Observer (PO) for every meeting — both in the off-site, safe workshops AND back in the challenging workplace.

Much of organizational life occurs in groups, such as formal subunits, small work groups, cross–boundary teams, and the like. *For the purpose of improving group functioning in both the off-site workshops and back in the workplace, it's important to appoint one member as the Process Observer (PO) at the start of every meeting.* The PO is responsible for observing how well members are applying what has been learned in the completely integrated program. And then, at the end of every meeting, the PO summarizes what the group members did particularly well and in what ways the group fell short. The members then decide what to do differently – and better – during their next meeting. A different member should be appointed to this role every time the group meets.

Over a period of a few months, each member will thus have the opportunity to develop group observation skills and practice giving effective feedback. At a certain point, it will no longer be necessary to remind groups to appoint a Process Observer; the responsibility for improving group process will have become accepted and shared among all group members. After the first three tracks in the program, the use of a PO in each work group is automatic and habitual.

> CSF #16: Surveys and instruments should periodically be used to provide effective feedback to individuals and work groups, regarding their systems conflicts, culture-gaps, time-gaps, team-gaps, and more.

When members and their work groups try to improve their behavior and results, they need valid information to guide their good intentions; otherwise, "wishful thinking" and mere rhetoric about the need to change will never result in effective action or improved results.

Conveniently, various self–report assessments and surveys are used throughout the program that provide a lot of valid – and highly useful – information that members can easily use to: (1) identify various GAPS in the functioning of their systems, (2) determine the root causes of those identified GAPS, (3) develop action plans (solutions) to close those GAPS, (4) implement those carefully developed action plans, and then (5) evaluate if they have succeeded in closing those GAPS (hence, following the five steps of problem management). Assessment tools such as the Thomas–Kilmann Instrument (TKI), the Kilmann Organizational Conflict Instrument (KOCI), the Kilmann–Saxton Culture-Gap Survey, the Time–Gap Survey, and the Team–Gap Survey make it easier for members to determine: What has improved, stayed the same, or become worse? *Since these quantitative surveys and assessments enable repeat comparisons over intervals of time (e.g., every three or six months), organizational members have a systematic way of charting their progress and adjusting their efforts accordingly.*

As discussed earlier in this chapter, all the off–site workshops in the first three tracks include intact – natural – work groups. This arrangement makes it easy for members: (1) to remind one another of what was learned from all the previous personality, belief, behavior, and organizational surveys and (2) to average their individual scores on any of these assessment tools in order to calculate group profiles and then discuss the implications of the results for improving their group and the organization.

> CSF #17: Work groups should regularly present oral progress reports to other groups in the community on "what we have done differently since the program began."

> CSF #18: Individuals should regularly receive oral feedback from their fellow group members on "what I have done differently since the program began."

Feedback given in public (in front of other work groups in a workshop setting or in front of one's own group of colleagues) can motivate fundamental changes in behavior, because people are profoundly affected by the presence and opinions of others. Of course, these public exchanges should be done with effective and supportive communication (as practiced in the skills track) and members should also be open to try different approaches on the job, as a result of these public feedback sessions.

But even when members and their work group are utterly sincere in their attempts to change and improve, they may still demonstrate a significant GAP between what they *intend* to do differently and their *actual behavior on the job.* Receiving feedback from other people (who can directly observe the person or work unit in question) is essential to close the GAP between *knowing something* (i.e., declarative knowledge) and then *doing something* (i.e., procedural knowledge).

Consider for example, the following "public progress report" that should be conducted bimonthly for every group during the workshops (and also conducted periodically for each individual member): Each work unit first meets to discuss and answer these questions: "Since the program began, what has improved, stayed the same, or become worse? And what have you and *your* work group done differently during this same period of time?" Then each group is asked to present its responses – publicly – to the other work groups in the same workshop.

During the early stages of the program, a few work groups announce that "most things have stayed the same, nothing has improved, and some things have gotten worse," followed in that same sentence with this revealing explanation: "And we haven't had much time to begin – let alone complete – our homework assignments; we usually forget to appoint a Process Observer at the beginning of our group meetings; and we've not bothered to sanction anyone's behavior. We're just too busy."

Meanwhile, a few *other* work groups report that quite a few things have already improved since the program began: more sharing of information, better listening skills, less interrupting, and increased cooperation across subunits. These same groups then add: "We complete the homework assignments during our lunch breaks, we appoint a PO for every meeting, and we give both positive and negative sanctions to one another, based on our agreed–upon system."

As a result of these bimonthly public progress reports, it gradually becomes obvious to the membership that there's a cause-and-effect relationship between doing things differently and things actually improving in the organization!

Since these public reports are conducted at least every other month in a workshop session, it becomes increasingly difficult for work units to disclose publicly to their peers: "Nothing has changed and we haven't tried to do anything differently." Soon enough, community–wide sanctions (such as soft groans or mild laughter) are applied to those groups that seem unwilling to see the connection between applying the principles of the program and what happens in the organization as a result. ***After several months of these progress reports that are publicly presented by every work group in the organization, it becomes impossible for any group to proclaim that it hasn't been able to improve anything – when so many OTHER groups have already been able to improve their workplace in many ways.*** Besides, most people do not like to publicly disclose feelings of helplessness;

instead, most people prefer politically correct behavior: "Accept the need to change and faithfully embrace all the principles and practices of the program."

CSF #19: Transformational change should be further stimulated by recurring discussions on self-esteem and Internal Control.

If the public progress reports and relevant group sanctions are not sufficient to convince members to change and improve, there are two additional topics that will further propel quantum transformation: (1) self-esteem and (2) Internal Control. During workshop sessions, group members are exposed to the impact of a person's **self-esteem** on his emotional ability to adapt to loss and change. In most cases, people with low self-esteem have a greater difficulty in coping with loss in their personal and work lives than those with high self-esteem. ***The relevant implication is that people who have trouble adapting to change must have low opinions of themselves.*** Whether this implication is true or not for any given individual is totally besides the point: No one wants to acknowledge that he or she may have low self-esteem and definitely doesn't want such a possible fact to be believed publicly. As a result, whenever people consider how to change and improve, the mere mention of the negative impact of low self-esteem seems to convince group members to do their very best to improve themselves and their entire organization.

The second topic is **Internal Control:** whether members take personal responsibility for improving their workplace behavior. The distinction between Internal Control and External Control is especially helpful in asking members to examine themselves – rather than pointing their fingers at others. As we discussed in Chapter 5, External Control is when a person believes that what happens to him is primarily determined by *outside* forces (luck, politics, or other people's behavior). In contrast, Internal Control is when a person believes that what happens to him is largely determined by what he does or doesn't do – his *own* decisions, attitudes, and behavior. *A collective belief in Internal Control helps people take personal responsibility for change; External Control, in contrast, shifts all the attention and/or the blame onto someone else.*

Even after having participated in several workshops in the completely integrated program, some members *continue waiting for something to happen:* "My boss still doesn't keep me informed of what goes on." "The other groups still don't cooperate with us." "My assistants still don't complete their work on time." "When will this organization change?" But soon after group members have learned all about the two kinds of "control," such helpless complaints are met with public challenges: "You seem to have some strong beliefs in External Control!" "Don't you recall that nothing will ever change around here if you continue to believe that someone else has to change you?" "Don't you realize that you are the driver of organizational improvement and that it's YOU who must do something to improve things?" Most people would rather change their behavior than be regularly subjected to these public sanctions – including a good dose of "ridicule." As a result, passive observers (who believe in External Control) transform into active participants and enlightened participants (who now publicly announce their beliefs in Internal Control), which then shifts how members approach the challenge – and the true source – of organizational change and improvement.

> **CSF #20: An organization-wide, electronic newsletter should regularly highlight success stories (i.e., how individuals and groups improved performance); meaningful, widespread celebrations should be held periodically in order to recognize victories and encourage an even greater commitment to creating a quantum organization.**

Another way to reinforce change and improvement is to give organization–wide attention to significant events and successful outcomes beyond the relatively safe, off–site workshop setting. One approach for reaching all members is through the use of formal channels: company-wide newsletters or magazines, for example, and electronic bulletin boards. More interactive – and involving – approaches, including rites, rituals, and ceremonies, can be very powerful reminders and reinforcements of what has already been accomplished, which can further inspire members to succeed at quantum transformation.

CONCLUDING THOUGHTS

If these twenty Critical Success Factors are sincerely honored and seriously used for implementing the completely integrated program (and if the program's other principles and practices are also applied as well), then members have an excellent chance to achieve their organization's long-term strategic vision. Of course, there's always a possibility that some other organization might dream up a new technology that reforms the boundaries of the industry or significantly lowers the cost of providing the same products and services. Or the federal government might decide to revamp how organizations compete and whether particular technologies should be protected in the marketplace. **But if all members continuously monitor and improve their behavioral infrastructure, the formal systems, and value-added processes, they have the best possible chance of rapidly adapting to their chosen network of external stakeholders. In our increasingly turbulent world, that's about as good as it gets.**

Although an organization's long-term success can never be guaranteed, the probabilities are remarkably increased when all members become active and enlightened participants who are inspired to contribute all their wisdom, experience, passion, and mind/body/spirit consciousness to their revitalized – and fully aligned – quantum organization.

"I'm so delighted that you arrived on this page!
Hopefully, you've enjoyed learning about
the whys & hows of creating
a quantum organization.
The remaining sections include the
Bibliography, Index, and About the Author.
Thank you so much for reading my Legacy Book!"

Ralph Kilmann, 2021

BIBLIOGRAPHY
AND
REFERENCES

Allen, R. F., and C. Kraft. *The Organizational Unconscious: How to Create the Corporate Culture You Want and Need* (Englewood Cliffs, NJ: Prentice-Hall, 1982).

Allenbaugh, G. E. "Coaching: A Management Tool for a More Effective Work Performance," *Management Review,* May 1983, 21–26.

Amsden, R. T., H. E. Butler, and D. M. Amsden. *Statistical Process Control Simplified* (White Plains, NY: Quality Resources, 1989).

Aposhyan, S. *Body-Mind Psychotherapy* (New York: Norton, 2004).

Asch, S. E. "Opinions and Social Pressure," *Scientific American,* November 1955, pp. 31–34.

Atkinson, J. W. (Editor). *Motives in Fantasy, Action, and Society: A Method of Assessment and Study* (New York: Van Nostrand, 1958).

Bakal, D. *Minding the Body: Clinical Uses of Somatic Awareness* (New York: Guilford, 1999).

Blake, R. R., and J. S. Mouton. *The Managerial Grid* (Houston: Gulf Publishing, 1964).

Blake, R. R., J. S. Mouton, and R. L. Sloma. "The Union-Management Laboratory: Strategy for Resolving Intergroup Conflict," *Journal of Applied Behavioral Science,* 1965, Volume 1 (1), pp. 25–57.

Bohm, D. *Wholeness and the Implicate Order* (London: Routledge, 1980).

Bramson, R. M. *Coping with Difficult People* (New York: Ballantine, 1983).

Camp, R. C. *Benchmarking: The Search for Industry Best Practices That Lead to Superior Performance* (Milwaukee: ASQC Quality Press, 1989).

Churchman, C. W. *The Design of Inquiring Systems: Basic Concepts of Systems and Organization* (New York: Basic Books, 1971).

Combs, A. *Consciousness Explained Better: Toward an Integral Understanding of the Multifaceted Nature of Consciousness* (St. Paul, MN: Paragon House, 2009).

"Conversation with Edson W. Spencer and Foster S. Boyle." *Organizational Dynamics*, Spring 1983, pp. 30–45.

Crosby, P. B. *Quality Is Free* (New York: McGraw–Hill, 1979).

Davenport, T. H. *Process Innovation: Reengineering Work Through Information Technology* (Boston: Harvard Business School Press, 1993).

Deal, T. E., and A. A. Kennedy. *Corporate Cultures: The Rites and Rituals of Corporate Life* (Reading, MA: Addison–Wesley, 1982).

Deming, W. E. *Out of the Crisis* (Cambridge, MA: Massachusetts Institute of Technology, 1986).

Deming, W. E. *The New Economics: For Industry, Government, Education* (Cambridge, MA: Massachusetts Institute of Technology, 1993).

Drucker, P. F. *The Practice of Management* (New York: HarperCollins, 1954).

Duncan, W. L. *Just-in-Time in American Manufacturing* (Dearborn, MI: Society of Manufacturing Engineers, 1988).

Epstein, D. M., with N. Altman. *The Twelve Stages of Healing: A Network Approach to Wholeness* (San Rafael, CA: Amber–Allen, 1994).

Ewing, D. W. "How to Negotiate with Employee Objectors," *Harvard Business Review*, January–February 1983, pp. 103–110.

Flax, S. "The Ten Toughest Bosses in America," *Fortune*, August 6, 1984, pp. 18–23.

Gangaji. *Freedom & Resolve: The Living Edge of Surrender*
(Novato, CA: The Gangaji Foundation, 1999).

Gangaji. *The Diamond in Your Pocket: Discovering Your True Radiance*
(Boulder, CO: Sounds True, 2005).

Goswami, A. *The Self-Aware Universe: How Consciousness Creates the
Material World* (New York: Tarcher/Putnam, 1993).

Grof, S., with H. Z. Bennett. *The Holotropic Mind: The Three Levels
of Human Consciousness and How They Shape Our Lives*
(San Francisco: HarperCollins, 1994).

Hackman, J. R., and G. R. Oldham. *Work Redesign* (Reading,
MA: Addison–Wesley, 1980).

Hamel, G., and C. K. Prahalad. *Competing for the Future:
Breakthrough Strategies for Seizing Control of Your Industry
and Creating the Markets of Tomorrow* (Boston: Harvard
Business School Press, 1994).

Hammer, M., and J. Champy. *Reengineering the Corporation:
A Manifesto for Business Revolution* (New York:
Harper Business, 1993).

Harrington, H. J. *Business Process Improvement* (New York:
McGraw–Hill, 1991).

Harrington, H. J. *Total Improvement Management* (New York:
McGraw–Hill, 1995).

Harris, B. *Thresholds of the Mind: Your Personal Roadmap to Success,
Happiness, and Contentment* (Beaverton, OR:
Centerpointe, 2002).

Hart, W. *Vipassana Meditation as Taught by S. N. Goenka*
(San Francisco: HarperCollins, 1987).

Hawkins, D. R. *Power vs. Force: The Hidden Determinants of
Human Behavior* (Carlsbad, CA: Hay House, 2002).

Hayes, B. E. *Measuring Customer Satisfaction: Development and Use of
Questionnaires* (Milwaukee, WI: ASQC Quality Press, 1992).

Ishikawa, K. *Guide to Quality Control* (Tokyo: Asian Productivity
Organization, 1986).

Jois, K. P. *Yoga Mala: The Seminal Treatise and Guide from the Living
Master of Ashtanga Yoga* (New York: North Point, 2002).

Jung, C. G. *Psychological Types* (Boston: Routledge & Kegan Paul, 1923).

Jung, C. G. *Synchronicity.* In *Collected Works*, Volume 8, Bollingen Series XX (Princeton, NJ: Princeton University Press, 1960).

Juran, J. M. *Juran's Quality Handbook.* 4th Edition (New York: McGraw–Hill, 1988).

Juran, J. M. *Juran's New Quality Road Map: Planning, Setting, and Reaching Quality Goals* (New York: Free Press, 1991).

Katherine, A. *Boundaries: Where You End and I Begin — How to Recognize and Set Healthy Boundaries* (Parsippany, NJ: Touchstone, 1993).

Keen, P. G. W. *Shaping the Future: Business Design Through Information Technology* (Boston: Harvard Business School Press, 1991).

Keen, P. G. W. *The Process Edge: Creating Value Where It Counts* (Boston: Harvard Business School Press, 1997).

Kilmann, R. H. *Social Systems Design: Normative Theory and the MAPS Design Technology* (New York: North–Holland, 1977).

Kilmann, R. H. *Beyond the Quick Fix: Managing Five Tracks to Organizational Success* (Washington DC: Beard Books, 1984).

Kilmann, R. H. *Managing Beyond the Quick Fix: A Completely Integrated Program for Creating and Maintaining Organizational Success* (San Francisco: Jossey–Bass, 1989).

Kilmann, R. H. *Quantum Organizations: A New Paradigm for Achieving Organizational Success and Personal Meaning* (Newport Coast, CA, 2001; 2011).

Kilmann, R. H. *Workbook for Implementing the Tracks: Volumes I, II, and III* (Newport Coast, CA: Kilmann Diagnostics, 2011).

Kilmann, R. H. *Consultant Schedules for Implementing the Tracks: Volumes I, II, and III* (Newport Coast, CA: Kilmann Diagnostics, 2011).

Kilmann, R. H. *Logistic Manual for Implementing the Tracks: Planning and Organizing Workshop Sessions* (Newport Coast, CA: Kilmann Diagnostics, 2011).

Kilmann, R. H. *Work Sheets for Identifying and Closing Culture-Gaps* (Newport Coast, CA: Kilmann Diagnostics, 2011).

Kilmann, R. H. *Work Sheets for Identifying and Closing Team-Gaps*
(Newport Coast, CA: Kilmann Diagnostics, 2011).

Kilmann, R. H. *The Courageous Mosaic: Awakening Society, Systems,
and Souls* (Newport Coast, CA: Kilmann Diagnostics, 2013).

Kilmann, R. H. *Kilmann Organizational Conflict Instrument*
(Newport Coast, CA: Kilmann Diagnostics, 2020).

Kilmann, R. H., and Associates (Editors). *The Management of
Organization Design, Volume I: Strategies and Implementation*
(New York: North–Holland, 1976).

Kilmann, R. H., and Associates (Editors). *The Management of
Organization Design, Volume II: Research and Methodology*
(New York: North–Holland, 1976).

Kilmann, R. H., and Associates (Editors). *Gaining Control of the
Corporate Culture* (San Francisco: Jossey–Bass, 1985).

Kilmann, R. H., and Associates (Editors). *Corporate Transformation:
Revitalizing Organizations for a Competitive World*
(San Francisco: Jossey–Bass, 1988).

Kilmann, R. H., and Associates (Editors). *Making Organizations
Competitive: Enhancing Networks and Relationships Across
Traditional Boundaries* (San Francisco: Jossey–Bass, 1991).

Kilmann, R. H., and Associates (Editors). *Managing Ego Energy:
The Transformation of Personal Meaning into Organizational
Success* (San Francisco: Jossey–Bass, 1994).

Kilmann, R. H., and Associates (Editors). *Producing Useful Knowledge
for Organizations* (San Francisco: Jossey–Bass, 1994).

Kilmann, R. H., and Associates. *Kilmanns Organizational Belief Survey*
(Newport Coast, CA: Kilmann Diagnostics, 2011).

Kilmann, R. H., and Associates. *Kilmanns Personality Style Instrument*
(Newport Coast, CA: Kilmann Diagnostics, 2011).

Kilmann, R. H., and Associates. *Kilmanns Time-Gap Survey*
(Newport Coast, CA: Kilmann Diagnostics, 2011).

Kilmann, R. H., and Associates. *Kilmanns Team-Gap Survey*
(Newport Coast, CA: Kilmann Diagnostics, 2011).

Kilmann, R. H., and T. J. Covin. *Kilmann-Covin Organizational
Influence Survey* (Newport Coast, CA: Kilmann
Diagnostics, 2011).

Kilmann, R. H., L. A. O'Hara, and J. P. Strauss. *Organizational Courage Assessment* (Newport Coast, CA: Kilmann Diagnostics, 2011).

Kilmann, R. H., and M. J. Saxton. *Kilmann-Saxton Culture-Gap® Survey* (Newport Coast, CA: Kilmann Diagnostics, 1983).

Kilmann, R. H., and K. W. Thomas. "Developing a Forced–Choice Measure of Conflict–Handling Behavior: The MODE Instrument," *Educational and Psychological Measurement,* 1977, Volume 37 (2), pp. 309–325.

Kübler–Ross, E. *On Death and Dying* (New York: Macmillan, 1969).

Kuhn, T. S. *The Structure of Scientific Revolutions* (Chicago: University of Chicago Press, 1962).

Lawrence, P. R., and J. W. Lorsch. *Organization and Environment* (Boston: Graduate School of Business Administration, Harvard University, 1967).

Leahey, T. H., and R. J. Harris. *Learning and Cognition.* 3rd Edition (Englewood Cliffs, NJ: Prentice–Hall, 1993).

Lewicki, R. "Organizational Seduction: Building Commitment to Organizations," *Organizational Dynamics,* Autumn 1981, pp. 5–21.

Lewin, K. *Field Theory in Social Science* (New York: Harper & Row, 1951).

Lipton, B. *The Biology of Belief: Unleashing the Power of Consciousness, Matter, and Miracles* (Santa Rosa, CA: Mountain of Love, 2005).

Locke, E. A., and G. P. Latham. *A Theory of Goal Setting and Task Performance* (Englewood Cliffs, NJ: Prentice–Hall, 1990).

Lombardo, M. M., and M. M. McCall, Jr. "The Intolerable Boss," *Psychology Today,* January 1984, pp. 44–48.

Lorsch, J. W., and J. J. Morse. *Organizations and Their Members: A Contingency Approach* (New York: Harper & Row, 1974).

Lowen, A. *Bioenergetics: The Revolutionary Therapy that Uses the Language of the Body to Heal the Problems of the Mind* (New York: Penguin, 1975).

Mackenzie, K. D. *The Organizational Hologram: The Effective Management of Organizational Change* (Boston: Kluwer, 1991).

Mason, R. O., and I. I. Mitroff. *Challenging Strategic Planning Assumptions* (New York: Wiley, 1981).

McGrath, J. E. *Groups: Interaction and Performance* (Englewood Cliffs, NJ: Prentice–Hall, 1984).

McIntosh, S. *Integral Consciousness and the Future of Evolution: How the Integral Worldview Is Transforming Politics, Culture, and Spirituality* (St. Paul, MN: Paragon House, 2007).

Milgrom, P., and J. Roberts. *Economics, Organization, and Management* (Englewood Cliffs, NJ: Prentice–Hall, 1992).

Mitroff, I. I., and E. A. Denton. *A Spiritual Audit of Corporate America* (San Francisco: Jossey–Bass, 1999).

Mitroff, I. I., and R. H. Kilmann. *Methodological Approaches to Social Science: Integrating Divergent Concepts and Theories* (San Francisco: Jossey–Bass, 1978.

Mitroff, I. I., and R. H. Kilmann. *Corporate Tragedies: Product Tampering, Sabotage, and Other Catastrophes* (New York: Praeger, 1984).

Mitroff, I. I., and R. H. Kilmann. *The Psychodynamics of Enlightened Leadership: Coping with Chaos* (New York: Springer, 2021).

Mizuno, S. *Management for Quality Improvement: The Seven New QC Tools* (Cambridge, MA: Productivity Press, 1988).

Montgomery, D. C. *Introduction to Statistical Quality Control* (New York: Wiley, 1991).

Myers, I. B. *Myers-Briggs Type Indicator* (Sunnyvale, CA: The Myers–Briggs Company, 1978).

Myss, C. *The Anatomy of the Spirit: The Seven Stages of Power and Healing* (New York: Three Rivers Press, 1996).

Nonaka, I. "The Knowledge–Creating Company," *Harvard Business Review*, November–December 1991, pp. 96–104.

Ornstein, R. E. *The Nature of Human Consciousness* (San Francisco: Freeman, 1968).

Peat, F. D. *Synchronicity: The Bridge Between Matter and Mind* (Toronto: Bantam Books, 1987).

Peat, F. D. *Superstrings and the Search for the Theory of Everything* (Chicago: Contemporary Books, 1988).

Petri, H. L., and M. Mishkin. "Behaviorism, Cognitivism, and the Neuropsychology of Memory," *American Scientist*, 1994, Volume 82, pp. 30–37.

Porter, L. W., E. E. Lawler, III. *Managerial Attitudes and Performance* (Homewood, IL: Irwin–Dorsey, 1968).

Porter, L. W., E. E. Lawler, III, and J. R. Hackman. *Behavior in Organizations* (New York: McGraw–Hill, 1975).

Porter, M. E. *Competitive Strategy* (New York: Free Press, 1980).

Porter, M. E. *The Competitive Advantage of Nations* (New York: Free Press, 1990).

Rank, O. *The Trauma of Birth* (New York: Harcourt Brace, 1929).

Roethlisberger, F. J., and W. J. Dickson. *Management and the Worker* (Cambridge, MA: Harvard University Press, 1939).

Rotter, J. B. "External Control and Internal Control," *Psychology Today*, June 1971, pp. 37–42, 58–59.

Ruiz, D. M. *The Four Agreements: A Practical Guide to Personal Freedom* (San Rafael, CA: Amber–Allen, 1997).

Rummler, G. A., and A. P. Brache. *Improving Performance: How to Manage the White Space on the Organization Chart* (San Francisco: Jossey–Bass, 1990).

Russell, P. *Waking Up in Time: Finding Inner Peace in Times of Accelerating Change* (Novato, CA: Origin, 1998).

Sagan, S. *Awakening the Third Eye* (Roseville NSW, Australia: Clairvision, 1997).

Schrödinger, E. *What Is Life? and Mind and Matter* (London: Cambridge University Press, 1969).

Schwartz, G. E. R., and L. G. S. Russek. *The Living Energy Universe* (Charlottesville, VA: Hampton Roads, 1999).

Searle, J. *Minds, Brains, and Science* (Cambridge, MA: Harvard University Press, 1984).

Senge, P. *The Fifth Discipline: The Art and Practice of the Learning Organization* (New York: Doubleday/Currency, 1990).

Sheldrake, R. *A New Science of Life* (Los Angeles: Tarcher, 1981).

Sheldrake, R. *The Presence of the Past: Morphic Resonance and the Habits of Nature* (New York: Random House, 1988).

Shewhart, W. A. *Economic Control of Quality of Manufactured Product* (New York: Van Nostrand., 1931).

Shilling, E. G. *Acceptance Sampling in Quality Control* (New York: Marcel Dekker, 1982).

Shlain, L. *Art and Physics: Parallel Visions in Space, Time, and Light* (New York: William Morrow, 1991).

Singer, J. *Boundaries of the Soul: The Practice of Jung's Psychology* (New York: Doubleday, 1972).

Smith, P. C., and L. M. Kendall. 1963. "Retranslation of Expectations: An Approach to the Construction of Unambiguous Anchors for Ratings Scales," *Journal of Applied Psychology*, April 1963, pp. 149–155.

Smolin, L. *The Life of the Cosmos* (Oxford: Oxford University Press, 1997).

Squire, L. *Memory and Brain* (New York: Oxford University Press, 1987).

Stata, R. "Organizational Learning: The Key to Management Innovation," *Sloan Management Review*, Spring 1989, pp. 63–74.

Talbot, M. *The Holographic Universe* (New York: Harper Perennial, 1991).

Teilhard de Chardin, P. *Building the Earth* (New York: Discus Books, 1965).

Thomas, K. W., and R. H. Kilmann. 1974. *Thomas-Kilmann Conflict Mode Instrument* (Sunnyvale, CA: The Myers–Briggs Company, 1974).

Thompson, J. D. *Organizations in Action* (New York: McGraw–Hill, 1967).

Thurston, M. *Discovering Your Soul's Purpose* (Virginia Beach: ARE, 1984).

Trice, H. M., and J. M. Beyer. *The Cultures of Work Organizations* (Englewood Cliffs, NJ: Prentice-Hall, 1993).

Trist, E. L., and K. W. Bamforth. (1951). "Some Social and Psychological Consequences of the Longwall Method of Coal Getting," *Human Relations*, 1951, Volume 4, pp. 3–38.

Vosniadou, S., and W. F. Brewer. "Theories of Knowledge Restructuring in Development," *Review of Educational Research*, 1987, Volume 57 (1), pp. 51–67.

Vroom, V. H. *Work and Motivation* (New York: Wiley, 1964).

Wallach, E. J. "Individuals and Organization: The Cultural Match," *Training and Development Journal*, February 1983, pp. 29–36.

Walsh, J. P., and G. R. Ungson. "Organizational Memory," *Academy of Management Review*, 1991, Volume 16 (1), pp. 57–91.

Wheatley, M. J. *Leadership and the New Science: Learning About Organization from an Orderly Universe* (San Francisco: Berrett-Koehler, 1992).

Wilber, K. *The Atman Project: A Transpersonal View of Human Development* (Wheaton, IL: Theosophical Publication House, 1980).

Wilber, K. *Sex, Ecology, Spirituality: The Spirit of Evolution* (Boston: Shambhala, 1995).

Wilber, K. *A Brief History of Everything* (Boston: Shambhala, 1996).

Wilber, K. *Integral Psychology: Consciousness, Spirit, Psychology, Therapy* (Boston: Shambhala, 2000).

Windrider, K., and G. Sears. *Deeksha: The Fire from Heaven* (Novato: CA: New World Library, 2006).

Wolf, F. A. *Parallel Universes: The Search for Other Worlds* (New York: Simon & Schuster, 1988).

Young, A. M. *The Reflexive Universe: Evolution of Consciousness* (Cambria, CA: Anodos Foundation, 1976).

Zand, D. E. *Information, Organization, and Power* (New York: McGraw-Hill, 1981).

Zohar, D. *The Quantum Self: Human Nature and Consciousness Defined by the New Physics* (New York: William Morrow, 1990).

Zohar, D. *Rewiring the Corporate Brain: Using the New Science to Rethink How We Structure and Lead Organizations* (San Francisco: Berrett-Koehler, 1997).

Zuckav, G. *The Dancing Wu Li Masters: An Overview of the New Physics* (New York: William Morrow, 1979).

INDEX
FOR
FINDING THINGS

H

ABOUT THE AUTHOR

Ralph H. Kilmann, Ph.D., is CEO of Kilmann Diagnostics (KD) in Newport Coast, California. In this position, he has created all of KD's online courses and assessment tools on the four timeless topics of conflict management, change management, expanding consciousness, and quantum transformation.

Ralph's online products are used by such high-profile organizations as Amazon, Bank of America, DuPont, Exxon Mobil, FedEx, GE, Google, Harvard University, Microsoft, NASA, Netflix, Philips, Twitter, the U.S. Department of State, Verizon, Walmart, the World Health Organization, and Zoom Video.

Ralph earned both his B.S. in graphic arts management and M.S. in industrial administration from Carnegie Mellon University in 1970, and a Ph.D. degree in the behavioral sciences in management and social systems design from the University of California, Los Angeles, in 1972. After Ralph left UCLA, he was appointed an Assistant Professor at the Katz School of Business, University of Pittsburgh. In 1991, the faculty awarded him the George H. Love Professorship of Organization and Management, which he held until 2002, when he decided to relinquish his tenured faculty position. Instead of staying in Pittsburgh, Ralph moved to the West Coast, since he wanted to fulfill his California Dream, which eventually led to the creation of Kilmann Diagnostics.

Ralph is an internationally recognized authority on systems change. He has consulted for numerous corporations throughout the United States and Europe, including AT&T, Catalana de Gas, IBM, Ford, General Electric, Kodak, Lockheed, London Stock Exchange, Olivetti, Philips, TRW, Wolseley, and Xerox. He has also consulted for numerous healthcare, financial, and government organizations, including the U.S. Bureau of the Census and the Office of the U.S. President.

Ralph has published more than twenty books and one hundred articles on such subjects as conflict management, organizational design, problem management, change management, and quantum organizations. He is also the coauthor of more than ten assessment tools, including the *Thomas-Kilmann Conflict Mode Instrument (TKI)*, the *Kilmann-Saxton Culture-Gap® Survey (CGS)*, the *Organizational Courage Assessment (OCA)*, and the *Kilmann Organizational Conflict Instrument (KOCI)*.

In 2021, Ralph wrote and published his "legacy book," which integrates everything he's ever created and presented across all his previous books, articles, and assessment tools: *Creating a Quantum Organization: The Whys & Hows of Implementing Eight Tracks for Long-Term Success.*

Since 1985, Ralph's professional biography has been profiled in *Who's Who in the World*. And then, in 2017, Marquis Who's Who distinguished him as a "Lifetime Achiever" and featured his profile in "Sciences."

Ralph's hobbies include hiking, biking, golf, Ashtanga Yoga, and photography, as well as listening to many types of music (classical, opera, rock, pop, jazz, and country) and visiting all kinds of museums and art galleries. He has a passion for home theater – a setting that integrates music, art, science, and intimacy. Yet his long–term hobbies, since childhood, are writing, printing, and publishing.

To learn more about the author and his work, visit his website: ***www.kilmanndiagnostics.com.***

Publications by Kilmann Diagnostics

Self-Report Assessment Tools
Kilmann-Saxton Culture-Gap® Survey
Kilmanns Organizational Belief Survey
Kilmanns Time-Gap Survey
Kilmanns Team-Gap Survey
Organizational Courage Assessment
Kilmanns Personality Style Instrument
Kilmann-Covin Organizational Influence Survey
Kilmann Organizational Conflict Instrument (KOCI)

The Books That Explain the Eight Tracks
Quantum Organizations (2001)
Creating a Quantum Organization (2021)

Materials for Implementing the Eight Tracks
Work Sheets for Identifying and Closing Culture-Gaps
Work Sheets for Identifying and Closing Team-Gaps
Consultant Schedules for Implementing the Tracks
Logistics Manual for Implementing the Tracks
Workbooks for Implementing the Tracks

The Book for Expanding Consciousness
The Courageous Mosaic:
Awakening Society, Systems, and Souls (2013)

CPSIA information can be obtained
at www.ICGtesting.com
Printed in the USA
JSHW040802200921
18818JS00002B/221

9 780989 571